B E Y O N D
COLONIAL
ANGLICANISM

D1715935

B E Y O N D
COLONIAL
ANGLICANISM

THE ANGLICAN COMMUNION
IN THE TWENTY-FIRST CENTURY

EDITED BY
IAN T. DOUGLAS AND KWOK PUI-LAN

 CHURCH

Church Publishing Incorporated, New York

Library of Congress Cataloging-in-Publication Data

Beyond colonial Anglicanism ; the Anglican Communion in the
twenty-first century /
Ian T. Douglas, Kwok Pui-lan.
    p. cm
Includes bibliographical references.
ISBN 0-89869-357-8 (pbk.)
1. Anglican Communion—Congresses. I. Douglas, Ian T.
II Kwok, Pui-lan.

BX5021 .B48 2001
283'.09'051–dc21   2001028155

Church Publishing Incorporated
445 Fifth Avenue
New York, NY 10016

5 4 3 2 1

CONTENTS

ACKNOWLEDGMENTS

This book originated at a consultation on "Anglicanism in a Post-Colonial World" held at the Episcopal Divinity School from June 7-11, 1998. We would like to thank the V. Eugene and Rosalie DeFreitas Charitable Foundation for its generous support of the consultation that brought together Anglican theologians and church leaders from different parts of the Anglican Communion. Our colleagues at the Episcopal Divinity School, Professors Christopher Duraisingh and Fredrica Harris Thompsett, were involved in the consultation planning process from the beginning and offered invaluable insights and wisdom. We are deeply indebted to all of the participants in the consultation, including the Rt. Rev. Barbara Harris, the Rt. Rev. James Ottley, the Rt. Rev. Eliphaz Maari, the Rev. Mark Harris and several students from the Episcopal Divinity School. We are particularly indebted to those presenters who have revised their papers for this volume in light of the lively conversations generated at the consultation as well as subsequent developments in the Anglican Communion following the 1998 Lambeth Conference. Special thanks go to the Rev. Mark Wastler, who, as a seminarian, did most of the unglamorous administrative tasks related to the consultation and ensured that we had multicultural cuisine as food for thought.

There are many individuals and institutions we would like to recognize for their contributions to this volume. We have invited colleagues and friends to provide additional papers beyond the initial consultation in order to broaden and deepen the discussion. The essays by Archbishop Njongonkulu Ndungane and Professor Jaci Maraschin have appeared in the *Anglican Theological Review,* and we are grateful to the authors for allowing them to be published here. We are particularly thankful to the staff of the *Anglican Theological Review*, especially James E. Griffiss, Editor, and Jacqueline B. Winter, Managing Editor, who have graciously worked with us to reprint these articles. Financial assistance for the book was provided by both the Theological Writing Fund of the Episcopal Divinity School and the V. Eugene and Rosalie DeFreitas Charitable Foundation. We are deeply grateful for such assistance.

Editing a book with fifteen authors who are accustomed to English usage in diverse ways, and who write in different styles, is no easy task. As coeditors, we were very fortunate to have had the efficient and patient assistance of Anne L. Deneen, who edited each essay with meticulous care and cultural sensitivity. We are deeply indebted to her for her hard work and gracious presence throughout the project. Our research assistant, Gretchen Grimshaw, proofread the final text with eyes for details. We thank Frank Tedeschi, Managing Editor of Church Publishing Incorporated, for his interest in the book and for shepherding the manuscript through the different stages of production. We have also received much encouragement from church leaders, theologians, and friends in the Anglican Communion who are eagerly looking forward to the book's publication. We appreciate their observations, guidance and patience in the development of this book.

Finally, we want to express our gratitude to our family members for their support, companionship and love. Ian would like to dedicate his part of this work to his parents, Duncan and Gladys Douglas, and his in-laws, William and Nan Harris, for all that they have given him in his life. In addition, Ian wants to thank Kristin, and Pui-lan wants to thank Wai Pang, for their encouragement and understanding along the way. We are deeply grateful that they see our scholarship as important for the church and for society. May our children Anpu, Luke, Timothy, and Johanna, grow and flourish in a world with peace and justice that is beyond colonialism.

Ian T. Douglas
Kwok Pui-lan

Cambridge, Massachusetts
Advent, 2000

PREFACE

GLAUCO S. DE LIMA

In June of 1998, I participated in a conference addressing the theme of "Anglicanism in a Post-Colonial World" at the Episcopal Divinity School in Cambridge, Massachusetts. The sponsors were preoccupied with the question: What would be the message from the church at a time when colonialism was a thing of the past? This question drew varied responses from the participants in the conference. We came from different parts of the world, and from diverse positions within the church: lay people, priests, bishops, teachers, writers, theologians, and pastoral agents. In our papers, some of us surveyed the current expressions of colonialism in our local and global ecclesial contexts; some of us explored the particular global crises our churches face in the world today; some of us analyzed our ways of organizing worship, our methods of scriptural interpretation, and discipleship. The presentations and conversations broke open the ground for us, helping us to make visible our painful histories, and at the same time, engaging our creativity to imagine an Anglican Communion for the twenty-first century, filled with hope for a future church beyond the colonial legacy we inherited.

The Anglican Communion exists as a result of British colonial expansion, since the majority of the Anglican provinces are located in areas once colonized by the British. The Anglican Communion has been shaped by the old condition of "the crown next to the cross," meaning that the imperial power and the state should be set alongside the spiritual power, the latter providing the church's approval and justification of the mother country's economic expansion. The symbol of imperial power wedded to the symbol of spiritual power reflected a policy that the submission of the colonized people must be not only economic, but also ideological. During the course of the conference, we saw that the phenomenon of colonialism in the world and in the church has not yet been overcome. There are still strong signs of this within the church; and for this reason, we decided to change the title of this book to *Beyond Colonial Anglicanism,* indicating that we look ahead toward, we hope, a not very distant future where the structures and powers of colonialism have lost their efficacy. In these papers, we begin to discern a call from God for our churches. The Anglican Communion is called today beyond its history, into new imaginative and creative work, to participate with the actions of the Holy Spirit in this new century, to be a sign to the world that God does indeed make all things new.

SIGNS OF COLONIALISM IN THE CHURCH

Some years ago a bishop colleague of mine told me a revealing story. He went to witness a trial in a country on the east coast of Africa, and there he saw that the judges used the same kind of wigs as English judges. The African judges sat in court in their heavy wigs, perspiration trickling down their faces. We human beings are symbolical beings; we live among symbols. The symbols that we create are the products of culture. Among colonized peoples, the ruling culture dominates and appears in the symbols of the culture. In the case mentioned above, for the sake of showing the solemnity of the court and justice being served, the symbols bore witness to the authority of those from whom they originated. Therefore, in spite of the inappropriate climate, African judges appear with heavy wigs and vestments which are appropriate for the ruler's climate. This is an example of the way our colonial legacies operate today in shaping our cultures. Colonized peoples, aware of the ways colonial symbols function, have begun to question them, reinterpreting them, sometimes replacing them with symbols from their own context. This is a task which develops a critical, reflective, reconstructive reading of cultural symbols. If the Anglican Communion is to move beyond our colonial legacy, all of us must learn to examine the roots of our tradition, exploring ways in which we can transform the symbols we have inherited from a culture of empire and its expressions.

In our Anglican churches, the signs and power of colonial symbols may be seen not only in the liturgical order. The Hebrew and Greek sources for our liturgy come to us already filtered through British culture in the Book of Common Prayer, a wonderful Western and Christian inspiration, itself an example of a contextual theological process. Beyond the very order and linguistic sources of our worship, even our clothing bears witness to a colonial origin. In the vestments and trimmings of the clergy, for example, on the bishop's surplice, the sleeves finish up at the cuffs in the same way as those of the noblemen in the British court. Moreover, and perhaps more troubling, the influence of colonial symbols and patterns occurs in the methodology of theological elaboration, in the way our parishes or communities are organized, and in the canonical structures of the church. Colonial influence may be seen in the interpretation of the Bible. It is present even in the still dominant bias in many areas of the church regarding minorities who have an orientation different from the dominant cultural patterns, a bias which is profoundly oppressive for homosexuals.

Another recent example of theological elaboration influenced by British culture is the last report from the Inter-Anglican Theological and Doctrinal Commission, or the *Virginia Report.* If we examine the text closely, we will see that despite its merits as a compilation of essential points of Christian doctrine, it is basically conservative. The document contains strong traces of British liberalism, and does not manage to avoid certain ingenuous expressions regarding its view on Christian love. There are some strengths, however, which we may note. For example, the British cultural tradition brings to the *Report* an acceptance and positive interpretation of diversity. Another positive aspect of the *Report* is the view that God's manifestation in us has its origin only in community. Since the time of the British empire, there has been a strong, positive view of communal organization, where the concentration of power is not so much in one person, but in a group which becomes the spokesperson for the law and order of the community.

This inheritance affects the core structures of Anglican thought and expression, theological imagination, worship, ecclesial organization, and power. In the Anglican way of doing theology, based on the tripod of scripture, tradition and reason, one sees traces of British culture. Law and revelation are based on a sacred text. Tradition is used as a positive criterion to be able to judge what happens in the present and in the future against the experience and practices of earlier Christian communities. Reason reveals the pragmatic British spirit, which is successful in its undertakings, thanks to the recognition that reason provides a criterion of truth and is instrumental for us to position ourselves in life.

In our idea of divine grace in the life of the church, we see the bishop as a point of reference for order and doctrine. In our tradition, however, he or she may not be an autocrat, for together with the clergy and laity, he or she shares the responsibilities of managing the church. There is a substantial participation of lay people in the administration of the church. This shared authority is very indicative of the liberal British tradition.

The different types of church life reflect the strain which has always existed in the United Kingdom between the traditional catholic influences in the British court and the popular zeal for evangelical experience, with a strong emphasis on individualism and personal experience. In fact, the commercialism which marks the expansionist era of the empire reinforces individual initiative in the accumulation of wealth, which is the new way of exercising power. The presbyter as the local leader of the church reproduces analogously the whole scheme of organization of the imperial oligarchy, in which there is a local agent who represents in a collegiate manner not only the community of the empire, but also that of the church. In the *Virginia Report*, we see in item 3-26: "The expansion of the Church of England, as a consequence of British colonization, resulted in the formation of Provinces, each with its own episcopal structure and synod to keep the Church alive." Here, the organization of the empire is reflected in the ecclesiastic structure.

For those of us who believe that the church is a sign and foretaste of the reign of God in the world, the task of undoing colonialism in our mission is urgent. Herc there are two matters we must explore which seem to be merely theological, but if we examine them more profoundly, we find that they have sociological dimensions. The first one is a question of conversion, of a radical change of life for those who are touched by faith. We know that there is no pattern by which to measure the degree of conversion of a person, because this is an internal experience. The subject of conversion has already caused much hypocrisy, especially by those groups of Puritan origin who measure conversion by external acts of abstinence from human pleasure or ad hoc forms of piety. There has been a great appeal for the so-called conversion by those more connected with the common people. In conversion, these people unconsciously saw that the life patterns of such a change were connected with the "establishment" or with the court which, on the contrary, always supposed that they had a compromise with the "status quo."

The second question is that of the interpretation of Christian love that is preached, in most cases in an uncritical and sometimes childish way, with sufficient emphasis on conformity with the established order, something very useful for avoiding revolutions. Whilst the idea of conversion favors the idea of a new elite, the "saved," which should not be confused with the imperial elite, the idea of love implies, for the colonized, the idea of submission to the members of the dominant group, endeavoring to love them as God loves us. Authentic conversion to faith and the practice of Christian love must not be tied to hidden colonialism and its agenda of conforming to a ruling culture.

I consider these two questions—that of conversion, as well as of love—to be two serious theological questions which must be considered in more creative terms. This critical reflection on mission and the transformation of mission practices are tasks that a church moving beyond colonialism must undertake.

AUTHORITY AND LEADERSHIP RECONSIDERED

As Anglicanism slowly ceases to be an English phenomenon and becomes a universal reality, the primacy of the Archbishop of Canterbury needs to be reconsidered. Considering the office's constitutional and canonical purposes, the Archbishop of Canterbury must of necessity be a British guardian. Even recognizing the necessity of a representative who symbolizes the Anglican Communion, I feel that the leadership of the Communion should continue being collegial as it is now, through the Primates Meeting and the Anglican Consultative Council. The leader of the Communion should be elected with no regard to nationality, and should be changed periodically. How can this be done? That is a challenge to our creativity.

The most incoherent and absurd thing is the action on the part of some conservative groups to transform Lambeth Palace into another central authority, a movement toward the model of empire rather than away from it. We are seeing now the manifestation of an authoritarian tendency in the Communion, even when it arises from the praiseworthy intention of maintaining unity. In the first place, we must remember that unity is not something which requires us to smother liberty. Unity should not be confused with uniformity. Uniformity is not possible in the pluralistic world of today. In the second place, it is well to remember that no person or group can save the church. It is the Holy Spirit who maintains the unity of the church, in spite of our limitations. Beneath our divisions, we are united by the Spirit, that is, the spiritual reality in which we live. Our community has up to now remained united. This unity, although not perfect (due to our sin), is a fruit and miracle of the Spirit. So let us rely on that. In the third place, we should not build a unity which is based on concessions. Our challenge is to remain united, while respecting our differences. "Unity in what is essential, diversity in what is secondary, and charity in everything."

What kind of leadership do we need in the Anglican Communion for the future? Let us start with the episcopate. I agree that we need to maintain the historic episcopate as articulated in the Chicago-Lambeth Quadrilateral as an expression of our unity with the apostolic church, and through which we can maintain historical ties. I think it is important for us to have in the church that which is recognized as its *plene esse*, its fullness of being. However, we should not envelop ourselves in a sterile legalism which, in an uncritical way, sticks to canonical documents. Above all, and for the benefit of unity in the church, we must value the maintenance of the apostolic spirit that cares for other people and for their evangelization, which is characteristic of the apostolic college. If a bishop comes from a tradition which broke off from the legal succession, but which maintained an apostolic spirit, then why not recognize that? Let us avoid falling into a mechanical legalism; let us maintain the line of succession, but be open to the influxes of the Spirit which come to us from other historical traditions.

In order to speak about presbyters and deacons, we shall have to revise our own notion of the parish. In our tradition, as in its etymological origin, the parish is connected with the place where we live. The parish church is the one that serves the people who live in the neighboring community, either in a village or a town. In previous eras, the parish church was where you registered for church and state: baptisms, marriages, deaths, as well as any other civil acts. Since the parish community had such influence, it was necessary that it become bureaucratic in nature with the clergy being part of this. With the secularization of the world and consequent separation from registers and bureaucratic systems of the church in most parts of the Anglican Communion, the canonical structure will have to be revised. In a secularized world, instead of parishes with all the canonical and bureaucratic display that we now have, we should have communities of adoration and service that would endeavor to give the members of the larger community some signs of God's presence through a mystical awakening, and relief to the people who suffer.

We should be prophetic communities that teach the people to criticize power when it corrupts, and institutional structures when they become instruments of domination rather than well-being. In a renewed Christian community, there is no room for posts, but only for functions. Some of the functions have to be carried out by ordained persons, such as sacramental acts and pastoral counseling. Other functions, however, can be engaged by lay people who have a vocation for them, such as administration, social work, visiting the sick, and the like. What we need to banish from our communities is the clerical conception of the clergy as well as the clerical caste that manipulates the sacraments as if they were acts of magic, and who act as intermediaries of the (colonial) dominating power toward the people. All leadership functions need to be chosen by the community in recognition of a gift and preparation for the fulfillment of that gift. The Christian community is one of the few organizations of our globalized society which acts in the interest of others, and not just in its own. We need leaders who always keep this alive in the conscience of its members.

There was a time when the church used to be the center of the life of the local community, at least in our Western Greco-Roman civilization. The church used to care for people's health, community administration, education, and the arts. In the society we live in today, the church is marginal; it has been placed in the perimeter as an axis of social influence. This has been very good for us; we have no problems with secularization, but only with the ideology of secularism. It has been good in this sense: to belong to the church is to have a vocation, which at first sight is not valorized according to the patterns of the time, because this vocation is that of questioning in a prophetic manner the foundations of the type of society in which we live. It is the vocation of bringing a vertical perspective of life to humanity. In our world, reality is generally looked at from the societal and horizontal dimensions, which makes us insensitive to that which comes from the depths of reality. To be church is the vocation of giving with solidarity for those who suffer. To fulfill this vocation, there is no room for mediocre people. This is the time when our leaders are required to have an excellent existential, emotional, and intellectual formation. For in a world in which it is difficult to believe, we really need to know in whom and in what we believe.

In a post-Christian era, the phenomenon of Christendom is a thing of the past. It must be mentioned that it was through Christendom that much colonialism has been preserved in the church. We are in a different world; new structures of reality are being built. Not just our structures, but our faith in all its manifestations needs to be reconsidered. There is no formula for this. With our creativity, we are called into this reconstruction. I hope and pray that the essays in this book will foster the reconstruction of Anglicanism beyond our colonial past.

INTRODUCTION

In the spring of 1997, Kwok Pui-lan sat with Ian Douglas in the refectory of the Episcopal Divinity School (EDS), talking about the imminent return of Hong Kong to China in a few months' time. To mark the end of a chapter of British colonial history, Pui-lan suggested to Ian the possibility of organizing a conference on "Anglicanism in a Post-Colonial World," inviting Anglican theologians and leaders from around the world to join in the conversation.

Born and raised in Hong Kong, Pui-lan teaches theology and spirituality at the Episcopal Divinity School and prefers to put her family name, Kwok, in front of her given names to honor her Chinese heritage. Her parents went to Hong Kong as refugees from southern China after the Second World War and practiced Chinese folk religion at home. She became an Anglican in her teens due to the influence of a family friend, a descendant of the first Chinese pastor in Hong Kong. Her church in Hong Kong was built in the Chinese architectural style, with Chinese symbols as well as Christian motifs adorning the walls of the sanctuary. She comes from the diocese that first ordained a courageous woman, Florence Li Tim-Oi, to the priesthood in 1944, while her own vicar, Jane Hwang Hsien-Yuin, became one of the first women officially ordained in the Anglican Communion in 1971. Pui-lan has been active in the ecumenical movement since her college days, and has given lectures and led workshops throughout Asia and in many parts of the world.

Ian Douglas, who teaches world mission and global Christianity at EDS, has a much different experience of Anglicanism. While his maternal grandparents were Roman Catholic French Canadians from Quebec, his paternal grandparents emigrated from England to work in the paper mills of the industrial northeast United States. In his hometown, Fitchburg, Massachusetts, church identification was based on the immigrant community with which one identified. Finnish folk went to Messiah Lutheran, Greeks to Holy Trinity Orthodox, Quebecois to St. Francis's, Acadians to St. Joseph's, Italians to St. Leo's (these latter three being Roman Catholic churches), and immigrants from England to Christ Episcopal Church. Growing up in Christ Church as a second-generation American from English working-class stock, Ian identifies himself as an "ethnic Anglican." After his theological training, Ian served as a Volunteer for Mission in *L'Eglise Episcopale d'Haiti* (The Episcopal Church of Haiti) where he was exposed to the richness of Haitian culture and the challenges of Anglicanism in a non-English setting. Ian's combined interests in the changing nature of the Anglican Communion and in Christian mission led him to work in the World Mission Department at the national offices of the Episcopal Church, as well as to pursue doctoral studies in missiology. At the Episcopal Divinity School, Ian directs Anglican, Global and Ecumenical Studies, a study area that assists the seminary and the wider Episcopal Church USA to engage the realities of contemporary global Christianity. He has been secretary and chair of the Standing Commission on World Mission of the General Convention of the Episcopal Church and is the convener of the Episcopal Seminaries' Consultation on Mission.

Although coming from two very different experiences of Anglicanism, Pui-lan and Ian are both concerned about how political, economic, and cultural factors affect their church in the past, present, and future. For nearly a decade they have worked closely as faculty colleagues promoting global and ecumenical awareness in the classroom, in adult forums and continuing education in the diocese, and through their involvements in the national church.

As teachers and scholars, their work has contributed to an understanding of Christianity that is multicultural, justice-focused, and spiritually grounded.[1] A pioneer in Asian women's theology, Pui-lan insists that Asian people are not *missiological objects* of the West, but *theological subjects*, who can reflect on God's actions in the world through their own cultures and histories. An astute scholar of mission history of the Episcopal Church, Ian is interested in the theological foundation of mission and believes that mission is not an add-on, but is at the center of the life of the church.

In June of 1998, Ian and Pui-lan, with assistance from two other faculty colleagues, Professor Christopher Duraisingh and Professor Fredrica Harris Thompsett, organized a week-long consultation on "Anglicanism in a Post-Colonial World" at their seminary in Cambridge, Massachusetts. The consultation brought together approximately a dozen Anglican theologians, educators, and church leaders from a variety of contexts, including Brazil, Panama, Barbados, England, Aotearoa New Zealand, South Africa, Uganda, Hong Kong, India, and the United States. Participants had a taste of different meditations and worship from diverse cultures, as well as various kinds of ethnic food in Harvard Square. In formal sessions and over coffee breaks, they had animated conversations on some of the key questions facing the Anglican Communion: What does it mean for a family of churches historically identified with the Church of England that the majority of Anglicans today are from the South with very different cultures from that of the English? What does it mean that contemporary global Anglicanism is increasingly moving away from the cultural, political, and economic hegemony of Anglo-American colonialism? The reflections begun at the consultation gave birth to the present volume in the hope that it will invite more people into the continuing dialogue.

Those gathered in Cambridge in June of 1998 had a sense that the topic before them was timely and crucial to the life of the Communion. It became more evident the following month when bishops throughout the Anglican Communion met at the thirteenth Lambeth Conference in Canterbury, England. Ten years earlier, at the twelfth Lambeth Conference, the bishops from Africa, Asia, Latin America, and the Pacific slightly outnumbered their counterparts from the industrialized West. In 1988, however, the centers of power in the Communion had not yet changed dramatically, so that the historically privileged could avoid the reality that Anglicanism was in transition. Such could no longer be said after July 1998. It became vividly clear to all present in Canterbury—bishops, press people, consultants and pundits alike—that a profound power shift had occurred within the Anglican Communion. For the first time, bishops in the southern hemisphere found their voices in ways never before heard. From discussions on international debt to human sexuality, church leaders from Africa, Asia, Latin America, and the Pacific stated their opinions and made their presence known. Lambeth 1998 signaled for all that the colonial structures of the first two hundred years of the Anglican Communion were giving way to something new. What shape this new Communion will take in a new world is still to be discovered. How and if Anglicanism will be able to move beyond colonialism is the question of the day.

These shifts in demographics and power are not unique to the Anglican Communion. The number of Christians worldwide has done a topsy-turvey flip-flop within the last century, with the rate of change being especially steep within the last four decades. Mission scholar and statistician David Barrett has documented that at the turn of the twentieth century, close to three-quarters of the world's 558 million Christians lived in Europe or North America. Today 63 percent of the close to two billion Christians live in Asia, Africa, Latin America, and the Pacific.[2] For the Anglican church, David Hamid, director of ecumenical affairs for the Anglican Communion, estimates that almost 60 percent of Anglicans live outside the industrial countries of Europe, North America, and Oceania.[3] Although such facts are undeniable, many Christians in the West continue to function as if old structures of power and identity continue to have efficacy.

The demographic change and the shift of power within Anglicanism have not escaped the notice of scholars and theologians. Because of unequal access to resources, information, publishing, and promotion, the majority of publications on issues of common life in the Anglican Communion, however, continue to be dominated by scholars and writers from the West. A brief review of books published on global Anglicanism within the last decade demonstrates the bias toward Anglo-America. *Unashamed Anglicanism* by Stephen Sykes, Bishop of Ely in England, draws heavily on history to articulate an Anglican doctrine of the church and outline possible future directions for Anglicanism.[4] *The Transformation of Anglicanism: From State Church to Global Communion* by William L. Sachs does consider the stories of Anglicanism outside of England and the United States, but assumes the primacy of the Anglo-American context in defining identity and authority in the Communion.[5] The anthology *No Easy Peace* includes newer issues facing the Anglican church, such as women's leadership and sexual orientation, but addresses primarily the American context for these issues.[6]

Two other white, male authors, Alister McGrath and Mark Harris, have engaged more deeply the realities of an Anglican Communion that is no longer primarily English or American.[7] Both McGrath and Harris draw upon postmodern theory in their analysis of contemporary Anglicanism but end up in very different places as to their prescriptions for the future of the Communion. While McGrath argues for a new Anglican via media between the poles of "fundamentalism" and "liberalism," Harris commends a "vocational manifesto" for Anglicanism based upon provisionality, fellowship, mutuality, and common prayer.

The decennial meeting of the Lambeth Conference generally produces a series of new books on Anglicanism both before and after the meeting. In addition to the official report of the 1998 Lambeth Conference, such books as *Anglican Life and Witness: A Reader for the Lambeth Conference of Bishops, 1998* edited by Chris Sugden and Vinay Samuel, and *Diversity or Disunity? Reflections on Lambeth 1998* by James E. Solheim, give us glimpses into some of the more difficult issues before the Communion today.[8] The collection by Sugden and Samuel includes many authors from around the world, most of whom would share the editors' more conservative and evangelical theological position. Solheim, on the other hand, is an American journalist of a more liberal stance who wants to peel back some of the subtleties and strife of Lambeth 1998. In addition to these commentaries, the published reports of the meetings of the Anglican Consultative Council are a wealth of information on contemporary inter-Anglican life and mission.[9]

Perhaps the most up-to-date volume that sheds light on the breadth of today's Anglican church is *Anglicanism: A Global Communion* edited by Andrew Wingate, Kevin Ward, Carrie Pemberton and Wilson Sitshebo.[10] A collection of over seventy short essays from theologians and church leaders around the world, including a significant number of women and lay people, *Anglicanism: A Global Communion* lifts up many voices from different cultural and geographic contexts. Many of the authors are wrestling with what it means to be an Anglican Christian in this increasingly diverse and postcolonial family of churches. Limited by the space given, the short pieces give snapshots of the mosaic of the Anglican Communion, rather than providing detailed analyses of the issues or general thrusts of the direction of the church in the future.

The present volume wants to advance conversations about the contemporary Anglican Communion in crucial ways. First, it takes seriously the colonial legacy of Anglicanism and examines in depth the philosophical underpinning, cultural hegemony, and social and political ramifications of colonialism and its effects on the life of the church. As Bishop Glauco S. de Lima has said in the preface, the Anglican Communion was formed because of the imperial conditions of "the crown next to the cross"; and the colonial heritage is still evident in most churches today. A careful and sustained critique of colonialism with the help of critical theories and historical investigations will unravel the uneasy relationship between the church and the state; the rationale of the formation of provinces and other ecclesial structures; and the cultural assumptions of the liturgy, symbolism, and theology of the church. Without such a critical scrutiny, any discussion of the future of the Communion will be premature and may even reinscribe the colonial paradigm.

Second, the book provides careful analyses and detailed information of how globalization is reshaping the world today. The old forms of colonialism through political domination and military control have been superseded by the far-reaching and insidious global market, dictated not by individual nation states, but by the multinational corporations and international financial institutions. Ethicist Larry Rasmussen has described the three sequential waves of globalization in modern history.[11] The first wave was colonization, characterized by conquest, commerce, Christianity, and the spread of European-based civilization. The second wave was development, when the "underdeveloped" countries after the Second World War were exhorted to follow the example of the "developed" countries to modernize and increase their economic output. The current stage of globalization is defined by the logic of market, with little control and participation of the masses through democratic processes. What is the role of the Christian church in general, and the Anglican Communion in particular, in this global restructuring process?

Third, this book projects powerful visions of the future of Anglicanism for the new millennium, taking into consideration challenges of the present moment. Instead of a postcolonial Anglicanism, we have chosen to speak of an Anglicanism that is *beyond* colonialism. The prefix "post" has created much controversy among scholars interested in postcolonial discourse. As cultural critic Rey Chow has pointed out, "post" may mean "having gone through," "after," or "a notion of time which is not linear but constant, marked by events that may be technically finished but can only be fully understood with the consideration of the devastation they left behind."[12] Chow's final point especially emphasizes the ambiguous legacy of colonialism that cannot simply be described as "before" or "after," for its effects can be found lingering on for a long period of time. We prefer to use "beyond" to avoid the connotations of a linear time narrative. "Beyond" does not mean leaving behind the past or leaping by faith to an outer unknown world. "Beyond" connotes an exploratory space, a disturbance of the present, and a future that is not entirely certain. As influential postcolonial theorist Homi Bhabha has described it so vividly, beyond is a "moment of transit,"[13] where new possibilities can be discerned, identity and difference reconfigured, and the old myths challenged. In our Christian understanding, beyond is the open space that allows the action of God to happen in history. The ability to see beyond requires the discernment of the prophets, the courage of the truth-tellers, and the hope that history is not a contest of human wills, but an arena to show God's saving grace. *Beyond Colonial Anglicanism* signals a collective vision of the Anglican Communion to move beyond its colonial past to forge new identities and possibilities in order to respond to the calling of God in our present time.

The contributors to this book hope to share their insights and invite conversations for such a powerful vision. They write as bishops, priests, and lay leaders out of their long commitment to the renewal of the church. At the same time they write out of sustained involvement in issues such as the environment, feeding the hungry, the urban crisis, racism, and indigenous peoples' rights.

For a book that reexamines the colonial legacy, it is important to recognize the effects of English as a colonial language,[14] and to respect the ways that different authors—both native and non-native speakers—negotiate English in expressing their ideas.[15] Almost two-thirds of the authors in this collection of essays have grown up and lived in a cultural environment where English is a second, third, or fourth language. Even among native English speakers, the English usage and writing styles are different in England, North America, and Oceania. As editors, Ian and Pui-lan have tried to retain the liveliness of the authors' own voices and their diverse writing styles. For example, some authors are more sermonic and poetic, while others are argumentative and analytical. In all cases, the editors have done their best to respect the cultural milieu out of which each author has written.

Although some of the papers in this volume were originally presented at the consultation in 1998, they have all been revised for publication in light of developments in the Anglican Communion over the last two years. In addition, other authors were invited to contribute to cover new and emergent topics and to add a plurality of viewpoints and opinions. The book, thus, is not a conference proceeding, but points to next steps in a continuing conversation. The anthology covers a wide range of topics, but no single book can include all significant issues before the Anglican Communion. The editors have tried to present a multiplicity of voices, including women, lay persons, indigenous people, and individuals from diverse geographic, cultural and social locations. Most of the contributors have been trained in theology and religious disciplines, while a few are social scientists more adept in the fields of statistics and analytical figures.

It needs to be stressed that not all authors agree with one another on each topic. As a result, the articles represent the viewpoints of the individual authors only. Readers will notice, however, that similar issues are brought into the conversation across the contributions but manifest themselves differently in diverse contexts. For example, racism experienced by Africans in diaspora (Kortright Davis's chapter) is different from that experienced by indigenous peoples in the Pacific Rim (Jenny Plane Te Paa's contribution). Similarly, the global economy may link the urban crises in Western societies with the debt crisis of the Third World, but they each present different sets of problems and require appropriate contextual responses from the churches. The anthology also demonstrates that the same issue can be looked at from diverse angles and theological perspectives. For example, Pui-lan analyzes the debate of homosexuality at Lambeth through the lens of cultural politics shaped by the colonial past. Njongonkuku Ndungane interprets the issue within the contexts of diverse interpretations of the Bible and different understandings of the teaching authority of the episcopacy. Renée L. Hill articulates an emancipatory vision of the church, based on the experience of the struggles of gay men and lesbians in the United States. We hope that such diverse and contextually informed interpretations will enliven discussions on crucial issues before the Communion today.

Writing from diverse geographic, social, ethnic, cultural and theological locations, the authors do share some common hermeneutical assumptions as well as gospel vision. They all recognize the impact of global capitalism on the livelihood of people and on the restructuring of cultural and social processes. They are interested in looking beyond the colonial and globalization paradigms to articulate a future for the church beyond the Anglo-American understanding of Anglicanism. Toward this end, the authors highlight the importance of context in theological reflection and in discerning God's will in our world. Basic to this contextual hermeneutic is the imperative of listening to voices of the suffering and marginalized among us. The authors assert that the gospel of Jesus Christ means love, freedom, and inclusivity for all. The Anglican Communion, for them, must serve God's mission of justice, compassion, and reconciliation, by becoming a beacon of hope for the broken and fragmented of humanity and an advocate for the goodness and sustainability of all creation.

The anthology is divided into three sections. The essays in part one, "Colonialism and the Anglican Communion," trace the philosophical, social, and cultural roots of Anglicanism in a variety of ways. Ian Douglas's essay points to the increasing plurality within the Anglican Communion and the power shift that occurred at the Lambeth Conference 1998. He traces the rise of Anglicanism to the economic and socio-political results of colonialism as well as to the philosophical and theological underpinnings of modernity. Instead of constructing Anglican identity based on doctrinal agreements or on the centralization of authority, Douglas argues for celebrating apostolic catholicity when the gospel is translated into the vernacular in its local contexts. In the next chapter, Kwok Pui-lan focuses on cultural hegemony that has shaped the identity, history, and liturgy of the Anglican church. Engaging the works of Gramnsci and postcolonial theorists, she analyzes the dense web of connections between cultural representation and colonialism and presents her hopes for a multicultural and plurifocal Anglican church. David Hamid's essay presents much-needed facts and data about the churches of the Communion. For Hamid, the cultural diversity of the churches, uneven monetary contribution to the Anglican Communion, and the erosion of constants create tensions when we speak about autonomy and interdependence within the family of churches. Finally, Hamid argues that the future of Anglican identity is also shaped by ecumenical sensitivity and the increasing participation of churches in communion with Anglicanism.

The essays in part two, "Challenges of the Present World," focus on some of the significant global issues the church needs to reckon with in carrying out its witness and ministry. Denise Ackermann discusses the politics of violence that shapes the contemporary life of her home country, South Africa, and undergirds racial strife, ethnic cleansing, and domestic violence around the globe. She passionately calls for a ministry of healing for the church and delineates the markers of a feminist theology of healing praxis. Kortright Davis's essay uses his personal experience as a Caribbean theologian to highlight the burden of racism and the struggles of the black church. After describing the abusive cultures that contribute to racism and other oppressions, he elucidates the cultural and religious principles needed for Christians to "sail life's rugged sea."

The next two chapters deal squarely with economic injustice and environmental degradation brought on by the growing gap between the rich and the poor in the world. Jeffrey Golliher articulates the relationship between the web of life and the body of Christ, and suggests a profound ecological reformation of the church and a spiritual revolution that sees human beings as "co-partners" with all living things. As social scientists, John Hammock and Anuradha Harinarayan provide data and analyses about problems in our current political economy and trade arrangements and point to ways that the churches can be involved in the debt relief process. In the following chapter, African-American theologian Renée Hill rejoins the hot debates regarding human sexuality from her perspective as a lesbian Episcopal priest. She challenges the church to live up to the promise of freedom, compassion, and justice based on God's love for all, and discusses the controversy around the blessing of same-sex unions within the Episcopal Church USA. The last essay in this section focuses on Christian responses to urbanization. Laurie Green, who has written many essays on the challenges of the city, reinterprets the traditional teachings of the church as one, holy, catholic, and apostolic to provide guidance for the church to be the body of Christ in the global and urbanizing world.

The final section, "Visions for the Future Church," presents the voices of theologians and Christian leaders on key issues facing the Anglican Communion from different continents and cultural contexts. Njongonkulu Ndungane's essay is based on his address given in January 2000 at the Church Divinity School of the Pacific as part of the conference, "Healing Leaves: The Authority of the Bible for Anglicans Today." While scripture plays a pivotal role in theology and liturgy, Ndungane argues that Christians have different approaches to biblical authority and hermeneutics influenced by culture, gender, and social location. He cites as an example how scripture has been used in the discussion on sexuality and gender at the 1998 Lambeth Conference. Fredrica Harris Thompsett's essay offers an expansive and collaborative vision of the church, based on the ministry of the whole people of God. Challenging a colonial and hierarchical ecclesiological structure, she argues for a reaffirmation of authority grounded in the baptismal promise. From Aotearoa New Zealand, Jenny Plane Te Paa shares the history and vision of how the Anglican church struggles to redress injustice done in the past to the Maori people. As the leader of the only indigenous Anglican theological college in the world, Te Paa describes the struggles of developing future leadership formation that is culturally appropriate and justice-based.

The final three essays discuss the crucial issues of episcopacy, worship, and faith and witness of the church. Simon E. Chiwanga's essay on "Beyond the Monarch/Chief" is a part of his doctoral thesis, in which he examines the cultural and colonial legacy of viewing the episcopate as a monarchy. Instead, he offers the image of *mhudumu* from the Tanzanian context that reorients episcopal leadership toward servanthood and mutual responsibility. Jaci Maraschin from Brazil discusses the interplay between culture, spirit, and worship. He points out the fact that contemporary Anglican worship is challenged by the commercialism of banalized and globalized culture on the one hand, and by the bondage to the tradition of the Common Prayer Book on the other. As an Anglican in the non-English-speaking world, he offers the hope that worship may be rooted in the beauty of a spiritual culture that is responsive to local needs and evokes the sense of God's mystical presence. The last essay, by Christopher Duraisingh, revisits some of the discussions of the postcolonial context and presents his visions of the gospel as multivoiced story, the dialogical witness of the church, and the polycentric communion. Using the Pentecost experience as a guiding metaphor, Duraisingh helps us to think through how the church may address diversity, radical pluralism, and unity in a postcolonial and non-Eurocentric world.

NOTES

[1] The phrase "justice-focused and spiritually grounded" is taken from a sermon preached by Bishop Barbara Harris on 15 October 1999 at the St. John's Chapel of the Episcopal Divinity School.

[2] David B. Barrett, "Annual Statistical Table on Global Mission: 2000," *International Bulletin of Missionary Research* 24 (January 2000): 24-25.

[3] See Chapter 3.

[4] Stephen Sykes, *Unashamed Anglicanism* (Nashville: Abingdon Press, 1995).

[5] William L. Sachs, *The Transformation of Anglicanism: From State Church to Global Communion* (Cambridge: Cambridge University Press, 1993).

[6] Carter Heyward and Sue Phillips, eds., *No Easy Peace: Liberating Anglicanism* (New York: University Press of America, 1992).

[7] Alistair E. McGrath, *The Renewal of Anglicanism* (Harrisburg: Morehouse Publishing, 1993); Mark Harris, *The Challenge of Change: The Anglican Communion in the Post-Modern Era* (New York: Church Publishing, 1998).

[8] Mark Dyer, et al., eds., *The Official Report of the Lambeth Conference, 1998* (Harrisburg: Morehouse Publishing, 1999); Chris Sugden and Vinay Samuel, eds., *Anglican Life and Witness: A Reader for the Lambeth Conference of Anglican Bishops, 1998* (London: SPCK, 1998); James E. Solheim, *Diversity or Disunity: Reflections on Lambeth 1998* (New York: Church Publishing, 1999).

[9] James M. Rosenthal and Nicola Currie, eds., *Being Anglican in the Third Millennium: Anglican Consultative Council X* (Harrisburg: Morehouse Publishing, 1997); James M. Rosenthal, and Margaret Rodgers, eds., *The Communion We Share: Anglican Consultative Council XI, Scotland* (Harrisburg: Morehouse Publishing, 2000).

[10] Andrew Wingate, et al., eds., *Anglicanism: A Global Communion* (New York: Church Publishing, 1998).

[11] Larry Rasmussen, "'Give Us Word of the Humankind We Left to Thee': Globalization and Its Wake," *EDS Occasional Papers* 4 (1999): 1-16.

[12] Rey Chow, *Ethics after Idealism: Theory—Culture—Ethnicity—Reading* (Bloomington: Indiana University Press, 1998), 150-51.

[13] Homi K. Bhabha, *The Location of Culture* (London: Routledge, 1994), 1.

[14] See Gauri Viswanathan, *Masks of Conquest: Literary Study and British Rule in India* (New York: Columbia University Press, 1989).

[15] For a discussion on how the formerly colonized peoples negotiate the writing of English, see Bill Ashcroft, Gareth Griffiths, and Helen Tiffin, *The Empire Writes Back: Theory and Practice in Post-colonial Literature* (London: Routledge, 1989).

PART I

COLONIALISM AND THE ANGLICAN COMMUNION

1

THE EXIGENCY OF TIMES AND OCCASIONS

Power and Identity in the Anglican Communion Today

IAN T. DOUGLAS

Even to the casual observer, the 1998 Lambeth Conference of worldwide Anglican bishops was not the garden party of yesteryear.[1] Following the conference, Anglicans in the industrialized West have had to wrestle deeply with the reality that the Anglican Communion is no longer a Christian community primarily identified with Anglo-American culture. Up until the summer of 1998, most Anglicans in the West could pretty well ignore the radical shifts in demographics that have occurred in the Communion over the last four decades and thus avoid hard questions of identity and authority. The cultural, economic, and political power of Western Anglicans shielded them from deeply engaging the realities of an increasingly diverse and plural church.[2]

But Lambeth 1998 signaled a turning point for Anglicanism. In debates over international debt and/or sexuality, it became abundantly clear to all that the churches in the southern hemisphere, or the Two-Thirds World, would not stand idly by while their sisters and brothers in the United States, England, and other Western countries continued to set the agenda. Whether aided or not by some in the West who stood to gain ground in sexuality debates by siding with bishops in Africa, Asia, Latin America, and the Pacific, Lambeth 1998 pointed out that a profound power shift has occurred within Anglicanism. For the first time ever, the Anglican Communion has had to face head-on the radical multi-cultural reality of a global Christian community. Old understandings of Anglican identity based on shared Anglo-American hegemony have broken down. Anthems of Titcomb and Tallis sung by boy choirs in chapels at Cambridge and Oxford can no longer hold Anglicans together. Even bishops taking tea with the Queen in the garden of Buckingham Palace during Lambeth is not what it used to be.

Astute watchers of Lambeth and the emerging Communion knew that such a profound shift has been in the works for decades. Speaking of the contemporary Anglican Communion, the Most Rev. Robert Runcie, past Archbishop of Canterbury, in his address to the 1985 General Convention of the Episcopal Church prophetically announced:

> We have developed into a worldwide family of churches. Today there are 70 million members of what is arguably the second most widely distributed body of Christians. No longer are we identified by having some kind of English heritage. English today is now the second language of the Communion. There are more black members than white. Our local diversities span the spectrum of the world's races, needs, and aspirations. We have only to think of Bishop [Desmond] Tutu's courageous witness in South Africa to be reminded that we are no longer a church of the white middle classes allied only to the prosperous western world.[3]

The changes in contemporary Anglicanism, from a white, predominantly English-speaking church of the West to a church of the southern hemisphere are consistent with the changing face of Christianity over the last four decades. Anglican mission scholar David Barrett has documented that in the year 1900, 77 percent of the 558 million Christians in the world lived in Europe or North America. Today only 37 percent of the close to two billion Christians live in same area. Barrett further predicts that in less than three decades, in the year 2025, fully 71 percent of the projected 2.6 billion Christians worldwide will live in Asia, Africa, Latin America, and the Pacific.[4] If we consider the church in Africa south of the Sahara, specifically, the numbers are equally astounding. In 1960, after a 150 years of Western missionary activity, the number of Christians in Africa was approximately 50 million. From 1960 until 1990, the Christian population in Africa increased from 50 million to 250 million![5] That change represents a five-fold increase in one fifth of the time, a fact not attributable to population growth alone.

What are we to make of this transformation in the global body of Christ? In particular, how has our own little corner of the Christian tradition, that part of the body of Christ that traces its origins to the holy catholic church first rooted in the British Isles and now known as Anglicanism, been transformed into a truly global Christian community? It is useful to reconsider our history.

For the majority of the nineteenth and the first half of the twentieth century the Anglican Communion (as it existed) was dominated by Western churches. Chief among them were the Church of England, the Episcopal Church in the United States, and the Anglican churches in Canada and Australia.[6] Each of these four autonomous Anglican churches supported and controlled their own missions around the world. In the case of the Episcopal Church USA, the three biggest mission fields in the nineteenth century were China, Liberia, and Japan. From the 1850s to the 1960s mission was inextricably linked to Western colonialism and imperialism.[7] This was especially true for the Church of England as the established church, for wherever the Crown went so too did the church.

All of this began to change, however, in the 1960s, for with political independence for countries in Africa, Asia, Latin America, and the Pacific came the desire for ecclesial independence for the mission fields. Over time the missions grew into autocephalous Anglican churches in their own right, ostensibly autonomous from their "mother" churches in England and the United States.[8] With the increase in the number of member churches in the Anglican Communion, Anglicans began to search for new ways of coming together, new ways of relating to one another as the body of Christ. The Anglican Congress of 1963, held in Toronto, Canada, was a watershed for the contemporary Anglican Communion. This meeting of Anglican lay people, priests, and bishops from every corner of the globe embraced the influential and far-reaching vision: "Mutual Responsibility and Interdependence in the Body of Christ" (MRI). MRI proposed a radical reorientation of mission priorities and stressed equality and partnership between all Anglicans. It stated in part:

> In our time the Anglican Communion has come of age. Our professed nature as a world-wide fellowship of national and regional churches has suddenly become a reality.... The full communion in Christ which has been our traditional tie has suddenly taken on a totally new dimension. It is now irrelevant to talk of "giving" and "receiving" churches. The keynotes of our time are equality, interdependence, mutual responsibility.[9]

"Mutual Responsibility and Interdependence" stood as a challenge to the Anglo-American preeminence in the Anglican Communion during the nineteenth and first half of the twentieth centuries. The Rt. Rev. Stephen Bayne, Bishop of Olympia (Washington, USA) and the first Executive Officer of the Anglican Communion, played a central role in the development of MRI. He knew that the changes afoot in the Anglican Communion of the 1960s would require a radical readjustment in understandings of Anglican identity and mission. Recalling his diocese in the United States, Bayne reflected on the changes in thinking that needed to occur if Episcopalians were to live into the truth of MRI.

> They [the people of the Diocese of Olympia] need, as I need, to rethink the whole meaning of mission, and that as this happens, the cost of it in the abandonment of old ways of thinking and old comforts and old priorities is going to be very great. Many people in the Diocese of Olympia between 1947 and 1960 had the feeling that the Church was an association of people, a kind of memorial association for a deceased clergyman named Christ, whose ideals were important and who was an early supporter of the "American Way of Life." To such people mission was something you did for somebody else. Mission was a way of keeping God in business.[10]

Unfortunately, Bayne's challenge to the church in the United States has remained largely unheeded. MRI remains a goal to be achieved rather than a reality that is lived. The prime question for Anglicans today is how does mutual responsibility and interdependence play itself out in a community of thirty-eight equal and autonomous churches? What are the challenges prohibiting us from realizing the vision of the 1963 Anglican Congress? I believe that there are two significant and related forces, one political and economic, the other philosophical and theological, that stand in the way of the Anglican Communion's genuine embrace of mutual responsibility and interdependence.

The first force prohibiting our living into the vision of a mutually interdependent community in Christ is the ongoing legacy of colonialism. As mentioned above, the Anglican Communion, for the bulk of its history, has been closely linked to of Western colonialism. If one considers a map of today's Anglican Communion, this fact is undeniable. The majority of Anglican churches lie in areas of the world that at one time or another were territories of either England or the United States. With the advent of political independence for colonies in the southern hemisphere, the missions of the Church of England or the Episcopal Church USA "grew up" into autonomous churches of the Anglican Communion. These churches were no longer to be considered outposts or provinces of the Church of England or the Episcopal Church USA.[11] Although many of these countries where the newly independent Anglican churches have come into being still suffer at the hands of economic colonialism (witness the sin of international debt), by and large with political independence has come ecclesial independence. Whether Anglicans in the West are prepared to accept it or not, the Anglican Communion today has begun to move from being a colonial church to a postcolonial reality. As a result, the political and economic structures of power associated with colonial dominance have begun to lose their efficacy in the new Anglican Communion.[12]

The second major force that hinders an embrace of the new Anglican Communion lies in the ongoing dominance of the philosophical and theological underpinnings of modernity. Whether one marks the beginning of the Anglican Communion at 1784 with the consecration of Samuel Seabury as the first bishop of an autonomous Anglican church outside of the British Isles, or with the first Lambeth Conference of Bishops in 1867, the Anglican Communion as a family of churches is approximately 200 years old.[13] The Anglican Communion therefore is a thoroughly *modern* phenomenon—with "modern" understood as the age of modernity, the last 500 years, the Age of Enlightenment.

The philosophical constructs of the Age of Enlightenment elevate rational thought and the modern scientific method to a place of preeminence and authority. Trusting in the reliability of human reason, Western scientists, one by one, seemed to unlock the inscrutabilities of nature. The subjugation of the natural world gave way to the advent of manufacturing and the Industrial Revolution. By the end of the nineteenth century the West, with its political, economic, military and industrial might, had been able to claim both knowledge of and power over peoples and places in all corners of the world.

> Subjugation perhaps properly defines the order of the Enlightenment; subjugation of nature by human intellect, colonial control through physical and cultural domination, and economic superiority through mastery of the laws of the market. The confidence with which the culture of the West approached the world to appropriate it reflected in the constructs of science, industry, and empire that principally represent the wealth of the period.... The scientific catalog of racial otherness, the variety of racial alien, was a principal product of the period.[14]

Enlightenment thought and colonial domination go hand in hand, with the former giving rationale to the latter and the latter ensuring the world view of the former.

The Anglican Communion has historically traded on the power of Enlightenment thought as much as it has on the power of Western colonialism. Anglicanism, up until very recently, has rested on the philosophical and theological formularies of the Enlightenment that value either/or propositions, binary constructs, and dualistic thinking. Anglicans formed in Enlightenment thought pride themselves on being able to figure things out, to know limits, to be able to define what is right and what is wrong, who is in and who is out. Modern man (and I use this non-inclusive term deliberately) values clear lines of authority, knowing who is in charge, a hierarchical power structure. Pluralities and multiple ways of seeing the world are an anathema to modernity and thus to many who have been in control in the Anglican Communion for most of its history.

But all of this is changing as the majority of Anglicans today are located in places where the constructs of Enlightenment thought have less efficacy. I do not mean here that sisters and brothers in the South and those who are more free from the constrictions of modern thought are less educated or caught in a world of superstitions, as the Rt. Rev. Jack Spong, now retired Bishop of Newark, New Jersey, asserted at Lambeth 1998.[15] Rather, the majority of Anglicans in the world today are able to live in multiple realities, which include Western Enlightenment constructs as well as their own local contexts. It is important to emphasize here that the marginalized in the West, especially women, people of color, gay and lesbian individuals, have always lived multiple realities, their own particularities and that of the dominant culture. It is only those in power, historically heterosexual, white, clerical, males in the West, who have the privilege of believing and acting as if there were only one reality, their own! The movement within Anglicanism from being a church grounded in modernity and secure in the Enlightenment, to postmodern or extra-modern reality is as tumultuous as the shift from colonialism to postcolonialism.

The transition in the Anglican world from colonialism to postcolonialism and from modernity to postmodernity is terrifying, especially for those individuals who historically have been the most privileged, most in control, most secure in the colonial Enlightenment world. The radical transition afoot in the Anglican Communion is terrifying, for it means that Anglicans in the West—especially heterosexual, white, male clerics—will no longer have the power and control that they have enjoyed for so long. They thus feel anxious, confused, lost in a sea of change. The movement from being a colonial and modern church to that of a postcolonial and postmodern community in Christ, with its concomitant specter of loss, is vigorously countered by those who have been historically the most privileged in the Communion. Various attempts to reassert control, reassert power, put Humpty Dumpty back together again, with all the King's horses and all the King's men, are dominating inter-Anglican conversations at this point in history.

Two attempts to maintain old structures of power and privilege in response to the changing face of Anglicanism are particularly insidious and thoroughly un-Anglican. The first is a rather diffuse attempt to claim "historic documents" of the church as authoritative for all time. Driven by fear of change, some want to look backward to a perceived simpler time to claim clear definitions of what it means to be an Anglican today. There are increasing attempts in various corners of Anglicanism, especially in the West, to raise the Thirty-nine Articles or some other theological affirmation to be the defining statements of what Anglicans are and are to believe.[16] What results is a new confessionalism, as insecure individuals and those who fear loss of power in these changing times struggle gallantly to nail down Anglican theology and beliefs. Armed with clear doctrinal definitions and limits, the same folk are then able to count who is in and who is out. Control is reasserted, ambiguity is overcome, and traditional authority is maintained.

The second response to these changing times are attempts to construct a new central structure of authority for the Anglican

Communion, what I call a new "curialization." There are those
who believe that without a clear, central authority structure (such
as the one the Roman Catholic Church has), the body of Christ,
the church catholic, will fly apart in a disorganized mess. And so
some gravitate toward a kind of Anglican curia with the Archbishop of Canterbury at its head. The much celebrated *Virginia Report*
of the Inter-Anglican Theological and Doctrinal Commission
attempts to define "four instruments" of Anglican unity, namely:
the Archbishop of Canterbury, the Lambeth Conference, the
Anglican Consultative Council, and the Primates Meeting.[17]
Implicit in these four instruments is a bias to episcopal and
archepiscopal authority. One of the primary authors of the *Virginia Report* has emphasized publicly that Anglicans should consider the Archbishop of Canterbury as "the personal embodiment
of (Anglican) continuity and unity in Christ."[18] Decisions made at
the 1998 Lambeth Conference of Anglican bishops have imbued
the primates, or archbishops of the Anglican Communion, with
enhanced responsibility for pan-Anglican doctrinal and moral
matters and unheard-of extra-metropolitical authority to intervene in the life of Anglican provinces locally, under the Presidency
of the Archbishop of Canterbury.[19] Even the most recent report of
the Anglican and Roman Catholic International Commission
(ARCIC II) challenges "Anglicans to be open to and desire a
recovery and re-reception of ... the exercise of universal primacy
by the Bishop of Rome."[20]

There are those within the Anglican Communion today that
celebrate and seek to advance the slide toward increased primatial authority within Anglicanism. This is especially true among
those who feel as if some churches in the Anglican Communion,
such as the Episcopal Church USA, are pursuing an errant path
with respect to issues of human sexuality. Encouraged and supported by conservative groups of Episcopalians in the United
States, such as the American Anglican Council and the Ekklesia
Society, eight archbishops, including seven primates, from the
Anglican Communion wrote an "open letter" to the Presiding
Bishop of the Episcopal Church, the Most Rev. Frank Griswold, in
April 1999. The letter called on Presiding Bishop Griswold to use
his perceived power to "take whatever steps may be necessary to
uphold [within the Episcopal Church] the moral teachings and
Christian faith of the Anglican Communion."[21] Bishop Griswold

responded by inviting the archbishops to "come and see" the many and fine ministries in the Episcopal Church and "listen to the experience of homosexual persons."[22] In late September and early October 1999, five archbishops or their representatives toured the Episcopal Church in the United States, seeing and listening to the stories of American Episcopalians who were both "liberal" and "conservative." The following month these visitors were joined by other "conservative" Anglicans from the United States and around the world in a meeting in Kampala, Uganda, to formulate a response to the visit and next steps of action. The nine primates at the Kampala meeting rejected a bid by First Promise, a network of conservative American Episcopalians, to consecrate alternative "orthodox" bishops for the Episcopal Church USA, to minister to disgruntled congregations; although some among the group were prepared to go ahead with such a plan.[23] The archbishops who had visited the United States, however, did respond to Bishop Griswold by suggesting "that the Presiding Bishop find ways to strengthen the framework that will make possible both obedience and dialogue ... by some arrangement for alternative [episcopal] oversight" for the conservative congregations.[24]

Two primates who remained convinced that immediate alternative episcopal oversight was necessary for the Episcopal Church believed that it was within their authority to take steps to effect such. On January 29, 2000, in Singapore, the Most Rev. Emmanuel Kolini, Archbishop of Rwanda, and the Most Rev. Moses Tay, then Archbishop of South East Asia, consecrated two American conservative priests, the Rev. Charles Murphy and the Rev. John Rodgers, as "missionary bishops" to the United States. Such action was intended both to provide alternative episcopal leadership to conservative congregations in the Episcopal Church USA, as well as to cause an international crisis within the authority structures of the Anglican Communion. The "irregular consecrations" of Murphy and Rodgers were planned to push the archbishops of the Communion, who had a regularly scheduled Primates Meeting in Oporto, Portugal, in March 2000, to take some decisive action on issues of human sexuality. Archbishops Harry Goodhew from Sydney, Australia, and Maurice Sinclair, Primate of the Southern Cone (two of the original signatories of the April 1999 letter to Bishop Griswold), emphasized both the perceived authority and responsibility of the Primates to establish moral norms for the Communion.

> With respect to the resolution of the sexuality controversy it is important though to return to the responsibility of the Primates meeting under the chairmanship of the Archbishop of Canterbury. At Lambeth '98 there was the reaffirmation of a Lambeth '88 resolution which urged 'that encouragement be given to a developing collegial role for the Primates Meeting under the presidency of the Archbishop of Canterbury, so that the Primates Meeting is able to exercise enhanced responsibility in offering guidance on doctrinal, moral and pastoral matters.' This resolution complements what we have already noted for the Primates in terms of giving guidelines on the limits of Anglican diversity ... in full respect for the leadership of the president, decisions backed by the majority [of Primates] should be observed by all. In relation to human sexuality, one would anticipate the need for the Primates to delineate a Biblical vision for teaching and ministry and to commit themselves and their bishops to consistent observance of the historic disciplines while any further dialogue proceeds.[25]

For Goodhew and Sinclair at least, a strong central authority residing in the Primates Meeting was not only positive and necessary for the Anglican Communion but a *fait accompli.* The fact that the Portugal meeting of the primates did not follow Goodhew and Sinclair's lead nor give a clear and unambiguous mandate on "the limits of Anglican diversity," demonstrates that not all archbishops see eye to eye with Goodhew and Sinclair on the role and function of the Primates Meeting. The most the primates could say about the limits of Anglican diversity is that "the unity of the Communion as a whole still rests on the Lambeth Quadrilateral: The Holy Scriptures as the rule and standard of faith; the creeds of the undivided Church; the two sacraments ordained by Christ himself; and the historic episcopate. Only a formal and public repudiation of this would place a diocese or province outside the Anglican Communion."[26]

Perhaps the Bishop of Mpwapwa, Tanzania, the Rt. Rev. Simon Chiwanga, Chair of the Anglican Consultative Council, said it best in his address to the eleventh meeting of the Anglican Consultative Council in Dundee, Scotland, in September 1999. "In these times and change, many who are fearful of the future seek secular solace in what they perceive as safe and sound.... Whether on or curia, catechism or conference, constitution or council, the fearful are looking for easy answers."[27] But easy answers based on a shared Anglo heritage will no longer hold the Anglican Communion together. In these changing times we must not put our hope in either tighter doctrinal definitions or a more centralized authority structure. Instead, a new understanding of Anglican identity is needed if we are to remain in communion across the colors and cultures, nations and nationalities, that Anglicanism now embodies.

BACK TO THE FUTURE WITH ANGLICAN IDENTITY

The roots of a contemporary understanding of Anglican identity lie not in a newly constructed form of Anglican self-definition but rather in a reclamation of the historic processes of contextualization which lie at the heart of the English Reformation. In the sixteenth century, Christians in England struggled to formulate a Christian community that was both genuinely English and genuinely connected to the church universal. The advent of the Church of England marked a reconception of the body of Christ on the English shores that was at once profoundly particular and profoundly catholic. This process of contextualization, in which the church becomes grounded in the local realities of a particular people while remaining in communion across the differences of culture and geography, particularly through a shared history with the See of Canterbury, is where Anglican identity lies. Anglicanism thus can be understood *as the embrace and celebration of apostolic catholicity within vernacular moments.* Such an understanding warrants unpacking if it is to be used for advancing conversations about Anglican identity in these postcolonial times.[28]

First, what is the meaning of embrace and celebration? Embrace begins with an affirmation of the incarnation. In Jesus, God took human form and became one with humanity. To heal the sins of division and separation between God and humanity, and between humans as individuals and nations, God crossed the divide and became incarnate in a first-century Jew. God embraced a particular culture, nation and people in Jesus. Fully human and fully divine, God in Jesus became one of us and lived the human condition in all of our glory and all of our failings. God embraced humanity in the incarnation of Jesus.

The wonder and joy of the embrace of humanity in a first-century Jew is that God's incarnation in Jesus did not stop with him.

The new creation effected in Jesus has continued to spread to the ends of the earth in the ongoing life and body of Christ, the church. The miracle of the incarnation is that God's embrace of humanity in a particular person, at a particular place and time, was not limited but universal. Empowered by the Holy Spirit, the incarnation of God in Christ gave way to the plurality of Pentecost. The embrace of humanity in Jesus the Jew became the embrace of all of humanity in the worldwide body of Christ.

The ongoing incarnation of Christ is thus both profoundly particular and profoundly universal. All Christians share a oneness in Christ, but the reality of the incarnate one among us can only be known and experienced contextually. God's embrace of humanity, and our embrace of God in the incarnation of Jesus, is at the heart of God's reign made real in both our particular localities and across the universality of time and space.[29]

The church, as the body of Christ in the world today, thus lives and celebrates the reality of the incarnation, locally and globally. As Anglicans, we believe that each time we gather to hear God's word and share in the sacraments, we are joined anew with God and with each other in Jesus. As a liturgically centered people, we affirm that the celebration of the eucharist is an expression of genuine communion with God and each other. The eucharist becomes for us the place where we herald and experience anew that incredible good news that God has embraced us, individually and corporately.[30] Whether graced with handbells in Houston, drums in Dar es Salaam, or choirs in Canterbury, the celebration of our commonality with God and each other in Christ is at the heart of our worshiping community. The embrace of us by God and God by us in the incarnation of Jesus, and the celebration of this profound and life-giving truth in our sharing of the body and blood of Christ is basic to understanding Anglican identity today.

Anglicanism, however, does have a specific historical expression of how the body of Christ has developed over time. This is where an emphasis on apostolic catholicity informs Anglican identity. As Anglicans we believe that the body of Christ is genuinely catholic—that is, genuinely universal. There is an ongoing continuity of the church today with the first band of believers who gathered around Jesus. We are not divorced from either those who have gone before us or those who will follow us. Rather, God's redeeming, reconciling embrace of the world in Christ is true for all humanity, for all of time. Those of us who are brought into the body of Christ through baptism share in a universal, catholic community of faith. Often divided by the failings and foibles of a fallen humanity, the unity of the body of Christ is the eschatological reality that we affirm as catholic Christians.

Anglican commitment to catholicity has emphasized over time some apostolic norms, particularly as to the nature and authority of the episcopate. The Chicago-Lambeth Quadrilateral of 1888, originally intended as a generous ecumenical venture outlining the basics of the Christian faith, offers what has become a classical view of Anglican apostolicity.[31] The fourth affirmation of the Quadrilateral outlines the importance of "the Historic Episcopate, locally adapted in the methods of its administration to the varying needs of the nations and peoples called of God into the unity of His Church."[32] For Anglicans, the historic episcopate, locally adapted, gives way to our valuing of apostolic succession. The fact that Anglicans believe we can trace our episcopate back to the apostles through the historic See of Canterbury is a source of great joy, confidence and pride—one that frankly some of our reformed sisters and brothers find from time to time off-putting and exclusive. The emphasis on "manual transmission" (as a Lutheran colleague has described it), namely the ongoing continuity of episcopal ordination through a perceived unbroken laying on of hands, contributes to an Anglican understanding of apostolicity.[33] For Anglicans, the unity of the church through time and across geographic and cultural boundaries is connected to the exercise of *episcopé* located in the historic episcopate as it has been conferred to us through the Chair of St. Augustine, the first Archbishop of Canterbury.

Apostolic catholicity for Anglicans does value the succession of episcopal authority through, and in relationship with, the historic See of Canterbury. But such is not the only understanding of apostolicity in the body of Christ. Lutheran sisters and brothers in the United States, in particular, take exception to what seems to them our over-emphasis on "manual transmission" to define apostolicity.[34] Anglican affirmations of the universal catholicity of the body of Christ, however, maintain that the apostolic nature of the church is intimately bound up with the exercise of *episcopé* as manifested in the historic episcopate.

The emphasis on the universal body of Christ, our Anglican apostolic catholicity, can only be known and made real, however, within vernacular moments. What are vernacular moments? Lamin Sanneh, Professor of Missions and World Christianity at Yale Divinity School and originally from Gambia in West Africa, has emphasized the importance of the "translatability" of the gospel. Professor Sanneh, in his study of the missionary impact on culture, maintains that the gospel finds its truth and validity only as it is translated into the local vernacular and idiom of the cultures into which it travels.[35] He stresses that as the gospel is translated into the vernacular, the new local body of Christ, as the primary agent of translation, discovers life and hope in the liberating good news of Christ. The imperative on the translatability of the gospel into the local context presupposes that the incarnation of God in Christ is an ongoing reality that can be known and made real across the diversity of the world's cultures and peoples. In the translation of the gospel into the local vernacular and idiom, the particularities of the translating Christian community are both affirmed in their cultural and ontological constructs while at the same time connected to a greater whole across the worldwide Christian community. Sanneh would assert that the whole truth of the gospel can only be known as it is fully translated by and into the vernacular and idiom of local cultures.

The imperative on the translatability of the gospel into the local vernacular and idiom of individual cultures is central to the process known as contextualization. In the contextualization of the gospel, Christians find new life in the gospel story as the incarnate God comes to live and dwell among them, no matter how culturally distant the Christian community might be from first-century Palestine where Jesus walked. A fully contextualized Christian community will discover God's embrace of their cultural realities as good and pleasing, while at the same time connecting the community to something greater and more real than their own limited experience. The imperative on the translatability of the gospel thus results in contextually relevant and culturally grounded Christian communities in communion with other fully contextualized gatherings of the faithful.

It is in the vernacular moments that this ongoing process of the translation of the gospel into local cultural realities, resulting in a fully contextualized Christian community, occurs. Vernacular moments are always the present reality, or realities, where the word of God becomes the living word, ever new and ever changing.

Vernacular moments are not once-and-for-all points in time, a "been there, done that" by which the gospel has been translated definitively. Rather, vernacular moments are those places where ongoing revelation of the universal incarnate God, in the changing particularities of specific Christian communities, occurs. Vernacular moments are those places where God in Jesus meets believers again and again, in all of our uniqueness of culture and contextual specificity. Vernacular moments are where we experience God's ongoing embrace of us and our embrace of God in the incarnation of Jesus Christ.

And so the discussion has come full circle in this understanding of Anglicanism as the embrace and celebration of apostolic catholicity within vernacular moments. The Anglican Communion is a community of God's incarnation in Jesus, enlivened by the ongoing revelation of Christ in eucharistic fellowship, connected to the universal church, particularly through the historic episcopate as transmitted through the See of Canterbury, and forever new in the contextualization of the gospel in local cultural realities. This contextualization of the incarnational community in local cultural realities, while remaining part of the church catholic, is what the English Reformation was all about. Tyndale's English Bible was first and foremost an exercise in the translatability of the universal truths of the gospel into the vernacular and idiom of English culture. Cranmer's Book of Common Prayer further sought to locate the formularies and worshiping traditions of catholic experience within the Anglo-Saxon reality. Both undertook to live the incarnation in a genuinely English context as part of a greater whole. The genius here is not that our Anglican forebears were English but rather that they arrived at a particular way of being the church which was both genuinely local and genuinely universal. It is only with the rise of the British empire and its political and economic hegemony that the unique experience of Anglo-Saxon contextualization became codified and was made normative for Anglican churches the world over, thus betraying the genius of the original English Reformation. Today the growing plurality and multicultural reality of the Anglican Communion forces Anglicans to see that our common identity lies not in a shared English culture but in the experience of locality in universality, described as the embrace and celebration of apostolic catholicity within vernacular moments.

A Lesson from Aotearoa

Recently, I was blessed to spend two weeks with sisters and brothers in Christ in the Maori tikanga of the Anglican Church of the Province of Aotearoa, New Zealand and Polynesia.[36] This was a particularly rich learning experience for me as Maori (the indigenous peoples of Aotearoa) church leaders generously gave of their time and energy to introduce me to their land, church and world. The Anglican Church in Aotearoa, New Zealand and Polynesia is a particularly interesting Christian community as their new constitution of 1992 genuinely attempts to embrace a postcolonial polity that shares power between the Pakeha (or white English colonizers) the Maori (or colonized indigenous population) and the wider community of Pacific Islanders.

While in Auckland, I was asked to address an evening class on theology and church history attended by approximately twenty catechists, priests, and lay leaders from the Anglican Maori community. I was particularly sensitive to the fact that as a heterosexual, white, male, American cleric, I was not in a position to define what is normative in theology and church history for these indigenous Christian leaders of Aotearoa. I began the evening class by asking how many class participants considered themselves to be Anglican. Without exception, everyone in the classroom raised hands, with some of the leaders emphasizing that they were in fact fifth- or sixth-generation Anglican. I then asked: "What does it mean to be Anglican?" A variety of rather curious answers were given, most of which referred to characteristics such as "white," "English-speaking," and "Church of England." When I asked how their positive response to my first question about being Anglican related to these cultural and racial definitions of what it means to be Anglican, which they seemed less likely to own, there was silence in the room. Clearly, definitions of Anglicanism relying upon being white and English were difficult to reconcile with the Maori experience of being Anglican.

With this problematic, I proceeded to try out my definition of Anglican identity as the embrace and celebration of apostolic catholicity within vernacular moments. I attempted to draw parallels between the processes of contextualization by the likes of Tyndale and Cranmer in the English Reformation and the drive to greater relevance, cultural ownership and power sharing of the 1992 constitutional reforms of the Anglican Church in Aotearoa,

New Zealand and Polynesia. By comparing the drive toward vernacular expression of the gospel in relationship with the church universal through the historic See of Canterbury, implicit in both the English Reformation and contemporary Maori contexts, those gathered in the classroom that night discovered that perhaps the Maori are in fact being more genuinely Anglican as they struggle to live into Maori forms of worship, theology, and polity, than when they pray in English and follow the ways of their colonizers. Becoming more Maori does not mean becoming *less* Anglican, it means becoming *more* Anglican.

Anglican divines through the centuries have maintained that the fullness of God is to be experienced in the "inbetweenness" of the local and the universal, the particular and the catholic. There is an Anglican hesitancy to canonize as ultimately authoritative for all time either local experience or the received tradition. Anglican priorities of worship in the language of the people and an openness to liturgical change and renewal demonstrate that God in Jesus Christ is best encountered in the dialectic between that which is on the ground and that which has been received. The Preface to the 1662 Book of Common Prayer thus states:

> ... the particular Forms of Divine worship and the Rites and Ceremonies appointed to be used therein, being things in their own nature indifferent, and alterable, and so acknowledged; it is but reasonable, that upon weighty and important considerations, according to the various exigency of times and occasions, such changes and alterations should be made therein, as to those that are in place of Authority should from time to time seem either necessary or expedient.[37]

Neither the compilers of the early Prayer Books in the Church of England nor their American successors who celebrated the "various exigency of times and occasions" in the preface to their own 1789 American Book of Common Prayer could have envisioned the radical multicultural reality of today's Anglican Communion.[38] The urgent demand of today's times and occasions is that Anglicanism is no longer limited to Anglo-American experience but has grown beyond anything ever imagined by our forbears.

Max Warren, the great Anglican missiologist and General Secretary of the English Church Missionary Society from 1942 to 1963, is credited with saying: "It takes the whole world to know the whole gospel." This simple, yet profound statement points to a possible way forward for Anglicans in the exigency of these multicultural, postcolonial, and postmodern times and occasions.

Warren's statement shows first an openness to the world and to God's intervention in human history. It affirms that God has used the church, including the church of the colonial Enlightenment world, to effect God's purpose on earth. It is an open, hope-filled statement that, while recognizing the truths of the gospel already revealed in the world, emphasizes that God is not yet done with us. Christians need not fear the future nor the radical changes that the church in general, and the Anglican Communion in particular, is experiencing. For the more diverse and the more plural the Christian community becomes, the greater the promise of living into the fullness of God.

Second, Warren's statement affirms the universality of the whole gospel while lifting up the particularities of the good news as it is known in the many and diverse contexts of the whole world. Christians cannot know the fullness of God without one's own unique experience of God in Christ. Likewise, we cannot know the fullness of God without coming into relationship with others who experience and know Christ in a radically different context from our own.

Finally, Warren's embrace of the whole world and the whole gospel as being mutually interdependent and of one substance with the Creator points to the new creation. In the living of the whole gospel in the whole world, the vision and the hope of God's mission of reconciliation, redemption, and liberation for all creation are made real.

If our calling as Christians, as Anglicans, is to participate with God in this mission (and I believe it is), then the end to which we all need to be working is that *shalom*, that reign, that kingdom, where all will be restored to unity with God. The *shalom* of God will be that place where all Anglicans, all Christians, all people of faith, in fact all creation, will find a renewed oneness and renewed wholeness with and in God. In the *shalom* of God, the breaches and tensions in the body of Christ, and the violence, poverty, and oppression in our own neighborhoods and around the world, will all be overcome and made new. In this important time of change and transition for the Anglican Communion, let us pray that we will grow in our commitment to God's mission and be driven by a call to restore all people to unity with God and each other in Christ.[39]

NOTES

[1] Portions of this paper have appeared in Ian T. Douglas, "Authority after Colonialism," *The Witness* 83:3 (March 2000): 10-14.

[2] For a discussion of the politics of hegemony in the Anglican Communion, see Ian T. Douglas, "Radical Mutuality Still Out of Reach: Lambeth Analysis," *The Witness* 81:11 (November 1998): 24-27.

[3] "Pastoral Letter from the House of Bishops to the People of the Episcopal Church" in General Convention of the Episcopal Church, *Journal of the General Convention of the Episcopal Church: 1985* (New York: The General Convention, 1985), 12. The statement is a little misleading in that English remains the primary language of the Communion but the majority of Anglicans today do not speak English as their first language.

[4] David B. Barrett, "Annual Statistical Table on Global Mission: 2000," *International Bulletin of Missionary Research* 24 (January 2000): 24-25.

[5] Ibid.

[6] The nomenclature "Anglican Communion" describing the family of churches historically related to the Church of England did not come into usage until the mid-nineteenth century. See: Mark Harris, *The Challenge of Change: The Anglican Communion in the Postmodern Era* (New York: Church Publishing, 1998), 5-6.

[7] David J. Bosch, *Transforming Mission: Paradigm Shifts in the Theology of Mission* (Maryknoll: Orbis Books, 1991), Chapter 9 "Mission in the Wake of the Enlightenment," 262-345.

[8] The nature and meaning of "autonomy" and "autonomous" in reference to churches in the Anglican Communion is somewhat problematic. Each church in the Anglican Communion is free to establish its own canons, liturgies, and polity structures independently from other Anglican churches. In that respect there is no international, inter-Anglican authority that can speak for the life and ministry in any one church. "Autonomy" in polity structures does not mean that there is not a common life that all Anglican churches share as a global body of Christ; a community of churches where no one church can say: "we have no need of another."

[9] E. R. Fairweather, ed., *Anglican Congress 1963: Report of the Proceedings* (n.p.: Editorial Committee of the Anglican Congress, 1963), 118.

[10] Ibid., 130-31.

[11] The fact that many of these newly autonomous Anglican churches still maintain the word "province" in their names, such as the Church of the Province of Uganda or the Church of the Province of South East Asia, reflects the colonial legacy of seeing these churches as outposts of historic Western churches.

[12] For a discussion of how colonial and neocolonial power relationships still affect the Anglican Communion, especially with respect to debates over human sexuality, see Ian T. Douglas, "Lambeth 1998 and the 'New Colonialism'," *The Witness* 81:5 (May 1998): 8-12.

[13] Samuel Seabury was consecrated for the newly formed Episcopal Church USA.

[14] David Theo Goldberg, *Racist Culture: Philosophy and the Politics of Meaning* (Cambridge: Blackwell, 1993), 29.

[15] As first reported by Andrew Carey in the 10 July 1998 edition of *The Church of England News*, Bishop Spong is quoted as saying that African Christians had "moved out of animism into a very superstitious kind of Christianity" and have "yet to face the intellectual revolution of Copernicus and Einstein that we've had to face in the developing world."

[16] Some "conservative" groups within the Episcopal Church, such as the American Anglican Council or Forward in Faith, North America, subscribe to "confessional" statements of belief and action such as "A Place to Stand" and "Declaration of Common Faith and Purpose" respectively.

[17] See Fredrica Harris Thompsett's chapter in this volume for a fuller discussion of the Inter-Anglican Theological and Doctrinal Commission and the *Virginia Report*.

[18] From the address by the. Rt. Rev. Mark Dyer on the *Virginia Report* to the 11th meeting of the Anglican Consultative Council, Dundee, Scotland, 15 September 1999.

THE EXIGENCY OF TIMES AND OCCASIONS **45**

[19] See Resolution III.6 (b) and (c) on "Instruments of Anglican Communion" in Mark Dyer, et al., eds., *The Official Report of the Lambeth Conference 1998* (Harrisburg: Morehouse Publishing, 1999), 396-97. For a fuller discussion of the "new curialization" see Ian T. Douglas, "Authority after Colonialism."

[20] Anglican-Roman Catholic International Commission, *The Gift of Authority* (New York: Church Publishing,1999), 42.

[21] From "An Open Letter from Primates of the Anglican Communion to the Most Rev. Frank Griswold, Presiding Bishop of ECUSA," 24 February 1999.

[22] From "The Presiding Bishop's Response to Archbishops Bazley, Gitari, Goodhew, Kolini, Malik, Mtetemela, Sinclair and Tay," *Episcopal News Service* 10 March 1999.

[23] Leon Spencer, "Archbishop of Rwanda joins in 'irregular' ordination of two American bishops" *The ANITEPAM Bulletin* 25 (February 2000): 10.

[24] Harry Goodhew and Maurice Sinclair, *Way of Faithfulness: A Report on a Visit to the Episcopal Church in the U.S.A. and a Considered Proposal to Address Current Controversies in the Anglican Communion* (Carollton, Tex.: The Ekklesia Society, 1999), 18.

[25] Ibid., 75-76.

[26] "Final Communiqué from the Primates of the Anglican Communion," The Primates Meeting of the Anglican Communion, Oporto, Portugal, 22-29 March 2000.

[27] Simon Chiwanga, "Address by the Chair—What is the Communion We Share?: The Anglican Communion in a 'time of change and transition'" Anglican Communion News Service Press Release no.16, The 11th Meeting of the Anglican Consultative Council, Dundee Scotland, 16 September 1999.

[28] A first draft of this understanding of Anglicanism appears in Ian T. Douglas, "Anglican Identity and the *Missio Dei*: Implications for the American Convocation of Churches in Europe" *Anglican Theological Review* 82:3 (Summer 2000): 459-74.

[29] For a full discussion of the implications of living the reality of the incarnation, particularly within the American Episcopal experience, see Fredrica Harris Thompsett, *Courageous Incarnation: In Intimacy, Work, Childhood, and Aging* (Cambridge, Mass.: Cowley, 1993).

[30] The current emphasis on the eucharist as a point of celebration of God's embrace of humanity does not deny that many Anglicans through history have found connection with God and each other in the common prayer of the daily offices.

[31] See "Communiqué from the Primates Meeting."

[32] "The Chicago-Lambeth Quadrilateral, 1886,1888," in The Book of Common Prayer (New York: The Church Hymnal Corporation, 1979), 876-78.

[33] The historical authenticity of the unbroken chain of Anglican episcopacy is an important question but beyond the scope of this paper. Most Anglicans, however, subscribe to the ongoing continuity of episcopal ordination.

[34] See, for example, recent conversations between the Episcopal Church USA, and the Evangelical Lutheran Church in America on the "Concordat of Agreement" and its successor "Called to Common Mission."

[35] See Lamin Sanneh, *Translating the Message: The Missionary Impact on Culture* (Maryknoll : Orbis Books, 1989).

[36] Tikanga is translated as "culturally correct ways of being" or "household" and is used to describe the three polity "houses" of the Anglican Church in Aotearoa, New Zealand and Polynesia. See Jenny Plane Te Paa's chapter in this volume.

[37] From "The Preface" of the 1662 Book of Common Prayer.

[38] See the 1789 Preface in The Book of Common Prayer (New York: The Church Hymnal Corporation, 1979), 9-11.

[39] From the question in "The Cathechism" of the American Book of Common Prayer. "What is the mission of the Church? The Mission of the Church is to restore all people to unity with God and each other in Christ," Ibid., 855.

2

THE LEGACY OF CULTURAL HEGEMONY IN THE ANGLICAN CHURCH

KWOK PUI-LAN

Nineteen ninety-seven marked the end of 155 years of British rule over Hong Kong. The return of Hong Kong to China signified the end of the British colonial era and the decline of European influences over the destiny of formerly colonized peoples. In 1800, the British empire consisted of 1.5 million square miles and 20 million people. By 1900, the Victorian empire was made up of 11 million square miles and about 390 million people.[1] From 1815 to 1914 European colonial domination expanded from 35 percent of the earth to about 85 percent of it.[2] Most of these colonies were established in Africa and Asia, though all the continents were affected in the process. Today, these colonies have gained political independence, and until June 30, 1997, Hong Kong was one of the few remnants of the colonial past.

About 500 years ago, African, Asian, Latin American, and Pacific peoples were gradually forced to join the emerging world order with Europe as its center. The nineteenth century, often referred to as the great century of Christian mission, was also a period of political expansion and empire building by the West.

Missionaries were sent to convert the so-called "heathens," while their lands were forcibly taken from them. Since the Second World War, most of the colonies have become independent political entities; but they have been subjected to the continued control of the West through the mass media, neocolonialism, political influences, and military intervention. The Cold War era divided the world according to different ideologies. Since the late 1980s, the rapid transformation of the world has led to the redrawing of the world map, the re-examining of the legacy of the Cold War, and the revisioning of the world order. A leading political scientist, Samuel Huntington, predicts the "new world order" to be a clash of civilizations instead of ideologies.[3] Benjamin Barber, on the other hand, suggests it will be a struggle between the "Jihad" and the "McWorld"—"Jihad" refers to religious and tribal fundamentalism, and "McWorld" means global consumerist capitalism.[4] What will be the prospects of the formerly subjugated and colonized peoples in this "new world order"?

This chapter contributes to the dialogue by discussing cultural hegemony and its implication for the Anglican Communion in the postcolonial world. The term "postcolonial" has been variously interpreted, dependent on different social locations and academic disciplines. On the one hand, "postcolonial" can be understood in the historical and political sense. Scholars argue over whether "post" refers to the period after the colonies have regained their political independence, or to the period since the onset of colonization that continues to the present, because colonialist strategies persist in new forms.[5] Given the domination of the global market economy and the insidious forms of neocolonialism, some even question whether it is premature to speak of a "postcolonial" world. Furthermore, indigenous peoples have challenged whether the theories of postcoloniality can be applicable to their situation, since their prospects of gaining political sovereignty seem remote. On the other hand, "postcolonial" can also refer to cultural practices and reading strategies that resist and confront colonialism and imperialism. Biblical scholar R. S. Sugirtharajah has said postcolonial discourse is:

> ... an active interrogation of the hegemonic systems of thought, textual codes, and symbolic practices which the West constructed in its domination of colonial subjects. In other words, postcolonialism is concerned with the question of cultural and discursive domination. It is a discursive resistance to

imperialism, imperial ideologies, and imperial attitudes and to their continual reincarnations in such wide fields as politics, economics, history, and theological and biblical studies.[6]

Since the Anglican Communion was formed as a direct result of colonization, it is imperative for Anglicans to face the challenges of postcolonial realities. Anglican churches were established beginning in the seventeenth century in settler colonies in what would later become Australia, New Zealand, Canada, South Africa, and the eastern part of the United States. The term "Anglican Communion" was coined around the 1860s, when Anglican churches proliferated in the Third World as a result of the expansion of the British empire. Today, among the 70 million members of the Anglican Communion, the majority live in the southern hemisphere and speak a language other than English. In *Who Are the Anglicans*, Charles H. Long has observed, "The Anglican Church is rapidly outgrowing its Englishness but has not yet established its own identity as a multiracial, multilingual, multicultural family."[7] Postcolonial theories help us to re-examine the historical trajectory through which the state church of England became a worldwide Communion of churches and to envision the future of the Anglican Communion in our postmodern and postcolonial world.

In the following, I discuss the concept of cultural hegemony as developed by Antonio Gramsci and insights from postcolonial theorists regarding cultural representation and colonialism. Only those themes and concepts that I have found important for re-examining Anglican identity and cultural practices will be highlighted. Then I proceed to analyze the identity, history, and liturgy of Anglicanism, followed by some visions for a multicultural and plurifocal Anglican Communion in the twenty-first century.

CULTURAL HEGEMONY AND POSTCOLONIAL THEORY

Edward Said, often hailed as the founder of postcolonial studies, grew up in a Palestinian family closely related to the church. His father studied at the Anglican St. George's School in Jerusalem, and he grew up in Cairo attending Sunday school in an English preparatory school, followed by matins at All Saints Cathedral.[8] In his 1978 pioneering text, *Orientalism*, Said argues that colonization implies not only political and military domination, but also cultural hegemony and colonial representation of the Other. Analyzing British and French writings on the "Orient,"

Said links directly the structures of colonialism with Western knowledge production and cultural representation. The "East" was presented in these writings stereotypically as female, passive, despotic, backward, and irrational; while the "West" represented the masculine, aggressive, democratic, progressive, and rational. Such skewed misrepresentation contributed to creating in the public mind the prejudice that the "East" was inferior: these people could not rule themselves and had to be ruled.

In analyzing the cultural and religious dimensions of colonialism, Said builds on the theory of hegemony by Italian Marxist thinker Antonio Gramsci. Said writes: "It is hegemony, or rather the result of cultural hegemony at work, that gives Orientalism the durability and the strength I have been speaking about."[9] The word "hegemony," in its etymological sense of "leadership" and in its derived sense of "dominance," usually refers to relations among social groups and states. Gramsci had a rather broad definition of culture and understood human beings as products of history and culture, rather than of nature. Writing in 1916 he said:

> Culture is something quite different. It is organization, discipline of one's inner self, a coming to terms with one's own personality; it is the attainment of a higher awareness; with the aid of which one succeeds in understanding one's historical value, one's own function in life, one's own rights and obligations.[10]

Gramsci's concepts of culture and human consciousness were more dynamic and fluid than those of Marx, who adhered more strictly to an ideology of economic determinism. For Marx, law, politics, arts, and religion are ideological and false distortions because they reflect the interests of the ruling class. For Gramsci, they are not false or simply expressions of the infrastructure; they are crystallizations of the contradictions of life itself, representing the inadequate expression of the ideals of human beings, given the stage of their human consciousness.[11] In this way, Gramsci recognized the impact of culture and its role in influencing social reality and institutions.

Facing the ascendancy of Fascism in Italy, Gramsci was concerned to challenge the apparatus or mechanisms of the hegemony of the dominant class, unmask the contradictions in religion, ideology, and the arts, and create a popular culture that would promote the interests of workers and their political allies. He astutely observed that the hegemony of the ruling class was maintained by both the civil and political society. While the civil society taught and propagated ideas and values of how people should think and behave according to bourgeois interests, the state had the disciplinary power to coerce by force when people rebelled or resisted. Gramsci's theory was borrowed by Said in his discussion of how cultural hegemony facilitated colonial rule:

> Gramsci has made the useful analytic distinction between civil and political society in which the former is made up of voluntary (or at least rational and noncoercive) affiliations like schools, families, and unions, the latter of state institutions (the army, the police, the central bureaucracy) whose role in the polity is direct domination. Culture, of course, is to be found operating within civil society, where the influence of ideas, of institutions, and of other persons works not through domination but by what Gramsci calls consent.[12]

As a professor of comparative literature and an accomplished pianist, Said can readily cite well-known literary and cultural figures, such as Jane Austen, Charlotte Brontë, Joseph Conrad, Giuseppe Verdi, and Albert Camus, whose works on the surface may have nothing to do with colonialism, but in fact, participate in and are influenced by the colonial paradigm.[13] Charlotte Brontë's novel *Jane Eyre*, widely read in English literature classes in the colonies, seems to be a romantic novel with no political interest. But Said shows that the world as represented in *Jane Eyre* would not have been made possible without the growing British influences in the Caribbean. The madwoman, Bertha Mason, a West Indian, would not have ended up in Thornfield Hall. Said makes the bold observation that the so-called high culture in Europe during the imperialistic era, including literature, arts, and philosophy, were much influenced by empire building and the imperial gaze. From his own experience as a Palestinian boy growing up in Cairo, Said demonstrates the significant roles played by missionary schools, churches, English soccer, and Western music and fashion in furthering colonial cultural domination.

Following Said's lead, postcolonial critics have developed and elaborated on the concepts of cultural representation, colonization as a transcultural and transnational process, racial and sexual cultural politics, cultural hybridity, social temporality, and subaltern speech. I will briefly introduce some of the key postcolonial theorists and their contributions to these key topics, since they provide a valuable interpretive framework to examine the ways the Anglican church participated in and continues to maintain cultural hegemony during and after the colonial era.

Stuart Hall, a significant postcolonial thinker, is also widely acclaimed as a pioneer in cultural studies. Born and raised in Jamaica, Hall was a founder of the Birmingham University Center for Contemporary Cultural Studies. As a black sociologist living in England, Hall maintains that one of the myths that sustain the cultural hegemony of the West is none other than the construction of "the West" itself. He argues that discourses that deploy the binarism of "the West and the Rest" undergirded the ascendancy of Europe, shaping "its image of itself and 'others,' its sense of 'us' and 'them,' its practices and relations of power towards the Rest."[14] Instead of treating "the West" as infinitely superior to and different from the rest of the world, Hall investigates the intricate relations between the cultures of the colonizers and the colonized. On the one hand, the colonizers superimpose their language, schools, churches, marriage systems, and legal codes onto those they rule. On the other hand, the colonized raise issues the colonizers must face, and provide rich diversity of customs, food, arts, and music that form an integral part of metropolitan culture. Colonization, for Hall, is never a one-way street, but a transcultural and transnational "global" process that challenges an easy binary construction of "here" and "there," "then" and "now," and "home" and "abroad."[15]

Hall has written extensively on race, ethnicity, and identity, and has commented on black popular culture and black cinema. Well versed in Marxist thought, Hall finds Gramsci's ideas relevant in theorizing racism, though Gramsci had not written explicitly on the subject. Specifically, Hall regards Gramsci's non-reductionist approach to social analysis, his discussion of the roles of the state and civil society, his reflections on ideology and popular consciousness, and his emphasis on historical specificity and regional differences important for any discussion of race, especially regarding its complex relationship to class.[16] Commenting on the cultural representation of blacks in the British media, Hall laments that in literary, visual, and cinematic forms, blacks have typically been the objects and rarely the subjects of representation. He condemns the fetishization, objectification and negative figuration of the black subject in popular culture. Black cultural politics thus consists of the struggle for access to the rights of representation by black artists and cultural workers and for the creation of "positive" black imageries to counteract the dominant stereotypes.[17]

Similar to Hall, Indian postcolonial critic Homi Bhabha critiques British colonialism and pays attention to race, culture, and history. His densely argued book, *The Location of Culture*, explains why the culture of Western modernity must be critiqued from the postcolonial perspective.[18] The beliefs in rationality, liberty, and liberal humanism failed to challenge racism, slavery, and colonization in the modern period. In fact, the racist and colonial discourses were based on the fantasy of the difference of the other, constructed often in racial and sexual terms. Colonial discourse assumes the identity of the subjected people as fixed and unchanging, and the difference between them and the colonizers as unbridgeable. For Bhabha, the necessity of the creation of stereotypes points to the unstable psyche of the colonizers and the contradictory nature of colonial authority.[19]

Besides the concept of colonial fantasy, Bhabha contributes significantly to postcolonial theory through his articulations of mimicry, cultural hybridity, and reconceptualization of history. Since colonialism violently impinges one culture upon another, the colonial subjects have to learn a foreign tongue and the cultural idioms of their oppressors. In the colonies, one can easily discern imitations of the colonizers' writing and speaking styles, social habits, customs, and religious practices. Instead of simply treating such cultural practices as identification with the colonial regime, Bhabha argues that mimicry can also function to mock the power which the colonizers hold to be a model, that power which supposedly makes it imitable. Thus, mimicry can serve as a double vision "which in disclosing the ambivalence of colonial discourse also disrupts its authority."[20]

Bhabha rejects the idea that cultural boundaries are airtight, demarcating clearly the insiders from the outsiders. He insists that cultures interact with one another and that all cultures are continually in a process of hybridity.[21] Cultural hybridity challenges the myths of purity of cultural lineage, homogeneity of identity, and monolithic understandings of national cultures. Hybridity in postcolonial discourse demystifies the power of representation, for it can function as camouflage, contest, or a space in-between so that denied knowledges can be articulated and recognized.[22] Hybridity and the "in-between" spaces, for him, "provide the terrain for elaborating strategies of selfhood—singular or communal—that initiate new signs of identity, and innovative sites of collaboration, and contestation, in the act of defining the idea of society itself."[23]

Bhabha also calls for a radical re-imagining of the category of time and the reconceptualization of history. At the boundaries of the white, colonial, and male histories, he writes, are a range of other dissonant histories and voices—women, peasants, slaves, minority groups, and the subaltern. He destabilizes the binary construction of the "center" and the "margin," because for him "the boundary becomes the place from which *something begins its presencing.*"[24] Thus, history requires a radical revision of social temporality in which emergent histories can be written and histories of different peoples can be seen and analyzed as occupying the same time frame.

Although most of the well-known postcolonial theorists are male, Gayatri Chakravorty Spivak distinguishes herself by her sophisticated analyses, combining deconstruction, Marxist theory, and psychoanalytical analysis. Her most important contribution to the discourse on cultural hegemony is her controversial essay "Can the Subaltern Speak?"[25] Using the example of multiply-oppressed native women, Spivak argues that the subaltern cannot speak, otherwise she would not be a subaltern. In the ensuing debate about her essay, her critics accuse her of constructing the native, both male and female, as a historically muted subject. In response to her critics, Spivak now says the more important question is not "Who can speak?" but "Who will listen?" For even if the subaltern speaks, her voice will not be heard by the First World and Third World elite.[26]

Spivak adamantly critiques the hegemony of white feminist discourse. In an essay entitled "French Feminism in an International Frame," Spivak denounces the domination of feminist theory by the discourse of the world's privileged societies. She criticizes Julia Kristeva's travel memoir *About Chinese Women* as following the binary logic of the East and West, and appropriating Chinese women in her self-serving interest to define her own identity.[27] Her criticism is also directed toward English-speaking feminists as well. In her widely read essay, "Three Women's Texts and a Critique of

Imperialism," she challenges readers to think about the kind of subjectivity Charlotte Brontë constructed for Jane Eyre and Bertha Mason, the madwoman in the attic. In the rush to reclaim the female subjectivity of Jane Eyre by white feminists, Spivak asks why they have conveniently forgotten the imperialist impulse that set the stage for the story.[28]

Although postcolonial theory constitutes one of the most significant and controversial discourses in academia today, theologians and church historians have not yet fully engaged this body of literature. People in the pews have hardly heard their pastors talk about the roles Anglicanism has played in colonialism. In the following, I will apply some of the insights gleaned from the above discussion to examine the legacy of Anglicanism.

ANGLICANISM FROM A POSTCOLONIAL PERSPECTIVE

There has been much discussion on the identity, integrity, and authority of Anglicanism in recent decades. The meaning and unity of the Anglican Communion have been repeatedly debated in the Lambeth Conferences, especially since 1948. Archbishop Michael Ramsey, Bishop Stephen W. Sykes, theologian Paul Avis and others have produced important works on the subject. The question of identity is a critical one for the Church of England, partly because of the declining numbers of communicants, and partly because of its decreasing influence over other Anglican churches as the glory of the empire has faded. Some of these writers harken back to the past, to the writings of Richard Hooker, the liturgy of Cranmer, the institution of episcopacy, and the religious establishment in England to find unique characteristics of Anglicanism. Using our postcolonial language, they look back to the "point of origin" in order to find the unity and identity of the Anglican church. But as Kortright Davis has forcefully argued: "The Anglican Church must everywhere come to be known as the living church with the traditions of the living; no longer must anyone dare to call it a 'Royal Society for the Preservation of Ancient and Historical Monuments.'"[29] I propose to look at several important facets of Anglicanism as a living tradition from a postcolonial perspective.

The Anglican Church as a Cultural Hybrid

An important characteristic of Anglicanism is comprehensiveness. The Lambeth Conference of 1968 report says:

> Comprehensiveness demands agreement on fundamentals, while tolerating disagreement on matters in which Christians may differ without feeling the necessity of breaking communion. In the mind of an Anglican, comprehensiveness is not compromise. Nor is it to bargain one truth for another. It is not a sophisticated word for syncretism. Rather it implies that the apprehension of truth is a growing thing: we only gradually succeed in "knowing the truth." It has been the tradition of Anglicanism to contain within one body both Protestant and Catholic elements.[30]

Many Anglicans value comprehensiveness, toleration of diversity, and the via media in their church, but few have thought about the cultural logic that makes these qualities possible. I suggest that Anglicanism was a cultural hybrid from the beginning, and this tradition should be celebrated in our postcolonial world. As a cultural hybrid of Catholicism and Protestantism, the Church of England in the sixteenth century assimilated elements from both traditions to create a very fluid identity. Adopting the via media approach, the Church of England was able to hold together the evangelicals and the anglo-catholics in the nineteenth century. The encounter with diverse cultures during the colonial age presented both risks and opportunities to the cultural identity of Anglicanism. But instead of continuing the process of hybridity, Anglican churches were formed during the imperialistic period as mimicries of churches at the metropolitan center. The report of the Lambeth Conference of 1988 laments:

> Thus when Anglicanism was exported to other continents, it came not only with the "Englishness" of certain styles of clothing, music and worship, but with certain assumptions about who made decisions, who had authority in social life, who had ultimate control in economic affairs, markets, production, land ownership. The dominance of the English style ... could be seen as a reflection of the plain facts of political and economic dominance.[31]

Although we have entered the postcolonial age, Anglican churches in many parts of the world remain cultural representations of the colonial era. Africans and Asians living in tropical climates continue to wear English clerical dress, even under the hot blazing sun. The African bishop is addressed as the Lord Bishop of Cape

Coast or Freetown. John Pobee of Ghana has called this phenomenon the "Anglo-Saxon captivity of Ecclesia Anglicana."[32] In many cases, such mimicry of the "mother church" serves not as a mockery of colonial authority, but as a sign of privilege by association.

To get out of this captivity, the newer churches of the Anglican Communion must take seriously its hybrid identity as both Anglican on the one hand, and African, Asian, Latin American, or West Indian on the other. The 1996 Conference on World Mission and Evangelism with the theme "Called to One Hope: Gospel in Diverse Cultures" recognized the renewed quest for identity for oppressed people around the world. But as Christopher Duraisingh has observed, such an ethno-cultural quest for identity can lead to new forms of ethnic nationalism and cleansing, the oppression of religious minority groups, and the breakdown of community[33] The urgent question is how to construct identity in community so that the result will not be fragmentation, fundamentalism, or balkanization. The Anglican Communion can offer a unique prophetic model. On the one hand, it should encourage the experimentation of new cultural forms among member churches. On the other hand, the different cultural hybrids are in communion with one another, so that each can serve as a mirror for others, without absolutizing one's specific cultural form.

ANGLICAN HISTORY FROM THE PERIPHERY

When Anglicans think of their tradition, they often trace it back to the ancient apostolic tradition, mediated through the Church of England, and later brought to different parts of the world. Most historical works on the Anglican tradition, including the recent book *The Transformation of Anglicanism*,[34] follow such a time frame. The influential book, *The Study of Anglicanism*, traces the history and authority of Anglicanism and dissects various aspects of the church, sacraments, and ministry, but devotes only two chapters out of thirty to the younger churches.[35] From a postcolonial perspective, this is reading history from the metropolitan center, relegating the histories of other peoples to the periphery.

If colonization is a transnational and transcultural process, affecting both the colonized and the colonizers, how can we reinterpret the history of Anglicanism as a continued interaction between "the center" and "the periphery," thereby destabilizing both? Furthermore, how can we reimagine a different temporality so that we can resurrect the histories and stories of people not represented in metropolitan history? This requires a multicultural interpretation of the history of Anglicanism, a task that has hardly begun.

I will offer a few examples as several possible directions this multicultural interpretation can take. During the colonial days, the Anglican congregations in America had to coexist with those of other denominations, especially with the strong presence of Puritans in the northeast. After the Episcopal Church USA separated from the Church of England, it could not follow the model of the religious establishment. The Episcopal Church adopted a national structure which paralleled that of the government. The General Convention was divided into two houses: the House of Bishops and the House of Deputies that included clergy and laity. It drew its members from the middle and upper class, and included leaders in the public sector.[36] The Episcopal Church offers the longest historical example of the relationship between the church and state in a postcolonial setting. It will be especially enlightening to analyze the role of the Episcopal Church USA when the United States became a colonial power, following Britain, in the nineteenth century, and the sole superpower in the twentieth.

Another example is discerning racial politics in the Anglican Communion, especially in its important gatherings. In the Lambeth Conference of 1948, black bishops made up only 6 percent of the 37 bishops from Africa, but by 1978, they made up 80 percent of the 102 African bishops, representing almost 20 percent of all participants.[37] Most recently, the increased presence and influence of bishops from the South during the 1998 Lambeth Conference was evident. The first Anglican Consultative Council, which met in 1971 in Limuru, Kenya, was perhaps the first time that a world council with non-whites as the majority had met since before the Council of Nicea.[38] During the Lambeth Conference of 1867, churches in the Third World were referred to as "Colonial Churches," but many have become fully autonomous provinces since 1950. Bishop Desmond Tutu was the chair of a Section in Lambeth in 1978, and Bishop James Ottley served in that capacity in 1988. Christopher Duraisingh, Emilio Castro, and John Pobee have each played significant roles in recent Lambeth Conferences. The contributions of these bishops and theologians in Anglican gatherings have to be lifted up, since the official reports failed to highlight them.

The third example regards the inclusion of women in the ordained ministry within Anglicanism. As always, such an innovative attempt began at the periphery, but had rippling effects in the whole church. Because of war circumstances, Bishop R.O. Hall ordained Florence Li Tim-Oi to the priesthood in China in 1944. Later, in Hong Kong, Bishop Gilbert Baker officially ordained Jane Hwang Hsien-yuin and Joyce Bennett to be the first two women priests in 1971. At the crucial Anglican Consultative Council meeting in 1971 when the matter was discussed, Professor John Mbiti and Archdeacon Jabez Bryce of Fiji spoke approvingly of women's leadership in their African and Polynesian cultures.[39] The ordination of these pioneering women opened the doors to the consecration of women to the episcopate. The 1998 Lambeth Conference welcomed eleven women bishops for the first time. The ordination of women symbolizes the long struggle of women to gain access to full ministry in the church. After a quarter of a century, the Church of England finally decided to follow a practice, first adopted in a tiny British colony, to recognize the leadership of women in ordained ministry.

CULTURAL TRANSLATION OF LITURGY

As many have observed, the Anglican churches are not bound by a body of doctrines, but more by a common liturgy. The Book of Common Prayer (BCP) drew from many ancient and contemporary sources and phrases of its time, and Cranmer added touches of his own creation. Since the BCP serves as a "grammar" to understand the language and religious practices of Anglicanism, it is important to analyze the cultural and linguistic world created by it.

The first Book of Common Prayer was known as the First Prayer Book of Edward VI (1549), while subsequent revisions had close connections with the accession of a new monarch to the throne: the Elizabethan Prayer Book (1559), the Jacobean Prayer Book (1604), and the revision of 1662 when Charles II restored the monarchy. The images of king and empire are found frequently in the liturgy, canticles, and hymns. God is imaged as the "the King eternal" (Collect for the Renewal of Life), a "great King above all gods" (Venite), and the "heavenly King" (Gloria in excelsis).[40] Cultural imperialism is often unchecked: "Grant that people everywhere may seek after you and find you, bring the nation into your fold," and "At the name of Jesus every knee shall b

[handwritten annotation: perhaps this is the main question I need to answer by the end of Seminary?]

Since many new revisions of the BCP are now available, the question of how much diversity can be allowed without losing the identity of the church becomes urgent. In addition, there are bold attempts to use cultural resources other than English. The Prayer Book of Aotearoa, New Zealand and Polynesia, for example, adopts material from the language, poetry, and wisdom of the Maori and Polynesian peoples. I find the analysis of "translation" in postcolonial theory helpful to point to new ways to look at the dilemma. Translation, for Stuart Hall, is more than finding a linguistic equivalent, but "a continuous process of re-articulation and re-contextualization, without any notion of a primary origin."[42] When the BCP enters a new cultural space, its terms and the world it represents unavoidably change. The unity and identity of the church can never be and have never been guaranteed by the sameness of liturgy, unless it is not translated. But a liturgy that is not translated into the local context is dead, not living.

CAN THE SUBALTERN SPEAK IN THE ANGLICAN COMMUNION?

Since the Anglican Communion does not have a centralized governing body as the Roman Catholic Church does, the question of authority has been raised time and again. The Lambeth Conference of 1948 put the question succinctly: "Is Anglicanism based on a sufficiently coherent form of authority to form the nucleus of a world-wide fellowship of Churches, or does its comprehensiveness conceal internal divisions which may cause its disruption?"[43] Instead of opting for the universal primacy of Canterbury, the Anglican Communion chooses to be a fellowship of churches, autonomous entities, each in communion with each other. Since the Communion embodies the diversity of so many races and cultures, differences in opinion and even sharp disagreements are unavoidable.

The Lambeth Conference was first called by the Archbishop of Canterbury in 1867 in response to the requests of bishops and clergy in Canada that members of the same church family be brought together. Since then, the bishops have met about every ten years to discuss matters that concern the whole Communion. In between the conferences, some primates met as a consultative body of the conference, and such gatherings became the precursor of the Primates Meetings, which first convened in 1979. The Anglican Consultative Council was formed by the Lambeth Conference of 1968 and consisted of bishops, clergy and lay people. Meeting every two or three years, the Council shares information about development of the churches in the Communion, advises on matters arising from national and regional concerns, develops Anglican policies in world mission, and guides Anglican participation in ecumenical dialogues and fellowship.[44] Two Anglican Congresses were organized at Minneapolis (1954) and Toronto (1963). These Congresses provided opportunities for a large number of priests and lay people, as well as bishops, to meet people from all parts of the world and to experience the richness of the universal church.

The unity of the Communion is symbolized by the bishops of the churches getting together. Except for the two Congresses, the rank-and-file members of the church seldom have opportunities to share communion with each other. Only those lay people who participate in the Anglican Consultative Council have any real impact on the life of the whole church. The structure of the Communion is modeled after that of the British Commonwealth, with the bishops functioning almost as governors or heads of state. The hierarchical structure and its symbolic representation diminish the participation of the laity, both at the international and local levels.

But the laity are in fact the backbone of the church. As Fredrica Harris Thompsett has noted: "Contemporary scholarship demands that attention be paid to the common folk, to what has been described as 'popular religion.' Critical scholarship has rejected the implicit two-tiered 'producer/consumer' model of supposedly articulate clergy developing doctrine for presumably inarticulate laity."[45] But in the discussion of the authority of the church and other important matters, the voices of the laity are seldom heard. Even though the Lambeth Conferences repeatedly affirmed the ministry of all the baptized and the involvement of the whole people of God in mission, there are no adequate channels, either local or international, to mobilize the masses.

Third World women's voices have been particularly marginalized, even though the church is growing most rapidly in Third World countries. The Lambeth Conference of 1998 welcomed the women bishops, but none of them is from the Third World. Except for Bishop Barbara Harris of Massachusetts, all of them are white. The gathering of Anglican women in Brazil in 1992 was a good beginning, but most of the participants were from the First World, and there were few resources for follow-up work. The stories of Anglican women in Africa fighting the AIDS crisis, and the witness of their sisters in Asia struggling in the fast economic changes of their societies, have seldom been told to enrich the ministry of the church. As Spivak has asked, even when these subaltern speak, who will listen?

CULTURAL POLITICS OF OUR TIME

The old forms of cultural hegemony and political domination of the colonial period are now superseded by the information superhighway and global market economy. Using the mass media, satellite technology, and the World Wide Web, the postindustrial West continues to exert its power to create a "globalized" culture defined by Western taste and norms. The "McWorld" has extended itself exponentially in the past decade through the omnipresent tendrils of fiber optics. The logic of global capitalism becomes the logic of society itself, influencing cultural productions such as arts, sports, education, entertainment, and communication. At the same time, there is renewed interest and self-awareness of people searching for their cultural, ethnic, and religious identity. A section report of the 1998 Lambeth Conference notes: "In almost every part of the world, we find a search for cultural roots and tradition, a stress on cultural uniqueness, an insistence on 'difference' and the right of each group to its own specific ways of being and development."[46] Such a trend can lead to the affirmation of a plurality of cultures, but can also result in violent ethnic conflicts and the persecution of minorities. In many different parts of the world, various kinds of cultural and religious fundamentalisms have emerged, vehemently contesting and resisting the formidable forces of globalization. Some fundamentalists are deeply suspicious of Western liberal causes, such as the education of women, religious tolerance, and democratic political participation. But apart from the zealots, there are also conscientious people who view the preservation of their cultures and ways of life as crucial to maintaining a sense of cultural pride and autonomy. They may be open to adopting social and cultural practices of the West, but such acceptance is never without discrimination.

With such a broader picture in mind, we may be able to better assess the cultural politics at the Lambeth Conference of 1998.

At that multicultural and multiracial gathering, some North Atlantic bishops still tried to maintain their sense of superiority and their self-ascribed status as the old guards of tradition. The symbols of the British empire were prominently displayed, including worship at Canterbury Cathedral and afternoon tea at Buckingham Palace. But the presence of a large number of bishops from the South, representing the vitality and growth of the Communion, clearly demanded that the Conference pay heed to what they had to say and not conduct business as usual. Cultural contestation formed the backdrop of much of the debates on interpreting scripture, tradition, polity, and most poignantly on the issue of homosexuality.[47] With a sense of moral superiority and cultural pride, some of the bishops from Africa, Asia, and Latin America together with conservative bishops from the United States, denounced homosexuality as a sign of the moral decay of the West. Staged as a theological debate over the Bible and tradition, the bishops from the South took the opportunity to "talk back" to the West, assuming that truth was on their side. Some of the liberal bishops in the United States did not challenge these bishops with darker skin, for fear of being accused of racial bigotry.

The issue of sexuality has always crystallized cultural differences and brought to the forefront deep-seated assumptions about morality, social order, and gender construction. During the colonial period, missionaries condemned the cultural practices of footbinding, polygamy, women's veiling, and *sati* (the custom of widows burnt at their husbands' funeral pyre). The subordination and ill-treatment of women were taken as symptomatic of barbarous and uncivilized cultures, thus calling for the intervention and "benevolent" rule of the West. This kind of colonial feminism has hindered the receptivity of women's movements and other progressive causes in the Third World, because they were labeled as "problematically Westernized."[48] But ironically many colonized people, including leaders of the churches, have internalized the ideology of nuclear monogamous marriage brought by the missionaries as synonymous with modernization and the Christian way. While their cultures are generally more inclusive of diverse sexual practices, they have learned from the colonial masters and missionaries a much narrower understanding of sexual propriety and acceptable code of conduct. Thus, some African and Asian bishops at Lambeth considered homosexuality as abominable, to

NOTES

[1] Samuel P. Huntington, *The Clash of Civilizations and the Remaking of World Order* (New York: Simon & Schuster, 1996), 51, 91.

[2] Edward W. Said, *Orientalism* (New York: Vintage Books, 1979), 41.

[3] Huntingon, *The Clash of Civilizations.*

[4] Benjamin R. Barber, *Jihad vs. McWorld: How Globalism and Tribalism are Reshaping the World* (New York: Ballantine Books, 1996).

[5] Bill Ashcroft, Gareth Griffiths, and Helen Tiffin, eds., *The Postcolonial Studies Reader* (New York: Routledge, 1995), v x.

[6] R. S. Sugirtharajah, "From Orientalism to Postcolonialism," in his *Asian Biblical Hermeneutics and Postcolonialism* (Maryknoll: Orbis Books, 1998), 17.

[7] Charles H. Long, ed., *Who Are the Anglicans* (Cincinnati: Forward Movement Publications, 1988), 4.

[8] Edward W. Said, *Out of Place: A Memoir* (New York: Alfred A. Knopf, 1999), 7, 22.

[9] Said, *Orientalism,* 7.

[10] Antonio Gramsci, *Antonio Gramsci: Selections from Political Writings, 1910-1920,* ed. Quintin Hoare (New York: International Publishers, 1977), 11.

[11] See the discussion in Teodros Kiros, *Toward the Construction of a Theory of Political Action; Antonio Gramsci, Consciousness, Participation, and Hegemony* (Lanham, Md: University Press of America, 1985), 100-2.

[12] Said, *Orientalism,* 6-7.

[13] Edward W. Said, *Culture and Imperialism* (New York: Alfred A. Knopf, 1994).

[14] Stuart Hall, "The West and the Rest: Discourse and Power," in *Formations of Modernity,* ed. Stuart Hall and Bram Gieben (Cambridge: Polity Press, 1992), 318.

[15] Stuart Hall, "When Was 'the Postcolonial'? Thinking at the Limit," in *The Postcolonial Question: Common Skies, Divided Horizon,* ed. Iain Chambers and Lidia Curti (New York: Routledge, 1996), 247.

[16] Stuart Hall, "Gramsci's Relevance for the Study of Race and Ethnicity," in his *Critical Dialogues in Cultural Studies,* ed. David Morley and Kuan-Hsing Chen (London: Routledge, 1996), 435-40.

[17] Stuart Hall, "New Ethnicities," in Critical Dialogues, 442.

[18] Homi H. Bhabha, *The Location of Culture* (London: Routledge, 1994).

[19] See the discussion in Bart Moore-Gilbert, *Postcolonial Theory: Contexts, Practices, Politics* (London: Verso, 1997), 117.

[20] Bhabha, *The Location of Culture,* 88.

[21] Homi Bhabha, "The Third Space," in *Identity: Community, Culture, Difference,* ed. Jonathan Rutherford (London: Lawrence & Wishart, 1990), 211.

[22] Bhabha, *The Location of Culture,* 193.

[23] Ibid., 1-2.

[24] Ibid., 5. Emphasis his.

[25] "Can the Subaltern Speak," in *Marxism and the Interpretation of Culture,* ed. Cary Nelson and Lawrence Grossberg (Urbana: University of Illinois Press, 1988), 271-313.

[26] See "Subaltern Talk: Interview with the Editors," in *The Spivak Reader,* ed. Donna Landry and Gerald Maclean (New York: Routledge, 1966), 287-308; also her *A Critique of Postcolonial Reason: Toward a History of the Vanishing Present* (Cambridge, Mass: Harvard University Press, 1999), 308-11.

[27] Gayatri Chakravorty Spivak, "French Feminism in an International Frame," in her *In Other Worlds: Essays in Cultural Politics* (London: Routledge, 1987), 137.

[28] Gayatri Chakravorty Spivak, "Three Women's Texts and a Critique of Imperialism," *Critical Inquiry* 12 (1985): 244-47.

[29] Donald Henry Kortright Davis, "Present and Future Trends in Anglicanism," in *Anglicanism: Present and Future,* ed. Michael P. Hamilton (Washington, D.C.: Washington National Cathedral, 1992), 25.

[30] *The Lambeth Conference 1968: Resolutions and Reports* (New York:

Seabury, 1968), 140.

[31] *The Truth Shall Make You Free: The Lambeth Conference 1988* (London: Church Publishing, 1988), 88.

[32] John Pobee, "New Dioceses of the Anglican Communion," in *The Study of Anglicanism,* ed. Stephen Sykes and John Booty (London: SPCK, 1988), 395-98.

[33] Christopher Duraisingh, "Editorial: Gospel and Identity in Community," *International Review of Mission* 85 (1996): 6-7.

[34] William L. Sachs, *The Transformation of Anglicanism* (Cambridge: Cambridge University Press, 1993).

[35] Sykes and Booty, eds., *The Study of Anglicanism.*

[36] Sachs, *The Transformation of Anglicanism,* 67-68.

[37] John Howe, *Anglicanism and the Universal Church* (Toronto: Anglican Book Centre, 1990), 14.

[38] Ibid., 19.

[39] Joyce M. Bennett, *Hasten Slowly* (Chichester: Little London Associates Publishing, 1991), 16.

[40] Quotations are from The Book of Common Prayer of the Episcopal Church USA (New York: The Church Hymnal Corporation, 1977).

[41] *The Truth Shall Make You Free,* 67.

[42] Hall, *Critical Dialogues,* 393.

[43] *The Lambeth Conference 1948* (London: SPCK, 1948), 84.

[44] Howe, *Anglicanism and the Universal Church,* 87-88.

[45] Fredrica Harris Thompsett, "The Laity," in *The Study of Anglicanism,* 245-46.

[46] Mark Dyer, et al., eds., *The Official Report of the Lambeth Conference 1998* (Harrisburg: Morehouse Publishing, 1999), 186.

[47] For the resolution on human sexuality, see Ibid., 381-82.

[48] Uma Narayan, *Dislocating Cultures: Identities, Traditions, and Third-World Feminism* New York: Routledge, 1997), 1-39.

[49] R. S. Sugirtharajah, ed., *The Postcolonial Bible* (Sheffield: Sheffield Academic Press, 1998); Laura E. Donaldson, ed., "Postcolonialism and Scriptural Reading," *Semeia* 75 (1996).

3
THE NATURE AND SHAPE OF THE CONTEMPORARY ANGLICAN COMMUNION

DAVID HAMID

If we could take a snapshot of the contemporary Anglican Communion, what would it look like? How many Anglicans are there, and how are they distributed around the world? What are the Communion's sources of funding? This brief paper is intended to provide such background information, to be a lookout point as we gaze beyond the colonial legacy of Anglicanism toward a vision for the Communion in the twenty-first century.

Much of the information in this paper consists of basic facts and figures about our global family of churches which were compiled just prior to the 1998 Lambeth Conference, with some recent updates as appropriate and available. These facts and figures come with some caveats related to the often slippery business of statistics and demographics.

Beyond the statistical data, I have made some comments on what I believe to be some underlying issues for the churches of the Communion. The matters which were emerging, globally, prior to the 1998 Lambeth Conference became the focus for Communion-wide deliberation at that event and were worked into the fourfold agenda of the Conference:

- Economic justice, ecological and biological questions, sexuality
- Mission and evangelism
- Authority, pluralism, identity within Anglicanism
- Unity, dialogue with other Christians, and relations with non-Christians

In this introductory background paper, I will not attempt to comment on these points directly, but to indicate what may be some undercurrents lying beneath the surface, which are informing the way Anglicans approach these contemporary questions.

THE BRANCH OFFICE

One caveat when compiling data relates to the question of who keeps the figures and who tells whom. I mention this in particular since I work in the one central bureaucratic structure of the worldwide Communion, the Anglican Communion Office (ACO). But it is revealing, and perhaps characteristic of Anglicanism, that this central structure is quite limited in its connections and influence. Perhaps it is not central at all, but at the periphery.

Some might assume that from the vantage point of the ACO, I would be in a choice position to have an overview of the contemporary worldwide Communion. Just over a month before the ten-yearly gathering of bishops in the Lambeth Conference, one might have thought that our ACO Secretariat (which is the Lambeth Conference Secretariat) would be swirling with statistics, trends, facts and figures which will be part of the raw material for the bishops' discussions in Canterbury. Not so!

A four-month project, headed up by Jane Gitau, the present director of communications of the Anglican Church of Kenya, who was seconded to our office in order to prepare statistics for the Lambeth Conference, actually resulted in up-to-date data from only 18 of the (then) 37 Provinces. Part of the problem is related, understandably, to the difficulties of communication in some parts of the world. But since returns were not received from such places as England and Australia, it was clearly not just the technology of communication which was the problem.

Anglicans appear to be somewhat shy, even reluctant, about compiling and sharing hard data on our membership. This, in itself, might be telling us something about this Anglican Communion of ours. Have we inherited a certain (dare I say characteristically English) reticence about such matters? Or, do we have a different understanding of church and of membership that does not want to be too sharp in terms of who is in and who is out. Some denominations have absolutely no difficulty in telling, at any given moment, who is a member and who is not. Anglicans appear to be somewhat more flexible and even elusive on this issue. Across the Communion we do not even have a common understanding of what constitutes membership for the purposes of a government census. It could be baptism, confirmation, church attendance figures, or even cultural/tribal affiliation. There is no standard method of reporting.

Another important factor which contributed, no doubt, to the lacunae in our Communion data has to do with how we as Anglicans understand the role of our central structures, and how much information (because information is power) we feel we ought to share with the central office. You see, due to the decentralized nature of our global Communion, the ACO is not at all like a "head-office." We do not function like a Vatican curia. The real head offices or central structures in our Communion, one might argue, are the provincial headquarters. As there are now 38 of these, it would be fair to say that I work for the one *branch* office of the *38 head offices.*

I am grateful to Archbishop Michael Peers, the Primate of Canada, for this understanding of power-sharing in the Communion. It comes from his experience (which I am sure is the experience of many who work in provincial offices) that the real "head office" *within a province* is not the provincial headquarters at all, but the diocesan offices! Just as provincial offices at times feel a certain distance from diocesan structures, it follows that information, statistics, and membership data from around the world are not naturally and as a matter of course shared by the provinces with the ACO in London. It follows that only with extreme caution and considerable limitation can someone from the ACO speak from a position of overview.

The accompanying chart brings together some figures about the member churches of the Anglican Communion. Before I examine these numbers in more detail, I wish to make some comments about the ambiguities associated with this data.

THE CONVENTIONAL FIGURES

Despite a certain shyness when it comes to compiling and sharing hard membership data, Anglicans actually have at the tip of the tongue an oft-quoted sound bite: "We have over seventy million members worldwide, in more than 165 countries." A statement like this is often heard in sermons and addresses, and even appears in official publications of provinces and of the Communion itself. But if one were to ask where the speaker or writer obtained this figure of seventy million, or, indeed, where one could obtain a list of the 165 countries with an Anglican presence, the details become rather foggy.

In fact, the figure itself of seventy million is problematic. It does seem to have semi-official, or even official sanction in the Communion. But is it not about time that this sound-bite figure is updated, as it has been in circulation at least since the Lambeth Conference of 1988? This statistic, just prior to the Lambeth Conference of 1998, got the Anglican Communion into a bit of hot water. I refer to the case of the missing Anglicans. A headline appeared in the *Church of England Newspaper* in 1997 which read, "Numbers reveal 17 million missing Anglicans." The article went on to say:

> New figures compiled by one of the Christian church's leading statisticians show that while the number of Christians worldwide has increased by 53,000 per day there are about 17 million Anglicans missing.
>
> Over the past few years the Anglican Church has used the oft-quoted figure of 70 million as a tally of members of the Anglican Communion worldwide. However, 'The World Church Handbook', issued by Peter Brierly of the U.K.-based organisation, Christian Research, lists the total number as 53,200,000 or about one per cent of the world's total population.
>
> Canon James Rosenthal, a spokesman for the Anglican Consultative Council, said that there are plans underway to do some research on Anglicanism worldwide. However, he admitted that a statistical survey had not been conducted for some time. In fact, in 1960, there were 41 million Anglicans and the church was estimated to grow to 58 million by 2010—a growth rate of 42 per cent—by that reckoning the numbers may well be on target.

Despite the alarming headline in the *Church of England Newspaper* (which along with other church press was looking to stimulate discussion and debate before the Lambeth Conference), Anglicans continue to toss about the figure of seventy million as the global membership. But if this figure has been in constant use for about twelve years now, does this mean that there has been no growth in the Communion in that period? If so, the Anglican Communion is in a rather embarrassing predicament: this twelve-year period embraces the decade of evangelism, and therefore questions must be raised about another oft-quoted sound bite, namely that the Communion is growing rapidly, especially in the global South.

WHOM DO WE COUNT?

Even a simple fact such as the number of provinces in the Anglican Communion can be rather ambiguous for Anglicans. For instance, it is not universally understood that we include among the list of Anglican provinces the churches in South Asia which incorporate former Anglican dioceses into new United Churches with which we are in communion. These are the churches of Pakistan, North India, South India, and Bangladesh. These four churches are members of the Anglican Consultative Council (ACC), and send their Moderators to the Primates Meetings, and in 1998, sent all their active bishops to the Lambeth Conference. Moreover, they contribute to the inter-Anglican budget. So in terms of their participation in the life of the Communion, these churches are as Anglican as the Church of England or the Episcopal Church USA. Yet, in terms of global Christianity, we have the anomaly that these churches may also appear in lists of the Methodist or Reformed families. Ecumenically, this anomaly is good news, but ecumenical progress can cause confusion as communions seek to compile membership figures for their own family. Despite the ambiguities involved, Anglicans officially include these four churches in the list of Anglican provinces, bringing the total to 38.

There is also a situation which arises from time to time, where a new province is formed but is not immediately a member of the Anglican Consultative Council, for that body only meets every three years, and must give assent to the admission of new members. At the time of the 1998 Lambeth Conference, such a situation arose concerning *La Iglesia Anglicana de la Región Central de América,* the Anglican Church of the Central American Region. This province had just been granted autonomy from the Episcopal Church USA in 1997 and was inaugurated, and its new Primate installed, early in 1998. Since the ACC would not meet until 1999, the Central American Province had not yet been approved for membership in ACC. So there was at the time of the Lambeth Conference some question as to whether it should appear among the list of provinces in the report. Fortunately it did, but it was not included in the official list maintained in our website until this year. It would be astonishing if Anglicans were to decide which church is a province of this branch of the One, Holy, Catholic and Apostolic Church simply by constitutional membership in a body formed a scant thirty years ago! But we do not, as Anglicans, have a clear, consistent and inclusive way of listing who we are, at a given moment. This causes confusion when other communions or organizations like the World Council of Churches seek information from our official sources.

Other anomalies crop up in the yearbooks and directories of provinces. *The Church of England Year Book* is often used as a good source of Anglican information by bodies such as the World Council of Churches, given the lack of anything that resembles an "Anglican Communion Directory." But it continues to list the *Chung Hua Cheng Kung Hui,* the Holy Catholic Church in China, among the provinces of the Communion. Apart from the diocese of Hong Kong, which divided into three dioceses, and recently became a province in its own right, the *Chung Hua Cheng Kung Hui* has become subsumed into the post-denominational China Christian Council. I asked officials at the Church of England why they still list the Holy Catholic Church in China as a province in their yearbook. The answer was that there are former Anglicans in that (former) province who are now members of the China Christian Council, but that they had to be accounted for. But, for argument's sake, I pointed out that, similarly, the *Church of England Year Book* should also list among the provinces the Church of India, Pakistan, Burma and Ceylon, whose Anglicans, with the exception of those in Sri Lanka and Myanmar, are now to be found in the United Churches in the Indian Sub-Continent.

The following is the present official list maintained in the ACO of the churches of the Anglican Communion.

CHURCHES OF THE ANGLICAN COMMUNION

Provinces

The Anglican Church in Aotearoa, New Zealand and Polynesia
The Anglican Church of Australia
The Church of Bangladesh
Igreja Episcopal Anglicana do Brasil
    (The Episcopal Anglican Church of Brazil)
The Episcopal Church of Burundi
The Anglican Church of Canada
The Church of the Province of Central Africa
Iglesia Anglicana de la Región Central de América
    (The Anglican Church of the Central American Region)
Province de L'Eglise Anglicane du Congo
    (The Province of the Anglican Church of the Congo)
The Church of England
Hong Kong Sheng Kung Hui
The Church of the Province of the Indian Ocean
The Church of Ireland
The Nippon Sei Ko Kai
    (The Anglican Communion in Japan)
The Episcopal Church in Jerusalem and the Middle East
The Anglican Church of Kenya
The Anglican Church of Korea
The Church of the Province of Melanesia
La Iglesia Anglicana de México
    (The Anglican Church of Mexico)
The Church of the Province of Myanmar (Burma)
The Church of Nigeria
The Church of North India (United)
The Church of Pakistan (United)
The Anglican Church of Papua New Guinea
The Episcopal Church in the Philippines
La Province de l'Eglise Episcopale au Rwanda
    (The Province of the Episcopal Church of Rwanda)
The Scottish Episcopal Church
The Church of the Province of South East Asia

The Church of South India (United)
The Church of the Province of Southern Africa
Iglesia Anglicana del Cono Sur de América
    (The Anglican Church of the Southern Cone of America)
The Episcopal Church of the Sudan
The Anglican Church of Tanzania
The Church of the Province of Uganda
The Episcopal Church in the USA
The Church in Wales
The Church of the Province of West Africa
The Church in the Province of the West Indies

Extra-Provincial Dioceses and other Churches

The Anglican Church of Bermuda
Iglesia Episcopal de Cuba (The Episcopal Church of Cuba)
Igreja Lusitana, Católica, Apostólica, Evangélica
    (The Lusitanian Church of Portugal)
Iglesia Episcopal Reformada de España
    (The Reformed Episcopal Church of Spain)
Iglesia Anglicana en Venezuela
    (The Anglican Church in Venezuela)
Iglesia Episcopal Puertorriqueña
    (The Episcopal Church of Puerto Rico)
Falkland Islands

STATISTICS BY REGION, INCLUDING CONTRIBUTION TO INTER-ANGLICAN BUDGET

Region	PROVINCE or CHURCH	Bishop	Diocese	Congregations	Members	% of Budget
Oceania	Aotearoa, New Zealand & Polynesia	16	9	991	220,659	2.46
	Australia	43	23	1,400	3,998,444	9.75
	Melanesia	8	8	948	163,884	0.12
	Papua New Guinea	6	5	100	246,000	0.12
Latin America & Caribbean	Bermuda	1	1	17	24,000	0.16
	Brazil	8	7	167	103,021	0.47
	Central America	5	5	80	13,409	0.12
	Cuba	1	1	45	6,000	0.00
	Haiti (Episcopal Church USA)	1	1	82	71,000	**
	Mexico	5	5	100	21,000	0.12
	Province IX (Episcopal Church USA)	5	5	130	25800	**
	Puerto Rico	1	1	40	20,000	0.00
	Southern Cone	11	7	247	22,490	0.27
	Venezuela	1	1	9	2,000	0.00
	Virgin Islands (Episcopal Church USA)	1	1	161	16,089	**
	West Indies	12	8	900	770,000	1.09
Africa	Burundi	6	5	140	425,000	0.03
	Central Africa	12	12	451	600,000	0.67
	Congo	7	6	N/A	300,000	0.05
	Indian Ocean	6	6	95	90,486	0.28
	Kenya	25	27	779	2,500,000	0.83
	Nigeria	2	76	3,167	17,500,000	1.59
	Rwanda	9	9	500	1,000,000	0.11
	Southern Africa	31	22	1,200	2,000,000	1.29
	Sudan	24	24	1,440	2,000,000	0.27
	Tanzania	17	16	725	1,379,366	0.55
	Uganda	29	27	9,720	8,000,000	0.55
	West Africa	12	12	N/A	1,000,000	0.21
North America	Canada	41	30	2,390	740,262	6.64
	USA	145	110	7,000	2,500,000	29.67
Europe	England	117	44	13,000	26,000,000	30.65
	Ireland	12	12	1,150	410,000	2.46
	Portugal	1	1	16	5,000	0.05
	Scotland	7	7	337	53,553	1.61
	Spain	1	1	26	5,000	0.05
	Wales	7	6	1,129	93,721	2.46

Region	PROVINCE or CHURCH	Bishop	Diocese	Congregations	Members	% of Budget
Asia	Bangladesh	2	2	40	13,000	0.05
	Ceylon	2	2	130	52,500	0.12
	Hong Kong	3	3	45	29,000	1.92
	Japan	11	11	282	57,273	1.36
	Jerusalem & Middle East	4	4	62	10,000	0.38
	Korea	3	3	92	14,558	0.36
	Myanmar	8	6	120	49,247	0.12
	North India	24	24	2,000	1,250,000	0.12
	Pakistan	9	8	300	800,000	0.12
	Philippines	7	5	559	118,187	0.17
	South East Asia	7	4	435	168,079	0.39
	South India	21	21	8,700	2,000,000	0.17

** Contribution to the Inter-Anglican Budget as Part of the Episcopal Church USA.

Wherever possible, the figures in the above table have come from data gathered in the ACO. These are supplemented by two other sources of statistical information, *The World Christian Handbook*, based on the database of Operation World by Patrick Johnstone, published by Christian Research, London, 1997; and David Barrett's magisterial *World Christian Encyclopaedia* (1982), as updated annually in the *International Bulletin of Missionary Research*.

In compiling the statistical information that was available in the office in London, I kept in mind the principle that the ACO is not a "head office"; and so I consulted with one of the "centers," the library of the General Synod of the Anglican Church of Canada, to have the figures corroborated. That library continues to be an excellent first resource for contemporary global Anglican information.

The table above is intended to be one element in the backdrop for this discussion on postcolonial Anglicanism. It is not a scientific census. Some figures are fairly hard, coming from direct, first-hand information reported by competent Provincial authorities. Some are no more than educated guesses, but which nevertheless seemed to be available in the ACO or the library of the Canadian General Synod.

The table, moreover, has built into it the complication, to which I have alluded earlier, that there is no accepted definition of whom to count as members. For example, the figure in the table for membership of the Church of England (26 million) clearly is based on affiliation. I think I can say with some certainty that there are not 26 million worshiping members in the provinces of Canterbury and York. The average Sunday attendance, according to the *Church Times*, is 803,700, while Easter communicants in 1998 reached 1,172,000[1]. Contrast these figures with the Canadian data. The figure for Canada in the table is that which comes from parish and diocesan lists. However, the census of the government of Canada reveals that there are more than two million Anglicans in that land, but the Church in Canada can only identify 740,262 of them. So, in the table one will find mixed apples and oranges, not just in the two cases cited of the Church of England and the Anglican Church of Canada, but likely with other figures as well. But that is the way the provinces themselves want to count their membership, and we have no other choice but to go along with this.

Despite these inherent deficiencies, I hope the table provides a rough sketch to serve as a starting point for a discussion of who the Anglicans are today.

WHO ARE THE ANGLICANS?

The figures reveal that there are more than 76 million members of the Anglican Communion worldwide. (For shorthand I will call them Anglicans, although four million or so are not Anglican by denomination but are members of the United Churches in Communion.) These Anglicans are distributed around the world in this way:

Europe	26,567,274	35%
North America	3,240,262	4%
Latin America and the Caribbean	1,111,920	1%
Africa	36,794,852	48%
Asia	4,561,844	6%
Oceania	4,628,987	6%

So what is often said appears to be true: most Anglicans live in Africa, about 48 percent of the total. About 43 million, or 56 percent, live outside the so-called developed countries in Europe, North America and parts of Oceania. If we assume that the Church of England figures are inflated because of the method of measurement, then the proportions are even more heavily weighted towards the developing world.

Of the 807 active bishops, 390 live in Europe, North America, Australia and New Zealand. Hence, 417 or 52 percent of Anglican bishops live in the developing world. These bishops serve 391 out of the 634 dioceses of the Communion, or 62 percent of the dioceses around the world. Of the more than 61,500 congregations of Anglicans throughout the world, close to 35,000, or 57 percent, are in the developing world.

Visually, this shift of Anglicanism towards the global South can be demonstrated by examining the Lambeth Conference photographs over the years. The 1998 photograph looks darker in complexion than ever before. At the first Lambeth Conference in 1867, the 76 bishops in attendance were all white and were either British or U.S. citizens. In 1878, 100 bishops attended, the sole black bishop being James Theodore Holly, the Bishop of Haiti. Already at the 1988 Conference, the black bishops were in the majority. In 1998, the white bishops were an even smaller minority. As 1998 was the first Lambeth Conference at which women bishops were present, one might envision a similar and parallel process with respect to proportion of women as the photograph is taken each decade. What will the Lambeth photograph in 2098 look like?

It is clear that the center of gravity of Anglicanism has shifted. Most Anglicans, and the majority of leaders exercising oversight, *episcopé*, in the Anglican Communion, now live in the global South. This, I believe, is an important point for our discussion on the postcolonial church. If the Lambeth Conference is a moment each ten years for the Communion to express its mind on matters touching upon the faith, order, mission and ministry of the church, then that mind will be one which increasingly is formed from a cultural, economic, and linguistic context which is non-Anglo-Saxon, and non-First World.

MONEY

It is one thing to look at where Anglicans are in the world. It is another to look at the sources of financing of the various instruments of the Anglican Communion. The table above lists the percentage of the total inter-Anglican budget by source church. The percentages in the table, I hasten to add, are fairly accurate, given by the Treasurer of the Anglican Communion. Finance departments of the church tend to prefer a little more certainty about their figures than other departments. The table lists funding only towards the official instruments of the Anglican Communion: the Lambeth Conference, the meetings of the Primates and the Anglican Consultative Council, and the programs of the Communion which principally relate to communications, mission, and ecumenical affairs. The figures do not reflect or recognize the considerable extra-budgetary funding and in-kind support which the Anglican Communion receives, which is almost entirely from the United States, along with some smaller amounts from Canada and England.

Sixty percent of the funding of the Anglican Communion comes from two provinces: the United States and England. If we add in Australia, Canada, Aotearoa New Zealand, Ireland and Wales, we get to 72 percent. There is one obvious question related to these percentages, which has to do with sustainability over the long term of such concentrated sources of funding. Could the Communion be held hostage to the financial well-being or policy of a particular province? For instance, as parishes of the Church of England assume more and more of the share of the costs of the pensions of the clergy, the result will be a tightening of funds available for dioceses, and hence the national church, with a sure effect on support to the Anglican Communion programs. Similarly, the World Council of Churches, dependent on almost 40 percent of its funding from Germany, began to feel the pinch when German churches in the 1990s began to prioritize support within their own borders to help with the reunification and reintegration of the two Germanys.

THE SIGNIFICANT ROLE OF MISSIONARY SOCIETIES

In addition to Anglican Provincial structures and the instruments of the Communion which function at the world level, there is another important dimension to church life internationally, which must be taken into account in considering the nature and shape of the contemporary Communion: the role of the missionary societies. The missionary societies, mostly based in the wealthier provinces in Europe, North America, and Oceania, exert considerable influence and channel significant amounts of funding towards programs and ministry around the world. However, there are no central sources of information and hard figures on the amounts of such support.

We have seen that the funding of the central institutions of the Anglican Communion betrays a heavy dependency on a very few provinces in the North. It may well be that the quotas paid to the inter-Anglican budget from some provinces in the global South may have their ultimate origin in funding received by those provinces from missionary societies. If this were the case, it would mean that the support to the Anglican Communion instruments and programs is even more heavily dependent on sources in the North.

Since the Anglican Congress in 1963, there have been attempts in the Communion to establish mechanisms to support the fair, responsible, and interdependent sharing of resources throughout the church to support ministry and mission. Mutual Responsibility and Interdependence in the Body of Christ, and later the Partners in Mission process, monitored by Communion bodies such as the Mission Issues and Strategy Advisory Group, and now the Mission Commission of the Anglican Communion, play a role in this endeavor. These initiatives started a process which is continuing today and which radically alters the understanding of mission in the church. The initiatives encourage a move away from paternalism towards a new interdependence of equal, sister churches, responsible for the mission in a particular place, but always acting in communion with, and with the support of, the global church.

Funding, however, is still not completely transparent, from all sources. Funding inevitably raises issues of control. Disputes about who really makes decisions in dioceses and provinces in the developing world go back at least as far as some famous quarrels between the Bishop of Jamaica and the Church Missionary Society in the 1830s over who should control where missionary clergy should serve on that island. It is still largely true that some of the best and most up-to-date information on what is happening in provinces around the world is not available through the central vehicle that all provinces support, that is the ACC, but through missionary societies, either voluntary or synodical. And as someone who once worked for a synodical missionary society (in the Anglican Church of Canada) and who now works for the ACC, I can testify that such information does provide the agency with a certain amount of power. It is not unusual, for instance, that the Anglican Communion Office, charged with the responsibility of maintaining the database of dioceses and bishops of the Communion, learns of changes in the episcopate and in jurisdictions not directly from the provinces involved, but via mission agencies. The agencies in the North are repositories of information on dioceses and leaders in the developing world. There are no comparable sources of inside information on dioceses and leaders in provinces in the "wealthy" provinces, outside those provinces themselves.

The mechanisms in place in the Communion to encourage transparency and interdependence are in need of constant refinement and are in a state of evolution even today. The general direction is towards the freeing up the control of resources (and the control of information), towards supporting the mission and ministry of the church in ways that are mutually agreed upon and are respectful of local autonomy and responsibility. Nevertheless, many Anglican leaders in the developing world would comment that there is a certain reluctance among the mission agencies to look at *radically* new and innovative ways of sharing resources. Mission societies and agencies thus remain significant centers of power and influence in the Communion.

NATIONAL LEADERSHIP

The indigenization of Anglican leadership throughout the world is a recognized fact, and not only were most bishops who attended the 1998 Lambeth Conference *from* the global South, they themselves were *born* in the global South. This is also evidenced if one looks around the table at the meeting of the Primates. Of the 38 members of that meeting, only one is not a person born of the soil of the province he serves, that being Presiding Bishop Maurice Sinclair, the Primate of the Province of the Southern Cone of South America (and he is English).

Along with the growing indigenization of leadership we can observe a trend away from existing linguistic imperialism in the Communion. At the 1978 Lambeth Conference the only official language used was English. In 1988 there was some translation provided at plenary discussions into Spanish, French, and Swahili. Nevertheless, when Archbishop Michael Peers, the Primate of Canada, presided over a plenary discussion in 1988 in one of the official languages of his province (French), there appeared among the petitions submitted for the intercessions at the next day's eucharist a prayer (in English) that the Primate of Canada be given the gift of tongues. The symbolic gesture of the Primate of Canada, much appreciated by the sizeable Francophone minority among the bishops, clearly irritated one of the English-speaking bishops to the extent that he appealed to the Almighty to intervene.

The pressure for greater linguistic inclusivity does not let up, however. In two pre-Lambeth 1998 gatherings, of the Francophone bishops and of the Latin American Bishops, the question of furthering the production of resources and materials within the Communion in Spanish, French, and Portuguese was on the agenda. So the pressure will be maintained for a less English sound to the Communion. At the 1998 Lambeth Conference there was simultaneous translation provided for all plenary sessions into Spanish, French, Swahili, and Japanese. Moreover, the parallel Spouses' Conference functioned in these languages, plus Arabic, in addition to English. For the first time, some preparatory documentation for a Lambeth Conference was translated into other languages, principally the *Virginia Report* of the Inter-Anglican Theological and Doctrinal Commission, which was translated into French, Spanish, Portuguese, and Japanese.

However, in the planning for the last Lambeth Conference, several linguistic battles were fought. For instance, an attempt was made to strike from the list a proposed consultant (an eminent Latin American theologian from Brazil), because he was not fluent in English. The Brazilians fought back hard and successfully challenged this somewhat insensitive move. There are other examples. A request was received from Central America that the Spanish-speaking bishops from that region be housed in close proximity at the Conference, so that in the off hours they could relax together in their own language. This simple and human request was met with the comment, "Oh, no. You see, we cannot allow the formation of ghettos at the Conference." It was only when the Lambeth Conference management staff was asked if they considered a group of English speakers to be "a ghetto," and whether the administration was planning to break up the English-language group, that the management retreated from this Anglo-centric position. Significantly, the report of the 1998 Conference is only available in English. In this matter, contrast the Lambeth Conference and the Lutheran World Federation Assembly held in Hong Kong in 1997. The latter functioned completely—in plenary, in groups, in preparatory materials, and in post-Assembly reports—in five official languages: English, French, Spanish, German, and Chinese. So, perhaps linguistically we are still very much "the English Church."

The indigenization of leadership means that the leaders of our global family of churches now do not come from the same cultural common pot, namely English. A century ago, the leaders would not only have been English, but probably "Public School" and "Oxbridge" as well. Today our bishops think, write, speak, and dream in diverse linguistic worlds. Attentiveness, the ability to truly listen to each other, will have to be increasingly a gift that the Communion's leaders need to possess or cultivate in order to maintain the bonds of Communion. And this will entail the increasing use of more than one language as the means of communication throughout the Communion.

RECEPTION

The Anglican Communion is on a journey discovering what communion or *koinonia* means, and we are discovering this as we seek to live together in the face of challenges that would pull us apart. Challenges to the unity of the Communion on matters of ministry (the ordination of women) have been addressed through a commitment to being attentive and courteous to each other, and respectful of distinct, but equally passionately held positions. The Eames Commission on Women in the Episcopate, in its report to the 1998 Lambeth Conference, details how a particularly Anglican way seems to be emerging in the Communion which will enable the church to discern the mind of Christ on a specific matter that may be potentially divisive. This Anglican way is none other than learning how to live in a period of reception. Anglicans are becoming well experienced in the theological process of reception as we face hard issues that threaten the unity of our Communion. We are discovering the bonds that keep us together. We are discovering that these bonds are bonds of love, and as such, stem in a profound way from the love which characterizes the inner life of God the Holy Trinity. These bonds of communion allow us to live together despite our differences—differences that are deeply held with equal conviction on all sides.

The continuing divergence in Anglicanism over the ordination of women is a good example of the Anglican Communion living in a process of reception. The final report of the Eames Commission indicates that only eight provinces do not allow women to be ordained to any order; two permit ordination to the diaconate only; eleven permit women deacons and priests but not bishops; eight permit women to be ordained to all orders; and three provinces have women bishops. Accurate information could not be obtained from four provinces: Rwanda, Sudan, Congo and Myanmar. (The United Churches in Communion were not included in the Eames study.) Clearly the open process of reception of women's ordination is underway in the Communion, and there have been no major breaches of communion or unity. Only two bishops apparently chose not to attend the 1998 Lambeth Conference because there would be women bishops present. It is interesting, perhaps, to note that these two bishops, although both in Madagascar, are both expatriates, one English, the other Canadian. In this experience there are lessons to be learned about the way the churches of our Communion can hold together while wrestling with the discernment of truth over a matter that touches the very unity and communion of the church. Of course, these are lessons not only for Anglicans. There is much which we could share, and indeed are sharing, with the wider church.

The process of reception, involving an openness to a new thing being either accepted or rejected by the church, is becoming a regular feature in Anglican life. Such openness is, unfortunately, often tainted with the suspicion that there is manipulation by some interest group or other. Some conservatives quite often may feel that there is an inevitability to the outcome of a reception process and therefore may be cynical of its openness. Some liberals often may be impatient and may feel that periods of reception are stalling tactics providing time for opposition to the new thing to be marshaled. But the lessons we are learning about reception should not be quickly discarded. As long as Anglicans strive to maintain communion among the churches, these lessons will be invaluable.

The process of reception of new insights or developments in matters of faith and order is neatly summarized in *The Grindrod Report* which was submitted to the Primates of the Communion prior to the Lambeth Conference of 1988.

Whenever a matter is tested by the Church there is necessarily an openness about the question. The continuing communion of Christians with one another in faith and worship maintains the underlying unity of the Church while the reception process is at work. The openness needs to be recognized and accepted by those on both sides of the debate. There needs to be openness to the possibility of the new thing being accepted by the Church or rejected by the Church. It also entails a willingness to live with diversity throughout the 'reception' process. [2]

THE EROSION OF CONSTANTS

Some in the contemporary Anglican Communion feel a certain unease as it becomes increasingly apparent that one cannot take certain things for granted in the Anglican churches today. There is a growing worry about what the common assumptions and agreements among Anglicans are. As I mentioned above, when new situations and challenges arise, when we are called to reinterpret the gospel in a new light, Anglicans speak of a continuous process of reception in the life of the church. Does this mean that there are no longer some matters which remain constant in the church's life?

What were these constants to begin with? Here we get into very slippery ground in the Communion, because we use the same words to mean quite different things. Anglicans would all agree (or almost all would agree) that the truth of the revelation of God is attested to definitively in the canon of scripture. But there are no commonly held hermeneutical principles that allow Anglicans to interpret the scripture together. Nor is there agreement as to the precise relation among the three legs of the Anglican stool of scripture, tradition, and reason.

Before the 1998 Lambeth Conference there were rumors that a commission would be established to look at questions of human sexuality, homosexuality in particular. Many people envisioned that a body, similar to the Eames Commission which dealt with the question of the ordination of women to the episcopate, would be the way forward for the Communion to deal with this divisive issue. Although no such commission has been formed, if any body at the level of the Communion is going to address issues of human sexuality, it will need to begin with some basic work on scriptural hermeneutics. The Communion has never before had to address this issue of the *nature* of scriptural authority nor of the interrelation between scripture, tradition, and reason quite so explicitly.

In addition to the scriptures, there are also some other doctrinal articles and principles which Anglicans have received, but are they received for all time? I refer, for instance, to the other items in the Chicago-Lambeth Quadrilateral: the teaching set forth in the catholic creeds, the apostolic ministry, and the sacramental life of the church. Do not the demands from certain parts of the Communion to permit lay persons to preside at the eucharist implicitly call into question received sacramental practices summarized in the Quadrilateral? Another example would be the Anglican acceptance of the doctrinal definitions of the first four ecumenical councils. When Bishop John Spong, in his "12 theses" calling for a new Reformation which he posted on the door of the World Wide Web, states categorically that the christology of the ages is bankrupt, are these historical doctrinal agreements no longer secure touchstones for teaching and understanding the mystery of the incarnation?[3] Are such sure yardsticks and constants being eroded?

Some were hoping that the last Lambeth Conference would define explicitly what the constants are for the life of the church. Indeed a number of resolutions were passed which sought to do just that. For instance:

Resolution III.1:

This Conference, recognising the need in our Communion for fuller agreement on how to interpret and apply the message of the Bible in a world of rapid change and widespread cultural interaction,

(a) **reaffirms** the primary authority of the scriptures, according to their testimony and supported by our own historic formularies;

(b) **urges** that the Biblical text should be handled respectfully, coherently, and consistently, building upon our best traditions and scholarship believing that the Scriptural revelation must continue to illuminate, challenge and transform cultures, structures, and ways of thinking, especially those that predominate today;

(c) **invites** our provinces, as we open ourselves afresh to a vision of a Church full of the Word and full of the Spirit, to promote at every level biblical study programs which can inform and nourish the life of dioceses, congregations, seminaries, communities, and members of all ages.[4]

Resolution III.5:

This Conference:

(a) **affirms** that our creator God, transcendent as well as immanent, communicates with us authoritatively through the Holy scriptures of the Old and New Testaments; and

(b) in agreement with the Lambeth Quadrilateral, and in solidarity with the Lambeth Conference of 1888, **affirms** that these Holy scriptures contain 'all things necessary to salvation' and are for us the 'rule and ultimate standard' of faith and practice.[5]

Resolution IV.2:

This Conference:

(a) **reaffirms** the Chicago-Lambeth Quadrilateral (1888) as a basis on which Anglicans seek the full, visible unity of the Church, and also recognizes it as a statement of Anglican unity and identity;

(b) **acknowledges** that ecumenical dialogues and experience have led to a developing understanding of each of the elements of the Quadrilateral, including the significance of apostolicity, pastoral oversight (*episcopé*), the office of bishop and the historic episcopate; and

(c) **commends** continuing reflection upon the Quadrilateral's contribution to the search for the full, visible unity of the Church, and in particular the role within visible unity of a common ministry of oversight exercised in personal, collegial and communal ways at every level.[6]

More recently, the Meeting of the Primates in Portugal in 2000 seemed, in the communiqué which ensued, to reaffirm the central place of the Chicago-Lambeth Quadrilateral:

> We believe that the unity of the Communion as a whole still rests on the Lambeth Quadrilateral: the Holy scriptures as the rule and standard of faith; the creeds of the undivided Church; the two Sacraments ordained by Christ himself and the historic episcopate. Only a formal and public repudiation of this would place a diocese or Province outside the Anglican Communion.[7]

The Communion seems to be living in a time when a few seem to be challenging these common bases which underpin Anglican theology and ecclesiology. However, it is not just Anglicans who have received the scriptures, the creeds, the apostolic ministry and the sacraments, but the vast majority of Christians everywhere. Challenges to these constants in the life of the church are not simply challenges to Anglicanism but raise questions about much of the received framework of Christianity itself.

CULTURAL ISSUES

In some cases, the divergences that are seen and that are emerging within the Communion on many matters may be based upon cultural differences rather than upon different interpretations of scripture or its relation to tradition and reason, or as a result of challenging received doctrine. They are nevertheless critical divergences; and the church will have to examine the question of whether, with regard to a given development, it is appropriate to respect a particular culture and to recognize that a development might be appropriate or inappropriate in that culture. Even within a province, cultural particularity is being increasingly recognized. In many places in the Communion there is an openness to permitting diverse cultural groups to develop their own distinctive life within the one communion of the diocese or province. The Province of Aotearoa New Zealand and Polynesia is a good example, with the Maori, Polynesian, and Pakeha jurisdictions recognized constitutionally. In the Anglican Church of Canada, encouraged by the "First Nations Convocation" there is a movement towards a distinct jurisdiction within the Canadian province of indigenous people.

But to what extent does the church, with its new found cultural sensitivity and openness to diversity, allow distinct practices, which may be acceptable to one cultural group but not to others, to co-exist? For instance, in some areas Maori tradition does not contemplate, at present, women in leadership roles, apparently for deeply ingrained cultural reasons. The same could be said for the church in, say, the Arab Middle East. Can this be a barrier to greater communion? May cultural differences be church-dividing in the end?

Women and men in the Anglican Communion, across the boundaries of continents, oceans, cultures and nations, still live in relation with one another, through our common baptism and faith and our links to a particular ecclesial family. What happens when cultural and ethnic factors seem, however, to lead us in divergent directions? What if the deeply held belief of one cultural group within the church is understood to be a matter of justice same belief offends those of another cultural group? How balance sensitivity, inclusiveness, and tolerance with justice?

AUTONOMY, INTERDEPENDENCE, AND AUTHORITY

The ecumenical questions for Anglicans today, both the "extra-mural" questions and the "intra-mural" ones, relate to authority. The *Virginia Report* of the Inter-Anglican Theological and Doctrinal Commission, arguably the centerpiece of the Lambeth 1998 Conference, since it was the one document translated into most of the official languages of the Communion, offers important insights into the development of the structures of authority and unity in the Anglican Communion.

Within the Anglican family itself, there is an increasing tension between the concept of provincial autonomy on the one hand and interdependence on the other. At present in the Anglican Communion, binding decisions may only be taken at the provincial level. Some remain quite satisfied with this state of affairs. Others would argue that a global Communion needs some global mechanism of authoritative and binding decision-making.

Given the character of the present instruments of Anglican unity, a communal expression of the mind of the church at the international level can only be consultative. But if, at the world level, the Anglican Communion seeks at all to discover the mind and will of Christ in order to guide its mission and ministry, does that discernment not demand of the churches of the Communion a certain recognition of the authority of Christ speaking within the churches? Do the churches of the Communion need, not only to be able to consult with each other, but to be accountable to each other in order to grow in the gospel together? In certain cases, do the churches of the Communion not need to act and move together as a sign of unity in this broken and fragmented world? Does the seemingly inviolate Anglican principle of provincial autonomy have more to do with a latter-day culture of individualism and "doing one's own thing," rather than some ecclesiological rule or doctrine of the church? Does the reluctance to consider authoritative decision-making at the level of the Communion mean that divisive issues are being addressed effectively and authoritatively at the provincial level?

If, as the *Virginia Report* suggests, the interrelationship of the churches in the Communion is a sacramental reality which is related somehow to our communion with the Holy Trinity, then our relationship at the world level must be more than a political convenience or an alliance of like-minded Christians. We do not describe our global family as the "Anglican Federation," or the "Anglican Alliance," or the "Anglican Association." We are the Anglican *Communion*. Communion, from the Latin *communio* which translates the New Testament word *koinonia*, has to do with love—with loving, with an interdependent relationship, with equality, with giving and receiving, with sharing life. These are ultimately divine qualities. The Anglican understanding of the church as communion gives us the ability to understand the unity of the church and the potential unity of the human community in a unique way, because we can look beyond political and social organization to something that is a divine gift, something sacramental and graceful. As the Communion faces more and more divergence on key issues, does the reluctance to deal with authority at the communion level mean that the future shape of the Anglican family will be less a communion and more a loose federation? If so, we would need to ask ourselves if a federation is truly what God wants for a visibly united church. Ironically, some Christian families, such as the Lutheran World Federation, are now beginning to explore the implications of a deeper committed relationship, and are beginning to refer to themselves as the Lutheran Communion. Similar directions are being explored in the World Alliance of Reformed Churches. Are Anglicans, on the other hand, moving from communion to federation or alliance?

Most Anglicans do acknowledge a certain authority in the Lambeth Conference, and even in the Meeting of the Primates, but recognize these bodies of bishops to be exercising a moral authority which is not binding. But, if this is the case, Anglicans need to explore more fully the meaning of a moral authority for Christians which is not binding, especially when it relates to the ministry of a bishop, whom we understand to have oversight. The Anglican Consultative Council is advisory, but it is the only international instrument of the Communion in which all orders of the people of God are represented. In Anglican provinces, the synods—comprising bishops, priests and lay people—do have a binding authority for the province or diocese. On what basis is there a continued reluctance to bestow such a role upon the parallel body at the level of the Communion?

There are signs that provinces are desirous of a more concrete realization of their interdependence, of their need to share spiritual, intellectual, and material resources in order to effectively engage in the mission of Christ in their own locations. At the same time, there is a growing awareness, especially when we look at central authorities in other communions and in secular bodies, that not being able to instantly make an authoritative, communion-wide decision, may be a strength, since the Holy Spirit's action is perceived in the holy, and often lengthy, process of discernment and reception.

I said earlier that some Anglicans are becoming nervous because the hallmarks of the Communion are less readily visible. Some may fear that the Chicago-Lambeth Quadrilateral may be under reassessment—especially the article related to the historic episcopate locally adapted, as ecumenical agreements, particularly with Lutherans but also with other Protestants, begin to take shape. Liturgical heritage is no longer uniformly recognizable through a common ritual genealogy from the Book of Common Prayer of 1662. This, combined with a lack of central authority or a central body of canons, makes the landscape look less tidy. Perhaps this is why the call is even more urgent, from certain parts of the Communion, for a clear understanding of the place of scripture, and for an agreed hermeneutic. What is sure is that for the next few years, a frequent question for Anglicans will be, "What kind of authority do we really want or need across the Communion?"

ECUMENICAL SENSITIVITY

Anglicans have never understood themselves to be the whole church or the only true church. But we do believe we are a *part* of the whole, and that we share in the truth. So there is an inherent tension in Anglicanism. We are proud of our heritage, and there is a frequent desire to strengthen Anglican identity. Nevertheless, because we are part of the One, Holy, Catholic and Apostolic Church, we know that we must pay attention to a greater unity and be attentive to issues which touch the life of the wider Christian church.

In the task of continual discernment of the mind of Christ on particular issues before us as a Communion, to a considerable degree an ecumenical attentiveness must be a part of that discernment. Our basic bond as Christians comes from our baptism, relating us to every other baptized member of the body of Christ. Some would say that this has implications for us, that it is incumbent upon us to take into account the insights, and dare I say it, the Spirit-led wisdom of non-Anglican Christians. We increasingly recognize that the present state of Christian disunity inhibits our witness, weakens our *diaconia*; it makes provisional our decisions and partial our understanding of the faith. Pride in Anglican tradition and heritage must be balanced with an ecumenical vocation, outlook, and commitment.

There are some areas where a uniquely Anglican program or initiative is quite absurd. At the 1998 Lambeth Conference considerable attention was paid to issues of interfaith relations. In most provinces this meant relations with Islam. In some, particularly in Asia, it included relations with Hindus and Buddhists. But what does it mean for one part of a divided Christian family to pursue, alone, programs and studies related to interfaith relations? Should this not be one locus of intense ecumenical collaboration and initiative? It makes no sense (and is rather burdensome for the dialogue partner) if there is to be an Anglican-Islamic encounter, a Lutheran-Islamic encounter, a Roman Catholic-Islamic encounter, for example. Urgent ecumenical work needs to be done in terms of building a common platform and meeting place for interfaith relations.

THE FUTURE OF ANGLICAN IDENTITY

At the 1998 Lambeth Conference there were bishops present of churches in communion from Sweden, Norway, Germany, Netherlands, India, Pakistan, Bangladesh and the Philippines. They were not Anglicans, but came from Lutheran, Old Catholic, Mar Thoma, Philippine Independent, or United Churches. Bishops from the United Churches in South Asia were accorded the same status as Anglicans: full voice and vote. The others were members of the Conference, but with no vote. They were quite distinct, it must be noted, from ecumenical guests, who represented different world communions, but who were termed ecumenical *participants*, not *members*.

As the bonds of communion extend through the progress being made in ecumenical dialogues, the question is going to have to be asked about the future of structures within the Anglican Communion. Are they to remain "Anglican"? Is the Lambeth Conference of 2008 not likely to be an Anglican gathering at all, but rather a worldwide assembly of bishops from churches which are in communion?

Apart from the relationship already established through the Porvoo agreement between four Anglican Provinces in Britain and Ireland and six Lutheran churches in the Nordic-Baltic region, it is interesting to note that there is an initiative in Africa for a Pan-African Anglican–Lutheran relationship of communion. That would involve the continent where, as we have seen, most Anglicans live, and perhaps where most Lutherans live. In addition, in the United States (and likely in Canada before long), Lutherans and Anglicans will be living in relationships of full communion. Such communion naturally involves the churches' sharing in each other's instruments of oversight. Our relationship with the Roman Catholic Church is entering a new phase, following the meeting in Mississauga, Canada, in May of 2000, a relationship of "Communion in Mission." A new Anglican-Roman Catholic joint unity commission will work intensively towards the shared vision of full and visible unity in a eucharistic communion of churches. In future, our Anglican gatherings and instruments of decision-making are going to have to take into account these relationships; and Anglicans will be carrying with them to these councils the concerns and needs of our partners in the new relationships of communion. Eventually, perhaps, uniquely Anglican instruments of unity should give way to instruments which serve all Christians who visibly live in communion with each other.

How do Anglicans feel about the progress being made which underlines ever more strongly the vocation of Anglicanism to disappear, and to re-emerge as part of the coming greater unity? Perhaps the movements we are feeling, and the tensions, and the promptings are leading us to empty ourselves and be filled with a new vocation, a renewed identity in Christ.

Will Anglicanism in a postcolonial world not even be Anglican? A fascinating, and hopeful, thought.

Notes

[1] *Church Times,* 7 July 2000.

[2] John Grindrod, *Report of the Working Party Appointed by the Primates of the Anglican Communion on Women and the Episcopate to Aid Discussion in Preparation for the Lambeth Conference 1988* (London: Chameleon, 1987), paragraph 92.

[3] John Shelby Spong, *A Call for a New Reformation,* http://www.dioceseofnewark.org/jsspong/reform.html

[4] Mark Dyer, et al. eds., *The Official Report of the Lambeth Conference 1998* (Harrisburg: Morehouse Publishing, 1999), 394.

[5] Ibid., 396.

[6] Ibid., 404.

[7] *A Communiqué from the Primates of the Anglican Communion, 28 March 2000,* http://www.anglicancommunion.org/acns/acnsarchive/acns207 5/acns2094.html

PART II

CHALLENGES OF THE PRESENT WORLD

4

FROM VIOLENCE TO HEALING

The Struggle for Our Common Humanity

DENISE M. ACKERMANN

*I am filled with an indescribable tenderness towards this Commission.
With all its mistakes, its arrogance, its racism, its sanctimony, its
incompetence, the lying, the failure to get an interim reparation policy off the ground after two years, the showing off—with all of this—
it has been so brave, so naively brave in the winds of deceit, rancour
and hate. Against a flood crashing with the weight of a brutalizing
past on to new usurping politics, the Commission has kept alive the
idea of a common humanity. Painstakingly it has chiselled a way
beyond racism and made space for all of our voices. For all its failures,
it carries a flame of hope that makes me proud to be from here, of here.*
— Antjie Krog

FRAMING THE CONTEXT

The words from the above quotation are taken from the
remarkable book *Country of My Skull*[1] written by South African
poet Antjie Krog, who reported on the Truth and Reconciliation
Commission (TRC) for two years.[2] Week after week for the past
two years, South Africans have witnessed the testimonies of the
victims and the perpetrators of gross violations of human rights
during the apartheid years on our television screens and in halls

across our country. These stories have seared our souls with rage, feelings of vengeance, guilt, and with longing. They have also evoked more memories, stories as yet untold. The process of truth-telling, truth-seeking, the need for justice and accountability, relief to have spoken the unspeakable, horror, pain and the shattering of illusions—emotions in turmoil, and the ever-present longing for a new day—these are familiar realities.

Antjie Krog's phrase "the idea of a common humanity" encapsulates our present struggles in South Africa. The years of institutionalized racism have left deep scars on the psyches of our people, scars that remind us daily how fraught the search is for our common humanity. The idea of a common humanity is not intended to do away with our differences. South African society is profoundly multicultural, multireligious and multiracial. It is also a country which has a colonial past and which is experiencing a new brand of colonialism, one which is insidious, widespread, and which has serious consequences for our fragile democracy.

This new colonialism has many faces. Let me name a few: the colonialism of the World Bank, the International Monetary Fund, and the mighty dollar coupled with global economic policies, is wreaking havoc with the lives of the poor in the developing world. Chances for growth in sub-Saharan Africa are stifled by huge interest repayments on debts incurred, often by conscienceless dictators pandered to by lending agencies in the developed world, for which succeeding generations will have to pay the price. The raw materials of the South are a decreasing asset as they are traded at an ever-increasing rate simply to be able to make some repayment. In my country, where our currency decreases in value monthly against the power of the dollar, the pound, and the deutschmark, rich Europeans and North Americans are, for instance, buying up pristine wilderness areas for a pittance—playgrounds for the rich in a new type of colonization. It is estimated that one third of South Africans are unemployed.

Violence is an endemic reality in our society.[3]

Against the background of the TRC and its tales of our violent past, we are at present manufacturing more tales of terror and violence. The very fabric of our communities is fracturing as fear invades South African homes and lurks at stop streets. International drug cartels invade our townships with money, drugs and arms. Local gangs fight over territory, fights that almost always kill innocent bystanders. The infamous taxi wars claim lives daily. On average, sixty-seven murders are committed in South Africa every day, of which only fourteen percent end in a conviction. The physically less powerful members of society such as the elderly, women, and children are particularly vulnerable to acts of violence. Old people are murdered for the price of a cinema ticket. Women are raped and battered in their homes, on the streets, and in the veld at an estimated one every eighty seconds. Only six percent of reported rapes (some 37,905 in 1997) end in a conviction, while police estimate that only one in thirty-five rapes are in fact reported. Children are abused by those they trust, at a rate which has now made us the world's leader in child abuse.

Feminist ethicist Christine Gudorf writes that violence is narcotic. She describes a violent society in terms that are close to the South African bone: "A public caught up in violence cannot feel its own pain. It does not know that it is hungry, or tired, or wounded. It has no consciousness to spare for feeling, it only acts until the acting is done, until the public falls apart into its discrete individual persons."[4] Reactions to this ubiquitous violence vary. Many South Africans are resorting to numbness, others are increasingly angry, and still others are meeting violence with violence. Our hope for a democratic and peaceful future based on a culture of human rights is at risk, as evidenced by calls for a return of the death penalty and heavier sentences for criminals.

Violence is a theological problem, for it calls into question the very nature of humanity and it raises doubts about God's presence in, and care for, this world. It has ethical, doctrinal, and pastoral dimensions. The victims of violence cry out for healing; perpetrators of violence also need healing from the narcotic of violence.

Against this background, I wish to explore briefly the politics of violence and the idea of healing as a theological praxis. Thereafter, I shall look at the challenges to theologies, which speak the language of healing and liberation, and, lastly, I shall suggest some markers along the way in the struggle for communities of faith in violent times. I write as a white woman whose ancestors came to this part of the world over three hundred years ago as religious refugees. As a feminist theologian placing a particular emphasis on healing and liberating praxis, I speak from a Christian perspective with the hope that what I say will find resonance not only within multiple communities of faith but also beyond them.

THE POLITICS OF VIOLENCE

Not surprisingly, violence (and criminality) is one of the most debated social issues in our country today. The ways in which this topic is debated vary, depending on people's race, gender, class and social location. Our political ideologies, our social theories, and our personal histories shape our perceptions of violence as well as our desire to engage with it.

In a penetrating study on violence, Susanne Kappeler[5] points out that violence is named after its victims: violence against children, violence against animals, hatred of foreigners, and violence against women. Further, she makes the striking observation that when violence is spoken about it is usually about the violence committed by someone else: the violence of the structures, the violence of the criminals, the violence in Cambodia, Bosnia, Kosovo, Rwanda or the Congo. Projection on to others serves to blanket the common human propensity to violence. When violence is owned, it is not condemned but condoned. The violence perpetrated over decades to prop up the white minority government in my country was justified in terms of the "total onslaught" of atheistic communism. All wars are justified by the participants as just wars.

According to Kappeler, violence is recognized by its visible effects, such as bloodied bodies and the material destruction of objects. The invisible forms of violence, such as threats, insults, or humiliation, are seldom matters for general concern. These kinds of violence are recognized by the victims and defined from their perspective. Violence against women and against children is a prime example of an invisible form of violence. Rape, incest and wife battering are usually hidden acts of violence, whose victims often connive in blanketing them with silence for a number of reasons. Wives protect battering husbands because of their fear of further retaliation and because of ingrained relationships of dependency. Raped women remain silent because of feelings of shame and societal prejudice. Children who are victims of incest are too often subject to threats, or are simply not believed.

In the light of South Africa's racist history, there are compelling reasons for concluding that the roots of our continuing violence lie in the system of apartheid. The uprooting and destruction of communities of people, unemployment, poverty, and overcrowding, all contribute to the present climate of violence. Feminists, in analyzing the preconditions for violence based on women's experience, have found also that unequal power relations create conditions for violence. There is much validity in these arguments. Yet both contain a dangerous assumption and run the risk of being behaviorist. Human actions are seen as the exclusive product of circumstance, and human agency in acts of violence is ignored.

This underlying assumption has further implications. The ostensible aim of arguments based only on political and social analysis is to draw attention to the pervasive structural violence of race and class oppression. Yet, as Kappeler points out, such explanations "ignore the fact that not everyone experiencing the same oppression uses violence; that is, these circumstances do not 'cause' violent behavior. They overlook, in other words, the fact that the perpetrator has *decided* to violate, even if this decision was made in circumstances of limited choice."[6]

Kappeler continues:

> To overlook this decision, however, is itself a political decision, serving particular interests. In the first instance it serves to exonerate the perpetrators, whose responsibility is thus transferred to circumstances and a history for which other people (who remain beyond reach) are responsible. Moreover, it helps to stigmatize all those living in poverty and oppression: because they are obvious victims of violence and oppression, they are held to be potential perpetrators themselves. This slanders all the women who have experienced sexual violence, yet do not use violence against others, and libels those experiencing racist and class oppression, yet do not necessarily act out violence. Far from supporting those oppressed by classist, racist or sexist oppression, it sells out these entire groups in the interest of exonerating individual members.[7]

All situations of injustice, in whatever guises they appear, are intolerable and should be eradicated. But once violence is explained solely in terms of people's circumstances, the implication is that the solution lies wholly in changing the circumstances. The suggestion that people need to change is missing from this argument. "We turn the perpetrators of violence into the victims of circumstances, who as victims by definition cannot act sensibly...."[8] We find it easier to talk about changing circumstances than to address the equally fundamental need to change our attitudes and our behavior. It is simpler to appeal to the might of the state for more stringent law enforcement and more punitive measures by the courts than to examine our own hearts and our own proclivities to violence. *The recognition that people make choices demands that we take seriously both the will to violence as well as how we choose to respond to violence.* The question of agency, of choice, is extremely important in the search for an appropriate theological and pastoral response to violence.

A HERMENEUTIC OF HEALING

In the light of the situation sketched above, there is clearly a dire need for change and healing, for a discovery of the value of our common humanity. I now want to explore what a feminist theology of praxis that has a hermeneutic of healing at its core might contribute to the theological debate on violence and the search for our common humanity.

What would happen if all our theological theories and all our theological praxis were to be measured by their efficacy in the cause of human healing and the hope for wholeness? The search for healing is not to be seen merely as an individual quest for personal healing. Women know that the personal and the political cannot be separated. Our crying need is to "bind up the wounds" at every level and for all in different ways. In South Africa today, the phrase which best describes my quest is "the healing of our land."

Healing is inseparable from justice-seeking. In a context whose history is glutted with blatant injustices, doing justice is an inescapable priority. This is no easy task. A particularly relevant example here is the vexed question of perpetrators applying for amnesty to the TRC. As their atrocities are revealed, the relatives of victims experience afresh the trauma of loss and grief and, not surprisingly for some, feelings of anger and retribution. We are learning that justice is more elusive than we had thought and that the need for justice is, in this case, superseded by political compromises reached in our negotiated transition to democracy. We remind ourselves constantly that granting amnesty was a crucial ingredient in this negotiated settlement, one which prevented the inevitable blood bath that stared us in the face. Nonetheless, the hunger for justice remains. The moral significance of the victims' anger and the desire for retribution should not be trivialized or ignored.

For Christians a hermeneutic of healing rests on the belief that the reign of God brings good news to people in terms of their life situations. This news speaks of justice, love, peace, wholeness, and of the flourishing of righteousness. The life of Jesus discloses the critical and transforming vision of what it would mean for the fullness of God's presence to be known on earth. Seen from a feminist perspective, the good news calls us, like Jesus, "to a radical activity of love, to a way of being in the world that deepens relation, embodies and extends community, passes on the gift of life."[9] In order to be part of this vision we become agents of healing in the cause of the coming reign.

The quest for healing praxis is in essence, therefore, inspired by the dire need for the healing of creation. Humanity's social, political, and spiritual needs are both challenged and encouraged by a theology which places the values of a healed and mended creation at its center. This is not a solitary task. For healing praxis to be truly restorative, it has to be *collaborative and sustained action for justice, reparation and liberation, based on accountability and empowered by love, hope and passion.* It is not the prerogative of any one group of people. It can emerge from the actions and knowledge of those who are suffering, marginalized and oppressed as well as from those who have privilege and power, provided they too understand its genesis in the hope for a restored creation, and are willing to hear the pain of the suffering of "the others" and to act in response.

CHALLENGES TO A FEMINIST THEOLOGY OF HEALING PRAXIS

So far I have spelled out an approach which is familiar to all who have cut their theological teeth in liberation theologies: the talk of liberation, the utopian visions, the emphasis on justice, the longing for healing in our common humanity. This is not a language which is "in" today. More often, we hear the language of cyborgs, of nomads and of shifting discourses as appropriate to an age of technological and electronic revolutions. For radical-thinking theologians whose concerns over the past decades have centered on poverty, unemployment, racism, sexism, and the despoiling of the earth, it is all too often tempting to feel disappointment, even despondency, and to wonder whether our theologies have been merely words on paper leaving untouched the world in which we write and live. Are liberation theologies, including feminist liberation theologies, a spent force? Have the radical hope, the critical analysis, the energy and passion which characterize so many of these theologies exhausted themselves?

The demise of Eastern-bloc socialism and the present conservative world mood are also antithetical to the critical, analytical base and the utopian hopes of liberation theologies. The victory of the market place and the dominance of the drive for a global economy have largely replaced discourse on social justice, ethics and morals. Hope is vested in development, and development is seen as the concern of business, politics, and technology. The "free market" has become the economic metaphor for intellectual life.

A further challenge to liberation theologies comes from certain aspects of the social theories of postmodernity. Like most modern academics I find myself caught in a bind when talking about postmodernism. I have no trouble subscribing to some of its dominant characteristics: the tension between the global and the local, the ideas of difference and otherness, the contributions of new social movements for progressive change, and the critique of grand narratives and classical notions of truth, reason, identity and objectivity.[10] These categories of thought are, among others, deeply embedded in academic theological discourse in my part of the world. Yet, at the same time, the faith perspective from which I speak is predicated on hope, on a vision for creation, on a reaching out and beyond in order to live in the present with justice and compassion.

We do inhabit a terrain of tension between modernity and postmodernity. Neither is a comfortable nest from which we theologians can move forth into the next millennium. Postmodernism has, in my view, rightly been criticized for being too relativistic, for refusing to take sides.[11] Visions of social justice, which are so much a part of liberation theologies and which affirm the need for all that makes for the dignity of the human person, including a job, a roof over one's head and bread on the table, visions which clearly take sides, are scorned by some postmodernists as simply too utopian. They are antithetical to postmodernism's style which, in Terry Eagleton's words, is "... depthless, decentered, ungrounded, self-reflexive, playful, derivative, eclectic."[12] The philosophical notion of historical progress coupled with the idea of human equality is firmly modernist, and it is a notion which has taken a beating in present times. This is not surprising. On the one hand, the liberal view of progress measured in expanding capital growth and increased happiness has failed in the face of continued poverty, imperialism, colonialism, countless world and regional wars, environmental destruction, and the entrenchment of patriarchy. On the other hand, the historical-materialist view of progress as a classless society in which all partake in ownership of the means of production has also failed. We walk a tightrope between the legitimate concerns of postmodernity, and the concerns of liberation theologies for a healed world. Fortunately, however, in my country, we have known historical progress. The dismantling of apartheid shows that, though hard to realize, progress is indeed a worthy goal.[13] Utopias which have no grounding in present praxis for justice are indeed suspect. Nevertheless, holding on to a vision of a just world serves to remind us what we are fighting for, even when such a vision, because of unrealistic high-mindedness, may defer its realization.

Thus a feminist theology of praxis lives an uneasy existence. So it should. At the end of the twentieth century the terrain for all theologies is complex, challenging, marked with disagreement and ambiguity, and endlessly open-ended. A particular problem facing a feminist theology of healing praxis in my context is the relationship between identity and difference. As a theology concerned with justice and healing, the inevitable questions arise: Healing for whom? Do our different identities call for different healing processes? What is the relationship, if any, between identity, difference and healing?

Discussing identity and difference in our context is an exercise in ambiguity. Our history is one in which racial difference was reified, legislated, and enforced to such an extent that apartheid achieved universal notoriety. Now, on the one hand, the dominant political discourse of the day speaks of non-racialism, a "rainbow people," new nationhood and national reconstruction while, on the other, conservative Afrikaners and Zulus claim identity and difference. Identity is also a concept I shrink from, at least initially. It has a fraught history in our context; I think here of the contortions of "*identitiet in eie kring*"[14] which permeated apartheid's theology. Yet I know that for some it is quite simply the word which describes who each one of us is. It is a bond: "the affinity and affiliation that associates those so identified, that extends to them a common sense or space of unified sameness. It is a tie that holds members of the collective together."[15]

This understanding of identity is admittedly affirmative, but this understanding can also cut both ways. Identity can be more than a bond; it can be a bondage, a tie that holds one captive to exclusionary criteria. If you don't meet certain criteria of belonging, you will be kept out. This experience has, for instance, been common for Afrikaners who opposed Afrikaner nationalism. And it is has been the dominant criterion of white racism. There are clearly chosen aspects to identities. We can within the limits of possibility make choices about our cultural affiliations. Choices can be made in bad faith. As Sartre pointed out in *Being and Nothingness,* "If I take myself for someone else" and come to think of myself as that other, "then, as it were, I have broken faith with myself."[16] Peter Caws comments: "This stricture would include the case in which I simply accept without critical reflection the identity with which I am provided by family and culture of origin—and also the case in which I adopt a full-blown identity from an alternative culture with no more critical reflection than is involved in a passionate rejection of the dominant one." In both cases I am deceiving myself.

When identity becomes exclusionary, it is dangerous, often treacherous and can, in extreme cases, spell *elimination,* as Miroslav Volf points out.[17] "If you are not like me, I shall eliminate you." This leads to genocides like those against the Jews in Germany or the Tutsis in Rwanda. Volf continues to explain that the more benign face of exclusion is *assimilation.* "You can survive even thrive, among us, if you become like us; you can keep your life if you give up your identity."[18] This type of exclusion is experienced by many Tibetans in their struggle against Chinese rule. A third manifestation is exclusion as *dominance.* The other is deemed inferior as a human being and as such, must be kept out of the center, be subjugated and then exploited. This form of exclusion is the one which was practiced for centuries in our country, first by the colonialists and then by the policies of apartheid. The last form of exclusion is one which I suspect will be increasingly prevalent in the next decades. It is exclusion by *abandonment.* Today the rich developed world relates to the poor of the developing world in a manner which spells abandonment. If we in the developing world cannot deliver the goods and perform the services demanded by the rich North, they simply close themselves off from our predicaments, many of which are a direct result of past economic and political exploitation by these very countries.

Grappling with one's forming identity always entails drawing boundaries. In her wonderful book *Love's Work,* philosopher Gillian Rose wrote, "A soul that is unbound is as mad as one with cemented borders."[19] I am not advocating boundaries as an act of excluding others from what is considered "my territory." Boundaries have their own ambiguities. On the one hand, I see forming boundaries as being a healthy and necessary strategy to make space for the nurture and growth of what is the unique self of every person. On the other hand, if a boundary excludes me from the kind of conversation with the other which contributes towards a healthy shaping of my self, boundaries are not healthy. "Hence the will to be oneself, if it is to be healthy, must entail the will to let the other inhabit the self; the other must be part of how I am as I will to be myself."[20] Situations arise when the other wants one to be something which one knows is foreign to one's self. That is when boundaries are necessary. Otherwise we will react violently to incursions made on ourselves or retreat into exclusion. A sound understanding of boundaries helps us immeasurably to negotiate the long, difficult walk to wholeness.

Similarly the notion of difference is also double-edged. It can quite simply spell exclusion, and as such is dangerous. Differences are always differences in relation, "they are never simply free-floating."[21] As a woman and as a white person, I know that there is a long history of race and gender exclusion in the name of difference. Those who are deemed different are not only excluded, they are also not granted the respect and dignity they are entitled to as human beings. At the same time, assumptions of universality are equally damaging for the integrity of persons and smack of essentialist assumptions and the denial of cultural, racial, ethnic, and gender identities.

Identity and difference are not the same, although the ways in which their characteristics are played out are often similar. They are in fact two sides of a coin. Both need deconstructing, both need affirming, both need to be treated with care so that in doing our theologies, women do not ignore the challenges and nuances present in these concepts. We reject master narratives as much as we reject the reifying of identity and difference. We know that identity politics are showing themselves around the world to be dangerously divisive, as seen in the rise of fundamentalism and in ethnic conflicts, for instance. Identity can, as David Goldberg points out, "sustain fascist social movements as readily as emancipatory ones, and difference may license genocide almost as easily as it does celebration."[22] The question is: What would make a discussion of identity emancipatory and contribute to an understanding of our common humanity?

Against this complex backdrop, theologies which are interested in healing praxis have to deal with the cultural politics of difference and identity. Why? Simply because the struggle to name, expose and challenge assumptions about our identities, our differences or our commonalities, which enable dominant groups to exercise power and dominance, has to continue in the interests of healing. The wounds on our souls arise from different sets of circumstances. Yet all South Africans need healing, victims and perpetrators alike, in the struggle for our common humanity.

TOWARD A FEMINIST THEOLOGY OF HEALING PRAXIS

Acknowledging the deeply felt tug to pursue agendas which will hopefully alleviate human suffering in a highly complex, pluralistic, broken, often alien and unstable world, theologians of praxis can understandably feel daunted. We have no blueprints for ever-changing situations. Our theologies are forged in communities of difference. The only common factor for all is our shared humanity. Ours is an exercise in testing, in listening, in caring, in sharpening our awareness, and in ceaselessly reminding ourselves of the modesty of our enterprise. In this final section, I want to explore certain notions which may serve as markers for praxis along the way in our struggle for the healing of our communities of faith. The notion of practice lies at the heart of the Christian gospel.

First, we begin with confession and lament. We confess that, in the words of Dorothee Sölle, we have been "screaming too softly"[23] in the face of the unending, relentless quality of human suffering. We confess our role as agents in its causes. We lament as an act of reclaiming our tongues, giving voice to pain, fear and hope. We become confessing mourners.

In Zakes Mda's wrenching novel, *Ways of Dying*, the main character is Toloki, a professional mourner. In Toloki's life and mission, the narratives of suffering in the lives of black township dwellers in South Africa is interwoven with the need to lament the suffering, to mourn the dead. Mda writes: "[Toloki] has a mission in the world, that of mourning for the dead. It is imperative that he does his utmost to stay alive, so that he can fulfill his sacred trust, and mourn for the dead."[24] Toloki knows that his story and the stories of those he buries simply show that "Death is with us every day. Indeed our ways of dying are our ways of living. Or should I say our ways of living are our ways of dying?"[25]

The act of lament is one of self-expression which re-establishes communication, opens the blocked channels and makes ready the ground for change. These very obvious truths are too often lost in our liturgies. We no longer lament, we hastily confess and then move on. What I am seeking is an acknowledgment of the heart, which is in essence also a confession of my/our role in causing the suffering of others. We may not shy away from issues such as the dominance of world capital in which we partake and which causes untold suffering in the developing world. We look at our human greed, which is destroying the environment, our selfishness and instincts to be war mongering. We mourn the abuse of children and women and the lack of care for the poor. A theology of praxis is, in essence, a theology of passion, critical and committed passion. A passion for human well-being is its driving force. It is not afraid to confess. At the same time, this passion for making things right is balanced by critical inquiry and reflection. "Whatever steps we may take toward ameliorating the misery of existence, we must always recognize that they are practical, provisional, tentative, and therefore, always demand sustained critical reflection," Marsha Hewitt points out.[26] Passion is not dimmed by a critical edge; it is sharpened and tuned into flexible and creative intention. As tools in the hands of believers, confession and lament are always *de profundis*, words of compassion in the cause of healing and wholeness.

Second, the material for a theology of healing praxis emerges from the stories in our different contexts. These stories are often from the outer circles of discourse, stories which refuse to be silenced and which break the silence that too often surrounds the lives of women and other marginalized peoples. When the changes sought by those who have been oppressed are seen to entail only loss for those who are more privileged, when whites in South Africa see sharing as a loss of self "instead of the invitation to explore an alternative construction of selfhood,"[27] more than rational argument is needed to change hearts and minds. Hearing and engaging in informed reflection on the life stories of those who have been oppressed has the potential to change and enlarge the selves of the privileged hearers. But we do not only hear others' stories. We have our own stories to tell, although for some their stories have been stolen, crushed, or denied. Such circumstances are in themselves stories.

Stories evoke dangerous memories. Stories require the unflinching admission of participation in oppressive practices and systems. A number of perpetrators of human rights abuses, who justified their actions in the cause of Afrikaner nationalism, have not yet chosen to tell their stories and seek amnesty. This stance has meant that they have forfeited the opportunity to redeem their souls in the wider community in my country. Commenting on the TRC process, Antjie Krog writes: "If its interest in the truth is linked only to amnesty and compensation, then it will have chosen not truth, but justice. If it sees truth as the widest possible compilation of peoples' perceptions, stories, myths and experiences, it will have chosen to restore memory and foster a new humanity, and perhaps this is justice in the deepest sense."[28] As we tell our stories and hear the stories of others, they intersect, and they change. Sometimes they conflict, accuse, and even diverge greatly. Sometimes they attract, connect, and confirm. As our stories touch one another, they change and we too change. Not all stories evoke liberation; stories can reinforce oppressive structures and patterns of behavior. In my context they are too often full of fear and violence. It is only when hearing and telling stories begins to be a process of openness, vulnerability and mutual engagement that alienation of class, race and gender can be challenged.

Third, actively seeking change requires a collaborative effort between women and men from different cultures, religious traditions, and social locations. No one can effect the kind of healing we require on their own. The task is simply too unnerving. Collaborative efforts raise questions of difference and accountability. In a context such as ours, scarred as it is by legislated racial difference in the past and by patriarchal structures, we should expect to encounter suspicion and even hostility when differences are either not respected or when they are ignored in the rush to find commonalities. We all have our communities of accountability. These communities shape our identities and our theologies through transmission of traditions, cultural norms, social mores, customs, ritual, and myth. The healing we require is one which combines both a rigorous accountability to our different communities and histories with reaching out across differences to those who are other. A collaborative effort in the cause of healing requires that we be open and vulnerable across our differences, as concerned citizens with a common purpose.

Fourth, a theology of praxis is embodied practical theology. It accepts that all reality and all knowledge are mediated through our bodies. Our senses are sources of our knowledge. The power to love one another, as much as the power to injure one another, begins in our bodies. We *are* our bodies. This reality is so patent in the processes before the TRC. We have witnessed extremes—from the sight of a portly security policeman demonstrating how he applied the water bag torture method to victims (some of whom were at the hearings watching him), to the keening bodies of mothers mourning the memories of their lost sons—we have seen how both alienation and reconciliation are bodily events. Action for healing means becoming involved in the work of justice and healing with one's body. Ethical practices are in essence what we do, day by day, step by step, in our bodies. They are not merely abstract theological doctrines or moral principles. They are where and how we put our bodies on the line for justice and for healing.

Community is made in the body. We Christians speak of ourselves as the body of Christ, a wonderful metaphor with powerful political implications. This metaphor teaches us that we all have an equally important part to play in the health and welfare of the body, and that when part of the body hurts the entire body suffers. Eating the bread and drinking the wine at the eucharist are also profoundly bodily activities which have both personal and communal significance for Christians. We dare not be impervious to those with whom we share the cup. The struggle for healing is a struggle for the healing of the whole body.

Fifth, despite postmodern predictions of the demise of imagination,[29] the nature of a theology of praxis is essentially imaginative.[30] Both when it dares to dream its utopian dreams for a better world and when hopes are translated into actions for healing and wholeness, imagination remains a vital ingredient. Daring and imaginative praxis was at the heart of the struggle for liberation in South Africa: defiance campaigns, marches, innovative methods of protest. The stubborn resistance of those who defied the wrath of the oppressive authorities—even the writing of Antjie Krog, an Afrikaner—speaks of just such a praxis. Imaginative praxis also makes us practitioners of the future. We try, albeit falteringly, to image now in our bodies that for which we hope for the time to come.

The kind of imaginative praxis which is effective and constructive is one which calls for the creative convergence of the poetic and the ethical. To be ethically imaginative is to be prepared to stand in the shoes of "the others," the suffering and the marginalized, to hear the cry of need and then, compelled by the ethical demands of imagination, to respond to need with healing praxis. The poetic nature of imaginative praxis is expressed by Christians through symbols, stories and metaphors. The essence of what is perceived as real finds expression through poetic images because they are, in themselves, experiences of what is real. The retelling and re-enactment of our stories in our liturgies offer opportunities for communal participation in imaginative praxis which can bind up the wounds.

Sixth, the concern with healing is undergirded by the belief in the role of human agency in the mending of God's creation. In the face of relentless suffering, this remains our hope. In Elaine Scarry's words, "Belief is the act of imagining."[31] The Christian hope for the actualizing of the reign of God, when love, justice, freedom, peace and wholeness will flourish, provides the moral imperative for healing actions. In the language of liberation theologians, we have to struggle to hold on to this utopian vision while we act as agents for bringing it about. Our hopes are not only eschatologically garbed, but rest firmly in the desire for historical transformation. "This [hope] in Cornel West's term, is a utopian realism: an anticipation of a new, transfigured reality based on a realistic analysis of the sufferings and desires of the present age."[32] Living one's hope for a better world means realistically acknowledging brokenness and need, while at the same time engaging with life in such a way that deeds express that which one hopes for. Human agency and hope combine in the search for healing.[33] We have to make our hopes happen.

Finally, a theology of praxis should be characterized by stamina. Ambitious and risky, such praxis is an exercise in vulnerability, which rests on a spirituality of hope. It risks failing, it risks appearing futile in the face of often overwhelming odds. For those who choose not to be deaf, the cries of human suffering everywhere call us to seek healing, even when we have no illusions about the enormity of the task. This means, in Antjie Krog's words, being "naively brave in the winds of deceit, rancor and hate," while keeping alive "the idea of a common humanity." We dare not abandon the language of liberation and healing in our struggle against the forces of violence, in the cause of healing and wholeness.

A POEM FOR COMMUNITIES OF FAITH

I conclude with a poem by Antjie Krog written for the TRC, which I think directs us to where we ought to begin.

because of you
this country no longer dies
between us but within
it breathes becalmed
after being wounded
in its wondrous throat

in the cradle of my skull
it sings, it ignites
my tongue, my inner ear, the cavity of my heart shudders towards the outline
new in soft intimate clicks and gutturals

of my soul the retina learns to expand
daily because by a thousand stories
I was scorched

a new skin

I am changed forever. I want to say:
forgive me
forgive me
forgive me

You whom I have wronged, please
take me,

with you.[34]

Notes

[1] Antjie Krog, *Country of My Skull* (Johannesburg: Random House, 1998), 278.

[2] The TRC was set up in 1996 with the task of investigating human rights. The report was handed to President Mandela by chairperson Archbishop *emeritus* Desmond Tutu on 27 October 1998.

[3] See also Denise M. Ackermann, "For Such a Thing is not Done in Israel: Violence against Women," in *Archbishop Tutu: Prophetic Witness in South Africa*, ed. L. Hulley, L. Kretzschmar, and L. L. Pato (Cape Town: Human and Rousseau, 1996), 145-55.

[4] Christine Gudorf, *Victimization: Examining Christian Complicity* (Philadelphia: Trinity Press, 1992), 15.

[5] Susanne Kappeler, *The Will to Violence: The Politics of Personal Behavior* (New York: Teachers College Press, 1995), 1.

[6] Ibid., 3.

[7] Ibid., 3.

[8] Ibid., 4.

[9] Beverly W. Harrison, *Making the Connections: Essays in Feminist Social Ethics* (Boston: Beacon Press, 1985), 18.

[10] See Ben Agger, *Critical Social Theories: An Introduction* (Boulder: Westview Press, 1998), 34-55.

[11] See Richard Rorty, *Contingency, Irony and Solidarity* (New York: Cambridge University Press, 1989).

[12] Terry Eagleton, *The Illusions of Postmodernism* (Oxford: Blackwell, 1996), vii.

[13] Ibid., 44.

[14] Literally "identity in one's own circle," a slogan used in apartheid theology to justify a neo-Kuyperian view of independent modalities of peoples in which each could retain their own cultural and historical identities. This view ultimately resulted in the establishment of "homelands," largely infertile areas covering approximately 13 percent of land in South Africa to which millions of black people were assigned in the cause of a colossal social piece of engineering in the interests of white minority rule.

[15] David Theo Goldberg, ed., *Multiculturalism: A Critical Reader* (Cambridge: Blackwell, 1994), 12.

[16] Quoted in Peter Caws, "Identity: Cultural, Transcultural and Multicultural," in *Multiculturalism*, 384.

[17] The following four categories of exclusion are taken from Miroslav Volf, *Exclusion and Embrace: A Theological Exploration of Identity, Otherness, and Reconciliation* (Nashville: Abingdon Press, 1996), 74-75.

[18] Ibid., 75.

[19] Gillian Rose, *Love's Work: A Reckoning with Life* (New York: Schocken Books, 1996), 105.

[20] Volf, *Exclusion and Embrace*, 91.

[21] Peter McLaren, "White Terror and Oppositional Agency: Towards a Critical Multiculturalism" in *Multiculturalism*, 58.

[22] David Theo Goldberg, "Introduction: Multicultural Conditions" in *Multiculturalism*, 13.

[23] Dorothee Sölle, *Suffering*, trans. E. R. Kalin (Philadelphia: Fortress Press, 1973), 3.

[24] Zakes Mda, *Ways of Dying* (Cape Town: Oxford University Press, 1995), 88.

[25] Ibid., 89.

[26] Marsha A. Hewitt, *Critical Theory of Religion: A Feminist Analysis* (Minneapolis: Fortress Press, 1995), 226.

[27] Sharon Welch, "An Ethic of Solidarity of Difference," in *Postmodernism, Feminism, and Cultural Politics: Redrawing Educational Boundaries*, ed. Henry A. Giroux (New York: State University of New York Press, 1991), 97.

[28] Krog, *Country of My Skull*, 16.

[29] Richard Kearney, *The Wake of Imagination: Toward a Postmodern Culture* (London: Routledge, 1994), 360.

[30] See my forthcoming contribution in festschrift for Riet Bons-Storm: "The Substance of Things Hoped for: Imaginative Praxis."

[31] Elaine Scarry, *The Body in Pain: The Making and Unmaking of the World* (New York: Oxford University Press, 1995), 205.

[32] Cornel West, *The American Evasion of Philosophy: A Genealogy of Pragmatism* (Madison: University of Wisconsin Press, 1989), quoted in Rebecca S. Chopp and Mark L. Taylor, eds., *Reconstructing Christian Theology* (Minneapolis: Fortress Press, 1994), 2.

[33] Wesley Kort, in a response to this paper, pointed out that we are more than human agents. We are in fact human vessels of divine grace, co-operating with God who always acts first.

[34] Krog, *Country of My Skull*, 278-79. Permission to print this poem was given by Random House.

5
As We Sail Life's Rugged Sea
The Paradox of Divine Weakness

Kortright Davis

The words which I have chosen for the title of this chapter are taken from the "Alma Mater" song of Howard University, located in Washington, D.C., where I have been privileged to serve for the past sixteen and a half years in the School of Divinity. The text of the stanza is as follows:

> *Be thou still our guide and stay*
> *Leading us from day to day;*
> *Make us true and leal and strong,*
> *Ever bold to battle wrong.*
> *When from thee we've gone away,*
> *May we strive for thee each day*
> *As we sail life's rugged sea,*
> *O Howard, we'll sing of thee.*

The words come fairly close to sounding like words that would normally be addressed exclusively to God. But that is not the case. They are actually sung immediately before the benediction at our convocations. They serve to remind the Howard community of many things, especially of what life is all about, and the struggles and challenges for which Howard itself continues to prepare and equip us.

Howard University stands as an institutional and historical legacy of a Christian attempt to address, ameliorate, and correct the effects of an American historical wrong. The combined efforts of greed, racism, and slavery, having built for this American civilization the infrastructure for material growth and prosperity, were virtually unable to cope with the effects of the legacy that they created. The Civil War was ending, slavery was being outlawed, millions of black human chattel were now being left on their own. How would they be led and fed? Who would perform such tasks? Howard University began as one such attempt, as the direct result of a Bible study and prayer meeting in Washington, D.C., the federal capital. The mission of Howard University has never changed since its inception in 1867, even if there have emerged, over time, various approaches to the interpretation of that mission.

My own participation in the Howard process has been very important to me, important enough to be linked thus far with my personal sense of divine vocation. For if I am to address the question of what God is doing in history, I am obliged to begin with my own personal history as the center, and to work from there outward. Howard University actually recruited me from the Caribbean, and was persistent enough to allow me two years to make up my mind to come. Over these past years, then, I have been actively involved in the pursuit and promotion of black scholarship. I have participated in the creation of black leadership for America, especially being conscious of the fact that black leadership and black religious leadership are virtually synonymous in America. I have come to appreciate the divine significance of the black church in this country, its struggles, its shouts, its sharings, and its sufferings. I have learned so much more about the beauty and the bounty of the black experience, and have come to a heightened sense of awe and reverence for how God has so wonderfully created and adorned black people in God's own image, just as God has done the same for all those who do not share in the joys of ebony grace. In no small way, Howard University has helped me shape and appropriate an understanding and exegesis of history that is guided by a certain vision of freedom, justice, peace, and divine resolution. By "divine resolution" I simply mean that God will work out all the paradoxes and contradictions and injustices sooner or later, and that the words of the Magnificat will no longer be just a pipe dream in human history.

This kind of exegesis of history has enabled me to focus on history through the lens of the "Other" side, or the "Our" side— that is, the side of the poor, marginalized, oppressed, and dehumanized. Now this other side may be substantially different from the dominant side, but that does not make it inferior in any way. Exegesis from the other side looks at the history of the Exodus in the biblical story, for example, from the point of view of the Egyptian children whose fathers were drowned in the Red Sea. It looks at the history of the European balkanization of Africa from the experience of the Africans whose land was exploited for the sake of Europe's survival and unbridled greed. It looks at American history on Thanksgiving Day from the point of view of Native Americans and what such a season must mean to them and their heritage. Yes, history is exegeted in various ways and through different lenses. In the fullness of time, for example, it will be interesting to see how future exegetes will deal with the true realities of the Reagan era in America's history, as far as social compassion is concerned.

I was invited to reflect from my own personal perspective on the question of what I consider that God is doing in history at the end of one millennium and the dawn of a new one, and these are some of the contours that are guiding my thinking. Of course, much will depend on the answer to the basic question: "Which God do we mean?" For it is possible to sustain a polytheistic life style with a professed monotheistic religion. It is possible to revel in a deistic culture, with all its liberty and self-centered joys and delights, while professing a theistic faith. It is even fashionable to practice an agnostic/atheistic morality while engaging in, or leading, religious rites and ceremonies. So we need always to be clear to identify which God we really mean, when speaking about God. There is hardly any need for us to remind ourselves about how easy it is to create a God in our own image, even to the point of engraving that notion on our currencies of monetary exchange with the words, *In God we trust.*

The challenges of life break in on different groups of people in different ways, and the meaning of life is often circumscribed by some harsh realities. Because of these harsh realities, groups of people have often found it necessary to move—to move out, move away, move across, all in the quest of moving up. The history of this millennium has demonstrated time and again that people have taken to the seas to reach other pastures. They have sailed life's rugged seas both figuratively and literally. Life has been a sea of adventure and discovery, a sea of battles and conquests, but also a sea of bondage and loss. The use of the sea to find new life has been accompanied by the use of the sea to take away life. There are those who have used it as a passage to new freedom; and there are those who have experienced it as a middle passage, a middle passage to enslavement and loss of hope. The God who has supposedly guided religious pilgrims to safety and prosperity in lands belonging to other people has also been present in the middle passage of those who were wrenched away from their own lands to labor without pay for the prosperity of others. Is it really the same God? If so, how does one explain such vastly differing effects of that divine presence? Who is this God? Whose side really counts? Or does this God behave differently to different groups of people? Do we encounter a paradox here? Yes, indeed, I think we do. I have chosen to call this a "paradox of divine weakness."

As we scan the centuries of the millennium and try to summarily interpret what life has been like in the light of world history, and through the lens of a faith in the God of Moses of Egypt and Jesus of Nazareth, we do indeed recognize the ruggedness of human life and the paradox of God's weakness. Yet, to speak of divine weakness is not to undermine the centrality of our belief in divine sovereignty or divine omnipotence. It is for us to uncover what these words actually mean for us, since we can never know what they mean for God. At the end of the twentieth century, the Roman Catholic theologian Gregory Baum has this to say: "Despite certain episodes of betrayal, the story of twentieth-century theology is one of fidelity and anguish—fidelity to God's revealed word under changing historical conditions, and anguish over the unanswered questions and the powerlessness of truth in a sinful world."[1] It is this encounter between fidelity and anguish that I wish to reflect on in the rest of this chapter. I shall do so by looking at five cultures of this millennium, and then by proposing that we nail five sails to the mast of the ship of the life of faith, as we continue to sail on life's rugged sea.

Five Cultures of the Millennium

When we speak of "culture," we often tend to refer to the patterns of living which distinguish one set of people from another. We generally refer to their language, tastes, styles, outlook, and relationships. When I speak of culture here, however, I wish to indicate something much deeper: that which envelopes vast groups of people over time, whose tastes and styles might be significantly different, but whose cumulative efforts at survival and growth are linked together with interlocking bands of beliefs, self-identity, and creativity. In other words, I am sticking closely to Paul Tillich's understanding of culture in its wider sense as the "sum total of the creative human spirit." The five cultures I refer to are these: (1) The Culture of Self-Determination; (2) The Culture of Whiteness; (3) The Culture of Technology; (4) The Culture of Materialism; (5) The Culture of Dominance.

THE CULTURE OF SELF-DETERMINATION

From the event of the Magna Carta in 1215, through the era of the European Renaissance, the Reformations of Europe, the expansions of Western civilization through conquest and exploitation, revolutions across the globe—whether French, Haitian, American, Spanish, Russian, Chinese, or African—this millennium has been a continuous spectacle of people's efforts to wrest the power over their own affairs from others. This wresting has been done for political, social, economic, cultural and religious reasons. At the center of it all has been the cry for greater freedom, greater freedom for some, but not necessarily for all. The feudal barons in King John's day did not mention the ordinary freedmen and peasants in their charter, who comprised the bulk of the English population at that time. The American Declaration of Independence was drafted and signed by those who owned slaves and had no intentions of voluntarily setting them free. Although the Haitians went to the aid of the Americans in their revolution, the Americans did not return the favor to the Haitians.

So the culture of self-determination has been a mixed bag of a struggle for unconditional freedom and rugged individualism, reinforced by a combined force of common interests and exclusivist ideas. At the back of all this has been the role and function of conscience. This was given prominent sanction in the sixteenth century by the Italian statesman Niccolo Macchiavelli (1469–1527), who promulgated the view that leaders should not allow their religious consciences to prevent them from accomplishing what they wanted to. For since the state was like an organism, and the leader was like the head of the body, the leader should use any means necessary to preserve the state—whether by deception, or cruelty, or force—the ends always justified the means. Thus pragmatism has reigned supreme in this ongoing culture of self-determination. The principles of "zig" and "zag" have flourished unabatedly, and we have all inherited, and thrived in, a culture that gives warmth and comfort to the dictum that *"you have to do what you have to do."* This has been mightily undergirded by the virtually genetic attitude that reverences the primacy of the individual, and the almost irrefutable command to always be on the lookout for "Number One."

THE CULTURE OF WHITENESS

Human beings have always been afraid of darkness. The absence of light often represents a serious threat to well-being, loss of control, uncertainty about the environment, and the possibility of incipient negation. So the "prince of darkness" is not really a prince, but a devil. Darkness has thus stood for the face of evil, a face to be feared, conquered, or repelled. Western civilization has historically been made to flourish on the undying assumption that dark-skinned people are the wretched of the earth, endowed with brawn for others' benefit, lacking in brain for their own development, and devoid of souls—and thus unqualified for heavenly salvation. Accordingly, while it is difficult to find any large group of white people starving anywhere on the face of the globe, black people have continued to be the only people in modern history who have distinguished themselves in two ways. First, they have contributed much more to the prosperity and protection of others than they have ever done for themselves. Second, they have remained the only people in history whose claims to being fully human have not yet been universally acknowledged.

The culture of whiteness, or Eurocentrism, therefore made it axiomatic that Europeans would fight for their own survival and expansion of influence and control by exercising their power of whiteness. They would establish the Americas as the permanent and historic incubator of white racism for all time, and would create such religious and social structures as would exclude non-whites from ever sharing in the command of the heights of their own decision-making and public affairs. Thus, the history and sociology of racism in Europe and the Americas need no further explication. The transcendent doctrine of white supremacy in the world needs no further illustration. The apparent powerlessness of God to give people of color a break from their cries for justice and liberation creates its own paradox, even to the point where some have asked if God is a white racist. The rise and fall of Afrikaner politics in South Africa, and the horrible apartheid poison which it injected into twentieth-century history are there for all to remember. Yet, white racism continues to rise like a phoenix, as white supremacist young men roam the streets of our towns and villages, seeking whom of our children they might devour in order to be accepted into the corridors of white infamy. White racists are made; they are not born. Our black sons and daughters are born; they are not made. And there is nothing that we can do about it.

It was the white American professor of political science at Queens College, New York, Andrew Hacker, who asked the question in 1992, "Are we one nation under God, or two nations manacled by race?"[2] Hacker convinced me, at any rate, that the most powerful human being on the face of the earth was a white American male, and I have not met any such person who might cause me to forget that. The culture of whiteness germinates and sustains the power of whiteness, and I know of no exceptions or exemptions to this rule, fame and fortune notwithstanding.

Here is what Hacker suggests:

> ... all white Americans, regardless of their political persuasions, are well aware of how black people have suffered due to inequities imposed on them by white America. As has been emphasized, whites differ in how they handle that knowledge. Yet white people who disavow responsibility deny an everyday reality: that to be black is to be consigned to the margins of American life. It is because of this that no white American, including those who insist that opportunities exist for persons of every race, would change places with even the most successful black American. All white Americans realize that their skin comprises an inestimable asset. It opens doors and facilitates freedom of movement. It serves as a shield from insult and harassment. Indeed, having been born white can be taken as a sign: your preferment is both ordained and deserved. Its value persists not because a white appearance

> automatically brings success and status, since there are no
> such guarantees. What it does ensure is that you will not be
> regarded as *black*, a security which is worth so much that no
> one who has it has ever given it away.[3]

In this culture of whiteness as we see it today, the question of
equality is always of paramount importance, if for no other reason
than that America itself emerged as a result of a fight against
inequality. The pilgrims landed here in the seventeenth century
in search of their religious liberty. The framers of the War of Independence were driven by a revolt against inequality meted out by
the British Crown, and actually made their declaration of equality the first line of their proclamation. Yet, at the end of the millennium the culture of whiteness drove an intelligent and committed African-American scholar, Derrick Bell, who was formerly
a law professor at Harvard, to make the following assertion:

> Black people will never gain full equality in this country. Even
> those herculean efforts we hail as successful will produce no
> more than temporary "peaks of progress," short-lived victories
> that slide into irrelevance as racial patterns adapt in ways that
> maintain white dominance. This is a hard-to-accept fact that
> all history verifies. We must acknowledge it, not as a sign of
> submission, but as an act of ultimate defiance.[4]

As if that were not bad enough, Bell describes us blacks in
America as people who are "tolerated in good times, despised
when things go wrong, as a people we are scapegoated and sacri-
ficed as distraction or catalyst for compromise to facilitate resolution of political differences or relieve economic adversity."[5]

THE CULTURE OF TECHNOLOGY

Whenever we try to find an appropriate label for the age in
which we are now living, various words suggest themselves.
Philosophers speak of the postmodern age. Scientists speak of the
nuclear age. NASA would readily call this the space age. Industri-
alists speak of the age of technology. Journalists speak of the information age. It seems to me, however, that technology wins out on
all of them, since it represents the sum total of all that we have
invented, discovered, and adapted to satisfy our human needs and
desires. We are basically misfits in a world that is driven by a cycle
of irruption, expansion, and expiration—just as gasses do. We
irrupt at birth; we expand through natural growth; and we expire
at death. Nothing is able to eliminate the fact of our mortality. But

between the points of irruption and expiration we use all that we know and have to make life less uncomfortable. We use our technology.

There are those who have outlined for us the major benefits of technology. For example, they speak of these benefits in terms of increased productivity and production, reduced labor, easier labor, and better living standards. They also list such side effects as higher unemployment, depletion of natural resources, environmental pollution, and the creation of unsatisfying jobs.[6] But when I speak of the culture of technology here, I am referring mainly to the overarching effects of behavioral and attitudinal modifications which we have brought on ourselves because of the technological mastery which we have achieved. Three brief illustrations of what I mean should suffice.

First, the horrible spectacle of the Challenger space mission exploding before our eyes some years ago sent shivers up our spines. Precious human lives were lost in a second, for something had gone wrong with something that was not expected to fail. Those who knew most about the inner workings of the space ship were practically convinced that everything had been done to eliminate the possibility of failure. But they, like the rest of us, were shocked at what they saw. The words I heard used at the time were "virtual infallibility." The parts that failed were taken to be virtually infallible. It raised for me then, as it raises for all of us now, the basic issue with our culture of technology. Can a fallible being ever create an infallible object? Does our technology give us the power to eliminate fallibility?

Second, we have now become consumed by the power of the microchip, not only by what it can do, but also by the wealth that it can produce. William Henry Gates III, age forty-four, with his worth of over US $100 billion, founder and chairman of Microsoft Corporation, has virtually redefined the meaning of wealth, information, technology, and society, all in one fell swoop. Gates's biographer, Paul Andrews, has said of him: "People have only begun to see the impact of his wealth on education, medicine, poverty and social causes, a legacy that may overshadow his technological contributions."[7] But Bill Gates is more than all of this. He is a metaphor for the culture of technology at the end of the millennium. He places the emphasis on two simple factors, the flow of digital information, and the value of velocity. He himself says that the key to success in the twenty-first century will be the use of a digital nervous system that enables us to do business at the speed of thought. The question for us here is, are there limits to speed and growth? If so, what are they, and who sets them? In the meantime, however, the effects of our limited intelligence are upon us in the threats of our self-imposed Y2K calamity. Shortsighted glitches in our technology were poised to affect our life and livelihood—our information, utilities, transportation, banking, medical technology, and military precision, to name a few.

Third, there is the area of biotechnology. This is also an area to which Gates has said he would like to turn his attention later. In his own words: "... The advances we're seeing today and the ones to come in the near future are going to revolutionize the world of health care. That would be a fun area to spend more time in."[8] While there are innumerable and miraculous uses to which technology might be put for the benefit of the human species, there is still the awful spectacle of genetic engineering and selection that is already on the way. Given the wide range of moral imbalances in our world today, the continuing belief in a God who creates human beings in the divine image will be under serious assault. Human procreativity is likely to undermine, if not overtake, the basic Christian understanding of God as creator of heaven and earth, the author and giver of life. How we handle this issue in the culture of technology will be a critical challenge for Christians in the new millennium.

THE CULTURE OF MATERIALISM

Throughout the course of the millennium, we have been able to enhance our capacity to create wealth, right up to the point where Bill Gates is now worth much more than the combined sum of a large number of countries' national budgets. We have watched how, over time, people have made attempts to deal with modes of production and distribution, the generation of labor and technology for industrial advancement, and the coordination of markets and governments. We have seen where in 1776 the American War of Independence coincided with the publication of Adam Smith's book *The Wealth of Nations*. Having imbibed the *laissez-faire* economic philosophies of the French *physiocrats*, Adam Smith, the Scotsman, returned to Britain to urge his country to stimulate the economy by reducing governmental involvement, and by encouraging free trade and a self-regulating economy. He preached the gospel of individualism, insisting that human order and social progress were best possible in a society where individuals were enabled to follow their own interests.

Thus, for the past two centuries, the forces of the market and the culture of materialism have combined to create both wealth on the one hand and unimaginable poverty and undevelopment on the other. Materialism has placed primary attention and interest on material needs, material objects, and material considerations, while urging a rejection of spiritual and moral values. Materialism has treated matter as being of ultimate significance, placing profits before people. It has virtually won the triumphant victory of the verb *to have* over the verb *to be*. Materialism rejects the dictum of Jesus that a person's life does not consist in the abundance of the things which one possesses, and it feeds on the various manifestations of greed and avarice.

This culture of materialism is sustained by the forces of the market culture. The forces of supply and demand, the urges of power to get, spend, or control, are of paramount importance in the way we establish our values, or pattern our relationships. Market values drive our decision-making processes to such an extent that our very definitions of mission and ministry, of vocation and formation, of success and failure in the church, are governed by their practical outcomes, or their functional relevance to sectional interests. The theology of the bottom line—as in profits—is increasingly more important in our churches than the theology of the cross—as in the crucified prophet of Nazareth. Many of the debates and controversies in our churches are laced with an incessant clash of ideologies and theologies which fight for satisfying answers to the question, *What's in it for me?*, rather than to the question of the old-time religion, *Lord what wilt thou have me to do?* It used to be said that the church had been called into being to bear witness to the greater glory of God, but the culture of materialism has now made it abundantly clear that we seem to exist as a church more for the greater glory of our own marketplace.

So what side effects do the culture of materialism produce in our own day and age? We see that a heartless pragmatism drives much of our decision making and human development. We see the supreme dominance of the market as it governs almost all of our deals and ideals. This dominance by the market and its forces provides sacred melody for the celestial choirs of Wall Street, and a papal tiara for the Federal Reserve Board. We feel the force of an endemic militarism at work everywhere—in boardrooms, church conventions, meetings of superintendents, bishops and church overseers, our playing fields, and college campuses. This materialistic militarism worships the sword or the gun as the best pruning hook, and triumphs in the belief that it is always better to fight than to switch. We see the rage of rabid individualism that not only sharpens our competitive edge, but also keeps us firmly rooted in the unswerving belief in the primacy of the individual rather than in the just demands of the community.

THE CULTURE OF DOMINANCE

A few years ago, in 1992, we were all urged to celebrate the five hundredth anniversary of the historic voyage of Columbus from Europe to the Americas. Did Columbus make a colossal navigational mistake, or was it a supreme manifestation of divine providence? Samuel Morison has written: "To few people in modern history does the world as we know it owe so great a debt as to Christopher Columbus."[9] For some people, 1492 was the year in which a new world was opened up for them—a world, however, that was not new to the original inhabitants. For others, 1492 represented the beginning of a process of under-development that has continued to this day. At the end of the millennium, therefore, we have the very intriguing scenario of a country that was discovered for the benefit of those to whom it did not belong becoming the only super power on the face of the globe. Over the second half of the millennium, therefore, patterns of domination and control, of conquest and resettlement, of plunder and exploitation, of realignment and extinction, of revolution and containment, have all been witnessed in some form or other.

At the center of it all, there has been a driving belief that there are those who are destined to be in charge, and those who are destined to be ruled and governed by others. This culture of dominance has run rampant through all the patterns of colonialism and neo-colonialism over the past two centuries. It has manifested itself in the expanded doctrines of national security, which have caused nations to arrogate to themselves the right of uninvited entry into other countries. It has been aided and abetted by the mercantilist expansion of transnational corporations and conglomerates across the globe, reaping where they have not sown, and eating what they have not produced. It has manifested itself in much of the missionary activity of the century, where in the name of God and the gospel, peoples have been robbed of their cultural heritage, assaulted by a foreign spirit, and torn asunder in their souls by the lure of material gain wrapped in pious fantasy. For to control people's fears and people's faith is to exercise a reign of dominance that is hard to overcome.

Gregory Baum has offered the following reflection in the light of the fall of communism. He says:

> The collapse of communism has led to a new world order. Because of the absence of an alternative, capitalism, it would seem, is now able to show its ugly face, promote a global economy based on competition and the quest for gain, and become indifferent to the growing sector of people excluded from society's wealth—massively in poor countries, and significantly in rich ones. A single, unchallenged military superpower is now protecting the ongoing globalization of the self-regulating market system. Thanks to the power of the large corporations and the international financial institutions, national governments have lost the capacity to protect the material and cultural well-being of their citizens.[10]

As we came to the close of this second millennium, then, we recognized that although there had been a collapse of the Berlin Wall, the Soviet Union, and the apartheid regime in South Africa, there had been no collapse of global capitalism or Western civilization as such. But what does that say about the moral order? How morally justified are we to say and act as if might is always right? How ethically sound is the judgment that money speaks louder than morals? What human edifice do we construct when patterns of justice are determined by who is fair looking, rather than by what is fair? For in the end, I believe that the true and lasting culture of dominance will be demonstrated in the triumph of good over evil, and the victory of human dignity over the tyranny of material prosperity. It will not be a question of whose side is God on, but rather an open manifestation of who is truly on the Lord's side.

In reflecting on the Christian theological responses to the Great War of 1914–1918, John Douglas Hall has written this:

> That Christian peoples could face one another as deadly enemies, each claiming the Christian God for its "side," made clearer than ever before that a religion aligned with nationalism and racism could only end in self-contradiction and violence…. Christianity may no longer pretend to dominate the

course of our secularized and pluralistic planet, but from a position outside the realms of worldly power and prestige it may have greater influence for worldly good than it ever possessed as Christendom.[11]

We have been reflecting on five of the cultures of our times, which have in some way been representative of the human fight for survival. But it has largely been a survival of the fittest. In the cultures of *self-determination, whiteness, technology, materialism, dominance,* we have witnessed in our times the emergence of a greater divide between ourselves, and a more painful separation of those who have from those who do not. Our world is quantitatively richer but qualitatively poorer at the close of the millennium. Where then, in all of these cultures, one may ask, is the paradox of divine weakness? How does God show up? Is the rumor true that God is still around? Or is it that the traditional attributes of God—love, righteousness, omnipotence, omnipresence, compassion, justice, and the like—have merely been the pious projections of our religious imagination? What has happened to the millions of sermons, and the billions of prayers and praises, in the millennium? Does this God hear the prayers and acknowledge the praises? Or have we just been talking and singing to ourselves? Could the atheists be right after all? Where is the evidence that God is still in control, that God has the whole world in God's hands? Who hears the cries of those whose God-given endowments of skin are their major source of oppression and social pain? Does faith require sight, or does it thrive best in confronting the contrary evidence? Where is God's reign of peace, and purity, and love? When shall all hatred cease, as in the so-called realms above?

The cultures that we have explored have all been created, managed and controlled by those who name the name of Jesus as Savior and Lord. And yet, the injunction of Jesus to put up the sword and take up the cross is still being either laughed at or ignored. As we sail life's rugged sea, we prefer to set our own compasses and follow our own course, and as we say in the gaming business, we let the chips fall where they may. But life is not a gamble. Life is a gift— given by God, redeemed by God, and sustained by God's enlivening Spirit. Thus when the cultures of this world appear to work against the culture of Christ, even in the name of Christ, then we need to set our sails against the winds of cynicism, despair, and unbelief, and move forward. The God who has been our help in ages past will surely be our hope for years to come. That God will be our shelter from the stormy blasts of life, and even now provide for us a sure and lasting home.

Five Sails for the Mast

What do we carry with us in the boat as we sail into God's certain future? What do we possess that needs no reinvention? Well, for sure, we have a growing catalog of evils from which we daily pray that the good Lord will deliver us. We have the testimony of the saints who were also sinners, and whose witness provides us with the assurance that the life of faith is livable in spite of its many challenges. We have the treasury of sacred scripture that we accept as the word of God in a mysterious and mystical, yet profound and powerful way. We have the gift of the church, that wonderful and sacred body of Christ that is both sacramental and historical at the same time.

The church belongs to God and to no one else, and so far the prediction of Jesus has remained true that the gates of hell shall not prevail against it. We may wreak havoc within it with our tastes and styles, with our prejudices and our fears masquerading in theological garb, but the gates of hell will never prevail against it. We have our central message in the Great Communication—the Sermon on the Mount. We have our method in the Great Commandment to love God and one another. We have our mandate in the Great Commission to make disciples of Jesus, and not disciples of ourselves, wherever and whenever we can. We have the guarantee of the Great Companion—Jesus Christ himself—who has promised through the Spirit to be with us from millennium to millennium, until the end of time.

How then do we sail along on life's rugged seas? How do we fix our sails to the mast of the ship of life? Let me in conclusion briefly suggest five points of focus for our ongoing witness as Christians. These points of focus are offered in the context of the ongoing search for answers to the basic Christian question: What does it take to be a faithful Christian in this postmodern and sinful world?

First, let us work for the *devolution of moral authority* in our lives. We must truly come to believe that as many as are led by the Spirit of God are the children of God; and if children, then heirs of God's promise. This devolution involves the sharpening of our awareness that God's will and God's way are not prescribed by external and alien sources of authority, but rather they are made known to us in strange yet personally transforming ways. For while our consciences may not be the voice of God, they are certainly the primary means by which Christ's indwelling Spirit continues to sanctify and enlighten our lives. The role of religious leadership then is to enhance and strengthen God's indwelling Spirit in our lives, not to replace it.

Second, let us seek to *transform the cosmology of power*. This means that with all the cultures of self-determination and technology, all the threatening forces of domination and enforced dependence, we are to withstand the pressures of power that dehumanize us, or seek to negate our full personhood. We are to take our Christian mandate seriously by striving relentlessly to embody and promote the power of God's love, and through courageous modern-day martyrdom, renounce all pretensions to the love of power, whether in the church or in the world at large. We must never forget the force of Jesus' contempt for Pilate who reminded him of his power to kill or to release him. Pilate may be alive and well, but God has raised Jesus from the dead. O death, where is your victory?

Third, we must keep under constant review the true *anatomy of freedom in our lives*. The message of the gospel is clear. Jesus Christ has set us free from fear, from the threat of death, from the law of self-centeredness, from the powers, and from sin itself. This is the glorious freedom of the people of God. Not only are we free from these evils, but we are also free for the new life. That new life involves forgiveness, and justice, and sharing, and hope. We are to stand fast in the freedom that Christ has already won for us, and not return again to any yoke of slavery (Gal. 5:1). America may claim to be the land of the free and the home of the brave, but there is a freedom and a level of courage that America itself cannot provide. We are free to be members of Christ and citizens of the kingdom; and no visa, no green-card, no voter's registration, is required for that.

Fourth, we are to devote our intellects and our rational endowments to the *true sanctity of knowledge*. In this new age of information flows and technological skills, and increasing mastery over the vagaries of pain, poverty, disaster and disease, let us ensure that what we know and understand becomes an instrument in service of the greater good of all humanity. Let it not become a weapon of war to create divisions among God's people. If human life is sacred, then human knowledge is also sacred, given to us by God for the strengthening, not the weakening of human life, nor the assault on human dignity. We must never bring ourselves to believe that there yet exist types or groups of people for whom Jesus Christ did not die, nor did not come to save. For in that way we would relegate such to a level of disposability, not fit to be served or be saved. If knowledge is power, knowledge is also salvation. It must become available for all of God's children, who are indeed the objects of God's love. We must use it as a sacred gift for all humankind, and not just for the empowerment of the few over the many.

Finally, we must never relax *our spiritual and moral quest for that which is human*. At this turn of the millennium, we are bombarded on every side by patterns of experiment and surges of adventure, which seek to de-personify us and challenge our basic rights to be human. While the human body itself continues to be a sacred and wonderful mystery to us, we must strive by God's help to further understand what it really means to be truly human both in community with each other, as well as in a better relationship with God as our Creator. The quest for the truly human is not a quest that must make us God-like—for God-almightiness is a sin. Rather, it must help to make us more human, for that is the agenda which Jesus had set for himself in John 10:10: "I came that they might have life, and have it abundantly."

What does the new millennium hold in store for us? I really do not know, and quite frankly, I am not that much concerned. The one great hour on God's clock of time is simply NOW. Today is the accepted hour. Today is the day of salvation. Harvey Cox has this to say:

> If the qualities of most of the new religious movements presage anything, we may expect a world that prefers equality to hierarchy, participation to submission, experience over abstraction, multiple rather than single meanings, and plasticity rather than fixedness.... Ultimately, of course, only the future will disclose what the future will be.[12]

As we sail life's rugged sea, therefore, and continue to deal with the apparent paradox of an all-loving, all-powerful, and ever-present God who often appears to be weak, we can say with Doris

Day of old: "Que sera, sera, / Whatever will be will be, / The future's not ours to see, / Que sera, sera." Or we can jump into Paul's boat as his missionary journey continues, and shout with meaning and might the doxology with which he marched victoriously into Rome: "For I am convinced that neither death, nor life, nor angels, nor rulers, nor things present, nor things to come, nor powers, nor height, nor depth, nor anything else in all creation, will be able to separate us from the love of God in Christ Jesus our Lord" (Rom. 8:38-39).

NOTES

[1] Gregory Baum, ed., *The Twentieth Century: A Theological Overview* (Maryknoll: Orbis Books, 1999), viii.

[2] Andrew Hacker, *Two Nations: Black and White, Separate, Hostile, Unequal* (New York: Scribner's, 1992).

[3] Ibid., 60.

[4] Derrick Bell, *Faces at the Bottom of the Well: The Permanence of Racism* (New York: Basic Books, 1992), 12.

[5] Ibid., 10.

[6] Mevin Kranzberg, "Technology," in *The World Book Encyclopedia 2000*, (Chicago, World Book, Inc., 2000) 19:77.

[7] *Entrepreneur*, December 1999, 14-15.

[8] Ibid., 18.

[9] Samuel Morison, " Christopher Columbus" in *The World Book Encyclopedia 1985*, (Chicago, World Book, Inc., 1985) 4:697.

[10] Baum, "The Impact of Marxist Ideas on Christian Theology," in *The Twentieth Century*, 184.

[11] John Douglas Hall, "'The Great War' and the Theologians," in *The Twentieth Century*, 12.

[12] Harvey Cox, "The Myth of the Twentieth Century: The Rise and Fall of 'Secularization'," in *The Twentieth Century*, 143.

6

THIS FRAGILE EARTH
OUR ISLAND HOME
The Environmental Crisis

JEFFREY M. GOLLIHER

Virtually everyone on earth has heard by now that the ecological crisis is real. On a global scale, this crisis will in all likelihood worsen before it improves—assuming, hopefully, that it does. Greater personal and social awareness and more intense political action are urgently needed. These alone, however, will not be enough to avert the catastrophe we have already been witnessing for several years. We must fall in love with God and God's creation, so much so that the way we live and see ourselves as religious people will be transformed.

As Christians, together we make up the body of Christ, a visible sign and expression of God's love for the world. The body of Christ must also be understood as present in the web of life and in our relationship with it. The web of life generates the diversity which is God's creation on earth. It makes human life possible. The Spirit weaves together this diverse mosaic around the person of Christ in whom "all things hold together" (Col. 1:17). Awareness of life's interdependence, which predates the church, is new only in the modern, scientific sense. The early Christian theologians enshrined it in their teaching: Christ's sacramental presence in the eucharist reveals God's love for the world as the doorway to salvation. Our essential task now is to remember humankind's purpose in God's creation, because this will renew a loving relationship on our part, both spiritually and ecologically.

Let there be no mistake about how seriously broken our relationship with God and God's creation actually is. Undergoing the greatest loss of life since the last ice age, the earth has entered a sixth period of massive biological extinctions:

- one third of the world's fish are facing extinction;
- two thirds of all birds are on the decline;
- one fourth of all forests have been destroyed in the last fifty years;
- the extinction rate among mammals today is one thousand times greater than it was during the Pleistocene Epoch (10,000 years ago).

What do these scientific findings mean? In the nightmarish word of David Quammen, biogeographer, the web of life is "unraveling."[1] Obviously, no sane person or society would want to destroy the web of life; and yet, as the 1998 Lambeth Conference stated, human activity is the primary cause: poorly planned economic development, unsustainable levels of consumption by the rich, pollution of groundwater and soil, climate change resulting from greenhouse gases and fossil fuels, deforestation, and overpopulation. People may agree or disagree about the methods of calculating extinction rates or the reliability of climate change predictions, but the profound urgency of the larger picture is now clear and beyond reasonable dispute.

If the human impact on the ecological crisis is staggering, so is the impact of this crisis on millions of our brothers and sisters who experience the dire consequences of environmental destruction on a daily basis. Homeless refugees on several continents face starvation as they evacuate soil-depleted regions which were once fertile farmland. In tropical areas where whole habitats have been lost to deforestation, people migrate to expanding megacities in search of paid employment, shelter, and some form of community. Millions of people worldwide experience life-threatening illnesses such as cancer and asthma as a result of radiation poisoning or the dumping of hazardous substances into the air, soil, and groundwater. If the present course continues, the promise of human rights, as proclaimed by the Universal Declaration of Human Rights, may eventually have no meaning whatsoever.

Assuming that unsustainable economic development continues into the immediate future, one can reasonably expect the gap between the rich and poor to widen further, the environmental quality of life for both to diminish even more, and competition for affordable, if not healthy food, clean water, shelter, and energy to increase dramatically. In fact, this is a realistic description of the way things are now across much of the Anglican Communion and the world. Taking into account the impact of global climate change and habitat loss on extinction rates, the picture may rapidly become much worse. Yet, for many people in economically "developed" nations, the apparent "success" of the global economy for even a small portion of the world's peoples, the lure of consumption and personal gain, and the perceived need for security too easily distort the meaning of scientific facts and the anguished testimony of living beings. The contradiction between what seems to be abundant life, on the one hand, and the horrible loss of life and injustice, on the other, is apparently too great. We must not turn our backs to this unparalleled suffering or to the warning signs of an ecological catastrophe that threatens all. Especially now, the Holy Spirit is drawing out an overwhelming love from the deepest core of our being. It is absolutely essential that we express that love, because we are in deep trouble with God.

THE WEB OF LIFE AND THE BODY OF CHRIST

To stop our suicidal destruction, we will need both an ecological reformation of the church and a spiritual revolution in reverential love. The church must become God's creation in a process of renewal. A significant first step in that direction will necessarily involve a serious re-examination of the utilitarian values that shape the global economy and which treat the creation as a warehouse of inexhaustible resources for human consumption. The assumption that market forces are "value free" has so overwhelmed our reverence and appreciation for the intrinsic value of creation that we act as if we have no choice in the matter. That it has become so easy to believe we have no choice strongly indicates that our ideas about what the world is like (cosmology) have become confused and widely separated from our beliefs about how to live (ethics). We must bring them back together. If we continue to act as if there is no choice to make, then the web of life will, in fact, continue to unravel until our own extinction is guaranteed.

How do we face the facts and move forward with hope? Today, people in all parts of the Anglican Communion look for guidance in honoring the essential spiritual traditions of the church, while recognizing that the web of life is sacred and worthy of our instinctive love. For Anglican Christians, we usually turn to the Reformation period in England, especially to the writings of Richard Hooker, in search of a model of how to live or direction in how to create a new one. As suggested by Archbishop Michael Ramsey, the religious and political issues facing Elizabethan England might be more relevant to our lives today than we usually assume. The religious fanaticism and threat of economic and political chaos which were facts of life in sixteenth-century England are still present in the lives of many Anglicans on several continents.[2] In his own time, Hooker was committed to a higher principle of order in human institutions for one overriding reason: severe political divisions had created a chasm between reason and revelation to such an extent that institutional power and stability were seriously threatened. His solution was to affirm that the holy scriptures are sufficient as the complete revelation of God, while asserting that natural law is the presupposition, the necessary background, for our understanding of them. In its highest form, "reason," which is the "light of nature" according to Hooker, reaches perfection in humankind as the expression of the divine *logos*.[3]

Those principles were the foundation of Hooker's ecclesiastical framework for the church and the state as redemptive agents in the world. The genius of this framework is found in its humanistic anthropocentrism; namely, the belief that religious and political institutions must not become frozen in time, but remain vital and responsive, through human reason, to the changing circumstances of the present. This was only one of the very positive roles that anthropocentrism played during the Reformation and Enlightenment periods. It contributed to the advancement of science and to the adoption of political and civil rights in many parts of the world, eventually leading to the United Nations Universal Declaration of Human Rights. On the other hand, this anthropocentrism would develop its own shadowy side. Drawing upon an

earlier dualistic separation of soul from body, runaway anthropocentrism would dislodge the sacred from the center of the western worldview and sever the human soul from the soul of the
earth. It led to the social-Darwinist "ladder of evolution," which
provided the racist ideology for a colonial economy based on
political and military power and the belief that people could and
should be separated from the environment. This edifice of colonialism remains with us today, but in the form of the "value-free"
global marketplace. In practice, it relegates the life of the planet
into an essentially dead machine, treats animals as soulless creatures, and rationalizes economic and political exploitation as
forms of utilitarian virtue. It continues to be used, directly and
indirectly, to support the domination of nature, women, people of
color, and indigenous peoples.

Anglican theologians of the nineteenth century, led by
Charles Gore, hoped to counter the dehumanizing and despiritu-
alizing impact of these forces as they became manifest during the
industrial era. They expanded Hooker's emphasis on reason with
a vision of the incarnate, self-emptying Christ at the center of the
web of life and the Holy Spirit present in its diverse threads. Their
theological vision, along with Hooker's, forms the groundwork
for a contemporary Anglican response to the ecological crisis.
Although this groundwork is essential, it will not be enough to
heal our broken relationship with the web of life. To heal that
relationship, the shadowy side of runaway anthropocentrism must
be understood, released to the light of day, and transformed by
the power of the Spirit present in God's creation.

As we move forward, we will inevitably be influenced by the
dualisms of the past, not as the ghosts of our ancestors, but as necessary tools in the process of theological reflection and discernment. All cultures rely on cognitive categories and structures of
meaning. They help to organize the creative energy of human
awareness, making it possible for us to share our feelings,
thoughts, and perceptions with others. Our ideas about contemplation and action (or spirituality and justice), for example, represent different aspects of life and ministry to which people may
be called in different degrees, depending on the mind of the Spirit and the mundane circumstances of life. But they are never truly
separate.[4] Similarly, we must recognize the spiritual and ecological interdependence of the church and God's creation—the body

of Christ and the web of life. Of course, we will instinctively protect the lives and well-being of our families and communities,
whenever we are presented with difficult, immediate choices
about health, justice, and ecosystems. However, we do not want to
perpetuate a situation which is the outcome of runaway anthropocentrism, in which a "both/and" cosmology of people and the
living planet disintegrates into ethical decisions based on
"either/or" criteria. The tradition of Anglican spirituality affirms
the importance of this inclusive perspective. To seek communion
with God through prayer and meditation or by revering the divine
presence in women and men, in our friends and in strangers, in
the birds, in the lilies of the field and in hazelnuts, but especially
in our enemies, draws us closer to the holy mystery which lies
beyond and within the meaning that dualistic categories represent. Their ultimate purpose is to reveal the interdependence of
all living beings in God's creation, rather than to enshrine their
division in a worldview that undergirds colonialism.

From an ecological perspective, the fundamental issue concerns the relationships of power that these categories of language
and thought convey. To seek domination of one against the
other—matter against spirit, men against women, people against
the environment—distorts their meaning in human consciousness and corrupts everything we know intuitively about the purpose of authority and order in our institutions.[5] Ultimately, it
leads to an apocalypse of cruelty, if not death, rather than the liberation which is our hope in Christ. The unraveling web of life tes-
tifies that this apocalypse is happening now, which is why the ecological crisis is a crisis of the church. The model of domination
has misled us into behaving as if (while not necessarily believing)
the relationship between God and God's creation is a dualism
which should be overcome, rather than a creative tension which
we are called to embrace with love and joy. If we continue to sub-
mit to this spirit of domination in our consciousness, then we will
prolong the captivity of the church and other institutions by the
forces that destroy the web of life.

This understanding is important, because how we think and
feel about the ecological crisis can carry our most well-intentioned
plans forward or undermine them. Our revision of theology and
language will not be the sole answer to the ecological crisis. Self-
serving impulses concealed within the human heart can subsume

even the most earth-friendly philosophies and linguistic structures to achieve their aims. This should make us always vigilant about the condition of our own souls, but without submitting to cynicism or despair for the human prospect. Cynicism and despair can bolster the assumption that religious traditions are essentially unchanging, static, or frozen in time. Both crystallize a form of existence that thwarts the creative energy of human emotions and intellect. This temptation turns our hearts away from the very real suffering which is the outcome and brutal reality of the ecological crisis and denies the joy and liberation that ecological healing can bring.

Some ecofeminists and ecopsychologists have been working with forms of psychological denial and "ecological grieving" in a therapeutic process for those who experience the traumatic effects of environmental destruction. They have identified the existence of disturbances deep in the human psyche which are tied to ecological systems. The source of these psychological disturbances is found not so much in the human mind, but within the web of life of which human consciousness is an integral part.[6] The therapeutic process of ecological grieving can help people identify, express, and act upon the hidden sources of love which bear witness to the unraveling strands of the web of life within us. These disturbances may also reveal the human impact of what the Ecumenical Patriarch Bartholomew I and others at a recent interfaith gathering on the Isle of Patmos called "ecological sin."[7] As a possible catechetical doctrine, ecological sin affirms a neglected part of Christian theological tradition: God's love is manifest in the most basic way through the web of life which supports humankind and every living creature, while the human destruction of the web of life demonstrates our collective estrangement from that love.

The meaning of "ecological sin" has significant implications for the doctrine and practice of ministry. As a dimension of moral theology, it acknowledges something the human conscience already knows, but too often fails to express—namely, that acts of environmental destruction are morally wrong. In pastoral ministry, the depth of repentance and forgiveness on which ecological healing depends goes well beyond any emphasis on guilt and moral discipline, although these may be involved. The rite of reconciliation, in this context, takes on a profound significance as the sacramental means of expressing the creative energy of reverential love which will restore healing relationships with the earth. This kind of reconciliation speaks directly to the congregational and community basis of worship, and reminds us that the human community is part of the earth community, as Thomas Berry has so eloquently described.[8] His simple but profound insight into the interdependent nature of the web of life tells us that healing today requires the establishment of sustainable human communities. The church has had centuries of experience in nurturing and building communities; now our challenge is to create the kind of communities that will embody our love for God and God's love for us through the web of life.

SIGNS OF HOPE: LAMBETH 1998 AND THE STRUGGLE FOR A GLOBAL COMMUNITY

A great deal has been said in a variety of media, both positively and negatively, about economic globalization. However, its overwhelming ecological impact is felt most severely in the widespread uprooting of human communities from the web of life.[9] This is precisely what we want to avoid, and it confirms the wisdom of Rene Dubos, microbiologist and modern prophet of the ecological movement, who formulated the well-known maxim, "think globally, but act locally."[10] Currently, economic globalization is an extension of the same patterns of exploitation known to the colonial era. The spirit of domination, which it exemplifies, has become so intense that it culminates in an apparent attempt to replace the web of life as our common home with the World Wide Web, a manufactured world existing in cyberspace, and the human control of life's processes on the microscopic level of genetics.[11] The conceptual difference between the global and the local has become less significant than the enormous impact that globalizing forces have on local communities and ecosystems everywhere. This movement toward a far-reaching consolation of the global economy is matched by a dispersed but emerging countermovement (present, in part, at the recent World Trade Organization meeting in the United States) whose aim is to reverse its destructive economic and environmental consequences. The dynamic interplay between these two movements defines the process of ecological healing, as it occurs on a global level, as a struggle for justice and for the soul of the living planet. It lies at the heart of the highly contentious and complex effort to create a genuinely global community based on local interdependence, systemic solutions to poverty, sustainable economic development, human rights and environmental protection, and the recovery of democratic decision-making processes.

We should not be surprised that positive steps taken to avert the ecological crisis are usually accompanied by formidable obstacles. Loss of livelihood and self-respect, racism, the breakdown of family and community ties, unwise economic consumption and passive compliance with corporate values that support it—all these come into play and shape how we see ourselves and act in relation to the web of life. Each positive step becomes a test of commitment and faith as these obstacles are gradually encountered and worked through. When the obstacles become great and the outlook seems especially bleak, we may, in fact, be entering the most crucial, hopeful and liberating stage of the healing process.

The environmental resolutions of the 1998 Lambeth Conference are best understood in that context; and as a contribution to the international struggle of globalization, they are a significant sign of hope.[12] The involvement of the church in this struggle for justice and sustainable development is crucial on the international scene because that is where policies are made and enacted which will resolve or worsen the ecological crisis. The Lambeth resolutions, which affirm the search for integrated solutions to global problems, also reinforce the awareness that a genuine global community cannot emerge unless it is rooted in local cultural traditions and ecosystems. The resolutions themselves begin with a set of principles regarding an Anglican theology of creation.

> Creation is a web of inter-dependent relationships bound together in the Covenant which God, the Holy Trinity, has established with the whole earth and every living being: (i) the divine Spirit is sacramentally present in Creation, which is therefore to be treated with reverence, respect, and gratitude; (ii) human beings are both co-partners with the rest of Creation and living bridges between heaven and earth, with responsibility to make personal and corporate sacrifices for the common good of all Creation; (iii) the redemptive purpose of God in Jesus Christ extends to the whole of Creation. (Resolution 1.8)

Concerning "unbridled capitalism, selfishness, and greed" as the primary cause of environmental destruction, the text says the following:

> ... the future of human beings and all life on earth hangs in the balance as a consequence of the present unjust economic structures, the injustice existing between the rich and the poor, the continuing exploitation of the natural environment and the threat of nuclear self-destruction ...

Resolution 1.9 calls us to take specific action in four principal areas: (1) "to work for a sustainable society in a sustainable world," (2) to "recognize the dignity and rights of all people and the sanctity of all life, especially the rights of future generations," (3) "to ensure the responsible use and re-cycling of natural resources," (4) "to bring about economic reforms which will establish a just and fair trading system both for people and the environment." Lastly, Resolution 1.9 "calls upon the United Nations to incorporate the right of future generations to a sustainable future in the Universal Declaration of Human Rights." These statements underscore the urgent attention that we must give to raising awareness of the causes of environmental destruction and to the importance of collaborative action among organizations like the United Nations and the churches.

From an ecological standpoint, the significance of these resolutions is found in their implicit acknowledgment that economic globalization in its current form, while it promises to be the solution to global problems, is actually destroying the web of life. The source of this contradiction lies in the ambiguous meaning of "sustainable development," especially as it relates to large-scale economic forces and marketplace values. The contradiction itself can be traced to the "Earth Summit" in 1992, which, despite its overriding problems, was a remarkable achievement whose credit lies almost completely with the United Nations.[13] Without the work of that body in collaboration with countless non-governmental associations, including the churches, there would be no global effort among governments to eradicate poverty and to reverse environmental destruction. In effect, the Lambeth resolutions not only affirm the integrative vision of the United Nations for the Anglican Communion, but also acknowledge that we are a global community among ourselves and a functional part of many others working to preserve the web of life for the sake of every living being.

Still, the numerous conceptual and practical problems with "sustainable development" should not be underestimated. As it is understood within the United Nations, "sustainability" means "meeting the needs of the present without compromising that ability of future generations to meet their own needs." The problem(s) lie not with the definition itself, but with its implications: Sustainability for whom? That is, whose way of life will be sustained? Will the environmental ideals of economically developed nations be imposed on developing nations, despite the fact that the former are the primary consumers of the earth's natural resources? The Universal Declaration of Human Rights, for example, affirms the right to water, food, and shelter; but how will we respond if the earth, through the continued degradation and loss of whole ecosystems, loses the capacity to provide these resources? Economic exploitation, materialism, the equation of "economic growth" with "development," and the massive power of international lending institutions and transnational corporations figure prominently in all these questions.[14] Political and economic domination based on the nation-state has been replaced by a new kind of colonialism engineered by transnational corporate power. From an ecological point of view, we are not moving into a postcolonial world, but exchanging one kind of domination for another. So far, international plans for sustainable development have been closely tied to forms of economic globalization that dislocate communities and circumvent democratic decision-making on which environmental conservation depends. Steps toward clean energy, watershed restoration, forest preservation, and sustainable agriculture may be components of these makeshift solutions, but their promise reaches a severe limit when the long-term cost is the loss of local communities, human rights, and whole habitats. If global capitalism can be transformed in the direction of life-affirming values, rather than cost/benefit analyses which now seem to determine the value of ecosystems and living beings (including people), then our hope for the future may be realized.

The ongoing struggle for a genuine global community underscores a second, easily overlooked sign of hope. We have come a long way toward the resolution of an old opposition between science and religion, or knowledge and faith. This opposition has been fueled by two sources of fear, which are sometimes expressed within the church. The first is that our love for creation may indicate a tendency toward paganism. The second is that our willingness to work with organizations like the United Nations may bring the church under secularizing influences. The fact that we have moved to a great extent beyond both fears is crucial. The depth of this fear and mistrust was revealed in 1967 when Lynn White, an American scientist, placed the largest share of blame for the ecological crisis on the church, and yet identified St. Francis of Assisi as the positive example of ecological virtue and the "patron saint" of the emerging environmental movement.[15] White's criticism, which was much more controversial then than it is now, paralleled the vital work of ecofeminists who have traced the origins of the environmental crisis to the exploitative dualisms of patriarchal structures worldwide. These criticisms have prodded representatives of the world's religions to recognize that their own positive traditions of earth stewardship have not been adequately realized or taught. Nevertheless, any period of reformation requires discernment and consensus within the whole worshiping community. In that connection the more pressing issue today in some parts of the Anglican Communion concerns a reluctance to question the sometimes close relationship between science and corporate interests. This is especially relevant to a widespread concern about genetically engineered foods and pesticides, the corporate ownership of seeds and other life forms, and their ecological as well as economic and political impact.

A third sign of hope lies in the persistent effort to resolve the conflicting loyalties and allegiances that a rapidly globalizing world creates. These conflicts are a serious obstacle to the formation of a global community rooted in the web of life and a clear indication of the shallow sense of unity manufactured by globalization industries. As Bishop Michael Hare Duke observed in the opening address of the October 1994 meeting of the ACC Peace and Justice Network in Perth, Scotland:

> The processes of the market divide groups into competitive rivalry. Poverty, deprivation, unemployment, make for opposition and not collaboration. Yet on the other hand, the theme of the global village has become cliché. We all know how everything connects. The most remote political events in Afghanistan can affect the stock prices on Wall Street. Once upon a time we could have looked, with the unconcern of strangers, at distressing conflicts in the Balkans. Now we know that their existence impinges on ours....

This awareness of integration can disempower us. If decisions in one place are negated by actions in another it can feel like an invitation to irresponsibility. When it seems impossible to persuade everybody into concerted action, we hive off into a selfish concern to maximize our own advantage. This seems to be partly what happened to the decisions taken at the Rio Summit. The protocols become too costly when translated into local action. No one government was prepared to risk being disadvantaged for the sake of the common good. So decisions which required concerted action were undermined by individual rivalry. Yet this is in direct contradiction to the perception that global problems require global action.[16]

While Bishop Duke's comments were made as a reflection on the agreements of the Earth Summit, they apply to the continuing difficulty we face in forming a genuine global community. This difficulty has a direct bearing on the establishment of a popular consensus around a global environmental ethic. The primary purpose of such an ethic would be to affirm the preservation of the web of life as the primary commitment of the global community. Steps taken through the United Nations toward the creation of a global ethic, e.g., the World Charter for Nature and the Earth Charter, have helped to raise awareness about the urgency of the ecological crisis. By stating the environmental dimensions of their own beliefs through the Assisi Declarations, the major world religions have clarified the spiritual principles necessary for this global consensus.[17] In addition, "The Declaration Toward a Global Ethic" of the Parliament of the World's Religions affirms many spiritual principles which are already shared among the world's religions.[18] More recent efforts by the InterAction Council to supplement the Universal Declaration on Human Rights with a "Declaration on Human Responsibilities" also represent a significant step in a similar direction, but in more secular language.

All the ingredients of a global ethic are present, but the popular will has not yet been marshaled to make it a reality. Clearly, institutional and corporate loyalties are an issue here. These loyalties often come into serious conflict with the profound love for creation that people feel almost universally. At the moment, the media-based public relations arms of transnational corporations operate educational campaigns that short-circuit the full expression of this love. Their messages work simultaneously as "corporate greenwashing" efforts, designed to reassure the public of their commitment to the common good and as educational tools which convey implicit messages about "citizenship" in the global community. These media-generated images of good citizenship, which are thoroughly anthropocentric, define "good citizen" almost exclusively as the active consumer. The implicit belief that participation in the global marketplace (rather than active involvement in the decisions about how our lives are organized) is the essential ingredient of a global community only perpetuates the exploitation of peoples and ecosystems. Our global religious institutions must become more actively involved with this issue by creating educational campaigns about our love for creation as an integral dimension of religious faith. This will be necessary to counter the false sense of community created by consumerism and to redirect our commitment to a genuine community rooted in the web of life. For Christians, faith in God necessarily involves a commitment to the two great commandments. The rapidly deteriorating state of ecosystems everywhere suggests that allegiance to the web of life is a prerequisite for the fulfillment of Christ's command to love God and our neighbors.

ECOLOGICAL HEALING:
THE CHURCH AS GOD'S CREATION IN A PROCESS
OF RENEWAL

While the struggle for a global community carries hope for ecological healing and reveals serious obstacles to its realization, it also teaches an ancient lesson—ultimately, our true adversaries are the pride, fear, greed, and prejudice which we all face every day. We need the power of Christ to heal the earth; but even more, we need Christ to heal ourselves, because our relationship with the earth is clearly broken. A genuine global community will not appear unless it is built upon the foundation of interdependent local communities rooted in the web of life. The effectiveness of our efforts to build those communities depends on the presence of the Holy Spirit, which draws us into the mystery and awakens our love for God's creation. On the most local, flesh-and-blood level of community life, the process of ecological healing can sort out the difference between allegiance to the worldly powers, on the one hand, and to God's creation, on the other. This is where the church can make its most significant contribution to the transformational process that we urgently need.

ECOLOGICAL HEALING REQUIRES AN ATTITUDE OF HUMILITY TOWARD GOD AND GOD'S CREATION

We always hope that our understanding of life's problems, whatever they may be, is based on reason and wisdom in the fullest sense; and yet we recognize that their solutions ultimately come from the healing power of Christ. If we claim that power for ourselves, then we have lost our way spiritually. This traditional understanding of healing in the church, which applies to every aspect of our lives, has a profound significance for the ecological crisis. Lynn Margulis sheds light on this issue from the perspective of an eminent biologist who is deeply appreciative of the ecological value of humility. She says, "we cannot put an end to nature; we can only pose a threat to ourselves."[19] This statement encourages us to set aside anthropocentrism by turning our attention to how vast, complex, and resilient the web of life actually is in comparison with our generally unyielding attempts to destroy it. The interdependent ecological relations which support human life have become tenuous and uncertain, but the web of life as a whole is far from fragile. Having survived catastrophic extinctions on five previous occasions in geological history, it will survive again whether we change our unsustainable ways or continue on the present course.

If we do not have the power to put an end to nature, we might also ask whether we have the power to save it. The answer is both yes and no. From a spiritual point of view, we know that humankind can neither create nor destroy God's providence, although a great temptation of the twentieth century is to believe we can. The release of the tremendous power of atomic energy has magnified this temptation, combined with more recent advances in genetic engineering and cloning. We have the power, bestowed by God, to nurture the web of life or to exploit it, but we do not have the power to create it. At best, we can glimpse the outcome of the creative power of the Spirit constantly weaving the complex threads of relationship that generate life's diversity. Without question, compassion and dedication to justice for earth's creatures and ecosystems should propel us into immediate action to prevent the destruction of human lives, living creatures, and ecosystems; however, this is very different from claiming we have the power to put an end to nature or to save it.

This is a subtle, but important, point because it helps to clarify our dual role, noted in the Lambeth resolutions, as "co-partners" and "living bridges" in the process of ecological healing. As "co-partners" with all living beings, we are called to nurture the web of life for the common good of all. Co-partnership as a model of environmental stewardship differs from the more traditional anthropocentric, managerial image, in which the steward takes on the characteristics of a landlord. From an ecological perspective, co-partnership presumes a relationship of equality and mutuality with other living beings. Yet within this relationship of equality, we are still called to be "living bridges" between heaven and earth. If our role as "living bridges" is neither to create nor destroy nature, then what is it? Based on the spiritual tradition of healing, to become a "living bridge" is to set aside our egotistical and anthropocentric involvements, so the Spirit can weave creative communities of life through us and the whole of creation. These enigmatic words of Jesus recorded in the Gospel according to Matthew help us understand how we can fulfill that role:

> Therefore I tell you, do not worry about your life, what you will eat or what you will drink, or about your body, what you will wear. Is not life more than food, and the body more than clothing? Look at the birds of the air; they neither sow nor gather into barns, and yet your heavenly Father feeds them. Are you not of more value than they? And can any of you by worrying add a single hour to your span of life? And why do you worry about clothing? Consider the lilies of the field, how they grow; they neither toil nor spin, yet I tell you, even Solomon in all his glory was not clothed like one of these. But if God so clothes the grass of the field, which is alive today and tomorrow is thrown into the oven, will God not much more clothe you—you of little faith? Therefore do not worry, saying, "What will we eat?" or "What will we drink?" or "What will we wear?" For it is the Gentiles who strive for all these things; and indeed your heavenly Father knows that you need all these things. But strive first for the kingdom of God and God's righteousness, and all these things will be given to you as well. So do not worry about tomorrow, for tomorrow will bring worries of its own. Today's trouble is enough for today (6:25-34).[20]

In this passage, Christ poses the question at the heart of the ecological crisis: Are you not of more value than they? We would be mistaken to interpret this as evidence for Christ's anthropocentrism, which would justify the human exploitation of creation. Christ clearly affirms our kinship with the web of life—the birds of the air and the lilies in the field. Calling upon his and our intuitive wisdom based on the observation of nature, Christ then says that humankind is radically different from other creatures. A two-sided message is apparent here: We are different, in part, because we worry too much about the wrong things. We are also different because we have a distinctive purpose and creative activity: "Strive first for the kingdom and God's righteousness." This distinctive purpose neither excludes other living beings from the body of Christ nor exempts us from the responsibility to care for the web of life. It presumes that the web of life has a right to exist and that we are worthy to express our love for it as God's creation. By entering into the kingdom of God, we do not receive a special privilege to circumvent or disregard ecological wisdom. Such a self-serving claim would (and does) distort the distinctive purpose of humankind by elevating the very dualistic, spirit-denying forms of consciousness we want to overcome. Instead, we have the moral obligation to transform, through Christ's redemption, those forces that would destroy the ecological foundation of life which we all share. This suggests, ironically, that runaway anthropocentrism is a betrayal of the living Spirit, while the realization of our distinctive purpose liberates both humankind and the whole of creation.

Christ's teaching about worry is sometimes used to support the belief that our faith in God will provide us with material rewards. To let go of worry, however, is to remember who we are in God's creation by giving up the materialistic treadmill driven by greed, hatred, and fear in exchange for spiritual empowerment. Empowerment begins with the realization that all people, dehumanized and exploited by others and ourselves, are in danger of losing a sense of higher purpose and meaning, if we have not lost it already. This danger is the direct consequence of a world view which attempts to empty the cosmos of life-giving Spirit. The Holy Spirit is received to the extent that we search for our true purpose in creation by becoming "living bridges" between heaven and earth and "co-partners" with other living beings, including people. Runaway anthropocentrism has deceived us into believing that we could be "living bridges" without also becoming "co-partners" with all living creatures. Our dual role challenges us to deconstruct and move beyond the hypnotic power of the rapidly globalizing economic system. This in no way encourages us to be passive. Christ's radical call to critical awareness turns our attention here, as he points to the birds and the lilies and says, "do not worry about your life *and* strive for the kingdom."

ECOLOGICAL HEALING REQUIRES RESPECT FOR CREATION AS THE SACRED SPACE OF GOD'S CREATIVE PRESENCE

The fullness of creation encompasses everything: the web of interdependent relations that constitute ecological systems; all that we have not yet encountered or understood scientifically, which may be the greater part of the web of life; and the invisible supernatural forces present in creation, but beyond the scope of empirical methods of observation. Above all, there is the mystery of God, which we will never comprehend fully, and which we can yet recognize through our prayer and ordinary thoughts, feelings, sensations, and intuition.

The whole of creation is God's sacred space because the divine Spirit is sacramentally present everywhere. The trajectory of modern history has been to deface this sacred space by placing the golden calf of the marketplace at its center.[21] The church has contributed to this defacement in its own colonial past, one horrible example being its involvement in the destruction of indigenous peoples who have been the best stewards of God's creation. Professing to claim sacred space for Christendom, we were stealing it for our own and dishonoring everything sacred space really means. The church has, for the most part, confessed to this historical sin; and yet the destruction of indigenous peoples and lands continues, as the world remains hypnotized by the power of the global marketplace.

The church's ministry of ecological healing is to renew God's sacred space. Today, we recognize with our predecessors that not everything in sacred space is holy, but this applies overwhelmingly to the power of violence, greed, prejudice, and all temptations of pride. As we set aside anthropocentrism, which clearly involves egotistical pursuits and ethnocentrism, we can become co-partners with each other and with Christ, opening ourselves to the healing power present in God's sacred space. Ecological healing, which depends on reverence for life and respect for actual living beings and whole ecosystems, requires us to be vigilant about the dualistic assumptions that can undermine our good intentions and deface the sacred space of God's creation. Dualistic assumptions underlying the word "environment" exemplify this very point. Many scholars have called attention to these assumptions which have fueled the historical transition from an ancient appreciation of the fullness of God's creation to the recently despiritualized view of "the environment." In everyday usage "the environment" often refers to a sense of landscape which is understood as outside and separate from people. Because this meaning creates the false impression that the environment "surrounds" from the standpoint of the observer and forms a stage on which the human drama occurs, it suggests that we are somehow separate from the processes of life and exempt from ecological realities.[22] This meaning also encourages us to believe that the value of environment lies only in the resources it provides for human consumption.

For the same reason we want to avoid the false choice between the body of Christ and the web of life as the place of God's creative activity. This kind of either/or thinking epitomizes the propaganda machine of a war against nature and perpetuates the dualistic dichotomies we hope to overcome. Consider the predicament of millions of people suffering and dying from shortages of food and water, or from illnesses caused by environmental toxins transported illegally across continents. The body of Christ and the web of life must be present with them as the source of ecological healing and renewal. With ecosystems losing the capacity to sustain human life in many parts of the world, it would be easy to separate our faith in the resurrected Christ, which is our ultimate source of hope in any circumstance, from the incarnate Christ who works through human hands and bodies to create God's kingdom in this world. To reveal God's creation as sacred space, loyalty to the web of life must be brought together with our faith in Christ.

The Holy Eucharist is the Christian model for healing and sacred space in the broadest and most traditional sense. It creates an atmosphere of openness to the Holy Spirit, which we experience as joy, reverence, and holy mystery. In this sacred space, Christ's light is shed on hidden or forgotten places in the soul. Our mistaken allegiances and disordered loves are clarified. We experience forgiveness and reconciliation, while realizing that we are neither powerless nor isolated, and that life can be lived in new ways. To fill our liturgy with creation is to open our lives to the creative activity of the Spirit already at work in people, all living beings, and ecosystems. In the eucharist, we renew sacred space in order to redeem the fallen powers and release the web of life from the brute force of human exploitation. Our choice is not between a Christ-centered or a creation-centered spirituality. The universal saving message and vision of the church is Christ-centered and "creation-filled," as Esther de Waal has wisely put it.[23] When these become separated, then we have fallen away from the Christian vision we urgently need: the human community working within the earth community as one organic and superorganic whole.

ECOLOGICAL HEALING REQUIRES AN EXPANSIVE UNDERSTANDING OF THE INTEGRITY OF CREATION

In 1983 at its Vancouver Assembly, the World Council of Churches proposed the phrasing "Justice, Peace, and Integrity of Creation" as an integrative vision. Although this program for mission has been widely adopted by Christian denominations, its weak thematic link has been the "integrity of creation." In a nutshell, the "integrity of creation" includes more than the traditional theological image of *oikoumene*, the whole inhabited earth. It refers to the wholeness of living beings, ecosystems, and the entire web of life, whose existence depends on the interdependent relationships we think of as "communities."

The holistic implications of the "integrity of creation" have not been sufficiently explored, especially with regard to unity and diversity. The process of ecological healing expands our understanding of diversity and unity in the dynamic relationships which constitute community life. By saying that "diversity is creation," E.O. Wilson makes a scientific observation that affirms respect for diversity as an ethical principle.[24] The loss of biodiversity has consequences beyond anything statistical measures of endangered or extinct species can convey. It degrades whole ecosystems by altering the interdependent web of relationships that make their integrity real. Diversity as an ethical principle applies to human communities, which are inextricably linked to the ecosystems. Kortright Davis, an Anglican theologian, makes almost the identical point as Wilson, the biologist, but with regard to human communities and racism:

> The principal form of God's Oikoumene is that of diversity; we are daily confronted by the harsh realities of diversity which God's creative activity continues to unfold. The ecumenical endeavor then takes diversity into its system not as an optional extra, but as a primary focus of attention. This diversity

challenges the Christian in particular to seek the good of the
whole human race, regardless of differences of faith, or race,
or ethnicity. Diversity gives fullest religious expression to the
oneness of the Creator, and thus to the oneness of the Creator's family.[25]

Chief Oren Lyons, wisdomkeeper of the Onondaga in northern New York, extends diversity as an ethical principle to the
whole creation by summarizing the ecological wisdom of indigenous peoples: "Biodiversity" (which is too jargonistic) actually
means "all my relations," that is, all living beings.[26] This understanding of Chief Lyons and his fellow elders is expressed implicitly in Leonardo Boff's recent interpretation of Franciscan spirituality as a model of liberation. Boff argues persuasively that the
Franciscan vision of God's kingdom is based on two interwoven
threads. The first thread, which is cosmological, concerns our
spiritual birthright to express love for all life as a form of reverential kinship. The second thread, concerning ethics and economic justice, is the absolute moral imperative to meet the needs
of the poor.[27] The preferential option for the poor, in Boff's creation-filled theology, parallels an insight which originally shaped
the United Nations' global agenda for sustainable development—
the forces that impoverish the earth are the same as those that
impoverish people. For that reason, our goals of economic justice
and universal rights converge with reverence for the web of life.
The eradication of poverty is the most urgent goal of ecological
healing, and yet this must be accomplished without impoverish-
ing the web of life which supports the life of every human being.
    The value of biological and cultural diversity must also be
affirmed in order to counteract the present movement toward
imposed global unity at the expense of diversity. The globalized
economy uses stereotypic representations of diversity in advertisements in order to create an international appeal for its goods and
services. This image-driven celebration of diversity through the
airwaves and Internet may generate profits, but it results in uniformity; and the actual cost to life in its particularity is horrendous. Real living beings and whole ecosystems, whose integrity is
realized within the interdependent relationships of the web of
life, are lost to the demands of the so-called "value-free" global
marketplace. Precisely what we do not want to do is to replace real
people and ecosystems with images and ideas about them. Yet, in
the economically "developed" nations, this apocalyptic logic of

virtual reality drives as well as conceals the systemic destruction of peoples and ecosystems, and it exemplifies the dire ecological consequences of separating cosmology from ethics.

The church has traditionally seen one of its primary goals as the maintenance of "unity within diversity," and the importance of this cannot be emphasized enough. However, a Christ-centered, creation-filled spiritual vision must be as profoundly dedicated to preserving diversity, and even generating it, as it has been to maintaining unity. From an ecological perspective, this mission of the church thoroughly informs our understanding of what it means to be a "living bridge" between heaven and earth. Everything we do to affirm the vital importance of cultural and biological diversity in our congregations and communities, as well as in the global biosphere, is a step toward the resolution of the ecological crisis. Clearly, the diversity of life is not a problem to be overcome. Rather, diversity *is* the integrity of creation which we want to preserve on every level.

Our most urgent goal now must be to seek "diversity within unity" by forming ecologically harmonious relationships within the unity that already exists within the web of life. As an ethical and cosmological principle, "diversity within unity" must include practical knowledge of how to live as part of the ecosystems where our communities and congregations are located. This is sacred knowledge, which must be placed at the heart of the church for at least two reasons. First, a majority of people in economically "developed" nations have lost the practical knowledge of how to live in any real or immediate ecological sense. Obviously, these nations maintain a huge amount of knowledge concerning, for example, environmental protection and food production within government agencies, academic establishments, and transnational corporations. However, these institutions, which usually embody a domination ethic, either rule the global marketplace or operate as extensions of it, even as ecological reform movements exist within them. Second, those who have ecological knowledge at the heart of their culture, especially indigenous peoples, risk losing it as a result of cultural theft.[28] Transnational corporations obtain patents on genetic material and subsume ecological knowledge held by indigenous peoples, while the people themselves struggle to survive as their lives and ecosystems are destroyed. The rights of the people who have this knowledge must be protected as part of our most basic living tradition, which is the web of life itself and the knowledge of its care.

Everyone knows that the web of life can be demanding and even dangerous at times. Reliance on romanticized images of nature alone will surely distort the clear vision we need.

Nevertheless, to seek "diversity within unity" is to recognize that the web of life forms its own organic unity with Christ, rather than humankind, at its spiritual center. We are now learning to respect this deeper, yet practical unity by the ecological limits the Spirit has always imposed, if not by the rich diversity that it provides or the reverential love it calls forth from our souls.

TELLING NEW STORIES

To remember our purpose in God's creation necessarily involves a re-examination of the anthropocentric roots of the ecological crisis and of the church. Runaway anthropocentrism is a matter of concern for the individual who seeks to express love for creation as well as for communities that hope to establish a sustainable way of life. Perhaps the chief obstacle in this regard, however, lies in the underlying anthropocentrism which binds political, economic, and religious institutions into a single interlocking system and may uproot the entire global community from the web of life. Some deeply thoughtful leaders of the environmental movement believe that present-day institutions of all kinds are not inspired by the values, goals, and spiritual vision required to avert ecological catastrophe. To guide our way into an uncertain future, Brian Swimme and Thomas Berry have argued eloquently for the emergence of a "new story," a revolution in our understanding of God, the universe, and humankind.[29] Whether you accept or reject their assessment, it is reasonable given the unraveling web of life. Either way, the church will change because the web of life is drastically changing, and this will eventually lead to a new story of the church.

If all goes well, this inevitable transformation will lead to many new stories, each containing elements of the old, combined with the new. These new stories are already in the making, inspired by the examples of Chico Mendes from Brazil, Ingrid Washinawatok from the United States, Ken Saro-Wiwa from Nigeria, and countless other martyrs who have known that the future of humankind is not guaranteed. If all goes well, our lives will be supported by a flourishing web of life and unified by reverential love for God and the whole creation. These new stories may relate our struggle to express that love by overcoming anthropocentrism, false allegiances, and incessant worry about the wrong things. Thomas Traherne, the Anglican poet, had it right nearly three hundred years ago.

> When we dote upon the perfections and beauties of some one creature,
> we do not love that too much, but other things too little.
> Never was any thing in this world loved too much, but many things
> have been loved in a false way, and all in too short a measure.[30]

NOTES

[1] David Quammen, *The Song of the Dodo: Island Biogeography in an Age of Extinction* (New York: Simon and Schuster, 1996), 12-13.

[2] Dale Coleman, *Michael Ramsey: The Anglican Spirit* (Cambridge, Mass.: Cowley, 1991), 11-34.

[3] Richard Hooker, *Of the Laws of Ecclesiastical Polity,* 4 vols., ed. W. Hill (Cambridge, Mass.: Harvard University Press, 1977); see also *Creation and Liturgy: Studies in Honor of H. Boone Porter,* ed. Ralph N. McMichael, Jr. (Washington, D.C.: The Pastoral Press, 1993).

[4] Thomas Merton, *Contemplation in a World of Action* (Garden City: Doubleday, 1973).

[5] See Carolyn Merchant, *The Death of Nature* (New York: Harper and Row, 1980), and Val Plumwood, *Feminism and the Mastery of Nature* (London: Routledge, 1993).

[6] Joanna Macy, *World as Lover, World as Self* (Berkeley: Parallax Press, 1991), and Theodore Roszak, *The Voice of the Earth* (New York: Simon and Schuster, 1992).

[7] Sarah Hobson and Jane Lubchenco, eds., *Revelation and the Environment, A.D. 95-1995* (Singapore: World Scientific Publishing, 1997). See also William Becker, "Ecological Sin," *Theology Today* 49:2 (July 1992): 152-64.

[8] Thomas Berry, *The Dream of the Earth* (San Francisco: Sierra Club Books, 1988).

[9] Maria Mies and Vandana Shiva, *Ecofeminism* (London: Zed Books, 1993).

[10] Rene Dubos, *Celebration of Life* (New York: McGraw Hill, 1981), 83.

[11] William Irwin Thompson, *The American Replacement of Nature: The Everyday Acts and Outrageous Evolution of Economic Life* (New York: Doubleday, 1991).

[12] Lambeth Conference and Anglican Consultative Council resolutions have reflected this growing concern with regard to church mission at least since 1968.

[13] The Earth Summit's "Agenda 21" established a comprehensive plan for environmentally sustainable economic development with special conventions of forests, biodiversity, oceans. Today, nearly every nation of the world has a plan of action for environmentally sustainable development as a result of this conference.

[14] Herman E. Daly and John B. Cobb, Jr., *For the Common Good: Redirecting the Economy Toward Community, the Environment, and a Sustainable Future* (Boston: Beacon Press, 1989).

[15] Lynn White, Jr., "The Historic Roots of the Ecological Crisis," *Science* 155 (1967): 1203-07.

[16] Bishop Michael Hare Duke, *Opening Address,* October 1994 Meeting of the ACC Peace and Justice Network, Perth Scotland.

[17] Tim Jensen, "Forming the Alliance of World Religions and Conservation," in *Cultural and Spiritual Values of Biodiversity,* ed. Darrell Addison Posey (Nairobi: United Nations Environment Program, 1999), 492-99.

[18] Hans Küng and Karl-Josef Kuschel, eds., *A Global Ethic: The Declaration of the Parliament of the World's Religions* (New York: Continuum, 1998).

[19] Lynn Margulis, *Symbiotic Planet: A New Look at Evolution* (Amherst: Basic Books, 1998), 128.

[20] *The New Oxford Annotated Bible,* New Revised Standard Version (New York: Oxford University Press, 1991).

[21] Timothy C. Weiskel, "Selling Pigeons in the Temple: The Blasphemy of Market Metaphors in an Ecosystem," in *Cultural and Spiritual Values of Biodiversity,* 466-68.

[22] James Hillman, "Where is the environment?" in *Cultural and Spiritual Values of Biodiversity*, 486-89.

[23] Esther De Waal, *The Celtic Way of Prayer: The Recovery of the Religious Imagination* (New York: Doubleday, 1997), 141.

[24] E.O. Wilson, "Biophilia and the Conservation Ethic," in *The Biophilia Hypothesis*, ed. Stephen Kellert and E.O. Wilson (Washington, D.C.: The Island Press, 1993).

[25] Kortright Davis, "Ecumenical Dialogue and Divine Racism," *The Journal of Religious Thought* 50 (Fall-Spring, 1993-1994): 67-68.

[26] Oren Lyons, "All My Relations: Perspectives from Indigenous Peoples," in *Cultural and Spiritual Values of Biodiversity*, 450-52.

[27] Leonardo Boff, *Ecology and Liberation: A New Paradigm* (Maryknoll: Orbis Books, 1995).

[28] Vandana Shiva, *Biopiracy: The Plunder of Nature and Knowledge* (Toronto: Between the Lines, 1997).

[29] Brian Swimme and Thomas Berry, *The Universe Story* (San Francisco: Harper and Row, 1992).

[30] A.M. Allchin, ed., *Landscapes of Glory: Daily Readings with Thomas Traherne* (Harrisburg: Morehouse Publishing, 1989), 27.

7
DEBT RELIEF
Giving Poor Countries a Second Chance

JOHN HAMMOCK AND
ANURADHA HARINARAYAN

INTRODUCTION[1]

C itizens of over forty countries in sub-Saharan Africa, Latin America, and Asia are suffering the impact of overwhelming and severe foreign and domestic debt. As a result of past events, their governments are now liable to pay between twenty to fifty percent of their earnings towards debt repayments.[2] It is now recognized that such unsustainable debt restricts a country's ability to grow out of poverty. As governments cut back on basic social services like primary education, health care, and infrastructure to service this growing debt, it undermines the safety nets available to the citizens in the country, and contributes directly to an increase in poverty and inequality. This is made evident from the statistics used to demonstrate the quality of life in countries around the world. For example, of the forty-four countries ranked in the "low human development" category according to the United Nations Development Program's Human Development Index, thirty are identified as Heavily Indebted by the World Bank. This group of Heavily Indebted Poor Countries (HIPC), as defined by the World Bank, has among the highest levels of under-five mortality rate, the lowest levels of primary school enrollment, and among the lowest rates of life expectancy.[3] Without doubt, the HIPCs suffer some of the deepest levels of deprivation in the world and this extends across all spheres—economic, social and political. (A list of Heavily Indebted Poor Countries can be found at the end of this chapter).

Within this global economic reality, the church has opted to stand with the poor, based on the Jubilee tradition found in the Bible. The church has argued for the need for debt forgiveness by rich nations in order to give the poor a second chance. This paper will lay out the position of the Anglican Communion and will end with a call for a prophetic role for the church in today's world economy. Before turning to the issue of debt and the response of the church, it is important to discuss the global context shaping this issue.

LIVING IN AN INCREASINGLY INTERDEPENDENT WORLD

Perhaps no single event has received as much attention in the past decade as globalization and the proliferation of free markets worldwide. The push for integrated world markets, trade agreements like the North America Free Trade Agreement (NAFTA), and the establishment of agencies like the World Trade Organization, are all a reflection of the prevailing orthodoxy that promotes capitalism and free markets as the only way forward in the new millennium. The cycle of market openness and free trade is seen as the engine of growth that stimulates domestic growth and leads the way out of poverty. The theory is that unregulated capitalism will not only be good for the wealthy, but eventually will help to pull the disadvantaged out of poverty.

It is important, however, to look more closely at the impact of globalization.

TRANSNATIONAL CORPORATIONS

Every day we hear of corporate mergers, not only of American companies joining forces, but of American companies merging with European or Japanese companies. Transnational corporations are getting larger. Some of the world's largest economies are now not governments, but transnational corporations. They have worldwide alliances and operations. Often these corporations can move their operations to cheaper countries that have fewer restrictive environmental, labor, and human rights laws. These transnational corporations can exert tremendous influence and pressure on poor governments, extracting tax holidays and other incentives to attract them to the country.

Transnational corporations defend their increased size and power by arguing that they are more efficient and produce cheaper goods, and compete more successfully against other large conglomerates. They create jobs and tax revenue and disseminate know-how and technology worldwide.

The trend to "bigger is better" has clear negative impacts, among them that smaller businesses are squeezed out, governments have less power to regulate these large conglomerates, and inequality is heightened through their salary structures and unequaled power. The theory of open markets and free trade is premised on competition to keep prices lower. Unfortunately, the growth in the size of conglomerates makes it more difficult to have competition, and drives smaller competitors out of the market.

The playing field for modern capitalism is not level. Large multinational Western corporations enter a poor economy, control international markets, have unlimited capital, and have the newest technology. It is difficult to believe that local enterprises would be able to compete effectively against these capitalist giants.

TECHNOLOGY

The modern world is characterized by intense change in the field of technology, primarily related to the information superhighway. The rise in e-commerce over the last couple of years is the latest manifestation of this change. The constant in today's world is change. Many of the technological advances of the last decade will be obsolete not only in our lifetime, but in the next decade. This technological revolution is increasing the disparity between those who have access to it and those who do not.

TRADE

The impact of rapid trade liberalization has been to increase the external deficit that developing countries currently face. This primarily is due to rapid decline in the terms of trade of these countries. In plain English, this means that developing countries are losing money when they import and export goods. The external deficit means that after all goods are sold overseas and all goods are bought from overseas, the balance will show in the red; they will have lost money. One of the main reasons for this loss is the decline in the terms of trade. For every unit of coffee, sugar, beef, peanuts or copper produced, the price in the international markets has been declining. This means that the producers of these basic commodities (mostly poor countries) make less money, though they produce more of the same product, because the price of that good is going down in relation to the other goods in the market. They can then purchase less with each unit of a raw material in any given year. While the unit price on the international market for these staple raw materials is going down, the unit price for luxury items (higher priced goods obtained by import) is going up in value. The Trade and Development report for 1999 provides ample statistics that support this trend. For example, while the share of primary commodities (produced mostly by poor countries) dropped below 20 percent in the world market, private consumption in the United States rose by over 400 million, more than twice the total annual income of sub-Saharan Africa.[4] The result is that over the last decade, developing countries have been subject to a growing trade deficit and cannot earn the dollars to pay off their debt.

STRUCTURAL ADJUSTMENT

Closely tied to the prevailing capitalist mantra of open markets and free trade has been the policy of structural adjustment. Structural adjustment has been the cornerstone of policies recommended by free market economists and advocated and imposed by the International Monetary Fund and the World Bank. Developing countries must play within the global economic rules laid down by agencies created during the aftermath of the Second World War. The International Monetary Fund helps to regulate and control worldwide monetary policy. The World Bank provides loans and resources for developing countries to stimulate economic development and growth. Both agencies have promoted the concept of structural adjustment. The World Bank has made the adoption of structural adjustment policies a condition for receiving World Bank loans.

In a nutshell, these policies have advocated for a reduction in government spending and interference in the private economy, and therefore, an increase in privatization of all sectors of the economy. This has meant that in order to get loans, governments have had to reduce their bureaucracies. Governments have done this by cutting back on their social spending in the education and health sectors. (Military spending is almost impossible to cut.) Governments have competed for transnational corporate investments by lowering the environmental and labor standards and adopting special-incentive policies to stimulate production for the export market. This has often led to a reduction in basic food production (rice and beans), and has stimulated food production for exports (coffee, cut flowers, cattle).

Structural adjustment policies have fed into globalization and the free-market economic model. Its supporters point to the growth of more efficient corporations, the growth of the modern economic sectors in places such as Chile. They point to a new dynamism in these economic sectors, to increased gross domestic and national product of some countries, to job creation and to the dynamic economic activity fueling unprecedented growth and prosperity in many parts of the world. Unfortunately, the picture is not all rosy worldwide. Before moving to a discussion of debt and debt relief, it is important to take a brief look at some of the consequences of globalization by looking at the characteristics of the current political economy.

CHARACTERISTICS OF THE CURRENT POLITICAL ECONOMY

INCREASING WEALTH, INCREASING POVERTY

Worldwide, the rich are getting richer. There are more rich people than ever before. There is more wealth being accumulated by more people than ever before. Alarmingly, however, there are more poor people and the gap between the two continues to grow. The growing gap can be witnessed within national economies, as well as between rich and poor countries.

INCREASED UNCERTAINTY

Even in wealthy countries, people with jobs are more insecure than in the past. People lose jobs as corporations downsize or move their operations overseas. People are nervous that their holdings in an ever-expanding stock market will disintegrate if the stock market collapses. It is an era of economic boom that is fueling widespread prosperity in wealthy countries, but there is increased psychological stress as economic uncertainty breeds insecurity.

INCREASED WAR

The past decade has seen the proliferation of internal wars in developing countries, particularly in Africa. These wars spawned complex emergencies that have led to increased military and humanitarian interventions. These wars are fueled by an explosion of arms trade, the collapse of Western geopolitical interests in these regions, and economic greed. Several countries deeply mired in debt suffer from internal wars.

A RISE IN FUNDAMENTALISM

The spread of the globalized economy as well as globalized culture has led to a strong reaction to these forces. The reactions have been varied. Some have reacted by turning to fundamentalist religion. The economic and social chaos is so life-threatening that people react by embracing a religious fundamentalism that makes sense of their lives. Others turn to their ethnicity, language, and culture to provide a sense of identity, pride, and security. Others challenge the whole theoretical premise on which globalization and the neo-liberal capitalist model is based. These critics look for capitalism with a human face, argue that smaller—not bigger—is better, and seek an alternative model of economic development. Many of these critics participated actively in the Seattle demonstrations against the World Trade Organization.

A CHALLENGE TO THE NATION STATE AND NATIONAL SOVEREIGNTY

The nation state is challenged by globalization and by a rise in fundamentalism. On the one hand transnational corporations work at the global level. They move capital from country to country with little regard to nationalism; they look for ways to increase corporate profits, with little or no regard of the impact on nations. With their power and prestige they challenge and thwart national laws. On the other hand, ethnic, religious, and cultural groups challenge the nation state to allow more independence, more autonomy. Witness Quebec or the former Yugoslavia; witness Indonesia or Sudan. The economic and political world system that was structured around nation states at the end of the Second World War is crumbling.

The problem of unsustainable debt is intrinsically linked to many of the social and political characteristics described above. In the face of increasing competition and pressure to participate in the global economy, poorer countries have to deal with the insurmountable challenges of human and capital resources. As the following section indicates, unsustainable debt exacerbates this problem, further alienating these countries and reducing their prospects for growth and development. Given our increasing interdependence, it is in the interest of the rich nations to forgive unsustainable debt so that these extremely poor countries have a second chance to rebuild their economies and create wealth for their citizens.

MONEY SUPPLY AND CONTROL OF RESOURCES

WHAT IS DEBT?

We all know what debt is. If I lend you $1.00 for one month, I may lend it to you by charging you interest. If I charge you 10 percent simple interest, at the end of the month you will have to pay me $1.10. You now owe me $1.10; you are in debt to me by that amount. If you pay me back the full $1.10, then the loan is cancelled. If, at the end of the month, you pay me all or a portion of the interest that I charged you, but did not pay back the principal ($1.00), then you continue to be in my debt. You are servicing this debt by paying the interest. Of course, every month that you do not pay, I still charge you an extra 10 percent on the balance that you owe me. So, for example, if you pay back only five cents of the interest, then I will charge you 10 percent not only on the $1.00 that you still owe me, but now also on the $.05 of unpaid interest. Over time, this original $1.00 loan may grow substantially because of your inability to pay it off in a timely manner. This is the exact same principle that applies to debt in developing countries. Often countries will pay part or all of the interest due, thus keeping bankers and financial institutions happy. But all this payment does not reduce the original debt at all. If you do not pay off all the interest, the debt continually grows.

THIRD WORLD DEBT: WHY DID IT HAPPEN, TO WHOM ARE THEY INDEBTED?

In the 1960s and 1970s, loans were made to developing countries, spurred by optimistic development thinking that postulated that through investments, many of these countries could experience an economic takeoff. At times loans were made for political reasons—either to stop communism or demonstrate that a non-communist country was a better alternative to communism. Even when loans were not repaid, they were refinanced and incorporated into larger loans. In some countries, ruthless dictators amassed fortunes from these loans. Corruption ran rampant, and there was little political accountability within the developing countries for the massive future debt being incurred by the political leaders.

The 1960s and 1970s also saw many developing countries trying to develop through a policy called import substitution. This meant trying to develop local businesses to manufacture goods locally rather than importing them. This meant allocating more resources into building local factories and manufacturing capabilities. And yet, often these countries had no comparative economic advantage in these areas and could not compete in the globalized world.

The debt crisis in the 1980s was primarily viewed as a liquidity crisis, and multilateral and bilateral credit agencies mostly resolved the issues through short-term, non-concessional debt relief. In other words, lenders took short-term measures to ensure that the countries in debt could pay some of the interest on the loans, but holding on to the idea that the loan would be paid eventually. The primary aim of the credit agencies was to maintain the debt-servicing capacity of debtor nations. Macro economic stabilization, combined with controlled government expenditure, was seen as the solution to the problem. Through export-led growth, as described in the previous section, debtor countries were drawn into agreements that focused on debt servicing rather than resolving the underlying issue of debt repayment. While there was some consensus, even as early as the 1980s, that the strategy was not working, little was done to fix the problem. In Africa, the heavily indebted countries continued under the stranglehold of structural adjustment, as poor citizens suffered the consequences of declining public expenditure and falling real incomes. With declining exports, countries were forced to reduce the essential imports required to facilitate domestic growth, declining capacity and reducing investment in the country. Meanwhile the stock of debt[5] doubled over the period 1982-87, as current claims for repayments were rescheduled under the new adjustment policies.

WHAT DEBT DOES

"Should we really let our children starve, so we can pay our debts?"
— Julius Nyerere, President of Tanzania, 1980s[6]

One of the strongest reasons for canceling Third World debt is the severe damage that debt servicing has caused to human development. Not only are heavily indebted countries unable to mobilize human and capital resources to break out of the cycle of poverty and achieve internationally agreed-upon development goals, they are also rapidly losing many of the gains made in the last decades. The human development indicators for these countries are alarming:

- Average life expectancy is 51 years. This is 12 years less than in the developing countries as a group, and 26 years less than in the industrialized countries.

- The under-five mortality rate averages 156 per 1,000 live births. This translates into 3.4 million deaths annually, most of them resulting from infectious diseases, which could be averted through low-cost interventions.

- There are some 47 million primary school-aged children out of school—more than one third of the total worldwide. The majority of these children are girls. More than a third of the children who start school drop out before having gained basic literacy skills.[7]

In addition, about half of the citizens in these countries live below the one-dollar-a-day income poverty line. But perhaps even more distressing is that for a billion people, development is being thrown into reverse. After decades of steady economic advance, large areas of the world are sliding back into poverty and deprivation. In the heavily indebted countries, health systems are being stretched to a breaking point, as new threats like HIV/AIDS have emerged. Citizens from these countries account for most of the 5,500 AIDS-related deaths that occur every day. An estimated 10 percent of the children have lost one or both parents. The consequence of such threats in already impoverished societies is devastating. For example, in Zambia, where over half a million children are out of school and illiteracy is rising, debt servicing claims more of the national budget than health and education combined.

These extremely high rates of debt servicing are true for most of the thirty countries classified as severely indebted low-income countries, twenty-five of which are in the sub-Saharan Africa. For example in Ethiopia, where over 100,000 children die annually from easily preventable diseases, debt payments are four times more than public spending on health care. The same is true in Tanzania, where despite 40 percent of its citizens dying before the age of 35, debt payments remain six times higher than the spending on health care. The crushing effect of debt servicing on health has a downward spiraling effect, resulting in lower productivity, reduced capacity for growth, and more poverty—and hence decline in government revenues to repay debts, often leading to an increase of the debt burden.

The Heavily Indebted Poor Countries (HIPC) Initiative

Because debt kept growing in the poorest countries, a number of schemes were made available to individual countries to assist them with their debt repayment options. But none of them was comprehensive. Even as late as 1993, the International Money Fund and World Bank claimed that there was no real issue for consideration and there were no reasons to reassess the debt service options. The solution to the problem was still assumed to be the refinancing of debt, not its cancellation. However, at the behest of bilateral donors who were becoming increasingly worried about the preferential status of multilateral creditors, there was a comprehensive review of the debt situation in 1995. The Heavily Indebted Poor Country (HIPC) Initiative was born from that process.

HIPC brought together the industrialized countries and other bilateral and multilateral organizations to find ways of resolving unsustainable debt and give these most heavily indebted countries a second chance. However, while there has been general agreement about the need for assistance, there has been little consensus about the modalities and nature of assistance required to make a difference. The initial HIPC framework adopted in 1996 provided a comprehensive and integrated framework, extended debt reduction to multilateral creditors, and provided a basis for reducing debt obligations. This program required countries in debt to meet very stringent conditions in order to receive assistance. There were three thresholds for participating in the program, two tied to exports and the other to fiscal measures. The

HIPC process was subject to strengthened conditionality, with debtors required to adhere to two consecutive IMF structural adjustment programs over a six-year period in order to qualify. These conditions were imposed on the debtor nations and effectively excluded their participation. Very few countries were able to take advantage of this initiative that was supposed to reduce debt. Instead, the program came under increasing attack for being too little too late, for being in the hands of technocrats, for adherence to unrealistic time frames and stages, for not linking debt relief to poverty reduction, and for not viewing debt relief within a broader context of development.

By 1998, six countries had begun to benefit: Uganda, Bolivia, Guayana, Burkina Faso, Côte d'Ivoire, and Mozambique. But the case of Uganda, the first country to pass through the HIPC framework, is instructive. In 1999, collapsing world coffee prices meant that Uganda no longer met one of the criteria for participation. Debt relief needed to be far deeper in countries dependent on a narrow range of export commodities.

How Much Will Debt Relief Cost?

The cost of debt relief to the creditor nations and the multilateral organizations has been the subject of much debate. Economists and policy makers have argued over the methodology to calculate the total cost of a debt-reduction program such as the World Bank's Heavily Indebted Poor Country (HIPC) Initiative.

In the current World Bank framework for debt relief, the Bank identifies eligible countries, undertakes a country-specific debt-sustainability analysis and then designs a debt-relief plan. Within this framework the total costs for the HIPC Initiative (for 32 countries deemed eligible) will be an estimated US $26.6 billion.[8] With regard to implications for overall debt reduction, a rough estimate suggests that after HIPC and traditional debt relief, the net-present value of public debt in those 33 countries—presently estimated at about $90 billion—would be reduced by about half. This enhanced HIPC framework for debt relief, though more comprehensive than others in the past, will only minimally cancel unsustainable debt after the country undergoes structural changes and makes policy reforms. In other words, these countries will still have a serious debt problem.

The Jubilee 2000 and coalition of Non-Governmental Organizations, on the other hand, are calling for an unconditional cancellation of all Third World debt, and they estimate that it would cost approximately $75 billion to cancel all the debts owed by 52 of the poorest countries in the world.[9] These activists also point out that if all the countries on the current HIPC list were to repay their debts at the HIPC "sustainable" level, then the creditors would profit by $1.2 billion per year. This is because HIPC countries are only paying 55 percent of their debt service at present, while the initiative will require a complete payment of all "sustainable" debt over a period of time. They add that the costs of the HIPC Initiative is therefore only nominal, as it is merely a cost of writing off debts which would never be paid in the first place. The coalition calculates that the cost of debt relief, if poor countries are to achieve the human development goals for 2021, needs to be much deeper and faster and should be combined with effective development aid to the tune of US $12 billion. Their calculations are summarized in this table:

	Number of Countries	Cost $ bn/yr
Can pay debt service	27	0
Need reduction but not to HIPC levels	4	7
Reduction to HIPC	39	32
Further reduction	62	36
TOTAL DEBT SERVICE CUTS NEEDED	132	75

As the members of the Jubilee 2000 point out, "(t)here can be endless discussions about the validity of our assumptions and estimates, but what cannot be contested is that they show a need for debt cancellation going far beyond anything offered by creditors so far."[10]

OPTIONS FOR ACTION

A number of strategies are available to deal with the problem of debt. First, and the most radical, would be a simple forgiveness of debt. In this case, creditors would cancel debt with no strings attached. This option is not favored by most of the creditors or by many of the actors dealing with international development. However, in extreme situations, such as countries recovering from Hurricane Mitch, creditor governments have adopted this strategy. Second, debt forgiveness can be tied to strict economic conditions. Debtor countries would follow policies similar to the HIPC agreement, whereby countries would have to undertake macroeconomic structural adjustment policies, including increasing exports, decreasing public expenditure and increasing privatization. This policy has meant that very few countries have qualified for debt forgiveness, leading to a broad chorus of complaints not only from debtor countries but also from development agencies, churches, and other groups.

The third strategy, which has now gained some acceptance, is to establish a debt-relief or debt-cancellation and poverty-reduction program, linking debt forgiveness to a poverty-reduction plan. Eligibility for participation in this program would be the capacity of the debtor economy to absorb the savings of the debt reduction into national poverty reduction strategies. In other words, should debt be forgiven, does the country have a plan and the economic capacity to put these funds to use to develop anti-poverty or poverty reduction programs? In this case, eligibility would no longer be tied to economic indicators, and compliance would not be tied to compliance with structural adjustment programs. The program would move away from stringent economic conditionality. Conditionality would, instead, be the ability to absorb the funding made available by debt reduction into poverty-reduction schemes.

In this scenario, debt relief is seen as a financing mechanism for closing the gap between current extreme poverty and projected anti-poverty targets. Debt relief becomes a way of investing in the debtor country. For example, funds that the country would have used to pay off the interest and the loans to the creditor countries would now be used to fund a poverty-reduction scheme. In this strategy it is also important that, parallel to this debt reduction scheme, traditional development aid not be cut. Should it be cut, funds released by debt forgiveness would not be additional funds; rather, they would go to replace development funds and there would be no additional impact on poverty reduction.

The debt-for-development plan not only provides investment resources to help reduce poverty in the debtor country, it also insures the credit-worthiness of the country in that the debt is being repaid. The amount due of debt is being repaid in poverty-reduction schemes rather than in money transfers to creditors. This understanding is important to deal with the argument that these poor countries are "getting off the hook" with debt forgiveness. Governments would still have to invest the funds they would have paid in debt reduction into poverty alleviation.[11]

At a conference convened by the Global Coalition on Africa, ten principles on debt cancellation were agreed to. These principles call for debt cancellation to be untied from strict economic indicators and structural adjustment conditionalities. They tie debt cancellation to the preparation in these countries of social-action strategies to help meet the urgent human needs of their societies, and to policies dealing with corruption and the maintenance of a stable economic environment. They also called for not using debt reduction as an excuse for reducing concessional aid to these countries.[12]

POLITICAL ACTIVISM—JUBILEE 2000

Support for debt relief and cancellation grew throughout the 1990s to include a broad coalition of churches, non-governmental organizations, academics, and foreign governments. Taking its cue from the movement to ban landmines, this coalition built worldwide support for debt cancellation. Churches and non-profits mobilized their members. As debt continued to pile up, more and more people called for action.

In May of 1999, the Jubilee 2000 coalition undertook a massive demonstration simultaneously with a meeting of the Group of Eight (the world's most powerful economies) in England. More than 50,000 people joined hands in a human chain in Birmingham with plans to circle the Birmingham International Conference. In the end, "the human chain was not a circle but more of a wonky parallelogram."[13] The *Guardian* ran daily articles supporting debt cancellation and attacking the British government for not listening. The *Guardian* called for "a Big Bang of debt forgiveness."[14]

Jubilee 2000 complemented its public protests with direct advocacy to policy makers and leaders of international agencies. World Bank President Wolfensohn opened a dialogue on debt with religious leaders, including the Archbishop of Canterbury and representatives of Christian, Hindu, Jewish, Muslim and Orthodox groups.[15] Pressure was brought to bear on key governments, especially the United States, the United Kingdom, and Germany.

THE U.S. GOVERNMENT AND THE G-7

> I believe the American people to be loving and compassionate. I believe that if they knew about the conditions in your country, they'd say, "Forgive the debt." But they don't know. They know who's the No.1 football team. They know who won the fight in Las Vegas. But they don't know what you are going through. I didn't even know.
> — Rep. Spencer Bachus, October 1999[16]

With growing support for the issue of debt relief and intense lobbying and political activism by Jubilee 2000, the U.S. and the other G-7 governments met in Cologne in June 1999 specifically to discuss the issue of debt. The economic powers pledged US $100 billion of debt relief without any agreement about how and when the money was to be made available. With pressure mounting on this issue, there has been growing bipartisan support for meaningful debt relief in the U.S., and funds for debt reduction became a critical part of budget negotiations between President Clinton and Congress in the fall of 1999. The final budget produced an agreement on the following terms:

- Cancel 100 percent of bilateral debts owed to the U.S. by countries that qualify under a previously passed bill. (HR 1095–Debt relief for poverty reduction act)[17]

- Provide US $123 million for debt forgiveness to promote economic and environmental reform in countries. Of the total, US $110 million will fund the bilateral debt cancellation for eligible countries.

Analysts, however, point out that the budget makes no provision in terms of authorizing language for money to fund a U.S. contribution to the HIPC/Cologne Trust fund to pay for the multilateral debt cancellation. Instead, the budget authorizes the International

Monetary Fund to use its own resources to reduce the debts owed to it. While cancellation of bilateral debt is certainly a step forward, it fails to address the core issue of multilateral debt. Unless there is a greater and faster effort undertaken by the G-7, as Pope John Paul II correctly said, *"It is the poor who pay the cost of indecision and delay."*[18]

DEBT AND THE CHURCH

The church has called for total debt cancellation based on the Old Testament concept of the year of Jubilee, explained in the book of Leviticus. "You shall count off seven weeks of years, seven times seven years, so that the period ... gives forty-nine years ... and you shall hallow the fiftieth year and you shall proclaim liberty throughout the land to all its inhabitants" (Lev. 25:8,10). In that year of Jubilee, debts are to be forgiven; no interest will be charged to the poor.[19]

The Anglican Communion has worked to focus on this issue within its own structures, within ecumenical bodies, and within the broad Jubilee 2000 coalition. It has been an important player in the international mobilization for debt relief.

The Lambeth Conference back in 1988 passed a Resolution (#36) on poverty and debt. Among other things, that resolution called on national governments, transnational corporations, the International Monetary Fund and the World Bank together to consider:

> (b) offering relief from debt incurred with commercial banks in ways that will not leave debtor economies vulnerable to foreign manipulation by:
>
> > (i) lending directly to developing countries at reduced and subsidized interest rates
> >
> > (ii) improved rescheduling of existing debt repayments
> >
> > (iii) debt conversion arrangements
> >
> > (iv) establishing a multilateral body to co-ordinate debt relief
>
> (c) offering relief from official debts incurred with the World Bank and the International Monetary Fund through:
>
> > (i) improved rescheduling of existing debt repayment
> >
> > (ii) lending on conditions oriented to development objectives
> >
> > (iii) refraining from making demands on debtor countries which would endanger the fabric of their national life or cause further dislocation to their essential human services.[20]

But this was not enough. In the ten years leading up to Lambeth 1998, the voices of the Anglican Communion became sharper. The Episcopal Church in the United States worked with the Religious Working Group to launch a call to action. This Group has consistently called for:

- Cancellation of debt in countries burdened with high levels of human need
- Cancellation of debt that benefits ordinary people
- Debt cancellation that is not conditioned on policy reforms that perpetuate or deepen poverty
- Acknowledgment of responsibility to recover resources that were diverted to corrupt regimes
- Establishment of a transparent and participatory process to monitor and prevent recurring destructive cycles of indebtedness.[21]

While American church action was important, leadership within the Anglican Communion came primarily from Southern bishops. The First Article in 1997 "Report of the Second Anglican Encounter in the South" prepared in Kuala Lumpur, Malaysia, by eighty bishops and church leaders from the southern hemisphere decries "the crippling effect of international debt"

> and calls on the churches of the West to put pressure on their governments and on the World Bank and the IMF to respond to the many appeals coming from various quarters worldwide, to make the year 2000 a Year of Jubilee, to remit the Two Thirds World debt.[22]

This position was in keeping with ecumenical pronouncements on debt.[23] For example, the All Africa Council of Churches stated:

> With regard to the debt burden, we recommend a strong campaign for debt cancellation, collaborating with organizations already committed to this campaign based on the following conditions: true democratization, respect for human rights, demilitarization, [and] redirecting money thus saved for the benefit of the so-called ordinary people.[24]

In the Anglican Communion the Primate of Southern Africa, the Most Rev. Njongonkulu Ndungane, became a leading spokesperson on debt cancellation.[25] Early on, he called for the eradication of foreign debt of developing countries and worked to make this a central issue on the Lambeth agenda in 1998.

At Lambeth in 1998 debt relief was taken up as a major issue for discussion once again. The resolution adopted at the Conference has set the agenda for action in the new millennium. The Archbishop of Canterbury publicly proclaimed the need for debt cancellation. "The biggest and most crippling burden that the Third World countries have are the massive debts, which are totally unpayable and which engulf millions of people in slavery no less real than the terrible Atlantic trade of the early nineteenth century."[26]

Bishops from southern hemisphere countries made debt cancellation a top priority of the meeting. The 1998 Lambeth resolution on debt recognized the importance and urgency of international debt and economic justice and its support for debt relief is unequivocal. The resolutions issued are quite clear about the options for action:

> We see the issue of international debt and economic justice in the light of our belief in creation ... and the pattern of giving which God desires all to follow. Borrowing has its place only in as much as it releases growth for human well-being. When we ignore this pattern, money becomes a force that destroys human community and God's creation.
>
> • We conclude that substantial debt relief including cancellation of unplayable debts of the poorest nations under an independent, fair and transparent process, is a necessary, while not sufficient precondition for freeing these nations, and their people, from the hopeless downward spiral of poverty.
>
> • We welcome the HIPC initiative, the approach of bringing all creditors together to agree upon debt relief, the emphasis on debtor participation and the unilateral initiative taken by governments to write off some loans.
>
> • While recognizing these achievements, we wish to assert that these measures do not as yet provide sufficient release of ... (s)carce resources.[27]

The resolution further calls on political, corporate, and church leaders and on the people of the creditor nations to hasten the process of debt relief through an independent, transparent process by:

- accepting equal dignity for debtor nations in negotiations over loan agreements and debt relief;
- ensuring that the legislatures of lending nations have the right to scrutinize taxpayer subsidized loans and hold to account government-financed creditors, including the multilateral financial institutions, for lending decisions;
- introducing measures that will enable debtor nations to trade fairly with creditor nations.

It also calls for the establishment of a Mediation Council, under the direction of the United Nations, that will respond to appeals from debtor nations, assess the nature and severity of debt, and ensure that current and future policies prioritize basic human development needs with greater emphasis on poverty-reduction strategies.

At Lambeth, the Anglican Communion acted decisively to support debt cancellation. It must continue to take a prophetic stance on debt relief, based on the concept of Jubilee. In the postmodern world, the Anglican Communion needs to continue to drop the vestiges of colonialism and Western domination. It needs to take a leadership role in advocating not just for human rights, but for human responsibilities; not just for religious and spiritual freedom, but also for economic opportunity.

The cancellation of debt will not, in itself, solve the problems in the poorest countries. It is but one step to be taken in helping the poorest have a second chance. Anglicanism needs to embrace a global ethic that focuses on responsible economics, based on common ethical values shared by the Anglican community worldwide.

The Anglican Communion needs to represent the values and positions of its broad constituency by reflecting, understanding and advocating on the main issues confronting the postmodern world, such as transnational corporations, technology, trade, and structural adjustment. Anglicans must clearly understand the current political economy and speak out on the increasing poverty worldwide, the increase of war, the rise of fundamentalism, and the impact of the collapse of the nation state on religious and spiritual freedom.

CONCLUSION AND SOME REFLECTIONS

The postmodern world is a world in crisis. This is the time for the church to play a leadership role in advocating for the poor. It is a time for the prophetic voice of the church to be heard. The growing Third World composition of the membership of the Anglican Communion needs not only to be responsive to, but also to take a leadership role in addressing the needs of this constituency.

Within this reality, the Anglican Communion should continue to mobilize its constituency and world opinion for the program of debt cancellation and debt relief. Though the specifics can be quite complex, the general position is quite clear:

- Debt cancellation should not be tied to stringent economic performance, structural adjustment, export levels or any other economic prerequisite.

- In countries affected by conflict or devastating natural disas-ters such as Hurricane Mitch, debt should be cancelled outright. This means not just canceling debt servicing or interest on the debt, but the principal (initial amount loaned) itself.

- For the Heavily Indebted Poor Countries (HIPC), debt cancel-lation should take place on the condition of the establishment of a social-action strategy or a debt-for-development strategy that transfers the debt owed to foreign entities into national devel-opment programs assisting the poor. Such a strategy would set out measures to address human needs, establish monitoring mechanisms that are verifiable, and include intermediate targets for the use of funds released by debt cancellation. Governments would then still have to invest the funds they would have paid in debt reduction into poverty alleviation.

- Debt cancellation should not be taken as an opportunity for reduced aid or future flows of concessional aid.

- The church should press for the completion of the debt-can-cellation process for qualifying countries.

The West is experiencing a healthy, strong economic boom. U.S. government debt is being paid off at striking rates due to staggering budget surpluses. The same economic resurgence is not taking place in those countries suffering from massive debt. It is time for the world to adopt a system that gives poor countries a second chance. The prophetic church must be at the forefront of this effort.

REFLECTIONS: DEBT IN THE UNITED STATES

In 1994, the Episcopal General Convention resolved that "the Episcopal Church prepare for this Jubilee year by seeking to implement the biblical imperative of debt forgiveness by: "Participating in the development of sound financial plans for the reduction and cancellation of debt owed by the poor in our own society." The Jubilee 2000 campaign and the Anglican Communion have focused their attention on the cancellation of international debt, particularly on debt owed by the Heavily Indebted Poor Countries. The biblical concept of Jubilee, however, did not extend exclusively to debts owed by foreigners or to debt owed by those far away. Jubilee extends the forgiveness of debt to those in our own congregation and within our own societies. Within the United States, the Episcopal Church provides loans to churches in poor communities and holds them to strict repayment schedules. If there is room for forgiveness of international debt, there must be room to explore forgiveness of debt to our poor congregations as well.

It is always more difficult to implement policies that hit close to home rather than those whose impact is felt far away. The Anglican and Episcopal churches need to review the debt structure of the poor in their own communities and advocate for debt relief, not just within their own congregations, but also for the impoverished in their societies. Credit is often not available, or, when it is, is given at astronomically high interest rates. If it is serious about the concept of the Jubilee year, the Anglican Communion must also look into the structures of debt owed by the poor in Western countries and by its own congregations. A prophetic church would also develop plans and advocate for the reduction and/or cancellations of these debts.

The biblical concept of Jubilee was applicable to individuals, not just nations or congregations. Individuals who had much should share. Individuals who had surplus should give it away. Individuals who owed debt should be forgiven. The prophetic position of the Anglican Communion should also reach out to the individual members of its congregations. They should be asked to reflect on the tradition of Jubilee and asked to implement these strategies on a family and personal level.

The true meaning of Jubilee does not extend only to debts owed by the Heavily Indebted Poor Countries. The concepts apply within our own country and across the Anglican Communion.

HEAVILY INDEBTED POOR COUNTRIES (HIPC)

AFRICAN COUNTRIES

Angola
Benin
Burkina Faso
Burundi
Cameroon
Central African Republic
Chad
Congo
Côte d'Ivoire
Democratic Republic of Congo
Equatorial Guinea
Ethiopia
Ghana
Guinea
Guinea-Bissau
Kenya
Liberia
Madagascar
Mali
Mauritania
Mozambique
Niger
Nigeria
Rwanda
Sao Tome and Principe
Senegal
Sierra Leone
Somalia
Sudan
Tanzania
Togo
Uganda
Zambia

LATIN AMERICAN COUNTRIES

Bolivia
Guyana

Honduras
Nicaragua

ASIAN COUNTRIES
Laos
Myanmar (Burma)
Vietnam

MIDDLE EAST
Republic of Yemen

NOTES

[1] The authors want to thank Sarah Curie for her research on debt that contributed to this article.

[2] *From Unsustainable Debt to Poverty Reduction: Reforming the Heavily Indebted Poor Countries Initiative* (prepared by Oxfam GB Policy Department for UNICEF, August, 1999).

[3] Ibid.

[4] Overview, *Trade and Development Report,* United Nations Conference on Trade and Development, 1999.

[5] Debt stock indicators capture the accumulated burden of debt on the economy.

[6] *From Unsustainable Debt to Poverty Reduction: Reforming the Heavily Indebted Poor Countries Initiative.*

[7] For more information on the impact of debt servicing on human needs and development see, among others, a position paper by UNICEF and Oxfam International, "Debt Relief and Poverty Reduction: Meeting the Challenge"(paper resented at a World Bank Conference in Addis Ababa, July 1999).

[8] This is indicated in Net Present Value terms. NPV of debt is a sum of all future debt service obligations (interest and principal) on existing debt, discounted at the market interest rate. For more information, see Alex Van Trotenburg and Alan MacArthur, "The HIPC Initiative: Delivering Debt Relief to Poor Countries" (February, 1999); available from http://www.worldbank.org/hipc.

[9] See the Jubilee 2000 web site http://www.jubilee2000.org.

[10] What will it cost to cancel unpayable debt? Jubilee 2000, http://www.jubilee2000.org

[11] See position paper by UNICEF and Oxfam International, "Debt Relief and Poverty Reduction: Meeting the Challenge."

[12] The principles were agreed at a conference convened by the Global Coalition on Africa and Harvard University Center for International Development on 24-25 September, 1999. See www.cid.harvard.edu/cidhipc/tenPr.htm.

[13] "Gangrene of Debt: Time for Radical Solution," *The Guardian*, 18 May 1998; available from http://reports.guardian.co.uk/debt/news/19980515-10.html.

[14] Ibid.

[15] James Solhiem, "Religious Leaders Discuss Development Issues with the World Bank," *Episcopal News Service*, 3 April 1998.

[16] "GOP's Bachus Makes Debt Relief his Mission," *Washington Post*, 9 October 1999, Sec A, p. 3.

[17] For more information on this bill and other bills that address debt relief, see "Comparative Analysis of Several Debt Relief Bills;" available from http://www.J2000usa.org or the U.S. Senate web site, http://thomas.loc.gov/cp106/cp106query.html.

[18] *From Unsustainable Debt to Poverty Reduction: Reforming the Heavily Indebted Poor Countries Initiative.*

[19] For a closer look at the Sabbath Economics of the Old Testament, see Ched Myers, "God Speed the Year of the Jubilee," *Sojourners*, May-June 1998, 24.

[20] For more on the Resolutions of Lambeth 1998, see Report on "Christianity and the Social Order," para. 73.

[21] See Marie Dennis, "For a Dignified Life," *Sojourners*, May-June 1998, 30.

[22] Ian T. Douglas, "Lambeth 1998 and the 'New Colonialism'," *The Witness* 81:5 (May 1998): 8.

[23] For a concise position of the Catholic Conference of the United States and Catholic Relief Services, see Testimony of Most Reverend Theodore E. McCarrick, Archbishop of Newark and Most Reverend John H. Ricard, SSJ, Bishop of Pensacola-Tallahassee before the House Committee on Banking and Financial Services, 15 June 1999; available from http://www.cid.harvard.edu/cid-hipc.

[24] All Africa Conference of Churches, 7th Central Assembly, October, 1997.

[25] Read more on the role of the African church on http://www.fundy.com/churces/anglican/news/south_africa.html

[26] "International Debt Central Issue as Jubilee 2000 Looms," *Episcopal Life,* June 1998, 7.

[27] For more details, see Resolution I.15, International Debt and Economic Justice, at the 1998 Lambeth Conference home page, http://www.anglicancommunion.org/lambeth/1/sect1rpt.html.

8
POWER, BLESSINGS, AND HUMAN SEXUALITY
Making the Justice Connections

RENÉE L. HILL

- *Sherrice Iverson—eight-year-old African-American girl child sexually assaulted and murdered in a Las Vegas casino.*
- *Mathew Shepherd—a young, white gay man tortured and beaten. Murdered in Laramie, Wyoming.*
- *James Byrd, Jr.—forty-three-year-old African-American man dragged to his death, chained behind a pickup truck in Jasper, Texas.*
- *Billy Jack Gaither, Hattie Mae Cohens, Brian Mock, Alan Schindler, Amadou Diallo.*[1]

In preparing this essay, in my thinking about inclusion, justice, and blessing, I have not been able to keep these people out of my mind, these targets of hate crimes in the United States. I keep them in my prayers. I hold in my memory these victims of crimes that manifest the violence and symbolize the fear and rejection of difference in our culture. As we make our plans to turn the church toward justice in relation to gay men and lesbians, we do so in the cultural/social atmosphere that has called these crimes into being. We live in a cultural/social atmosphere in which racism, sexism, heterosexism, classism, ableism, continue to thrive and continue to shape and define our culture, including the culture of the church, in new and different ways. It is important to locate ourselves in an ever-changing contemporary context. It is essential that we ground our calls for justice not in abstractions, but in real life-and-death situations. We cannot do our work and speak as if wars are not raging, as if children are not starving, as if global economic chaos is not threatening the well-being of millions, as if AIDS and cancer did not continue to devastate individuals and communities. We cannot work for gospel justice without being affected by the challenges to thinking, being and acting that are required by our postcolonial and postmodern realities. To work for and speak about justice for lesbians and gay men in the church is to work and speak in this complex and challenging global social/cultural and political environment. We remind ourselves about this complexity not necessarily to solve all the world's crises, but to somehow ensure that our talk of and work for blessing, justice, and change is connected to all that is happening in the world. Our being the church, as individuals, as couples, as families, as communities must be rooted in the broad and real context of human life. Our being the whole living body of Christ must mean the commitment to manifest that body in the whole life of the world.

There is a desire in some parts of this culture/society, and in some congregations, to "simplify" our lives. We want to make our lives more simple, uncluttered, easier to manage. We believe that having fewer material possessions means less anxiety to accumulate and manage. What I am proposing is that the same impulse toward simplicity will not be effective in our work for justice for ourselves and for all people. In spite of wanting to be simple beings with uncomplicated lives, the truth is that we live in great complexity, movement, ambiguity and constant change. As an African-American lesbian priest in the Episcopal Church USA, I know that it is not simple. Life is not simple. The church is not simple. Our call to be agents of God's freedom and peace is not simple.

From where I stand, life, politics and spirituality are at the same time wonderfully and frustratingly complicated. I am an African-American who worships in a denomination that, in this country, is still predominately white. I am a woman serving in a church in which male power still dominates. I am a lesbian serving in a denomination that is still debating the worthiness of my being and the legitimacy of my family. I have given years of my time, talent, energy and focus to an institutional church in which my existence for some is a strange aberration or a horrible mistake. For others, my work and ministry as a priest, scholar, theologian, and teacher is some exaggerated sign of eschatological hope. (I cannot tell you how many times I have been told that Jesus is coming back as a black lesbian.) For each of us, more important than the exaggerations of friends or foes is our own groundedness in our baptisms and in the body of Christ. I claim the church as mine in spite of the multidimensional oppression that weakens it. I do not seek *inclusion* in the church because I know that by virtue of my baptism, I *am* the church. This is powerful, transforming knowledge. This is a powerful and transforming claim, a claim and a reality that is *most* frightening to some.

However, transforming knowledge is not the same as a transformed church. I am well aware of the church's acts of injustice and attempts at exclusion. I am equally aware of oppression and injustice as it is manifested in the wider society. It is always interesting to me that I am often counseled to leave the church, as if leaving would somehow shield me from the complex design of oppression that I was born into, that all of us are born into, not because of who we are, but because of the way that the world is set up. I also find it interesting that I have never been counseled to leave this country, to go into exile in a place that might be more hospitable. Even if I had been counseled to leave, the reality is that there really are no "safe" or uncontested places in which to hide. I do believe that there are places of rest and comfort, and I believe that some of them can even be found in the church. For now I choose to remain in the institution, to stake my claim and to *be* the church. I see this choice as part of a vision of God's love and freedom in both the church and the world.

In talk about justice-making in the church, I want to do away with the language of "inclusion" altogether. The idea of "inclusion" implies an acceptance of clear dividing lines and impermeable boundaries as markers that define "the church." This way of thinking portrays the "church" only in its most stilted institutional form, bricks and mortar and bureaucracy. It does not lend itself to an understanding of a living body of Christ, a dynamic ecclesiology that is in constant transformation in response to the suffering of the world. The language of "inclusion" and "exclusion" also lends itself to the worst kind of reformist theology and politics. The reality is that the inclusion of marginalized people in the church does not ensure the transformation of the church. Too often inclusion without transformation only means a different form of oppression for those who are asked to pay the price of silence and invisibility, all in the name of Christian unity. Reformist moves that do not invite critical questions about structures, governance, theologies, and liturgical practices are not likely to invite or welcome the potentially transformative presence of marginalized people. Indeed, one powerful way to neutralize the voices and actions of those outside of what and who is accepted as "the norm" is to co-opt through promises of inclusion. Those in positions of authority are happy to include "others" as long as they promise to be "just like" the dominant group. In this instance "inclusion" means erasure.

In addition, for many, the idea of being "in" or "out" of the church is antithetical to the multiple realities that most people live in. Many of us are simultaneously "inside" and "outside" of the institutional church rejoicing with some practices and policies, struggling with others, all the time faithfully showing up again and again to be challenged and comforted at the altar. Many of us have to work hard to walk in the sometimes divergent worlds that define our races, ethnicities and cultures, and that of the hegemonic anglo culture that still dominates the Episcopal Church's landscape. We are hybrid Anglicans who find power and meaning in the hyphenated places of our names. We recognize that our races, ethnicity, gender, sexual orientation are critical resources for defining our theopolitical ideas and practices.

Instead of the dialectical language of "inclusion/exclusion," we must talk about and act out of nurturing, just, emancipatory practices that will bring about a transformed church. We need to have a vision of a church rooted in freedom, compassion and justice. We must develop a process for getting there. Self-reflection and self-critique must be part of our emancipatory practice, part of our vision, part of our process. An important question is, Are *we* willing to be shaped by our own emancipatory practices? This is the risky business of admitting that we do not know all of the

answers and that we are in constant need of God's freeing and forgiving power. In talking about justice-making, we in the church
need to bypass reform in favor of radical transformation and
dynamic change.

One such emancipatory practice is to make a claim on what
already is ours by virtue of our baptism. We need to live as a
church already transformed. We need to practice the Christian
reality of the "not yet" *and* the "already." These are not independent, dualistic categories but *interdependent* signposts in the ongoing process of relationships that we have with God and with one
another. The kingdom of God, what I like to call "the freedom of
God," has not yet come, and yet, it is already here, an in-breaking
reality that began with the incarnation of Jesus Christ and continues with the presence of the Holy Spirit in our lives. Practicing
"alreadyness" will make clear to all that we are not simply begging
to be allowed into existing unjust structures, but that we are living
something that is both as new and as ancient as the ideas of Christianity themselves: an emancipatory community of faith in which
we are constantly called to fidelity, justice and freedom, not only
for ourselves but for all of creation. The blessing that we can bring
to the church is the opportunity to engage in a paradigm shift that
challenges us all to a new vision and practice of being the church
for all people.

We must also be conscious of the "not yet." Some of our disappointment with events that signal continued prejudice and
oppression in the church is a result of forgetting the "not-yet-
ness," the realities of oppression that still impact us all. For example, the judgment made at the 1998 Lambeth international conference of bishops that homosexuality was "incompatible" with
scripture and that same-sex blessings should be condemned are
signs of how far the church still has to go in order to be a location
of God's love and justice for all.

We must pay attention to the complex design of oppression
within the church and within society. As we focus our attention on
the blessing of same-sex unions, we must do so with a consciousness of the multiplicity and interconnection of oppressions and
unequal distribution of power within the church and throughout
the world. For example, the Episcopal Church USA continues to
struggle with racism and with the marginalization of people of
color in lay and ordained ministries. The Episcopal Church has

also not lived up to its promise to fully include women of all colors into its structures of power. In spite of the reality of a growing number of women bishops, both lay and ordained women, in the church continue to experience the intractability of a "stained glass" ceiling that limits full access to pulpits, offices, and roles that have the power to deeply transform the church. The Episcopal Church has not begun to address adequately issues of economic class. And as a church we must wake up and act on the reality of the global economic disparity that is suffocating poor nations with unpayable debt. A postcolonial reality requires the shedding of monocultural theologies and disconnected single-issue politics.

In recent years a number of individuals and organizations have been working to strengthen and change the Episcopal Church in relation to its gay and lesbian members. This work is based on a recognition that gay men and lesbians are valuable members of the body of Christ and therefore deserve the visibility, nurture, care, and responsibility that all members of the Christian community share. This work to recognize the gifts and the needs of gay men and lesbians takes many forms, including work to support the ordination of lesbians and gay men and efforts to officially sanction same-sex blessings. This work has been met with numerous forms of opposition and rejection.

The work for justice for lesbians and gay men in the church is not only or simply about rights and recognition. It is about a church transformed and brought into alignment with God's love and justice, a church that counters the violence of hatred with creative, constructive power. This work is about power. The power that we are dealing with is itself complex and has many forms. Power can be used as a destructive and oppressive force, or it can be a constructive element used in the service of justice and compassion. In her work on power and social-change movements, feminist theorist Chela Sandoval describes the ability of oppressive power to move and manifest in different forms, thus constructing complex systems of interconnected oppression.[2]

If we are going to be successful in our particular work to be a church that manifests the "already-ness" of God's justice and love for all creation, if we are going to have an impact on the landscape of our political, social, and economic lives in general, we have to be willing to work with the complexity of power in its constructive, destructive, and neutral forms. In other words, we must do our work grounded in theological, economic, sociopolitical analysis. We are going to have to be able to live with ambiguity, plurality, and difference, and draw on these as resources for creating the church that we want to be and the world that we want to live in. This involves developing long-term strategies as well as short-term tactics for doing change work that draw on our ability to be flexible and multifaceted in our approaches to challenging oppressive power. It also requires that we engage in thought and practice that reflects our postmodern, postcolonial times, and thus challenge the rigid categories and sharp dualisms that were born in Enlightenment thought and serve to maintain the oppressive structures of the status quo in the church and in society in general. This involves challenging hegemonic frameworks that so many in the church insist on under the guise of upholding "tradition," when in fact these frameworks are all about maintaining control and hegemony.

We are called to embrace the interdependent process of the "already" and the "not yet" of our faith tradition. It is when the "already" is held with the "not yet" that transformative power is unleashed. We must refuse to compartmentalize our identities, our issues, and our personal power, as if freedom and justice for ourselves were not tied up with freedom and justice for others, as if eradicating one manifestation of hatred is the balm that will heal the multiple wounds caused by the complex design of oppression. Single-issue politics are acceptable *only* as short-term tactics when they are engaged in with a long-term strategy and consciousness about the need to end *all* forms of oppression. For example, in the struggle for lesbian and gay voice and visibility in the church it is imperative that broader issues of sexuality (including those that impact heterosexuals) are discussed in the context of racial and gender justice.

As we celebrate the "already" through emancipatory practices, both small and large, we cannot let go of the "not yet." Steps forward for women and men of all colors, for lesbians, gay men, bisexual, and transgendered people do not automatically herald the expansive, justice-oriented church. Sadly, we all know that many in our communities have not shed the dominant culture's way of thinking and doing. As black lesbian poet Audre Lorde wrote, "the master's tools will never dismantle the master's house."[3] Within our communities and within ourselves we find those who are only too glad to continue to use the master's tools to advance their own cause—for example, closeted gay men and lesbians in positions of authority in the church who are all too willing to oppose the ministries of out gay men and lesbians. This is also true of men and women who hide behind sexist practices to deflect scrutiny of their own sexuality. In addition, there are those who insist of focusing on their own points of marginality without acknowledging their places of privilege. For example, white gay men and lesbians who are unwilling to examine their own part in the racism that still shapes our society. Those tools have nothing to do with God's freedom; they are only signs of "not yet." These tools are in fact hindrances to the building of a comprehensive freedom for all of creation.

BLESSING OUR RELATIONSHIPS/MAKING THE JUSTICE CONNECTIONS

There are many in the church who are strategizing and working toward blessing same-sex unions as one aspect of moving toward comprehensive justice in a transformed church. What does the movement for same-sex blessings in the Episcopal Church have to do with the urgency to challenge the complex design of oppression that we are faced with in and beyond the church? In engaging this tactical work/struggle we need to insist on understanding it in the context of the gospel call to be agents of God's boundless love and passion for all of creation. I believe that in our various and different work for freedom, no energy should be wasted and no effort can be exempt from the call that we share to be builders of God's comprehensive vision of compassion and justice. Our work for the official recognition of same-sex blessings (as well as for access to ordination processes and full access in the work of lay ministry for gay men and lesbians) must be deeply connected to blessings for *all* people in the form of justice.

I am one who fears that the movement for official blessings for same-sex unions is or will be disconnected from the complicated and arduous work of pulling apart and transforming the complex design of oppression that keeps our world in bondage. I disagree with the strategies for change that insist that we deal with justice for lesbians and gay men in the church "first" or in a way that understands this justice making as somehow disconnected from the urgent need to reinvigorate, and in some cases establish, anti-racist and anti-sexist work in the church. Racism and sexism cannot be set on a back burner. It is not as if racism and sexism have somehow been resolved and overcome. These single-issue strategies are deeply flawed in that they assume that race, gender, and class issues do not have a deep impact on justice for all people, including all lesbians and gay men in the church and in society. Too many of us still operate with the image of what it means to be "gay" as white and male only or primarily, thus replicating white patriarchal visibility and privilege in our work. To rephrase writer Barbara Smith's famous statement challenging popular images of the Black Power and Women's movements which ignored black women's presence and contributions, "all the women are white, all the men are Black, but some of us are brave,"[4]—too often it is imagined that all the gays are white, all the gays are men—and some of us are fed up with that perception.

A long-term strategy of rigidly defining and compartmentalizing identities without doing the work of broad-based organizing, without drawing on the power and creativity found in the reality of complex identities and difference, is a set up for failure and missed opportunity. For example, when race and class are not considered in justice work for lesbians, gay men, bisexuals, and transgendered people, the contributions and comprehensive concerns of lesbian, gay, bisexual, and transgendered people of color and those who are working class are marginalized. Only a partial story is told, and lesbian, gay, bi, and transgendered people of color and those who are working class are threatened with invisibility and silence. So the story of Stonewall[5] is threatened with becoming a story of respectable white gay men who want equal access, rather than the story of multiracial working-class gays and lesbians, many in drag, who were fed up with police brutality.

The serial strategy that governs single-issue identity politics also goes against my understanding of what it means to be the body of Christ working in the world. This body, this community of faith, knows that is has different parts, and that those parts have different roles to play in the life of the body; and yet those parts work together to maintain vitality, life, and healing. We are responsible for the parts that we cannot see or even don't want to see but that invariably we are connected to.

Oppressive power in its many different forms only feeds off of our inability to challenge it in a serious and comprehensive way. Many of us, because of the woundedness and real injury that we have experienced in our lives in general, and in the church in particular, often find it difficult to extend ourselves to work for justice for those parts of humanity that we don't think that we have any relationship with. Our lack of outrage at the exclusionary practices, prejudices, and acts of violence that do not appear to affect us directly only make it possible for oppression to continue to thrive in all its forms. For example, not challenging racist, sexist, classist incidents, language, and behavior enables oppressive power to go unchallenged. When we refuse to reflect critically on how we might benefit from or contribute to the marginalization of another person or group, we forestall the possibility of any real transformation of the church or society. We need to address the ways in which we have been injured in our churches, in our communities, in all institutions. We *do* need to insist on justice for ourselves. *And* we need to understand our "selves" beyond individual identities and see ourselves in a larger, more complex, interconnected communal context. A communally oriented self-understanding recognizes that what impacts the individual has an impact on the community and vice versa. We must do our work of healing in such a way as to be able to stand the discomfort of challenge to our own prejudices. In order to dismantle the complex design of oppression we must be willing to make connections, engage in self-critique, and faithfully work toward a comprehensive reality of love and justice. This is an ongoing process in relationship with the divine and with each other as we take responsibility to co-create God's freedom.

THE POWER OF BLESSING FOR ALL

In light of our call as people of God to work with strategies that will address the life-and-death matters in the complex design of oppression, let us turn our attention to same-sex blessing. Since the early 1970s there has been theopolitical movement in the church to ordain openly gay and lesbian people to the priesthood, as well as to recognize church rites for the blessing of same-sex couples. Access to ordination and the blessing of relationships are key components of the realization of full voice and visibility for lesbians and gay men. These issues in the Episcopal Church

USA, as in other denominations, have become a focal point of church politics.

As such, it is critical to understand them as themselves and also as signposts on the larger landscape of justice and freedom in the church.

The blessing that many hope to be officially recognized in the church and by the church should not, as theologian Mary Hunt writes, "limit our relational creativity."[6] We need to be clear that the blessing of same-sex unions is only one of a variety of options for recognizing and maintaining relationships. For justice's sake, we do not want to develop a norm that attempts to mimic hetero-sexual marriage blessed by the church as the *only* acceptable norm for a healthy relationship. As communities of faith we need to do more to uphold and recognize the inherent goodness and worth of single people, of extended families both biological and those created, of friendships and communal relationships that model care and nurture for all involved.

We also need to work through the sociopolitical dynamics of the rites of same-sex blessing to see whether or not in fact they maintain hetero-patriarchal structures not only within relation-ships but also in church structures and polity.

In the process of working to create blessing rites that are offi-cially recognized in the church, we need to be aware of and respect those who, like myself and my partner, have been in rela-tionship for years, have had community-based commitment cere-monies outside of church sanction and would not be interested in an official church blessing if it became an option. We have for years understood our relationship as "blessed" by both God and community. To require a different kind of blessing would be a denial of this previous blessing as legitimate. In other words, we need to be concerned that the theology behind blessings is not one that makes some of us more "legitimate" than others, some of us more moral than others. The issues should be access and choice, and not compulsion.

Same-sex blessings can be a tool of transformation for the church and for society. They are a vehicle for coming out that can have a deep impact on individuals and entire communities of faith. The "coming out" that is involved in the blessing of same-sex unions can be a model encouraging us all to live into the fullness of our creation. With these blessing rites we acknowledge the reality of who makes up our communities of faith. Not only do we pledge to uphold and support a couple, we work against the negative power of invisibility and denial that affects us all. We are able to celebrate the richness of sexual diversity within our communities of faith. Same-sex blessing rites can be a way to break silences and end invisibility that will affect entire communities. Who else is it that has been silent and hidden, whose "coming out" is a source, can be a source, for power and joy for us all?

Blessing same-sex unions is about sexuality. The transformative statement that can be made by blessing same-sex unions is that goodness and God's blessings can be found in relationships that are not founded on a procreative norm. This affects heterosexual couples, who either by choice or by circumstance, do not or will not have biological offspring. Blessing same-sex unions invites an expansive understanding of positive, healthy sexuality.

Working to affirm the blessing of same-sex unions can be part of an emanciaptory strategy that invites the church into new ways of being and doing the work of justice and love that God calls us to. It can be a blessing for all in affirming relational creativity, transforming invisibility and silence, and supporting positive, healthy sexual practices and identities. Or, it could be a curse: continuing to define single people as less than whole, of chosen families as less than legitimate, of silencing those who don't fit, and regulating sexuality such that it remains a taboo attraction rather than an integrated blessing in our spiritual lives. Blessing or curse, life or death, we are enmeshed in a complex design of oppressive power. How do we choose blessing? How do we choose life?

Same-sex blessings can be a blessing or a curse in our work to transform the church, and it is an issue of life and death. Sherrice Iverson, Matthew Shepherd, James Byrd Jr., Billy Jack Gaither—these are the names we know of people killed by the curse of hatred, a limited view of love, and a desire to silence those who interrupt a narrow norm of human life. There are scores of others unnamed and unknown. As individuals and as a church, we are offered a choice: blessing or curse, life or death.

The urgent call to action is now. These are matters of life and death. Let us choose life; let us choose blessing for ourselves and for all of God's people around the world.

NOTES

This essay was adapted from a talk originally presented at the "Beyond Inclusion Conference" in New York in April 1999.

[1] Those named here are murder victims whose murders have been classified by many as "hate crimes."

[2] Chela Sandoval, "Feminism and Racism: A Report on the 1981 National Women's Studies Association Conference" in *Making Face, Making Soul: Creative and Critical Perspectives by Feminists of Color,* ed. Gloria Anzaldúa (San Francisco: Aunt Lute Books, 1990), 55-71.

[3] Audre Lorde, " The Master's Tools Will Never Dismantle the Master's House," in Audre Lorde, *Sister Outsider: Essays and Speeches* (Trumansburg, N.Y.: The Crossing Press, 1984), 110-13.

[4] Barbara Smith, et al., *All the Women are White, All the Blacks are Men, But Some of Us are Brave* (Old Westbury, N.Y.: The Feminist Press, 1982).

[5] The demonstration against police brutality and harassment by gay and lesbians outside the bar Stonewall Inn in Greenwich Village in New York, 1969.

[6] Mary Hunt, "Variety is the Spice of Life: Doing it Our Ways," in *Our Families Our Values: Snapshots of Queer Kinship,* ed. Robert E. Goss and Amy Adams Squire Strongheart (New York: Harrington Park, 1997), 243-49.

9

GLOBAL URBANIZATION

A Christian Response

LAURIE GREEN

In 1950 just twenty-five percent of the world's population lived in towns and cities.[1] By the turn of the millennium it has reached that powerfully symbolic figure of fifty percent. What we have now to reckon with is that by the year 2010 it is estimated that no less than seventy-five percent of the world's population will be urban.[2] Other disciplines and interest groups have already begun to grapple with the new phenomena. Sociologists, politicians, economists, geographers, financiers, aid agencies, transnational companies, are all researching and redefining their strategies accordingly. But is the church, and is its theology, anywhere up to speed?

Theology that engages with the urban community is as old as the Bible itself. The biblical text draws our attention repeatedly to the theologically strategic significance of cities, each seen as a place of influence, symbolic of concerns, social power and ethical values—witness Damascus, Rome, or Babylon. They are places where spiritual battles must be joined, where the poor suffer, where sin and bloodshed are concentrated, and where pride is manifest.

In the latter half of the twentieth century urban realities have proved a prime focus for much exciting and dynamic urban theology,[3] but such theology has often failed to address the ways in which the internal dynamics of a city are largely related to external factors—such as the situation of its food producers in the countryside both near and far, or its national and international relationships with other cities and zones of manufacture and decision-making. It is our new awareness of the processes of globalization which brings many of these matters so aggressively to our attention and demands of us that we look again from these other perspectives to reassess our theology of the urban. This complexity of factors has made a city such as Bangalore, which only thirty years ago was a pensioners' paradise, now experience new intensities of interfaith rivalry and conflict, the marginalization of children and women, the ecological crisis of pollution, a palpable fear in the minds of the rich as they lock themselves away in their gated communities, and the daily violation of the poor. We can no longer have the optimism of Harvey Cox, who saw the modern city as the New Jerusalem[4]—for the newly expanding megacities of the Two-Thirds World are anything but! So it is that our theologies of the urban have become ever more ambivalent, telling the story of urbanization as a tale of complex relationships and human achievement at odds with the horror of human cost and environmental collapse.

Of late, capitalism's powerful economic forces have combined with new communication technologies just when the political bipolar segmentation of the world into East and West, capitalist and communist, has given way to a multipolar political environment which allows the global market new rein and scope. Transnational corporations, numbering only some seven thousand in 1969, now number more than forty-five thousand,[5] dealing mainly in petrol, cars, electronics, food, drugs and chemicals. They concentrate decision-making and control in the cities of the developed world while channeling production and manufacture to low labor-cost locations in the cities of the Two-Thirds World. This issues in an increasing global divergence between cities, whereby their earlier differences are emphasized by this specialist production, while at the same time we become all the more aware of a global convergence, whereby consumer preferences across the globe converge to North American and European tastes and patterns—the "McDonaldization" of the globe! A shopping mall in London will look suspiciously like its counterpart in Nairobi. But strangely, these same economic forces will also encourage localization, which may issue in tribalism, nationalism, anti-capitalist ideologies and anti-western religious fundamentalism, all driving for the strengthening of local identity against those dominating "Western" values. But for all this convergence and divergence, the cities are now bound together in a small "global village" where a *fatwa* can be issued in Tehran, taken up in Los Angeles and books burned in Bradford, England, all within twenty-four hours. A film can be shot in Bombay and edited in London the same day, and televised in New York that evening.

In the poor burgeoning cities of the Two-Thirds World, pre-industrial rates of fertility and post-industrial mortality rates combine to create steep natural population increments, while in-migration from the countryside of those seeking employment and food sends population figures skyrocketing. These vast cities can sustain a rich variety of sub-cultures, offering the possibility of solidarity for those who otherwise might find themselves in isolation, and this rich pluriformity issues in an exciting urban vibrancy. But for many the outcome of unbridled growth is abject poverty in dismal urban slums. As many as ninety percent of the urban dwellers of Addis Ababa live in slum-shanties, and more than a third of all the urban dwellers of the developing world have to eke out a life in these abysmal circumstances.

While all this is happening in the developing nations of the southern hemisphere, the poor of the cities of the northern hemisphere have also to face the debilitating and alienating international pressures of globalization, where its economic forces and its new technologies are constantly moving research and control to the northern hemisphere, and production industry to the South. For those in the wealthy "West" who are trained and positioned favorably, the economic standard of living can improve beyond their dreams; but those who are not equipped for the research and control functions of the market are left jobless and, due to the growing individualism of the dominant culture, left to their own devices. This is very evident in a country like the United States where, as *Forbes Magazine* recently reported, there are one hundred and forty-nine billionaires and yet thirty-six million people now live below the poverty line. Those in the developed westernized nations who have no access to the benefits of a society built on new technologies, financial systems, and high skills, go to the wall. So it is that the demanding processes of global urbanization leave the inner cities and priority-need estates of the northern hemisphere to decay and smolder—just as the southern cities become overloaded and advance nearer to chaos. The miracle is that despite all the horrendous injustices, corruption and terrifying growth of these great cities of the developing world, they continue, somehow, to operate. Their resilience and dogged stability in the face of such astounding pressure and lack of acceptable infrastructure defies belief.

Underlying all this change and challenge, it is important for us to acknowledge that globalization carries with it a culture of dominating values which impacts our world so vigorously that our cities reel under their pressure. We might name these values as "commodification" (everything and everyone is reducible to a cash value); "efficiency" (success is to be measured by its rate of productivity rather than its innate value); and "knowledge" (which is information rather than wisdom). Those who do not conform to these dominant values are excluded from the global society, as of no worth or value. They are therefore not only made financially poor but are alienated and demeaned spiritually, intellectually, and emotionally.

THE CHRISTIAN IN THE GLOBAL CITY: WHAT TO DO ?

Around the world the challenges of urban globalization are being studied and addressed. Every discipline acknowledges that answers which seemed appropriate only twenty years ago no longer apply in this extraordinarily new environment. The spiraling changes and challenges are political, geographical, social, developmental, cultural and, of course, economic and technological. Even the World Bank's recent World Development Report 1999/2000, "Entering the Twenty-first Century," acknowledges that they must shift their emphases to meet the challenge of globalization. The Bank's responses thus far, they now admit, have not sufficiently appreciated the importance of local communities amidst the pressures of global processes. Their report ends by saying, "The next step is to initiate an empowerment process that enables community-based groups to define their own goals and options ... and to assume responsibility for actions to achieve those goals." While it has not been easy for such mammoth institutions to rethink their policies in the face of the new learning, they have realized the necessity to do so.

Our question must now be: "Is the church up to speed on the situation?" Can its institutions appreciate that whereas its resources and structures have been largely targeted upon rural communities, urban life is now the dominant experience for the majority of the world's population, and will increasingly be so. If the church is not to repeat old irrelevancies, it must ask itself what God's will might be for the church in this new situation. Rather than address the issue from the perspective of the needs of our old institutions, the church will do well to seek to look from a more theocentric perspective and ask, "What is the mission of God in this urbanizing world and how can the church as the body of Christ live that out?" We must ask ourselves, "When Jesus weeps over the city, what is it about this urbanizing globe that makes it a world that he is still prepared to die for?" What must the church therefore do and be in order to play its part in that compassionate process of salvation? How can the church address an urbanized humanity and speak the appropriate good news in word and deed in our generation?

Having thus made such a call to action, I want, nevertheless, to suggest that our first step must be to pause and contemplate. Just as reflection without action is impotent, so action devoid of reflection is anarchic. All too often we rush past the truth in our search for answers. We fail to listen to the voice of the oppressed, to stand silently at the foot of the cross and listen to the cry, "My God, why have you forsaken me?" We must learn the discipline of attentive analysis, researching prayerfully and reflecting theologically before assuming that we can now be in "mission mode." Attentive listening and prayerful "standing alongside" will issue in a growing awareness of what God is and where God is in the present situation. Urban mission must include a multi-disciplinary and prayerful research of urban realities and the processes of globalization. We must listen in solidarity.

As we stand attentively at the foot of the cross and listen, so our hearts will be moved to repentance, to a *metanoia* or "new-mindedness" regarding the dominant values of the global, urbanizing culture in which we are now set. The church, alongside the poor and others of good will, must inculcate an alternative mind-set which illuminates the powers and dynamics at work in our midst. For the church to learn these lessons, it does not have to begin from scratch. In our traditional, credal teaching about the four marks of the church, as one, holy, catholic, and apostolic, we have in fact the signs of how the church can be the very body of Christ in our challenging, global, urbanizing world.

THE FOUR MARKS OF THE CHURCH

THE CHURCH MUST BE ONE

Given all that has been said about the importance of the global, we might want to declaim that any project which only addresses local reality is doomed to failure. But perhaps our inherited doctrine of the unity of the church allows us to think and act constructively even in our local (or parochial) enterprises. Our belief in the unity of the church sets great store by the recognition that in every local Christian church, the whole church is resident. This age-old doctrine of the universality of the church, even in its local manifestations, has in it already what modern geographers, sociologists and economists are seeking after when the slogan is rehearsed, "act locally, think globally." Just as the eucharistic presidency of an ordained minister indicates sacramentally that the local congregation is just part of the global and universal church, so also the obverse is manifest in that the priest is not allowed to preside alone, but only in the presence of the local laity, and in this way all "celebrate" together. Individuals know themselves to be in communion and never alone, just as the local knows itself to be always part of the whole. The Johannine perspective upon our belonging to the whole is emphasized in Jesus' repeated assertions that we should all be in him as he is in the Father (John 14:8-21), and that we as the branches must never understand ourselves to be separate from the vine, which he himself is (John 15:1-17). Our whole Christian mind-set then, as well as our action as the eucharistic community, must be at once both local and global.

A well-integrated global communion of churches can seek strategically to address issues at every pertinent level, be it local, national, continental, or global. But this is easier said than done. The diverse patterns and styles of church which emanate from the vast array of cultures within which it is set and incarnated inevitably produce tensions between its members when they seek to act strategically and globally as one. The inclusion in the gospel account of the prayer of Jesus that we should all be one (John 17) is clear evidence that the problem was there from the first. Clearly, St. Paul's reference to the need for the diverse limbs and organs of the body to work strategically together in unity[6] is yet another allusion to the difficulties which the early church had in trying to understand the interrelation between its own local and universal natures.

The Anglican tendency at present is to seek to address the opposing forces of globalization and localization, of centralization and subsidiarity, by turning to the doctrine of the Holy Trinity of God as its model and solace. But a brief look at the political history of that doctrine soon teaches us that the institutional church may find it difficult to learn the lesson the Trinity has to teach us. The history of trinitarian doctrine, like all theology, is contextually based and is, therefore, itself a ready symptom of how the church has sought to control the possible chaos of diversity and localization. In the Western church, due to the Roman Catholic political preference for a centralized papal authority, the central unity of the godhead has, therefore, understandably been the starting point for debate about the Trinity. Thomas Aquinas and Augustine stressed the stable, serene unity of the central godhead and only then spoke of the distinction of the Father, Son, and Holy Spirit within that authority. In the Eastern Orthodox Church, however, where the preferred way of managing pluriformity has always been through confederation, where not one bishop alone should stand above the others as Christ's vicar, their doctrine of the Holy Trinity has stressed instead the interrelationship of the three separate "Persons" of the Holy Trinity and only thereafter spoken of the unity of the One as an outcome of the qualities of the separate Persons.[7]

In today's postmodern world, theologians and church politicians turn again to the doctrine of the Holy Trinity as their inspiration (as they have done in the *Virginia Report* which was submitted to the 1998 Lambeth Conference) and recast it accordingly—perhaps unaware of its revolutionary implications when unfettered from the political needs to control. The real difficulty with the use of the doctrine as a model for the church in a global society is that the unity of the godhead would appear to rely upon the loving and deferential holiness of the three Persons[8] in their relationship one with another, whereas in the world of urban globalization we must also reckon with the demonic powers of greed and original sin, infecting both the structural dynamics of the local and global as well as the individual persons who play their part within them. Perhaps this is why the sacramental model offered by Professor Christopher Duraisingh[9] offers us a way through the impasse, for he recognizes that a totally repentant shift and sacramental belonging are both necessary if the global and local powers are ever to issue in a just and loving world. Duraisingh speaks of the change that is wrought in Christian witnesses through our sacramental belonging to the body of Christ, first through our baptism when our individuality is named and blessed, and then in the sacrament of the eucharist, when our personal identity is still honored but now within the wider global and universal communion of the one body. In both sacraments the three Persons of the Trinity must be named for the action to have validity so that we may then know ourselves to be operating in the image of the social triune God as we are sent out as baptismal communicants into a fallen global mission field.

But how will this redeemed unity in diversity "cash out" in our globalized, urban world? It is very important for all those engaged in Christian action that they should not allow themselves to be overwhelmed by the enormity of the issues of globalization. In the urban scene this can become an awesome temptation issuing in paralysis, for the challenges of urban living have been debilitating enough even before the addition of the complex forces of globalization intensified the dynamic. I would suggest that an awareness of the oneness of the church can helpfully direct us into liberating action by prompting us to engage in networking, advocacy, parabolic or sacramental action, and discernment.

Networking

Christian networking allows groups and individuals to relate together around common concerns and issues and to share information, stories, analysis, and planning. All this can today be greatly facilitated by the use of electronic communication media. It is a way to use the technology of globalization to seize upon its communal benefits without necessarily acceding to its dominant cultural values. Supportive friendships can be struck up and maintained between individuals and groups who gather around liberative action and key issues. In this way the best local action is both coordinated and reflected upon across the boundaries of the local so that local and global action can work together. The Jubilee 2000 Coalition[10] has been an inspiration in this regard, enabling a small local English initiative to gather pace and support, to link with like-minded groups across the world, to share theologically and philosophically, to pool resources and plan concerted action. Governments have had to respond, and transnational corporations have had to take notice. The populace in many countries have been made aware of alternative economic and social values, and Christian thinking about sin, debt, forgiveness and covenant has been shared. Such is the value and power of networking. The Anglican Communion has its own formally recognized networks, including its Family Network, its Justice and Peace Network and most recent of all, the new Global Urban Network, which will seek to share across the Communion on all matters relating to the issues of globalization and urbanization.[11] Networks allow us to act and reflect locally and globally, building coalitions with those of like mind and those who may come at the issue from a very different perspective. They relate, not in any hierarchical manner, but in a responsive openness to relationships and possibilities. They can become an expression of the eucharistic community at its best, not simply working for some intangible benefits "when the revolution comes" but for achievable goals for the benefit of the urban poor in the here and now—this is the power of networking.

Advocacy

Because networks allow action and reflection at so many levels in an integrated and strategically coordinated manner, those on the network who find themselves in positions to influence the outcome of events can do so having been well informed by those others on the network who are experiencing matters from the perspective of the downtrodden. However, advocacy of this sort has immense dangers, for the corridors of power have a subtle way of controlling those who visit them, issuing in patronizing attitudes and complicity with disabling forces. Better still is that form of advocacy which facilitates direct encounter between the poor and the powerful. The church universal must be a vehicle for the voice of the poor, and advocacy for others must always have as its goal the equitable sharing of power so that all human beings may become the subject of their own history by finding advocates from amongst their own community. A wonderful example of advocacy of the best sort occurred in South Korea, where a number of Anglican students mobilized slum-dwellers during the building clearances in preparation for the Olympic Games. They came together in "Houses of Sharing" and developed from that into a movement within the churches for the rights of the poor.

Sacramental Action

Just as networking will enable better advocacy, so global awareness will enable better local sacramental action, for Christians who know themselves to be part of the communion of saints will be inspired to initiate local action which speaks of issues much greater than themselves. Just as a sacrament participates in that which is beyond its own measure, so small but well-focused initiatives can bring change and illumination to issues which are local but participate in issues which are beyond themselves in the global interrelationships and issues of which they are but a symptom. Even a well designed local "bring-and-buy" sale can speak volumes about global sustainability, recycling, and waste awareness. An insightful embargo on a local shop can highlight the questions of unjust international trade. A project designed to help individual youngsters in Los Angeles who have entered into the gang culture can alert society to the international dimensions of the drug trade. Symbolic action and committed local campaigns on clean water or better housing can participate in and encourage a "movement" and strategy at a national or even international level. Each time a "mustard seed" is planted, the cultural battle might be joined. The best global thinking remains an abstract irrelevance if it is not rooted in local action, but local action that does not consider issues greater than the local will remain supportive of an unjust status quo.

As our church learns to be more aware of its own oneness, so it will find its local action ever more ecumenical and discerning of the whole body of Christ, for while experiencing itself as of many parts it will also become ever more mindful of its global power to confront the powers of darkness. It is then that the church must guard its holiness.

THE CHURCH MUST BE HOLY

The one, holy, catholic and apostolic church must above all things be God-directed, immersed in the concerns of the world, but at all times model its life upon God's holiness. The brutal realities of the urban world in which it is set must not be allowed to capture its vision, nor diminish its determination to play its proper part in God's transformation of those processes which work against the common good. In its reflection upon and engagement with the urban world, the church must always be asking where and how Christ is to be found within it, and act there with God in ways modeled upon the divine praxis. Therefore, we must expect the church as the body of Christ to be fractured and broken by its engagement if it is to partake of Christ's crucifixion within the urban world. In spite of this, the church must never forsake its ethical and essential holiness.

The crucifixion of Christ is to be found constantly in our urbanized world, for the commodification of people and things and the ruthless exploitation of technology and resources—the dominant values of globalized urban capitalism—threaten to enslave both rich and poor alike, coaxing the powerful to turn their backs on the downtrodden, and leaving the poor destitute and competitive with no sense of belonging, worth, or identity. For all its promise, there is a brutality in global urbanization. It promises the poor and the wealthy so much, but leaves them bereft of even what they had. The process runs as follows: the poor countries are awash with advertisements for and symbols of the benefits of the wealth of the rich, developed world and so look to it for aid. The World Bank offers to assist them, but only if they will emulate the values and priorities of the rich world. A loan will be offered only if the poor nation reduces its internal food subsidies, reduces spending on health and education, and ploughs its wealth into engagement in the international markets, by seeking to earn foreign currency rather than maintaining their own internal market. The international market is so designed that a poor country may never be able to win within it. The terms of trade and the advantages which the already wealthy have, lead to the poor new players being pushed ever lower down the league of trade; they eventually find that the initial promise of increasing wealth for all proves illusory. The poor country becomes ever more dependent, and the vast majority of its population is driven to deeper anguish and worse conditions than even pertained in their previous wretched state. All this is so far from the holy promise offered by Christ that when God's reign comes there shall be a banquet prepared for all the nations. The evidence of the streets of Mexico City, Calcutta, or Nairobi shows that the promise offered by globalization is hollow, driving the rich to hardness of heart and the poor to destitution.

We are not arguing here that the values of capitalism are essentially malevolent. Indeed, profit motive has proved its worth in providing a fallen world with wealth-creation and the opportunity for a higher economic standard of living; but the ruthless exploitation of those who are at abject disadvantage flies in the face of all that is decent. It is this process which is writ large across the features of global urbanization. When, by the very nature of the process, subjected human beings are systematically denied a share in the benefits of that system, and when the beneficiaries are so used to seeing everything and everyone as commodities, then the wrath of the holy God must be mirrored in the actions of the prophets of the holy church.

A holy church will not merely do different and alternative things—it must also be different and alternative. It must make an option for transformation of its very self. As we have noted from the work of Duraisingh, the church from its baptismal repentance and its eucharistic solidarity with the crucified must offer itself to transformation. Analysis and the experience of global urbanization must teach the church to recognize how, for too long, it has legitimized an exploitative status quo by its modeling of subservience to the powerful and obeisance to worldly success. The repentant church must step down from its pedestal before it is knocked off it by insightful ridicule. My hope is that those of goodwill within the church and without will see the crisis and respond together.

Jesus taught that right vision helps to elicit repentance and right action, for when asked about how the reign of God might be inaugurated, he told visionary parabolic stories and enacted sacramental signs of transformation. He spoke of the forgiving inclusivity of the father at the return of his prodigal son. He pointed to the way that loving action can cut across the barriers of race or tribe, in the parable of the good Samaritan. He warned of the crisis awaiting those who failed to care, in the stories of Dives and

Lazarus and the sheep and the goats. He indicated a new style of leadership as he rode a donkey into Jerusalem, and a new style of holiness as he threw money-changers from the temple. Whilst each of these, in itself, was such a small mustard seed of an action in the face of the global power of the Roman Empire, nevertheless each was significant of a new culture, a new way of being, a new logic, a new society whose participants were to change the world significantly.[12]

In the same way, there are small groups of globally networked Christians today acting with this reign-of-God logic, basing their style upon the sacramental, parabolic actions and the stories of witness that we see in the life and ministry of Jesus. But to emulate Jesus' method, they must take every care when engaged in Christian action to build in opportunity to reflect theologically, politically, economically, and culturally so that their actions may inform their thinking and their thinking inform their action. In this way the sacramental nature of the action may become more carefully defined and evident as it seeks to engage both locally and at the same time address global issues and structures of injustice which make that local action for justice necessary. This is what we can mean by the slogan "think globally, act locally." In this way real practical assistance is brought to those close to hand, while simultaneously there is a participation in the power of God and humanity to change globally the processes and cultures of oppression. This is acting according to reign-of-God logic, and I have elsewhere described how groups can best function in this way.[13]

The practice of such groups must, of course, be based in large measure upon how we see Jesus engaging with the local manifestations of the global issues of his day. This is why our praxis will begin by making the same basic option for the poor and outcast that we see him taking in his life and ministry. In the gospels, the poor are the first subjects of the good news. The social and economic status of Jesus and his family have been variously argued, although I am convinced that his skills in the construction and building technology of his day would have placed him above the peasantry on any financial scale.[14] Jesus, therefore, made a conscious option to work alongside the poor, downtrodden and disaffected, and there is clear evidence that he expected his disciples to follow him in that sacrifice: "we have given up everything to follow you" (Matt. 19:27). He opens his kingdom to those who by traditional and contemporary standards were considered unclean and of no account, and sets them instead at the very center of his affairs. He takes children and women, the blind, the lepers and the destitute, and speaks to their concerns and offers them inclusion. Jesus does not simply afford them dispassionate justice but aggressively positive discrimination. This is clearly evidenced in his parable of the laborers in the vineyard, for the logic of a market economy would see no justice in paying the same wage to laborers who have worked varying hours, but there is divine justice in sharing equally the benefits of a society which would otherwise treat its members unfairly. It is the new alternative logic of a holy church.

The international structures of global urbanization subject the poor and place women and children in powerless positions, today as then, while aggrandizing and further enriching the wealthy. Although this clearly means that both poor and rich are enslaved by the system, the Christian must make the option for the poor, as Jesus did, in order that all might be saved; and this will demand of the church that it hold tight to courage, vision and self-sacrifice, so that it may live by its own essential mark of holiness.

Because oneness is also a mark of the holy church, the holistic and systemic perspective this brings allows us to make this option for the poor in order that the rich may also be saved thereby. For the problem of poverty is beyond the poor and rich alike, and the new discipline of global studies is helping us to see this. We are now more able to analyze what factors drive modern exclusion and injustice, and this clarifies for us the structural nature of much of our predicament. Our fight is not so much against unjust individuals holding onto power and privilege, but against complex global and urban processes which incline and allow them to do so: "for our fight is not against flesh and blood but against the powers and principalities of this dark age" (Eph. 6:12). This is why Jesus places the so-called marginalized at the center, quite literally, time and time again,[15] in order to make more readily apparent that the cause of the injustice is in the larger dynamics of society, not merely in any one "marginalized" or "oppressive" sector. While not detracting from the responsibility which every human being must carry, we must assert that the global poor are not the cause of their own problems—they are much more sinned against than sinning. Likewise, it would be false merely to lay the blame entirely on the rich, as if to say there was never a rich person who did not act sacrificially and insightfully for justice. We are all in this dilemma together, and together we must seek liberation for all creation. Our urban mission must be open to all people of good will, but the driving stratagem must be God's option for the poor. Liberation theology has offered us a penetrating analysis of what salvation can mean in all its fullness, but it has never offered an adequately appreciative theology of wealth-creation and its complex challenges. Today we are challenged also to address that issue aright, but seek to bring to it not the scarring commodifying values of global capitalism, but those of the reign-of-God vision. Our repentant action must work for the release of both oppressed and oppressor as inclusively as our Lord bids us to pray, "forgive us our sins as we forgive those who sin against us."

The church should then adopt Jesus' direct strategy of being alongside the poor, asking always who is most benefiting from our actions—ourselves or God's poor, through whom he saves the world? Our servanthood alongside, for and as the poor, will result in a gospel integrity of vulnerability, whereby we share with those at risk a deeper appreciation of our need one for another and our dependence upon God's grace. Our servanthood will also assist us as church to fight against the church's greatest temptation, which is to consider ourselves a community of insiders who have all the answers. Being with the poor will remind us to see ourselves for what we really should be—a community, with Jesus, of "outsiders." From this perspective we can better judge whom is being served and where the injustice properly resides. It will also give us the heartache required to engage in courageous godly action.

The operation of a holy church in today's urban setting will often need to be in small, inclusive, issue-focused groups which have a prayerful heart and a courageous commitment to act locally. Such cells will gather together at the parish level in the larger eucharistic community of believers for grander worship, but usually they will also operate on a much smaller scale where more intimate worship is possible and where considerable networking with other women and men of good will is more likely.

The abiding concern of such groups when engaging in parabolic or sacramental action is whether or not the group's life is conforming to that of the man who rode into Jerusalem on a donkey. First, they must ask whether or not their action "rides into Jerusalem"—are they confronting the powers of injustice at the right level, as Jesus chose to do? And second, they must be certain that they "ride on a donkey"—that they come as servant, not concerning themselves too much with themselves and their church agenda. We will certainly need to be a self-sacrificial church for the new millennium, for to make the Jesus challenge fresh for our time will lead to crucifixion, as ever it did for a holy church.

THE CHURCH MUST BE CATHOLIC

The conflicting processes of globalization and localization are mirrored by equivalent dynamics in the church. The local parochial gathering must be jealous of its distinct particularity and identity, as well as being pleased to acknowledge its denominational identity shared with others as part of the church universal. A strong trinitarian doctrine will own the oneness of the universal and the differences of the parochial, but for each locally encultured parish to be thus accepting of the next will call for a Christian maturity which is not always readily to be found. Some sections of the church seem to treat our differences as if they were a design fault in God's creation, whereas for the church to be catholic it must own the fact that God has created us with exciting differences, and that to good purpose—so that we may learn that truth is not a statement, but a relationship. God gives us differences in order to teach us how to get on one with another—how to hold a mutually enriching conversation and so learn the wisdom of relationship. Holding our beliefs humbly in dialogue gives us the possibility of learning further truth from others rather than remaining the prisoners of our own dogmatic deafness.

One of the great benefits of urban life is that it concentrates so many people into close proximity that these differences become more readily apparent. The exciting possibilities of exchanging different foods, cultures, music, and languages are there for the taking, and many urban congregations become bridge-builders, practicing their ecumenicity and catholicity to the benefit of communities that are often otherwise fractured by these same differences. Cultural interchange, cross-cultural and multifaith dialogue is not, of course, exclusive to the urban scene, but it is often here that the reality of the differences is most sharply felt. It is one thing for academics from different faiths to discuss their differences in their senior common rooms; it is altogether more pertinent to engage the issues at the points of sharpest intercultural conflict on the streets of the inner city. When conflicting groups, multicultural or otherwise, seek to engage openly and respectfully in such places of strife, then the God of all creation is most graciously and evidently present, gifting participants with discernment, charity, and wisdom. This is the very stuff of catholicity, not the easy agreement over the coffee cups of academic debate, but charity forged in the furnace of global urbanization. This truly catholic church must be a bridge-builder for community and not prejudiced exclusivism, for the former is the only answer to the easy relativism with which globalization threatens and which is so alien to the Jesus of the gospels.

Community networking and bridge-building by Christians in the global city will necessarily entail giving attention to the treasures of our own Christian faith traditions and practices—thus reinforcing the solidarity of belonging among Christian members, telling the Christian story and living intimately together in eucharistic communities. At the same time it will give us the self-confidence to remain open to the possibility of engagement with different others so that our own faith traditions are put to the test to see whether they still carry God's truth adequately. The societal assumptions and opinions of others will also of course be critiqued from the perspective of the traditions which are part of our story as the Christian church. This mutually enriching dialogue can be Spirit-inspired if always the Christian community offers itself to continued encounter with the God who does not despise difference but creates it.

Such a rich, ecumenical catholicity will help those who live in our global urban world to guard against the sin of turning our backs on the "other." The fear of the other is very real in our present-day urban lives—be it the fear from those who gate themselves into their wealthy security-guarded ghettos because they fear those on the streets, or whether it is the fear at street level, where the poor demonize others and either withdraw into negativity and apathy or hit out with violent uprising or indiscriminate terror. Dialogue and meeting are the bridge-building gift of the catholic congregation to these alienated urban communities. Some, understandably, do not have the courageous faith to be thus vulnerably catholic amidst the urban scene. Instead they may retreat into fundamentalism in order to value only the local and particular, but this ploy disallows any open dialogue with the other. Another unrealistic escape is to treat everything and everybody as a commodity in the global market place, thus seeking to bring unity among the differences through enforcing a common method of exchange-relationship, while not owning the worth and value of local identity and difference. Only the new dialogical bridge-building of the reign of God—the vulnerable, loving logic of the open Trinity of God—will issue in a mutual ownership of our vulnerable humanity and a challenging but productive honesty within our globalized urban relationships.

To be catholic has been understood in the past to indicate that the church is both worldwide and unified in faith, but now in this new globalized frame of reference, we must include a third element—what Robert Schreiter calls "communication,"[16] but what I am here preferring to call "dialogue." First there is the dialogue of *culture*. Before globalization we were apt to describe cultures as confined complexes of place, language, and social coding. Now cultures have been blown apart by rubbing up against other languages, places, and social expectations. The globalized city is flooded with myriad cultural styles, and any one person or group may be expected to function within and across the boundaries of many. Young people particularly are assailed by so many possibilities and options in the city that the question of their own identity, place, and style of belonging becomes a battle ground for faiths and allegiances. Missional enculturation amidst the kaleidoscopic cultures of the global city is now one of the greatest challenges which our incarnational faith has to face. The missionary, unaware of this heady cultural mix, will die the death of irrelevance if he or she does not welcome intercultural catholic dialogue.

The second focus of our catholic dialogue, therefore, must be that of *identity*, for this complexity of cultures relativizes belonging, which is so much of who and what we are. The forces of global urbanization have produced what postmodernists refuse to acknowledge—the possibility of a new "metanarrative"—a new overarching story. Commodification is that story, introducing the market into all our relationships and transactions. In today's Western city we are born to shop, and in the urban poverty of the developing world people are reduced to economic units in the global market place or are ignored. Education, health, spirituality, family, and so much more are all to be judged in the balance sheet of economic worth and financial transaction. In this way erstwhile esteemed cultural values and meanings are blurred and muddled, ceasing to offer the securities which once they supplied. But while the market place is able to offer acquisition and efficiency, identity requires answers at a much deeper level. Identity requires shape and meaning; indeed, it requires some form of goal to which the proffered efficiency is expected to aim. The Christian faith offers this deeper meaning and identity in the cross of our Lord. The church thus knows itself as the servant body of Christ, challenging the metanarratives of global capital and vulnerably engaging in liberative dialogue.

The third element of catholic dialogue must focus upon *social change*. Globalization has relativized the particular to such an extent that one centrally imposed authority or truth is no longer thought of as universally viable. Old notions of authority no longer pertain. The chaos which lurks only just below the surface in many a city is, among other things, a symptom of a refusal to accept patronizing answers from distant hierarchies. Sometimes the rampant individualism of society is blamed for this breakdown of order, but that individualism is only itself a symptom of the fear that there is no universal meaning or truth. Likewise, no longer is a universal theology viable which comes imposed from above upon our experiences. The way forward is to learn from the New Testament that truth is never a statement but a relationship, in that God, who is the ultimate truth, is essentially to be known not as a concept but as relational trinitarian love. Contextual theology by definition affirms this relational quality of truth and therefore asserts the provisionality of all doctrinal and theological statements. This is why deep immersion in the context of the globalizing world will help us to understand both the nature of our mission and the nature of God's relational truth. The search is therefore on to find a way in which all our exciting new contextual theologies can weave together a global pattern of godly truth which would be supportive of personal and societal integration without the imperial impulse which has dogged mission and theology for so long.

Manuel Castells and Peter Beyer[17] helpfully utilize the social philosophical concept of "global flows"—where initiatives deriving from different particular contexts nevertheless evidence similarities which prove to be mutually intelligible and supporting.

Beyer in particular argues that recent theological flows are strongly evident where ideas flow together in opposition to the prevailing dominant values of modern globalization. Liberation theologies accuse the global economy of failing the poor; feminist theologies uncover globalization's inability to deliver equality and inclusion; while ecological theologies unmask the waste and unsustainability of the growth ethic of global systems. It is in the dialogue of such critiques that the biblical notions of justice then begin to appear in such contradistinction to those espoused by global capitalism. The latter understands justice as dispassionate—personified in the blindfolded figure with balanced scales in her hand—but biblical justice is partisan, symbolized as a torrential, dynamic river rolling down from the mountains as an ever-flowing stream crushing all before it which would stand in its way (Amos 5:24). We can expect therefore that these cultural flows will be intense, critical, and powerful.

So our biblical and faith traditions enter into dialogue with culture, identity, and social change, offering a way of being catholic which is more than simply acknowledging our global universality. Our catholicity will no longer be imposed from the center—for a homogeneous church is but an illusion—but we will discover our catholicity in the fragments, as they testify in each diverse culture and locality that the church is incarnated there in mission, to God's glory.

THE CHURCH MUST BE APOSTOLIC

The church is a movement, not a hobby-club. It has a gospel mandate upon it, and it is sent by the Christ who himself was sent as the summation of the mission of God. Yet the church contents itself time and again with its own concerns, its own well-being and its own future—and fails to recognize its *raison d'être* which is to recognize and adore God, and then itself enter into the very mission in which God is evidently engaged. Our Lord's style of missional operation was to act so as to entice the powers that be into a dialogue for real change. He deliberately and overtly operated so as to bring the processes of injustice into the open. He engaged with many of the social tensions of his day, especially its religious politics, and while suffering alongside the poor under those unjust processes and dominant cultural values, showed us a way to address those cultures and triumph over them. And he sends us to participate in that same mission as apostolic witnesses in a world now dominated by the powerful forces of globalization.

When the church seeks to be truly apostolic, it must drive forward, looking to the front, and at the same time looking behind so that it knows where it has come from and to whom it belongs, while simultaneously venturing out into the risk of the future. As the church enters into catholic dialogue with others, and builds bridges in shattered urban communities, it does not come empty-handed to that dialogue. For while respecting the "other," the church catholic must have respect for its own provenance. We are molded by and carry the story which in turn we seek to make fresh in each generation, and to this heritage we must be true. For one of the demonic effects of globalization is that it seeks to make us forget who we are and see ourselves only as transactional commodities in the global market place. But the eucharistic community is of its very nature a community which remembers. As it gathers so it re-enacts, rereads, rehearses, and is true to its Lord who says again, "Do this in *remembrance* of me." So it is that the whole future is opened up for us. This is not to say that we must as Christians always expect God to repeat God's actions from the past—that would be merely to think ideologically—but we can expect God's nature to be unchanging, and interpret the world and shape our actions accordingly. These traditions of Christian faith we therefore bring proudly to the catholic dialogue, and against them we judge the values which surround us. In our mission and proclamation there will therefore be judgment and critique—and the poor will not think kindly of us if we deny who we are and fail to offer ourselves honestly and intentionally as Christian believers.

The apostle must know that our past teaches us that history is important and God's involvement with it has always been intimate. The prophet Jeremiah offers us a deep insight into the way God is with us in the politics and history of each moment. He acts symbolically by laying the heavy yoke of history upon his shoulders (Jer. 28), but the false prophet Hananiah broke Jeremiah's yoke and proclaimed that God would not be constrained by the present historical struggles, but would transcend them and act as always God had done in the past. In doing this Hananiah was using religion as ideology, constraining God by his own prophetic predictions based upon what God had done in the past in an altogether different historical context. Jeremiah therefore returned with an even stronger yoke upon his shoulders, so demonstrating to his contemporaries as to us that if the contingent historical realities are not fully addressed, then we will be retreating from engagement with the God who makes all things new.

We therefore require wise discernment when we delve into our traditions and seek to make appropriate connections with our present situations, for inappropriate ideological usage will led to misdirected consequential action. To this end we must take note that the biblical traditions which carry much of our gospel story have themselves been interpreted by many generations in a thoroughly imperialistic manner, which scholars are only now beginning to perceive.[18] We must therefore bring to those biblical traditions our learning and increased sensitization to the imperialist processes of today's global urbanizing world, so that our scholarship can help us unearth the foundational gospel from its later interpretative accretions. So our apostolic endeavors and experience will inform both our biblical hermeneutics and our missiology.

Walter Brueggemann[19] shows from the biblical traditions how God helps us understand who we are and affirms our human identity by taking us from undefined or coerced "space" and locating us into treasured and trusted "place." In the Hebrew Bible, God's promise to a wandering people is confirmed in their inheritance of a place, a land, to call their own. This promised land thus becomes a signifier of an historical process of liberation rather than standing as an emblem of a victor's power over other weakening tribes and races—even though that imperialist reading can be seen in the canonical text. Those with whom we now work in our urban mission are often the misplaced ones—those who have had their sense of place threatened or even have been forcefully removed—the built environment around them changed without reference to their feelings or to the soul of their now decimated community. While the poor are driven to locate in vulnerable urban shanties, identical shopping malls and office blocks appear all around the world, depriving the local populace of the corporate memory which had hitherto helped them know who they are and where they belonged. The biblical tradition gives us many insights into what the land can mean for us and how easy it is for the victor to obliterate memories of a real oppression.[20] It was this awareness of the importance of treasured place which led the theologian Thomas Aquinas to write at length about the theories and practicalities of city planning,[21] and we must follow suit by playing our missional part in the critique of modern urban development and regeneration.

As an apostolic, remembering church, therefore, we will not let people be forgotten but will celebrate the promise and its fulfillment. We must revel in the good times—advertising the good experiences of urban living and reminding our colleagues of those times when God has been very evidently in our midst. Our urban mission must, in addition to our criticisms, celebrate community with street festivals and parties, publish histories and pictures of the magnificence and inspiring complexity of the urban project, and celebrate in bold liturgical worship the vibrancy of urban living. We must tell of the many times God is to be met in the solidarity and in the anguish of urban community life. We must be true to our church's *raison d'être*, seeing and praising God in every facet of our urban experience, and working with God, that God's will may be done here on earth as it is in heaven.

So it is that in our inherited credal traditions about the church as one, holy, catholic, and apostolic, the Christian community has at its disposal helpful signs of how it can live as the body of Christ in the new reality of a globalizing urban world. By thoughtful and prayerful consideration of those traditions the church can begin to take on the new repentant *metanoia* mindset for the sort of incarnational community action which our gospel faith requires.

An Anglican Program

Despite the fact that the economic and cultural thrust of this globalizing world is now predominantly urban, many of our church structures and our modes of mission are based upon our rural experience of earlier generations. Additionally, our style of missional activity has tended to stress individual piety and pastoralia at the expense of attention to social structures and cultural values. I have argued in this paper that mission must be about understanding the processes that oppress, enhancing the processes that build up and affirm, and being alongside the poor in all of it, so that they themselves may be the voice that is attended to and through which all may become blessed. Like Jesus, the church must make, in addition to his option for the poor, an option for politics.

Around the world many lay and ordained people work wonderfully together in sacrificial, inclusive action which addresses these complex issues within the context of urban globalization at all levels. Journals, conferences, worship, workshops, gatherings, the Internet, and word of mouth, tell us thousands of stories about women, men, and children fulfilling their apostolic calling effectively and uniting with God's mission in our urbanizing world.

The Lambeth Conference of 1998 resolved[22] to assist these exciting endeavors by establishing an international Anglican Network for those who are engaged in addressing the issues of urban globalization, and this Conference resolution was unanimously endorsed by the subsequent meeting of the Anglican Consultative Council at Dundee, Scotland, the following year. This Anglican Network will be facilitated by a program of study and urban mission research through engagement across the continents, in the hope that the profile of these issues will be heightened throughout the Anglican Communion. The intention is that such a program will provide significant support for those who are already substantially involved in these issues, both as researchers and as practitioners, by bringing them together in an action/research mode. Their work will, we trust, inspire the Anglican Communion as a whole through its next Lambeth Conference to redirect resources in response to new insights and learning. Already Dr. Andrew Davey, working from Church House in London, is drafting a primer on globalized urban process and theological practice, to be published by SPCK, in 2001 entitled *Resources for an Urban Future*. This work will, we hope, inspire the ongoing work of action/reflection.

Most of all, we will be praying for the gift of God's grace to effect *metanoia* in the minds and hearts of God's people so that the one, holy, catholic, and apostolic church may be gifted and liberated to discern the interrelated processes of urbanization and globalization which affect the new mission landscape and, alongside others of good will, it will be energized to tackle the issues which these processes spawn.

So it is that the Anglican Communion is being challenged to make a decisive shift towards enabling and supporting urban mission in this new globalizing world. If it does not rise to this challenge, the Communion will have misjudged the global challenges facing the church as it stands on the threshold of the third Christian millennium. This shift can only be achieved if the changes in our global context are acknowledged and the spiritual and material resources are found to discern the challenge we face and the responses that we are called to make. This paper is offered as a contribution to these endeavors.

NOTES

[1] Only London and New York had more than eight million inhabitants in 1950.

[2] David Clark, *Urban World, Global City* (London: Routledge, 1996), 47-48. It is however notoriously difficult to forecast population since many countries have no present reliable data from which to project. Wichmann states that not till 2005 will half the population be urban but suggests that ninety percent of future population increase will be urban and that in 2025 four-fifths of all city dwellers will be living in developing countries. See R. Wichmann, "The Link between Poverty, Environment and Development, Countdown to Istanbul," in *Habitat* No.5, November.

[3] For a useful overview see Michael Northcott, ed., *Urban Theology: A Reader* (London: Cassell 1998) and Peter Sedgwick, ed., *God in the City* (London: Mowbray 1995).

[4] Harvey Cox, *The Secular City: Secularization and Urbanizatin in Theological Perspective* (New York: Macmillan, 1967).

[5] The United Nations *World Investment Report 1997* enumerates some forty-five thousand transnational firms controlling two hundred thousand foreign affiliates. They account for fifty-one of the world's one hundred largest economic entities (the other forty-nine are countries).

[6] See for example 1 Cor. 12:12-30.

[7] We may note however that even then the fear of pluriformity has been so great that Eastern Orthodox doctrine has shied away from a true "confederational" model toward a subordinationalist model and has spoken of the Son and the Holy Spirit as but the two arms of the initiating Father. See examples of this in the word of J. Zizioulas.

[8] See especially the writings of Cappadocian Fathers.

[9] The Rev. Dr. Christopher Duraisingh is Otis Charles Professor in Applied Theology at Episcopal Divinity School, Cambridge, Massachusetts, USA and spoke to the Lambeth Conference, 1998 on this topic. I am grateful that he supervised my own sabbatical studies in the doctrine of the Trinity in 1998.

[10] See my own writing published by Jubilee 2000, and especially, *Jesus and the Jubilee, The Kingdom of God and Our New Millennium* (Sheffield: New City Special No.11, 1997).

[11] See the last section of this paper for further details about the establishment of the Anglican Urban Network.

[12] See my *Power to the Powerless* (Basingstoke: Marshall Morgan and Scott, 1981), especially Chapter 4, "Discovering How Parables Operate," 50-64.

[13] Much of my own writing has sought to describe the practicalities of how groups such as this can best function effectively, offering examples, methods and case studies, and I refer interested readers to those works. See Laurie Green, *Let's Do Theology—A Pastoral Cycle Resource Book* (London: Mowbray, 1990), and Laurie Green, *Power to the Powerless.*

[14] The special circumstances of the family soon after the birth of Jesus would account for the poor person's offering made at the time of his Presentation in the temple.

[15] See for example Luke 6: 6-11; John 8:8; Mark 9:36.

[16] Robert Schreiter, *The New Catholicity: Theology Between the Global and the Local* (Maryknoll N.Y.: Orbis Books, 1997).

[17] Manuel Castells, *The Informational City* (Oxford: Basil Blackwell, 1984), and Peter Beyer, *Religion and Globalization* (London: Sage, 1994), 96-111.

[18] Walter Brueggemann, *The Land: Place as Gift, Promise, and Challenge in the Biblical Faith* (Minneapolis: Fortress Press, 1977).

[19] Compare the fascinating unpublished paper by Timothy Gorringe on the "Theology of the City of Exeter."

[20] See for example the collection of essays entitled, *The Postcolonial Bible,* ed. R. S. Sugirtharajah (Sheffield: Sheffield Academic Press, 1998).

[21] Thomas Aquinas, "On Princely Government," in *Political Writings,* ed. A. P. D'Entreves, trans. J. G. Dawson (New York: Macmillan, 1960).

[22] The Lambeth Conference Resolution II.7 on Urbanization reads: This conference: a) calls upon the member Churches of the Anglican Communion to address the processes of urbanization across the world, both in our cities and all other communities; b) asks our Member Churches to give urgent attention to "Living and Proclaiming the Good News" in our cities so that all that destroys our full humanity is being challenged, the socially excluded are being welcomed and the poor are hearing the Good News (Matthew 11:3); and in order to assist this priority in mission c) resolves i) to ask that Anglican Consultative Council to give support to the formation of Anglican Urban Network to share information and experience on urbanization and urban mission; and ii) to support the establishment of a "Faith in an Urban World" Commission, after due consultation with ecumenical bodies.

Part III

Visions for the Future Church

10
SCRIPTURE
What Is at Issue in Anglicanism Today?

NJONGONKULU NDUNGANE

When I succeeded Archbishop Desmond Tutu as Archbishop of Cape Town, many questions were being asked as to how this relatively unknown young man was going to fill the shoes of such an effulgent personality. This was captured in a cartoon in one of the national newspapers. It showed me standing by the church door at the end of a service with a mitre almost covering my ears and my eyes. A parishioner was shaking my hand saying sympathetically: "Your Grace, it will fit in time."

If we reach the end of this address with more questions than answers, I shall be well satisfied. In my own exploration of this topic, the more I have delved into the questions, the less sure I feel about any of the answers. That, for me, is good theology. But it should serve as a warning to those who want sure and certain truths that I am not going to meet that need here.

There are two ambiguous words in the title we are set to explore: scripture and Anglicanism. Superficially, we assume we know what they mean, but I do not think it is all that clear. For example, when we talk of scripture, do we mean the Old and New

Testaments? the Apocrypha? the non-canonical texts? commentaries on and interpretations of the aforegoing? Then there is the tricky question of what is meant by Anglicanism. What is its essence? Is there something definitively "Anglican"? Can we even point to varieties of "Anglicanism"? Anglicanism, as we are all aware, grew out of the Reformation in England. In other words, it was formulated and developed in a particular context. Though the context remained quite similar for several centuries, there has now been a radical shift from Anglicanism's roots. One used to be able to point to the Prayer Book as the central essence, but in the last forty years or so there have been many new translations in various parts of the Communion, as we attempt to inculturate the Prayer Book and translate it into languages other than English. Inculturation has diluted or removed altogether the colonial English church. I am not suggesting this is to be deplored. Far from it. But it raises questions as to what is definitively Anglican. Are we simply to acknowledge that anyone who wishes to be called Anglican should be recognized as such? This is the debate surrounding the so-called "continuing" Anglican churches, which oppose women's ordination.

As if these questions were not difficult enough, we are faced with our rapidly changing global context. Though the church is slow, even loath, to recognize it, our context is now postmodern, and that reality influences our attitudes toward the reading of scripture and the question of authority—issues we will examine in more detail.

Then there are issues which are peculiarly twentieth-century phenomena and which have, depending on one's perspective, revolutionized, reformed, or severely harmed the church. I speak of the feminist movement, the growing recognition of the place of interfaith dialogue, and the issues debated most fiercely by the last two Lambeth conferences, namely, the ordination of women and the place of homosexual people.

Let us start, though, by looking at scripture and its place within the Anglican church.

SCRIPTURE

The place and role of scripture within the Anglican church, as an authoritative directive on issues of church order and Christian conduct, came under the spotlight at the recent Lambeth Conference, particularly in relation to the debate around homosexuality.

In this section I will be looking at the place and role of scripture within the Anglican tradition as it relates to the issue of authority.

Throughout the history of the Anglican church, scripture has played a pivotal role in theological discourse and liturgical practice. The Constitution of the Church of the Province of Southern Africa (CPSA)—my own province—states that it "receives and maintains the Faith of our Lord Jesus Christ as taught in the Holy Scriptures." This underlines the fact that the importance of scripture cannot be disregarded. In fact it is regarded as a primary source for doing theology, along with reason, faith, culture, experience, and tradition. However, although this is the formal position of the church—namely that scripture is one source amongst several others—it is certainly not reflected in terms of practice, where weight tends to be given to scripture. For instance, in the case of the debate around homosexuality, scripture was used as the predominant standard over and against which the different positions in the debate were measured. A significant number of bishops (arguing both for and against the acceptance of homosexuals) based their arguments upon the Old and New Testaments where, *prima facie*, homosexuality is condemned.

This debate has focused attention on fundamental questions relating to scripture, its authority and its interpretation. It is these questions to which we now turn as we search to find the significance of scripture for us today.

First of all, what constitutes scripture? This is not a simple question. There is no agreement even amongst Christians as to what constitutes scripture. For example, what is the position of the apocryphal writings? What is the position of those writings not generally even included in the Apocrypha, such as the Story of Norea, the daughter of Eve, and the Gospel of Mary, which present us with alternative interpretative frameworks?

Second, can the liberating sociocultural ethos, out of which the writings emerged and in which they served as a directive for contemporary readers and hearers, be appropriated in our contexts today in a way that is liberating?

Third, how do we determine whether scripture is authoritative or not in relationship to contemporary challenges facing us, such as gender and sexual orientation? And who does the determining?

Finally, which interpretations of scripture take precedence today in the church? The traditional interpretation of theologians and clerics? The current contemporary interpretations coming from marginalized groups (based on gender, race, culture, socio-economic status, sexual orientation)?

There are, in broad terms, three different positions which are upheld within contemporary Anglicanism with regard to calling upon scripture as a source of authority.

There are those who see scripture as the authority—the one and only source of authority. Here the text is used as a proof-text. This approach is aptly demonstrated by the story told by a priest who knew a woman who believed giving birth almost yearly was her response to God's injunction to increase and multiply (Gen. 1:28).

There are those who see scripture as one source amongst others. In other words, they see that scripture is not authoritative on its own. We need to place scripture alongside experience, reason, culture, faith, and tradition. For example, if one were to place these sources on a continuum, ranging from scripture on the one hand, to tradition on the other—one would then have the different variables placed in between (experience, reason, culture, and faith). For feminist theologians who use the oral and written experiences of women as the predominant sources for doing theology, the continuum might begin with experience, then faith, and somewhere down the line, scripture. For feminist theologians what may be most important is interpretation of praxis over and against or in light of scripture.

There are those who do not see scripture as the authoritative source at all. It is simply another text to be considered. For example, for some Christians outside the Western world, with their own cultural orientation, scripture is no more authoritative than other religious myths, gods, goddesses, and legends.

Are these three positions mutually exclusive? If one chooses one position, does this mean that one has nothing to say to or hear from those who adopt different stances? I think this will depend on the position one adopts. If one takes the first position, namely a literal reading of the scripture as the authoritative source for doing theology (what we would loosely call fundamentalism), one would not countenance the views of those who took the second and third positions. In other words, dialogue would not be possible. However, for those who see scripture as one source amongst others, whatever weight one gave to scripture, there would be a basis for some sort of dialogue. The relationship between these three stances, and the possibility or otherwise for dialogue, becomes important as we move to consider the issue of authority.

Before I consider the issue of authority, I would like to conclude this section on scripture by saying that we have to recognize an essential and continuing tension between the witness of scripture and the church's context, life, and teaching. It is this tension that gives vitality both to the church and to scripture. Many writers have stressed the existentialist position that the context and attitude of the interpreter have a deep effect on the meaning of the text. The African in a situation of poverty gives a different meaning to the text from that provided by an affluent believer in the U.S.A. The meaning does not reside simply in the text but in the reader's view of the text. Is one more correct than the other?

The importance of the Bible is that it provides a common reference point for all Christian people. It is a guide to life, not a lawbook, and its meaning and authority have to be worked out by the local Christian community. In this sense the authority of the church and that of the Bible go hand in hand, and their authority have to be *freely* accepted.

THE QUESTION OF AUTHORITY

One of the interesting side effects of the Lambeth debates on the ordination of women in 1988, and on homosexuality in 1998, has been a reexamination of the question of authority in Anglicanism. In those provinces where there is a disagreement with the majority stance taken on the homosexuality issue, people have been at pains to stress that decisions taken at Lambeth have no binding authority on any bishop or province in the Communion. Those bishops in the majority have not argued to the contrary. However some, including the Archbishop of Canterbury, have urged bishops to display unity and not to "go it alone." The issue is of course much broader and deeper than simply the debate on homosexuality. It goes to a fundamental question within Anglicanism: the nature and extent of authority. That is not a new question.

THE NATURE OF AUTHORITY

Authority "refers to the capacity someone has to commend free assent to another."[1] Edward Yarnold stresses that the word "free" is essential, and for this reason authority is not synonymous with power. However, the two cannot be divorced. Authority suggests the legitimate use of power. Legitimization may arise from agreement between those who have power and those who do not; or it may arise in a less mutual way. What is important is the recognition that authority implies relationship and is a dynamic process rather than a static rule. That this is so is evidenced by the changing attitudes towards all forms of authority, both ecclesial and secular, in the past twenty years.

The Lambeth Conference of 1948 argued that authority is grounded in the life of the Trinity, and that all other authority is secondary. I have recently come across a model proposed by David Cunningham in his 1998 book on trinitarian theology, *These Three Are One*. On the basis of the trinitarian relationship he suggests a relationship of persuasion rather than power or coercion.[2] Cunningham distinguishes persuasion (which is committed to nonviolence) from coercion or compulsion, with which he associates violence, oppression, and force.[3]

The 1948 Lambeth Conference went on to argue that secondary authority is distributed interactively between a variety of elements including scripture, reason, tradition, the creeds, ministry, the witness of the saints and the *consensus fidelium*, thus excluding any one of these secondary authorities from claiming primary status. Such understanding furthermore reinforces the understanding of the dynamic, relational nature of authority. An interesting observation on this dynamic interaction is made by Stephen Sykes, who suggests that conflict is a probability in such a persuasive, interactional model of authority.[4]

Cunningham's model of persuasion is, I want to suggest, peculiarly apposite for the Anglican situation. The Anglican Communion, unlike the Roman Catholic Church, has no formal teaching authority. There is no one body or organ charged with maintaining "sacred doctrine." Indeed it is a moot point whether there is any such thing as "core doctrine" in Anglicanism.[5] On the other hand, unlike some of the other Protestant churches, the Anglican church does not recognize scripture as the only authority. With multiple authorities (as recognized above) there are three possibilities: coercion, ostracism, or persuasion.

If this trinitarian model of persuasion were to be adopted, what would some of the consequences be for the way we are the church? Cunningham suggests three significant consequences:

First, multiple voices would be heard. Second, there would be an "interweaving" of the lives of those in authority with others. Finally, we would recognize the need for holding a space for particularity or difference.

THE QUESTION OF EPISCOPAL AUTHORITY

The place of episcopal authority has come under the spotlight recently with the Anglican–Roman Catholic International Consultation (ARCIC) statement *The Gift of Authority*, and the Anglican Consultative Council (ACC) has referred the ARCIC document for study and discussion over the next five years.[6] The document, however, operates from the assumption that authority and power are synonymous. The authority referred to in *The Gift of Authority* is primarily the authority of the Pope. What, though, would Cunningham's model of persuasion suggest for episcopal authority? I believe our current model, and the model presupposed by the ARCIC document, is challenged by Cunningham's vision of persuasion. However, Cunningham's vision does not exclude episcopacy. What is excluded is the model of authority which suggests that the church speaks with "one voice" from a fixed foundation of "truth." What is also excluded is the model of authority which gives power to one who is removed (either geographically or relationally) from the local context.

As we go on to examine some of the issues facing the Anglican Communion, namely, inculturation of the gospel and human sexuality, we will use the model of persuasion as a basis for considering approaches to those issues.

INCULTURATION

One of the key issues for the Anglican church, as well as for the church in Africa generally, is the issue of africanization. The need for the indigenization and africanization of the church in Africa has long been recognized. It has been felt all the more, now that most of the African countries have been decolonized, and since South Africa held its first democratic election in 1994. Earlier African theologians began with condemnation of missionaries' involvement in colonial rule, denigration of traditional rites and customs, attitudes of racial superiority, and of paternalism, and an unhappy desire to keep the African church for as long as possible under European rule. Some African theologians have proceeded in the search for African expressions of Christianity in terms of the need for Christianity to free itself from the influences of the colonial and apartheid eras. Thus they grapple with the relationship between Christian faith and political power. The liberation approach became a dominant model in this regard, and was popularized especially by theologians from the South. Other African theologians, like John Mbiti, sought to relate the Christian faith to African culture and tradition.[7] In theological circles, inculturation or indigenization has become the defining aspect of this approach. Yet others have argued for a symbiosis of both approaches. In all approaches the use of scripture was of significant essence, albeit approached differently.

THE USE OF SCRIPTURE TO LEGITIMIZE/VALIDATE APPROACHES TO THE AFRICANIZATION OF CHRISTIANITY

Early attempts towards the africanization of Christianity, informed by the inculturation model, used the methods learned from the early missionaries and colonialists, namely the reliance upon scripture as a primary text. All things to be included in the Christian fold had to be justified on scriptural grounds. Theologians who have used this approach include John Mbiti, Edward Fashole-Luke, and Kwesi Dickson. Fashole-Luke, for example, believed that biblical categories had to be "translated into the social milieu and thought forms of the African continent." The major weakness of this approach towards indigenization is that it sought to dress Christianity in African culture while maintaining its foreignness in terms of symbols, thought forms, and value systems. In practice this implied the adaptation of the European practices and thought patterns to the cultural life of the people of Africa.

Even more objectionable is the assumption that scripture has independence from the culture in which it is read, and therefore has authority over African traditions and values. The use of scripture to legitimize africanization of Christianity was an attempt to impose European domination and control upon Africa. It echoes the prevalent but unacceptable presumption that the North knows better what is best for the South. Scripture became a tool of domination in the sense that African Christians could not escape the colonial models of being Christian. All models of Christianity came from outside, rather than inside Africa. The approach was intended to maintain the status quo, even though the model was used by the African theologians themselves. Oppression through colonial domination had been internalized. Models of being church remained hierarchical and colonial.

In an article entitled "Is There an African Democracy?" Herbert Vilakazi, a South African academic and member of the Independent Electoral Commission, reminds us that a similar uncritical incorporation of Western-style government has resulted in postcolonial African governments slavishly following Western models rather than drawing on truly African understandings of community and government.

Theologians Who Took Expression of Local Cultures as the Primary Source

Another shift took place wherein African culture and tradition were treated as the primary source alongside the Bible, largely owing to the influence of liberation theology in the sixties. Theologians such as Parratt, Mosala and Manas Buthelezi exemplified this shift, which opened the canon of scripture to include the stories and myths of African people. This new method used such stories and myths as valid and authoritative texts for doing theology in Africa.

The value of this model is that it began to undermine some of the colonial models of being church—for example, by assuming that one does not have to go via England in order to come to Africa. The weakness of the model is that it continued to maintain patriarchy in the sense that it was unable to critique patriarchal models, and so it was self-defeating. Leadership in the church in Africa has remained almost exclusively in the hands of men. This is well illustrated by the debates at Lambeth 1988 and 1998 on the issue of polygamy. Here was an attempt to reincorporate an aspect of many African cultures, without any regard at all to the voice of African women.

Feminist Critique of the Use of Scripture

Significant contributions by women in the church in Africa began to be realized in the 1990s. Previously women were not only excluded from theological discourse but they were even excluded from theological education, thus denying them a voice. Having entered the debate, though, the feminist critique reminds us trenchantly of how patriarchal are our models of the interpretation of scripture. Feminists call for a different way of being church and look toward inclusivity.

WHO DOES INCULTURATION?

Whereas the colonial models, which intended to entrench control, were monocultural and exclusive, inculturation has come to mean not so much the revocation of non-African ways of being, but rather the inclusion of the tradition of the church whilst at the same time rooting its practice in the symbols and traditions of Africa. For example, the Christian symbol of the cross, whilst not especially African, is central to Christianity and stands at the center of African Christian worship. Where contextualization has taken place is in the replacing of a caucasian-featured Jesus on the cross with an African figure.

During the colonial period those who were the principal actors were the foreign missionaries. They were followed by Africans who still used the European way of doing things. This then gave way to a model which moved to an African way of doing things. In turn this model was criticized by the feminist theologians who pointed out that women were excluded from the circle. If we are to be truly inclusive, we need all these voices, together, rather than replacing one set of actors with another.

If we revert to Cunningham's model of persuasion we might note the following:

- All the voices of Africa—including missionaries, local people, women and men—are needed in order to develop a truly African Christianity.

- Both the traditional and contemporary symbols and interpretations are needed.

- There is no single definitive version of contextualized Christianity. There will be as many variations as there are influences and voices.

SEXUALITY AND GENDER

The next issue to which we turn is, like the issue of inculturation, not an issue peculiar to the Anglican church. It has, however, been given added prominence in the Anglican Communion since the last Lambeth Conference. No one who took even the remotest interest in the 1998 Lambeth Conference can fail to have observed that one of the major issues of this conference was homosexuality. The discussion centered on the place of homosexual persons in the church and the way the church should respond to homosexual persons in their chosen lifestyle—for example, those who seek the church's blessing of their union, or those who seek ordination.

I do not want to rehearse the debate again. However, those debates offer three significant insights within the context of this paper:

First, we might note the reliance on scripture to support a position condemning homosexuality *per se*, or homosexual activity specifically. Those who are convinced that homosexuality is sinful, or at best a lamentable condition which requires of homosexual persons a commitment to lifelong celibacy, point to scripture as self-evidently clear on the issue. Biblical texts were seldom examined in their context. The understanding of homosexuality in biblical times was not explored, or even questioned as being different from our own understandings. In the light of the three positions identified when we looked at the authority of scripture, this acceptance of the biblical position falls into the first or second of the two categories: namely, that scripture needs no interpretation, or secondly, that it needs interpretation, and those condemning homosexuality have the authority to interpret the scripture in the way they have done. In other words, it was assumed that the Bible spoke clearly on the issue and that homosexuality is sinful at worst, or at best is a condition which calls for lifelong celibacy. Given that the scriptures were written at least twenty centuries ago, before the advent and development of our current medical, psychological, and sociological studies, this attitude towards scripture might validly be accused of being simply a way to support a particular prejudice.

The second insight offered by the Lambeth debates derives from the obvious failure to look towards, let alone rely upon, other sources for doing theology—sources such as reason, tradition, culture, and most significantly, experience. Most of us are aware of the embarrassing refusal of the Lambeth group tasked with looking at the issue to listen to the stories of homosexual persons. However, it was not simply that the experience of homosexual persons was ignored. So, too, medical and psychological evidence was not considered.

Finally, there was no hesitation in assuming that Lambeth had the right (indeed some would say the obligation) to make a pronouncement on the issue. In other words, it was simply assumed that the bishops of the Anglican Communion had the right to make a decision as to how homosexual persons are to be received (or not, as the case may be) within the Communion. Unlike Cunningham's persuasion model, there was no consultation with the wider church, no engaging in debate with local congregations on their experiences.

On this emotional issue, as in similar issues, there appears to be a conscious or unconscious weighing in favor of the Bible as the primary source, an acceptance that "ultimate truth" is to be discovered in scripture—despite the Anglican assurance that theology is derived from a number of sources.

As we grapple with these issues, perhaps we need to take note of what Canon John Suggit says in his book *The Word of God and the People of God,* where he suggests that we need to discover the leading themes of the scriptures which can help control our interpretation.[8] Canon Suggit suggests that these are the loving faithfulness of God, and God's righteousness, resulting in effect in the supremacy of the two commandments of love of God and love of others. Others have suggested such themes as liberation and mercy as providing the key to interpretation. In this way we may be helped to let the local context become so important as to negate the universal appeal of scripture.

No doubt we have to be aware of the danger of allowing such diverse interpretations of scripture as would render the faith of one Anglican Province so different from another as to be unrecognizable. That was the problem in the early church, which led to a definition of heresy and which put the church's faith into a straitjacket.

CONCLUSION

How has the Lambeth decision affected the Anglican Provinces around the world? At a worldwide level it has highlighted divisions in the Communion. The pleas by a number of bishops for unity in the Communion evidence the recognition of this division. In my own context in the Church of the Province of Southern Africa, the decision has similarly divided people. Some are pleased that the church has taken a "strong stand" against homosexuality. Others feel that an injustice has been perpetrated. More than any other issue of our time, this one has served to illustrate the wide difference between us in theology, in theological method, in the use of scripture, in our response to authority, and in how that authority is defined.

The issue of homosexuality is not alone, though, in highlighting our differences. The debates at Lambeth in regard to interfaith dialogue, for example, have similarly exposed our very different approaches.

Underlying these differences is the unspoken but ever-present challenge to examine what exactly we mean by authority in our postmodern context. I am not suggesting a movement into anarchic antiauthoritarianism, but a critical questioning of what Cunningham describes as fixed foundations of truth giving rise to one voice. We are coming to recognize more and more that institutional authority is never independent of those who invest a person or body with that authority. To put it bluntly, bishops are authoritative in the church as long as the members of the church assent to allowing that authority to persist.

Does this suggest that Cunningham's model of persuasion is not just a nice alternative, but indeed the only viable model if we are to hold onto one another in our differences? Is the challenge to us, with all our differences and questions, to seek out in conversation with one another that which is good, healthy, and life-giving, with all the risk that that implies in having to let go of old securities? If this is our challenge it is indeed a radical one, but so too of course is the gospel.

Notes

[1] Edward Yarnold, "Teaching with Authority," *The Way* 21:3 (1981): 168.

[2] David Cunningham, *These Three Are One* (Oxford: Blackwell, 1998), 304.

[3] Ibid., 307.

[4] Stephen Sykes, *The Integrity of Anglicanism* (London: Mowbray, 1978), 87.

[5] See for example Charles Hefling "On Core Doctrine" *Anglican Theological Review* 80:2 (1998): 233.

[6] ARCIC Statement, *The Gift of Authority* (New York: Church Publishing, 1999).

[7] John Mbiti, *New Testament Eschatology in an African Background* (London: Oxford University Press, 1971).

[8] John Suggit, *The Word of God and the People of God* (Cape Town: The Celebration of Faith, 1994).

11

THE PRIMACY OF BAPTISM

A Reaffirmation of Authority in the Church

FREDRICA HARRIS THOMPSETT

AN IDENTITY CRISIS?

There is one thing on which most Anglicans can agree: faithful people across the world, and not simply within the Anglican Communion, are seeking greater understanding and clarity about their religious identity. This is indeed good news. Knowing who we are is foundational; it cannot be taken for granted in this pluralistic world. This search for identity occurs in conversations and conflicts experienced within our own congregations and denominational families, as well as amid the wider dialogues and challenges of ecumenical and interreligious life. In these and other contexts, the desire for deeper understanding and insight is as widespread at the start of this new millennium as it was among the multiple allegiances, cultures, and communities inhabited by our earliest Christian ancestors. Yet, many of us believe that in this rapidly changing world we face greater complexities than our ancestors. At the local and global levels we encounter a multicultural, multilingual, multiracial, and multireligious world. We live in societies marked by vast economic disparities of abundance and want. Most of the world's population struggles to live amid the devastations of abject poverty, homelessness, famine, and with the unjustified devastations of war, genocide, and other daily manifestations of violence. There is as well a raging global consumerism that creates greedy and unfulfilled populations, while our planet bears the ravages of increasing ecological devastation. This is a shared global context. There are other significant philosophical, economic and societal shifts that directly challenge the ways Anglicans and others look at authority, leadership, and identity. Ian T. Douglas has described these movements in an earlier chapter in this volume.[1]

Along the way, the character of the contemporary Anglican Communion has changed markedly from a predominantly white and English-speaking church dominated by Western and mostly-privileged male voices, to a global community of thirty-eight autonomous Provinces whose fastest growing populations are in the southern hemisphere. In terms of a more concretely embodied, incarnational image, we might best envision the average Anglican today as a black African who does not speak English as her mother tongue. Today few Anglicans can escape the fact that we are members of an increasingly multicultural Communion. Thus when speaking about the Anglican Communion it is important to be clear about who we have in mind. In fact, given this changing global reality, it may well be impossible for any single voice, no matter how well-intentioned, to encompass and speak authoritatively for Anglicans.

There are various responses to the multiple identities emerging in the contemporary Anglican Communion. As authority shifts globally and new leaders and populations emerge with greater prominence, former authorities are being challenged. Some of those who were and are accustomed to being in charge complain that the Communion lacks "unity." They question whether the center will hold and, as a remedy, seek enhanced centralized authority that will insist upon uniformity. In this call for unity, the issue of control, who holds the power, is central. Others believe that theological unity is a phony issue: "The only crisis in our church is the crisis manufactured by those who will not accept the reality of a pluralistic community."[2] They believe that the key issue at stake is sharing power and resources. Still others, working amid difference and conflict, commit themselves to naming common and emerging identities shaped within a multicultural plurality of traditions. They recognize that the gospel is pastorally and prophetically grounded in particular and diverse contexts, and seek to honor this reality as a traditional component of religious life. Various responses to these and other "identity crises" might be characterized on one hand by the demand to "tighten up" the structures of Anglican authority, and on the other hand by the opportunity for "opening up" liberating and reforming understandings of leadership and authority. Recently I heard this tension described as an ecclesiological contest between those in the church who wish "to keep the faith pure" and those who wish to respond by "keeping faith" in a rapidly changing world.

While I recognize truths claimed within and between these expressed tensions, I am attracted theologically toward the "opening up" and "keeping faith" stances. Indeed, as an historical theologian I find this direction is formative of traditional Anglican practice. This is an exciting and highly promising time for the church to seek both new and continuing truths about its identity. I bring to this quest experience as a Christian educator, a church historian, a feminist scholar, a former dean of an Episcopal seminary, an enthusiastic member of the laity, and an author of books emphasizing authority and leadership among the baptized.[3] Yet as a lifelong Episcopalian, a white, economically privileged member of a Western church, my assumptions about identity and authority have been repeatedly challenged, sobered, and deepened by listening to diverse global and local conversations. Still, the local parish with its members at work in the world remains for me the primary "school of the spirit."[4] In the 1990s my educational responsibility for understanding the broad living tradition represented within the Provinces of the Anglican Communion took on a new shape when I was asked to serve as an Episcopal Church USA representative to the Inter-Anglican Theological and Doctrinal Commission (known by the acronym IATDC). This global Commission of theologians—convened by resolution of the 1988 Lambeth Conference and by invitation of the Archbishop of Canterbury—was asked to reflect theologically on issues of Anglican identity and authority. By 1998 its work was summarized and presented to the Lambeth Conference in the *Virginia Report*.[5] From the vantage point of my own experience and that of the Province I represented at IATDC, I do not share this report's concluding call for greater centralization of hierarchical authority.[6] However, I do not regret learning from and contributing to the contextual storytelling and local theological wisdom evidenced by IATDC members.

My intent in this essay is not primarily to rehearse or reflect upon the work of IATDC, although this experience is directly germane to what I write below. Nor do I wish in this essay to detail the dramatic moves that are turning some Anglicans toward the historically unprecedented ground of advocating universal authority as a necessary component of life in a global communion. Others have told this story and critiqued its sense of direction.[7] I do want to point to two central lessons. First of all, I wish to underscore the role that theology, as disciplined reflection on lived practice, can and does play in illuminating questions of religious identity. In various ways when Anglicans and others address issues of "identity and authority," they are exploring ecclesiology, the theology of the church. *Where* we choose to begin sustained theological reflection provides a crucial and essential clue to the intent, direction and, perhaps, the conclusion of a conversation. The assignment that Lambeth 1988 handed to IATDC was occasioned by "a matter of urgency" challenging the "unity and order of the Church." Although the 1988 enabling resolution did not say so, the "matter of urgency" was widely understood to be the ordination of women to the presbyterate in various Provinces of the Communion and the likelihood that one or more Provinces of the church would soon elect women to the episcopate. The traditional episcopate, so some of the Lambeth bishops warned, was changing precariously. Authority at the top of the church's institutional life was shifting, here as elsewhere in society. Thus it was no accident that the 1988 Lambeth Conference sought to strengthen the unity of the church with "particular reference to the doctrine of the Trinity" and to contemplate "enhanced responsibility for the Primates Meetings."[8]

My second observation is that any continuing conversations about a "postcolonial" ecclesiological framework or expectation must come to terms not only with a long history of privileged colonialist assumptions that have marked the history of this church, but also with the fact that the last twentieth-century meeting of Anglican hierarchy—the 1998 Lambeth Conference of Bishops—focused on reinforcing and extending top-down, clerically driven assertions of oversight. Resolutions from Lambeth 1998 mandate a decade of future study led by Primates on this question: "whether effective communion, at all levels, does not require appropriate instruments, with due safeguards, not only for legislation, but also for oversight?"[9] A positive response to this leading question is assumed. In colonial and still in neocolonial settings, authority can be expressed by one identifiable voice, a centralizing authority that can and will speak for all others. A neocolonial questioner knows the response to the question before it is asked. Whatever "appropriate instruments" are devised, the overall direction of Lambeth's recent resolutions on identity and authority predict a future shaped by enhanced primatial authority.

Instead, in this chapter I will advocate a more expansive and collaborative vision of the church's future. While I draw primarily upon those local and provincial experiences that I know best, I invite others to bring their own experience to these reflections. The renewal of the Episcopal Church, as the recent *Zacchaeus Report* attests, is being shaped in the continuing vitality and power of local congregations.[10] The formative identity conveyed in baptism provides the foundational and sustaining base for exercising authority within the local church and the world. Structurally and theologically, authority for Christians begins with baptism. Shaping well-grounded ministerial communities depends upon baptismal affirmation of authority in the church. The primacy of baptism provides an ecclesiological identity for Anglican authority. What would "churches reborn" in the chaos and creativity of baptism look like?[11] What signs and theological clues would they manifest about God's covenant with humanity, about humane relationships that respect diversity, about Christian mission and witness in a postcolonial world, and about the structurally authoritative ways to express the witness of the baptized? What promise does a baptismally-based ecclesiology hold for living together ecumenically and with those of other faiths? In response to these and other everyday concerns about identity and authority, the centrality of baptism provides an open-ended affirmation of God's promises to humanity. The delineation of this alternative vision of authority shaped in the local church is the central focus of this essay. Along the way, however, it is important to observe that the formative ecclesiological character of baptism has at best been taken for granted when it comes to hierarchical consideration of authority. The *Virginia Report*, for example, notes parenthetically its "hope" for strengthening the "ministry and mission of the whole people of God" given in baptism. This report "necessarily dwells" on those who exercise structural ministries of oversight.[12] To put it more bluntly, the primacy of baptism as the sign of Christian identity and authority at work among God's people is, in the *Virginia Report*, secondary to the primacy of Primates Meetings.

OTHER STARTING POINTS AND APPROACHES

Preliminary to exploring baptism as an alternative ecclesiological identity, it is important to recall that global conversations among Anglicans about the theological structures do not typically result in augmenting the authority of those at the top of the church's hierarchy. Despite trends evident in the *Virginia Report* and resolutions of Lambeth 1998, other alternatives, structural processes, and theological directions have prevailed within officially convened international Anglican theological conversations. Even from Lambeth 1998, Section III of the Report observes "the Anglican Communion has developed an ecclesiology without a centralized authority which acts juridically on behalf of all its member churches."[13] In short, when Anglicans reflect with greater clarity on their identity and authority, it is not inevitable that they will call for enhanced primatial jurisdiction. Indeed, given understandings of authority which at least since 1948 have described authority as "dispersed" throughout the Communion, quite the reverse is true.[14] Anglicans have historically exhibited a family resemblance that dynamically engages the voices of tradition as well as innovation. Let me cite two relatively recent examples. I share these stories to illustrate the significance of affirming contextual differences, of engaging in open-ended processes that admit and learn from vastly different theological perspectives, and of claiming apt theological starting points. It is possible to envision the quest for clarity about religious identity as an opportunity that honors cultural differences with integrity.

The work of the first Inter-Anglican Theological and Doctrinal Commission—called for by the Anglican Consultative Council in 1976 and convened by resolution of the 1978 Lambeth Conference—provides an alternative vision. Its specific charge was to explore "the diverse and changing cultural contexts in which the gospel is proclaimed, received and lived." The 1985 report of this IATDC, *For the Sake of the Kingdom: God's Church and the New Creation*, affirmed the difficult ecclesiological labor of seeking comprehensive understanding amid seemingly incompatible views of the kingdom of God. It also noted that struggles for "belonging and pluralism" are centuries-old marks of Anglican life. These theologians emphasized a serious call to repentance as essential for engaging a variety of religious cultures and movements for liberation "particularly but not exclusively in the Third world." This first IATDC concluded by affirming pluralism as a continuing and valued component in the church's life:

> [Pluralism] means to assert that there is good in the existence and continuing integrity of a variety of traditions and ways of life [and] it means to assert that there is good in their interplay and dialogue…. At the same time, [pluralism] acknowledges that, in the dialogue between traditions, people's understanding of the meaning of God's Kingdom, and of the Christ who bears it, may be enhanced.[15]

This report bears rereading by those who assume that the search for Anglican identity is for the "sake of unity," rather than for the "sake of the Kingdom." The theological substance of this report identifies a critical and carefully defined affirmation of pluralism and a theology of repentance as essential components of contemporary Anglican ecclesiology.

Yet this theological legacy apparently did not register, at least at the top levels of the Communion. The resolutions of Lambeth 1988 do not even record customary thanks to the 1978 IATDC for its report, *For the Sake of the Kingdom*. Instead, as I've noted, only three years after this report was issued, the 1988 Lambeth Conference of Bishops (predictably meeting for the last time as the "Lambeth Fathers") called for a brand new IATDC to address those urgent issues of unity, identity, and authority.

My second story concerns the early work of the newly commissioned 1988 IATDC. The labors of this Consultation and the positive emphasis it placed on interdependence among Provinces have been overshadowed by the prominence given to the *Virginia Report* at Lambeth 1998. Still, there are lessons to be gleaned from IATDC's early life together. When this international group of Anglicans first met in 1991, we did not focus on women's ordination. We knew that another group, the Eames Commission, was addressing this matter. Nor did most of the twenty-two members of this Consultation frame our task as talking about structural "instruments of unity." Instead, we gradually came to envision our responsibility as holding up and strengthening ways that the Provinces could embrace a positive sense of identity and interdependence within the Communion. The results of our labors were printed in 1992 as a study document entitled "Belonging Together," a text that was circulated for response throughout the Provinces of the Communion.

The process used in this meeting directly contributed to its conclusions. Who was there and how we traveled together theologically shaped our identity.[16] For most members English was not their first language; still we wisely began by taking considerable time with storytelling from our local, diocesan, or provincial contexts. Again and again we heard stories of interdependence: an isolated Palestinian priest emphasized the importance of supportive prayer from Anglicans throughout the world; a woman leader from predominantly Muslim Pakistan shared with us the strength of women of that country as they pressed for solidarity and communication with other women; a Brazilian bishop told of widespread poverty, noting how everyone's attitudes toward food and possessions changed when inflation was thirty percent a month; and a six-foot-three Ugandan bishop who, when I walked with him to see the Lincoln Memorial, spoke of men as tall as Lincoln in his country and their families dying from the scourge of AIDS. Such stories can be multiplied and must not, as our text notes, "be measured lightly." These and other illustrations reveal how the church's life and identity are challenged by the diverse contexts in which Christians live. Reflecting theologically in the conversations that followed, we spoke (and argued) about what we believed the church could and could not accomplish, we identified commonalities shared by Anglicans, we named theological and traditional resources (including the doctrine of the Trinity) at our disposal for revitalizing interdependence, and finally we asked honest questions about what fuller interdependence might look like. Our work was far from perfect. A "neocolonial" description might suffice, given predominant voices and laptops from the West. Still we claimed:

> The concern about identity and authority is not a sign of weakness or anxiety. It is a mark of our determination to be faithful to the Triune God who is the ground and pattern of communion. This commits us to common dialogue and decision-making, locally, globally and ecumenically. Because we share a common faith in humanity, we are challenged to be interdependent in all the issues that touch our humanity and faith.[17]

We concluded this meeting by putting in place an open-ended process inviting responses from Provinces and other church bodies. We wondered whether our study document reflected their experience and understanding of church, and we bluntly asked how our "belonging together" might be strengthened without stifling diversity.

These two episodes illustrate the power of storytelling and of theological conversations that name difference and pluralism as part of the everyday realities of life together. They represent as well the value of naming and claiming those traditional commonalities—including worship and prayer, Bible study, commitment to mission and service, and the appeal to scripture, tradition and reason—shared by most Anglicans. They confidently point toward expansive theological futures that encompass pluralism, honor diverse cultural roots, and envision interdependent processes of consultation—locally, globally, and ecumenically—as formative for living together.

IDENTITY GROUNDED IN BAPTISM

The values named above can all be found within local churches. Indeed, I believe that local congregations are practical schools for shaping understanding of what the church is called to be. It is in such local sites that ecclesiology is grounded, that ministering communities develop and express the love, labors and authority of their members, and that connections between the global and local realities are nourished. In its totality the Anglican Communion is essentially a "virtual reality,"—a concept, and not a place we can visit. Lasting ecclesiastical identities cannot be shaped on paper; they grow out of communities living the gospel at the local level. When considering new possibilities for the church, and especially when dreaming vibrant visions of a church that sheds both colonial and neocolonial assumptions and structures, it is crucial that we consider the church realistically from the bottom up. Theology at its best is disciplined reflection on lived practice. "Theology," as Desmond Tutu once noted, "is also ethics."[18] It expresses the ways we work together, what we care to notice, who is included and whose voice is overlooked, dismissed or absent, and who are the active agents and authoritative leaders. In what follows, I wish to outline central characteristics of ecclesiology shaped in the dense communal sacramentality of baptism. What would a church reborn in the witnessing waters of baptism look like? What would be its identity? How would it exercise authority? I will look for, name and highlight signs—ancient and postmodern—that hold promise for our respective futures as people of faith.

Postcolonial visions of ecclesiology, of new and renewing churches, begin with God and the people God has called into covenant. We must reorient our theological compass from the start toward the holy character of all creation, including created humanity. The biblical story tells of a God pleased with the goodness of creation. Biblical scholar L. William Countryman observes: "God is the first source, the prime mover and the most lavish giver."[19] My parish priest speaks of God as an "inimitable profligate," the Holy One who withholds neither love, nor expectation, nor responsibility, nor forgiveness. The first theological clue I would expect in a church reborn without the oppressions of its imperial, colonial past is a church *that reaffirms and renews the holy character of creation*. The vast ecological devastations of the past century represent a genuine "crisis," an environmental one that faithful communities cannot ignore. Addressing this crisis is part of our continuing covenant with God. "Do you renounce the evil powers of this world which corrupt and destroy the creatures of God?" the parish priest asked; and the five-year-old girl next to me confidently responded, "He means pollution." Baptismal communities are called to live in harmony with creation and with God.

One of the characteristics expressed by churches that biblically ground their ecclesiology in baptism is an *intense interest in humanity*. I have drawn this theological hallmark from the work of Denise Ackermann, a South African professor of practical theology:

> All theological categories form part of the central drama of humanity's relation with God and the world we live in.... It is necessary for all theological inquiry to start from an intense interest in humanity—to do otherwise would be methodologically and ethically wrong.[20]

It is wrong-headed to believe that we can love the Creator and hate the created. Baptism as a structural reality asserts our common humanity, it affirms the "humanness" of blacks in pre– and post-apartheid South Africa, and it argues for the dignity of all people, especially the most vulnerable. The sacrament of baptism does not make a child or an adult "holy," rather it allows us to recognize how beloved and special each one is in God's creation. Country-man concludes that for laity as well as for clergy: "Nothing can sur-pass the gifts bestowed on you in birth and interpreted through baptism."[21] I would expect postcolonial baptismal communities to express an intense interest in humanity as "part of God's creation, made in the image of God," rather than an intense interest in man-made hierarchies.[22]

I have begun these reflections by focusing first of all on God's liberating activity and relationship with humankind, rather than with a singular focus on the institutional church. The most famous neo-orthodox theologian of the twentieth century, Karl Barth, is said to have introduced a sermon: "I have three points in mind this morning. First, God is omnipotent—all-powerful. Second, God is omniscient—all-knowing. Third, now some random thoughts on baptism." In the thoughts that follow my intent is to deepen understanding of the authoritative changes promised in baptism. Particularly when considering identity and authority, baptism must *not* be taken for granted, or assumed to be at best a passing, initial, identity for Christians.

The most familiar characteristic of baptism is that it *shapes our primary and continuing identity as Christians*. Biblically, through bap-tism new believers were forgiven, born anew in Christ and dis-persed as at Pentecost to be God's people at work in the world (see Acts 2). Theologically and structurally, baptism gives us our special character as Christians. From a postcolonial perspective it is important to emphasize that we are baptized into the body of Christ, baptized as Christians, not as members of this or that denomination. Baptism grounds us ecumenically, as illustrated in the World Council of Churches' influential document, *Baptism, Eucharist, and Ministry*.[23]

While in the early Christian communities interpretations and practices around baptism varied, our New Testament ancestors knew baptism as a powerful communal experience, not a private or singular observance. Paul in particular cherished the promise that *baptism overcomes all that alienates and divides human beings*. He and others emphasized the radical baptismal promise of unity wrought by God, that in Christ: "there is no longer Jew or Greek, there is no longer slave or free, there is no longer male and female; for all of you are one in Christ Jesus" (Gal. 3:28). This key biblical text, which recent scholarship agrees is part of a Pauline baptismal confession, presents baptism as a social definition in which "all the baptized are equal, they are one in Christ."[24] Biblical baptismal promises provide substance to the abolition of oppressive distinctions based on religion, race, class, gender, or nationality. In effect Christians are rendered equal in baptism. Biblical theologian William Stringfellow restates the implications of this promise:

> [Baptism is] the sacrament of the extraordinary unity among humanity wrought by God in overcoming ... all that alienates, segregates, divides, and destroys human beings in their relationship with each other, within their own persons, and in their relationship with the rest of creation.[25]

In social terms baptism creates continuing and expansive communities. Many of us already know and experience this reality within our local churches.

Let me hasten to add that this baptismal foundation does *not* work to render diverse peoples, languages, traditions, and cultures invisible. Baptism was originally an intracultural practice and *not* a single-group identity as Empire would later make it. Indeed, given the biblical and contemporary significance of different contextual expressions of the gospel, it is important to affirm interdependent relationships forged across difference. In her paper delivered at Lambeth 1998, "Becoming Fully Human: An Ethic of Relationship in Difference and Otherness," Denise Ackermann argues that "mutuality is the reciprocal interdependence of equals."[26] To paraphrase Ackermann's reinterpretation of the baptismal legacy: *baptism recognizes and values our mutual relational identity as one of difference and otherness.* Baptism not only shapes our primary identity as Christians, through baptism we are challenged to recognize and affirm our complementarity with others. These legacies of equality, mutuality, and respect for difference are not obvious hallmarks of the colonial past. They are, however, essential lifelines for moving beyond colonialist practices and structures.

A traditional and reaffirmed understanding of *baptism provides the liturgical grounding for mission and this in turn shapes Christian ministry.* Christians are baptized into God's mission, the *missio Dei* that seeks nothing less than the *shalom* of God.[27] Verna Dozier, a biblical theologian, observes: "the most important thing about Jesus' baptism is that by it his mission is set."[28] The form and ordering of ministries flow from the common mission of seeking reconciliation in the world. Fortunately new Prayer Book resources—including those used in the United States, Canada, and New Zealand—call forth the renewal of baptismal ministries. This contemporary liturgical renewal movement has again placed baptism at the center of the Christian life. In the Episcopal Church the service of Holy Baptism includes a "Baptismal Covenant" in which all present, not only the candidates for baptism and their sponsors, renew their commitment to Christian life in the activities of worship, forgiveness, proclamation, service and justice-making. Similarly, a new Catechism boldly describes "ministers" of the church as "lay persons, bishops, priests, and deacons."[29] Baptism shapes our primary and continuing ministerial identity. English theologian and bishop Stephen Sykes describes baptism as the "framework for the whole of Christian living." No one, he emphatically adds, ever moves "beyond" it.[30] Aiden Kavanagh, a liturgical scholar, agrees: "Christians thus do not ordain to priesthood, they baptize to it. While the episcopacy and the presbyterate do come upon one for the first time at ordination, priesthood per se does not; it comes upon one in baptism, and thus *laos* is a priestly term for a priestly person."[31] Clericalist assumptions that see clergy as the "real" or "serious" Christians distort the ordering of ministry by placing a higher prominence on ordination than on baptism. The witness of the baptized is primary and not secondary for the church's future.

AUTHORITY IN BAPTISM

When I was a child, three words stood out for me in the 1928 Book of Common Prayer: "Name this Child."[32] Naming was key to the ministration of baptism as the child (or older person) was received and welcomed as Christ's "own." The authority of Christians begins first with naming and then with baptism. Today as an adult who regularly participates in Holy Baptism and Holy Eucharist services celebrated in my local congregation, I am still caught up by the communal promises, responsibilities, and energetic responsiveness conveyed in baptism. Again it is theologian Verna Dozier who reminds us that "religious authority comes with baptism." Such authority, she continues, "is of God. Human beings do not give it. Human beings cannot take it away. Sinful human beings, however, can surrender it."[33] *The authority of baptism expansively grounds Christian witness in local, cultural, and socio-political contexts.* Since such authority is of God, we can expect to find it blossoming abundantly up from the people of God when the full potential of baptismal ministry is affirmed. Yet, even the most charitable reading of Lambeth 1998 resolutions on authority do not give this impression. This is ironic, given the *Official Report's* rhetorical praise for the extensive gifts bestowed in baptism.[34] Apparently such gifts do not lead to substantial structural recognition of the authority of both laity and clergy assembled for mission. Here again it is important to pay attention to William Stringfellow's warning that American and other churches persistently belittle "the authority that baptism vests in the laity."[35] What remedies, what opportunities for leadership and other interpretive practices are necessary to reaffirm the authority of the people of God?

Baptismal principles encourage recognizing, supporting, and sharing authority in community. Congregations and other religious communities are intimate sites for learning the ups and downs of communal life. Participation is more than showing up. At their best, baptismally centered communities nurture the authority that comes with baptism through prayer, worship, Bible study, service, justice-seeking and life together. One body with *many* interdependent members gathers regularly in common prayer, grounded in baptism and nourished in the eucharist, to be sent forth as trusted agents of Christ's reconciling mission in the world. Gifts can be identified communally, "tried on" and affirmed or not. Several of us know the formative and renewing role that the local congregation can play in developing ministry, authority and leadership. This is not easy work. Preparation, community support and follow up are repeatedly called forth in baptism. These same qualities are necessary as all members live into the fullness of the baptismal covenant in the church and the world. The local congregation can also be a school where members of all ages learn about the ethical exercise of religious authority, both internally within the congregation and in relation to the diocese and province. Here members learn that power can be exercised in liberating and transformative ways and also that power can be abused. Congregations typically discover a diverse polyphony of voices and, if they are lucky and observant, identify constructive ways to address inevitable conflicts. Disciplined theological reflection on the ways we live together locally, discerning the theology expressed and implied in such practices, will provide us with clues for affirming and renewing the witness of the baptized.

Communal formation in the sacrament of baptism invites attention to a sense of the church that is larger than an institution. Theologically, as Anglicans have traditionally insisted, the world is the church's working place. *Living into the baptismal covenant calls upon Christians to make a difference in the structures of the world.* This suggests that as we strive to live faithfully into baptismal promises our focus is not only on Sunday, but also on the fuller work we are given to do. A former Archbishop of Canterbury, William Temple, once quipped: "It is a great mistake to think that God is chiefly interested in religion." Temple cautioned against spending "the whole of our activity" in worship. He urged spending the "greater part of our time," the other six days of the week, expressing God's love through service in the world.[36] Baptism directs our attention to the everyday pastoral and prophetic experiences of life. Verna Dozier has argued that we are not called just to offer care to people in need, we are called to "challenge the systems that make these 'ministries' necessary."[37] Yet another reason for affirming the authority of the baptized is the promise this holds for encouraging Christians to join with others in addressing structural injustices throughout the world. The church's leadership needs for the future depend upon those who embody responsibility for furthering God's reign on earth.

We should expect congregations and other religious communities, perhaps the Anglican Communion as well, to develop in their understanding of baptism, ministry, and leadership. Historically it took more than a century for the transforming principle of the English Reformation to take hold: *that faithful living takes shape within communities where all members and not just a few leaders struggle to understand and live out the faith.* Communities, individuals, and institutions can develop spirituality. John Ackerman, an American pastor and parish consultant, has traced stages of growth within congregations which basically move from dependence to interdependence. Modes of exercising authority vary as well. If the goal of institutional religious leadership is producing informed followers, conformity and law-and-order thinking will likely prevail. This mode of relationship here is typically a paternalistic model of mutuality grounded in dependency. If the identity of members within the ministering community is one of increasing self-awareness and the desire for reconciliation and new insights, then church members will be more confident and interdependent in their exercise of authority.[38] While this kind of spiritual growth involves taking risks and reaching out to others, authority that develops in this direction is less coercive, more persuasive and promising for future life together. This vision is more than theoretical. The ministry development movement, as I have seen in practice in North American communities and dioceses, emphasizes the full participation of all Christians in the life of the local church. This collaborative vision, sometimes called "total ministry" or "mutual ministry" reinforces focus on the indigenous gifts within local congregations as they live out their lives in mutual interdependence with the diocese.[39] This movement also is changing understandings of ordination and of appropriate institutional structures for decision-making.

Theological reflection on the exercise of authority reinforces and reaffirms the importance of focusing on the local congregation. *Many of the same lessons about identity and authority gleaned in local communities inform and pertain to wider ecclesial structures.* This, of course, includes building and sustaining interdependent relationships with dioceses, synods, provinces, conciliar bodies, consultations and networks working on particular issues. While this is not true of all Provinces in the Anglican Communion, from the point of view of the Province of the Episcopal Church USA there is a long history of valuing representation of the baptized in decision-making. As early as 1784 an informal Convention declared "that to make canons there be no other authority than a representative body of the clergy and laity conjointly."[40] In 1968 the Lambeth Conference concurred when it resolved: "no major issue in the life of the church should be decided without the full participation of the laity in discussion and in decision."[41] These historical assertions point toward the importance of authority grounded in the baptized, representation from laity as well as clergy, involvement of members directly concerned in decision-making, processes that encompass pluralism and honor diversity, and consultative relationships that seek to express the reciprocal interdependence of equals. Most of these, and other, principles are currently represented within the Anglican Consultative Council (ACC), a body which not surprisingly at its post-Lambeth 1999 meeting critiqued the centralizing and hierarchical trends evident

in the *Virginia Report*.[42] ACC with its multiple provincial representations of laity, presbyters and bishops best expresses the authority of the baptized. *If* the authority of any of the "four instruments
of unity" named in the *Virginia Report* needs to be enhanced, ACC
is theologically the best candidate for speaking authoritatively
about the church.

*Authority grounded in baptism is also theologically formative for con-
sidering the exercise of episcopal authority.* As noted in "Belonging
Together," the Anglican Communion has inherited various models for episcopacy, including the "monarchical episcopate," and
practices still vary widely throughout the Communion.[43] One way
ahead for bishops is to underscore the implications of baptism for
the exercise of their authority. Bishop Sykes advises that *episcopé*,
like all other expressions of Christian service, "must be first
understood in relation to baptism."[44] Other authors in this volume—including Simon Chiwanga and Njongonkulu Ndungane—
have addressed the need for giving this order of ministry renewed
attention.[45] Chiwanga describes episcopacy grounded in mission
and responsive to the local context. Ndungane, also a Primate,
discusses the nature of episcopal authority and challenges the
model of authority that gives power to one voice, especially when
that voice is removed from the local context. Each suggests
dynamic directions that are not officially conveyed by *Virginia
Report* recommendations. Ndungane also argues from trinitarian
theology. The North American theologian he names, David Cunningham, advocates such "living" trinitarian practices as peace-
making, pluralizing and persuading. Cunningham suggests that
this model of relational authority, although it would be diversely
expressed in different contexts, would yet contain some common
virtues:

> First, it would need to allow multiple voices to be heard
> (polyphony). Secondly, the lives of those whose voices are con-
> sidered authoritative would need to be woven into the lives of
> others.... Finally, such an approach to authority would need to
> recognize a space for particularity—a difference that is shaped
> by the mutual formation of Christians by one another.[46]

One way ahead for bishops is to underscore the implications of
baptism, with its diversity and particularity, for the exercise of
their authority. Episcopacy shares in baptismal ecclesiology as
bishops also represent the human face of the church in the world.

Reaffirmation of the authority grounded in baptism enables us to look toward a hopeful future. It tests our readiness to address difficult social and ethical questions together, including in debates and conflicts within our own church family. Such struggles among us, if conducted with a spirit of reciprocal interdependence, may allow important differences to exist while we pursue questions of wider public urgency. This is as true for member churches of the Anglican Communion as it is for the whole *oikoumene.* Placing renewed emphasis on baptismal theology provides a broad ecumenical base, a large-minded foundation for life together. The vision of *Baptism, Eucharist, and Ministry* is consistent with the exercise of interdependent collaboration sketched above:

> All members are called to discover, with the help of the community, the gifts they have received and to use them for the building up of the church and for the service of the world to which the church is sent.[47]

These are large mandates. The gifts of all members of the body of Christ will be needed for "building up the church" and "service of the world." Further, baptismal theology is suggestive of ways for Christians and those of other faiths to live together. Not everyone needs to be baptized to participate in God's project. God's imagination is bigger than Christian experience. Mutual respect, self-knowledge, and readiness to concede equality in the pursuit of religious truth are all habits that the baptized can exercise, if we are willing. Years ago, David Jenkins argued: "neither in theory or practice should there be any conflict between absolute commitment to Jesus Christ and complete openness to the future."[48] Within the Anglican Communion we are still testing the implications of this claim.

Meanwhile, the church is not only being remade in Africa and Asia, it is being renewed in North America in ministerial communities seeking to practice fuller understandings of baptism. How might we on our best days understand authority at work in the church? The Gospel of Mark begins starkly with a full-grown Jesus meeting John the baptizer at the Jordan and "going under the water in solidarity with those he came to save."[49] When I think of promising images for the emerging church, this one comes first to mind. In this new era I look forward to welcoming markedly different manifestations of the church reborn and reaffirmed in the creativity and authoritative solidarity of baptism.

NOTES

[1] See Chapter One.

[2] This view of crisis was framed by Bishop Steven Charleston, President of the Episcopal Divinity School, in the spring of 2000 as part of his response to the power dynamics at work in the Singapore Episcopal consecrations.

[3] See, for example, *We Are Theologians* (Cambridge, Mass.: Cowley, 1989) and *Living with History* (Cambridge, Mass.: Cowley, 1999).

[4] Parker J. Palmer, *The Company of Strangers: Christians and the Renewal of America's Public Life* (New York: Crossroad, 1981), 123.

[5] The *Virginia Report* is printed in its entirely in Mark Dyer, et al., eds., *The Official Report of the Lambeth Conference 1998* (Harrisburg: Morehouse Publishing, 1999), 15-68. This Report is named for the site of the Episcopal seminary which generously provided its local meeting expenses.

[6] The Episcopal Church does not have a long history of favoring Primates and Archbishops. Indeed historically this Province has rejected the practice of metropolitical authority, speaking instead of a Presiding Bishop until the 1979 Canon defined the duties of the Presiding Bishop as "Chief Pastor and Primate;" for this history see Mark Harris, *The Challenge of Change: The Anglican Communion in the Post-Modern Era* (New York: Church Publishing, 1998), 56-58. The *Virginia Report* actually contains two contrasting directions of analysis. Roughly the first four chapters seek to ground the church's synodical life as one of biblically-based, interdependent relationships that are mirrored in the life and traditions of the Communion and that can be referenced theologically in the doctrine of the Trinity. When this Report, in the concluding two chapters, focuses on structural analysis, theological reflection becomes secondary to the assumed need (often shaped by asking leading questions) for an enhanced centralized hierarchy.

[7] See Ian T. Douglas, "Authority after Colonialism: Power, Privilege and Primacy in the Anglican Communion," *The Witness* 83:3 (March 2000). 10-14; and L. William Countryman, "Anglicanism's Entangled Sense of Authority: A Tradition that Allows for Great Disagreement," *ibid.*, 21-24.

[8] *Resolutions of the Twelve Lambeth Conferences, 1876-1988*, ed. Roger Coleman (Toronto: Anglican Book Centre, 1992), Resolutions of the Lambeth Conference, 1988, No. 18.

[9] *The Official Report*, Resolution III.8.h, 399.

[10] Thomas P. Holland and William L. Sachs, Co-Directors, *The Zacchaeus Project: Discerning Episcopal Identity at the Dawn of the New Millennium* (New York: The Episcopal Church Foundation, 1999), 15; while this text is worth reading in its entirety, particularly by those who assert that there is an identity "crisis" in the Episcopal Church, two conclusions are most germane here: "Creative ferment and vitality characterizes Episcopal life in local congregations," and "Episcopalians are successfully embracing diversity and changes in the life of their congregations."

[11] I have in mind renewed baptismal ecclesiology, in which a new church is reborn from the womb of the old, similar to that imaged by Leonardo Boff, *Ecclesiogenesis: The Base Communities Reinvent the Church* (Maryknoll: Orbis Books, 1986).

[12] *The Official Report*, 23.

[13] *Ibid.*, 200; this Section, on the other hand, does suggest the need for churches to have a "sense of connectedness and accountability to the wider Communion."

[14] Stephen W. Sykes, *The Integrity of Anglicanism* (London: Mowbrays, 1978), 87-100; in this chapter, "Authority in Anglicanism," Sykes refers to the influential statement on authority in the 1948 Lambeth Conference Report. In 1981 Sykes confirmed that this principle of dispersed authority "has not been superseded" or "bettered"; see "Authority in the Anglican Communion," in *Four Documents on Authority in the Anglican Communion*, Presented to the Anglican Primates Meeting, 1981 (London: The Anglican Consultative Council, 1981), 13.

[15] Inter-Anglican Theological and Doctrinal Commission, *For the Sake of the Kingdom: God's Church and the New Creation*, published for the Anglican Consultative Council in 1986; see the Preface and paras. 80, 85 and 98. I have used the North American edition published by Forward Movement Publications in 1988.

[16] The IATDC team that met in 1991 was comprised of 17 men and 5 women; there were 9 persons of color (including 3 Africans and 3 Asians); and the largest geographical representation (5) was from the United Kingdom. Together 15 members represented almost half of the Provinces within the Communion. The IATDC Commission that met twice in 1994 and 1996 and produced the *Virginia Report* was somewhat smaller and less diverse: 15 men and 5 women, 6 persons of color (only 1 of whom had served as a member of the previous Consultation), and 5 members remained from the U.K. English was the first language of all but 6 participants; not surprisingly, voices from the West dominated these proceedings.

[17] "Belonging Together," 1992, para. 15.

[18] Tutu as quoted in Michael Battle, *Reconciliation: The Ubuntu Theology of Desmond Tutu* (Cleveland: Pilgrim Press, 1997), 147.

[19] L. William Countryman, *Living on the Border of the Holy: Renewing the Priesthood of All* (Harrisburg: Morehouse Publishing, 1999), 64.

[20] See "Defining Our Humanity: Thoughts on a Feminist Anthropology," *Journal of Theology for Southern Africa* 79 (June 1992): 15.

[21] Countryman, *Living on the Border of the Holy*, 193.

[22] See the Catechism in the Episcopal Church's 1979 Book of Common Prayer, 845.

[23] World Council of Churches, *Baptism, Eucharist, and Ministry* (Geneva: W.C.C. 1982).

[24] See Elisabeth Schüssler Fiorenza, *In Memory of Her* (New York: Crossroad, 1983), 78, 213, and 205-220; and Krister Stendal, *The Bible and the Role of Women* (Philadelphia: Fortress Press, 1966), 33.

[25] From Stringfellow's 1976 book, *Instead of Death*, as cited in *A Keeper of the Word: Selected Writings of William Stringfellow*, ed. Bill Wylie Kellermann (Grand Rapids: William B. Eerdmans Publishing Company, 1994), 12.

[26] From a printed version of this paper, *EDS Occasional Papers* 3 (March 1999), 1-16, see especially, 4-5.

[27] See Ian T. Douglas, "Baptized into Mission: Ministry and Holy Orders Reconsidered," *Sewanee Theological Review* 40:4 (1997): 431-43.

[28] Verna Dozier, *The Dream of God, A Call to Return* (Cambridge: Mass.: Cowley, 1991), 131.

[29] The Book of Common Prayer, 1979, The Episcopal Church, 304-305 and 855. For similar statements see also *The Book of Alternative Services*, the Anglican Church of Canada, 1985, 158-159; and *A New Zealand Prayer Book, He Karakia Mihinare o Aotearoa*, 1989, 390 and 931.

[30] Sykes, *Unashamed Anglicanism* (Nashville: Abingdon Press, 1995), 14, 189.

[31] Cited in the *Anglican Theological Review* 66:1 (1984, Supp. Series 9): 40.

[32] Page 279.

[33] Verna Dozier, *The Calling of the Laity, Verna Dozier's Anthology* (Washington, D.C.: Alban Institute, 1988), 115-16.

[34] See especially the empowering description of baptism in subsection 2 of "A Faithful Church," *Official Report*, 191-98. Like the *Virginia Report*, the overall Report and Resolutions of Section III are not theologically and structurally congruent on issues of identity and authority.

[35] This warning is from the preface of an uncompleted book titled *Authority in Baptism*, see *A Keeper of the Word*, 158.

[36] William Temple, *The Church and Its Teaching To-day* (New York: Macmillan, 1936), 17-18. See also Arthur Michael Ramsey's assessment of Temple in *An Era in Anglican Theology* (New York: Charles Scribners' Sons, 1960), 146.

[37] Dozier, *The Dream of God*, 139.

[38] John Ackerman, *Spiritual Awakening: A Guide to Spiritual Life in Congregations* (Washington, D.C.: Alban Institute, 1994), 100-102.

[39] For a recent summary history of this movement, its visionary leaders and theological directions see Timothy F. Sedgwick, "Vision and Collaboration: Roland Allen, Liturgical Renewal, and Ministry Development," *Anglican Theological Review* 82:1 (2000): 155-71. For this vision of authority among the baptized I am indebted to Charles R. Wilson for a copy of his unpublished

paper, "The Order and Exercise of Authority in the Church," delivered as the Keynote Address at the "Living the Covenant Consultation," held 11 June 1999.

[40] Quoted in Stephen Neill, *Anglicanism,* 4th ed. (New York: Oxford University Press, 1978), 285.

[41] *Resolutions of the Twelve Lambeth Conferences,* 1968, No. 24.

[42] See the report of the Anglican Communion News Service, 1888, 18 September 1999.

[43] Paras. 78-79.

[44] Sykes, *Unashamed Anglicanism,* 188.

[45] See Chapters 10 and 13.

[46] David S. Cunningham, *These Three Are One: The Practice of Trinitarian Theology* (Oxford: Blackwell, 1998), 321.

[47] Quoted in *The Official Report,* 192.

[48] This is from his Bampton Lecture, see *The Glory of Man* (London: SCM Press, 1967), viii.

[49] See Mark 1:4-11 and Mary W. Anderson, "The Waters of Solidarity," *Christian Century* (December 22-29, 1999): 1249.

12

LEADERSHIP FORMATION FOR A NEW WORLD

An Emergent Indigenous Anglican Theological College

JENNY PLANE TE PAA

INTRODUCTION

In June 1998, a gathering of Anglican Communion representatives, mainly educators, was held at the Episcopal Divinity School in Cambridge, Massachusetts. The gathering was intended to stimulate a global conversation among key Anglican educators and leaders on some of the multitude of complex and often difficult issues, which arise for the church in our postcolonial world.[1]

It was also an opportunity for those attending the Lambeth Conference to be able to engage a preliminary dialogue with colleagues whose positions, experiences and insights could provide invaluable contextual evidence and information from "postcolonial" Anglican communities across the world.

I was asked to prepare a paper describing how I felt the newly revised Constitution of the Anglican church in Aotearoa,[2] New Zealand and Polynesia provided a mechanism for empowering previously oppressed minority indigenous Anglicans to become autonomous, self-governing, and self-determining. I was asked to pay special attention to the way in which training for leadership roles within the church might be impacted by the constitutional revision, with specific reference to the role of the Anglican theological college I have shared responsibility for leading.

In preparing my contribution, I first examined the disparate themes implied in the title for the gathering. There seemed at first glance, to be little or no possibility of thematic coherence. Anglicanism and consultation? Anglicanism and postcolonial? Anglicanism and indigenous people? Anglicanism, consultation, postcolonial, indigenous people and theological education!

However, when I paused to consider my own position as an indigenous Anglican woman, whose social, political, economic and faith history is inextricably linked with a relatively recent colonial past, I realized with confidence how well placed I was to be able to describe something of the *mixed* legacy of that experience.[3]

When I paused also to consider my position as a Lay Canon, as a woman enormously privileged by the experience of being entrusted with the responsibility for the academic and administrative leadership of the only indigenous[4] Anglican theological college in the world, I was reminded yet again of the critical importance of us each finding time and ways for sharing our stories, with generosity and with humility.

And so it was with both delight and a profound sense of obligation that I took to Boston an indigenous story, spoken with an indigenous voice and sourced from within an indigenous heart and mind.

This story begins as a classic "colonial" story, where all of the constitutive elements of imperialism, domination, abuse, unnecessary suffering, and sustained injustice against *the people of the land* are represented.[5] However, the story "concludes" somewhat differently than those typical of the twentieth-century colonial era; and as a result, I find myself uncertain about whether my story is postcolonial or not. My understanding of postcolonial is that the term is normally applied to the period immediately beyond the establishment of colonial settlement and governance, and that what is usually being defined by this term are those forms of societal reorganization which allow for, and thus assume the imposition of, the behaviors, values, attitudes, moral ideas and understandings, cultural norms and traditions of the colonials upon whomever already happened to inhabit various lands.

My uncertainty was heightened by my realization that my story refers to a period far beyond that of the establishment of colonial settlement and governance; therefore, it can hardly be viewed as strictly postcolonial. In Aotearoa New Zealand, there has been for some time a systematic movement toward mature re-evaluation of our colonial legacy; as a result of this re-evaluation, there has been an unequivocal rejection of some aspects of that legacy as being inherently unjust and irrelevant for our contemporary circumstances.[6] Furthermore, there has been a demonstrable willingness within some major public institutions to transform themselves away from the colonial type organizational management model, where the subordination of minorities or lower classes was key, into something more akin to truly egalitarian, efficient, inclusive, and pluralistic models of organizational management. This reconfigured form is not postcolonial and is certainly not neocolonial. Thus, I offer my alternative definition of "beyond postcolonialism."

AOTEAROA NEW ZEALAND—BEYOND POSTCOLONIALISM

In this South Pacific land, during the past twenty years, there has been a sustained and ultimately successful political movement led primarily by Maori activists, which has challenged many of the popular myths perpetuated in the name of the colonial era, particularly those concerned with history making. As a result, there is now a greater recognition and acceptance of the fact that Aotearoa New Zealand *was* populated by a sovereign people prior to the arrival of the colonials (representing the British sovereign); that there *was* an honorable covenant agreement struck between these two sovereign peoples, known as the Treaty of Waitangi; and that one partner to that Treaty *has* consistently and flagrantly dishonored their Treaty obligations and responsibilities, and, as a result, extreme disadvantage has accrued to the indigenous partner.

Maori people have consistently demanded that the only acceptable redemptive solution to redress the cultural devastation wrought by colonial dishonor be that the original Treaty partnership relationship of equals be restored. The political implications of a such a relationship have been, not unexpectedly, the primary focus for right-wing reactionary responses, especially given that Maori people now comprise around fifteen percent of the total population; that less than twenty percent of land is in Maori ownership; and that Maori are disproportionately represented in every official statistical indicator of negative social, economic, educational, health and welfare positioning in this land. The prospect of sharing power with such an "impoverished" Treaty partner initially appears simply ludicrous to the majority partner—the one which has benefited enormously at the expense of the colonized.

However, since the establishment by the Government in 1975, of the Waitangi Tribunal,[7] we have witnessed some truly extraordinary developments. The Tribunal has produced volumes of critical new research work, which provides irrefutable evidence of colonial dishonor. This new information has done much to validate the incessant historical cry of injustice from Maori activists. Most non-Maori New Zealanders now respond with a heartfelt willingness to redress that injustice. This is demonstrated in their support of, and interest in, the work of the Waitangi Tribunal,[8] and in their support for major legislative changes which commit the government to settling outstanding grievances.

It is my belief that significant instances of public reconciliation and forgiveness in response to our experience of colonial exploitation have occurred in Aotearoa New Zealand. In other words, I believe as a nation we have transcended our previously passive acceptance of imposed colonial settlement and governance, by challenging the assumptions, the rules, and the moral understandings implicit in the postcolonial period. San Juan describes this political movement as, "*embodying the resistance habitus of peoples attempting to transcend subalternity.*" He goes on however to describe what I believe has been achieved in this country, and that is the reconstruction of a Maori identity as a "*dynamic, complex phenomenon [which] defies both assimilationist and pluralist models [because] it affirms its antiracist counterhegemonic antecedent....*"[9]

I believe we have moved beyond the confines of grievance and sustained protest to an era where the potential is rich with creative possibilities for developing new relationships with those whose ancestors impacted upon our original indigenous society in myriad different ways.

This new era ought not to be ideologically constrained by the burden of precise definition, which can sometimes be so terribly limiting. Therefore, while I remain uncertain about whether or not my story is "postcolonial" or "beyond postcolonial," I leave that decision to readers whose scholarship in postcolonial studies far exceeds that of people like myself, whose political and academic energies have been of necessity primarily devoted to survival issues for the indigenous communities to which we are blessed to belong.

I am always conscious that in telling stories I will, of necessity, have intentionally selected certain pieces of information and omitted others. In so doing, I will have deliberately chosen to create a particular emphasis in keeping with my own particular indigenous feminist biases! However, I was reassured that because my paper was being prepared for a consultation, and this setting therefore invited and anticipated critical conversations among colleagues and friends, then all of my rather obvious personal assertions and biases would, as they ought, remain open to enquiry and to contestation.

What follows, then, is my story of the events which I see as being inexorably linked to the extraordinary gesture of redemptive justice taken in 1992 by the Anglican church in Aotearoa New Zealand.

THE CONTEXT FOR COLONIZATION IN AOTEAROA

Around a thousand or more years ago, the first migrations of those people who were eventually to become known as Maori voyaged intentionally across the Pacific and settled finally in Aotearoa. Around two hundred years ago, those people who Maori[10] call Pakeha,[11] voyaged intentionally from the British and Irish archipelago to Aotearoa New Zealand[12] and many eventually decided to settle permanently in "their" new land.[13]

For the first fifty years or so, the newcomers comprised a mixed group of traders, whalers, artisans of various types, and missionaries. Initially the relationships established between the "people of the land" or tangata whenua[14] and the "newcomers" or manuhiri,[15] were reasonably amicable. Each was enabled by the other to benefit from the relationship—Maori were willing to accommodate Pakeha needs for food and shelter; and in turn, Pakeha were willing to share agricultural and technological benefits and written literacy with Maori.

The Church Missionary Society (CMS), representing the interests of British evangelicalism, were the forerunners to mainstream (colonial) Anglican presence in Aotearoa.[16] In 1814, the

CMS began their official work of "civilizing" and then "christianizing" the natives. This work began through the missionary efforts of Samuel Marsden, an ex-Magistrate who had been earlier befriended by Ruatara, a chief of one of the northern tribes of Aotearoa. By virtue of his established relationship with a key Maori figure, Marsden, his family, and colleagues were able to be welcomed and protected in their early and largely unsuccessful missionary endeavors.

It was not until 1823, when ex-naval captain Henry Williams arrived from England, that there is any real evidence of Maori "conversion" to Christianity. However, once begun, Maori adherence to Christian faith teachings and practices was enthusiastic and unstoppable. Missionary *wives* were heavily involved in the work of introducing written forms of literacy to Maori people and missionary *husbands* set about establishing mission stations, often under extraordinarily physically and emotionally challenging circumstances. The Christian gospel thus arrived in the Antipodes[17] and under the benevolent tutelage of the earliest CMS missionaries, the *good seed* was strewn upon very fertile soil in a still relatively peaceful land.[18]

Throughout the 1830s, although Pakeha settlement was underway (albeit, not yet officially organized nor sanctioned as part of the British colonial expansionist effort), the CMS mission expanded; and relationships between Maori and missionary were mutually trusting and, by and large, mutually honorable. By the late 1830s, the colonial interests of Britain were firmly fixed upon the South Pacific. Initially, the British Colonial Office saw the need to introduce a political mechanism for dealing with distant social problems, rather than simply seeing Aotearoa as just another site for the imposition of British economic imperialism.

In 1839, the Colonial Secretary of Britain, Lord Normanby, dispatched Captain Hobson to negotiate some kind of treaty of cession with Maori, and in February 1840, a simple three-clause Treaty was drawn up. As a Treaty of its time, ours was relatively unambiguous and uncomplicated. It was, I believe, a Treaty of *accommodation* (Maori knew of, and accepted, the inevitability of increased settlement), and of *hospitality* (Maori social organization was governed by an understanding of reciprocity, and Maori recognized and welcomed opportunity for access to new knowledge, new technology, new social possibilities). The Treaty of Waitangi was drafted as a "covenant" type document,[19] which provided a framework for the offering of promises to establish and maintain relationships of mutuality and interdependence. It was intended to ensure that through the establishment of colonial governance and with genuine guarantees of protection for Maori rights and interests, justice would prevail in all things between Maori and Pakeha. The Treaty of Waitangi, albeit a political mechanism, thus envisaged a partnership relationship between indigenous Maori and Pakeha settlers—an opportunity for modeling the possibilities of bicultural development within one nation.

The local "agents" responsible for the drafting, translation, and promotion of the Treaty were, not unexpectedly, those Pakeha most trusted and thus most accepted by Maori—the CMS missionaries. Although the time frame between the signing of the Treaty of Waitangi by both partners and subsequent acts of statutory betrayal was indeed very short, it is important to note that there is no way that the CMS missionaries could be seen as *intentionally* complicit in the colonial treachery which eventually rendered indigenous Maori virtually landless, utterly impoverished, decimated by introduced diseases, disenfranchised and yet, astonishingly, ever faithful to God.

Within twenty years of the signing of the Treaty of Waitangi, indigenous Maori became "beggars" in our own land—land taken by either force or legislation.[20]

Ours is a tragic, and yet, very typical story of colonial oppression—we share our experience of cultural genocide with indigenous Australians, First Nations people in Canada and the United States, Hawaiian people, Tahitian people, Indians, Fijians, Puerto Ricans and many, many other colonized indigenous peoples throughout the world.[21]

COLONIAL CHURCH GOVERNANCE

Three years after the signing of the Treaty of Waitangi, the Church of England dispatched George Augustus Selwyn, first Bishop of New Zealand, to care for the interests of settler Anglicans and to care for the overall colonial church enterprise, which included overseeing the Maori mission work of the CMS.[22]

A complex of factors, not the least of which were simply lousy timing, inevitable tensions between the CMS evangelicals and Selwyn's high churchmanship, and his unfortunate colonial associations,[23] mitigated against Selwyn's ministry efforts among both the CMS and Maori. He was never to enjoy the depth of trusting relationships, like those that existed between CMS missionaries and Maori.

Selwyn eventually turned his attentions to matters of church order and governance, and in 1857 the first Constitution of the Anglican Church in New Zealand was officially signed. By this time, many Maori had experienced "being Anglican" for nearly forty years, and yet, not one Maori signature was attached to the first Constitution. Selwyn preferred to allow the CMS to continue their benevolent mission and ministry work, which included the provision of schooling, instruction in catechism, preparation for ordination, and of course, the regular experience of worship.

Because the CMS were financially independent of the settler Anglican church, economic tensions did not problematize their relationship. Because Selwyn's episcopal jurisdiction enabled him to control ordinations and appointments, he remained unperturbed by the fact that the settler church and the Maori church continued to develop as distinctive and relatively autonomous entities for much of the latter part of the nineteenth century.

True to their mission calling, the CMS always insisted upon a limited tenure, and to their credit, they signaled often and early, an intention to move away from Aotearoa New Zealand and a commensurate hope that the institutional or mainstream Anglican church would "adopt" or "embrace" Maori interests. The CMS finally withdrew from the Maori mission field in the early 1920s. Consistent with the prevailing colonial hegemony,[24] minority Maori Anglicans were to be simply "assimilated," (although in reality, subordinated, by sheer force of numbers), into predominantly Pakeha but ostensibly "democratic" episcopal church structures. Even a cursory glance through the first hundred years of New Zealand Anglican history reveals a dismal record of neglect by Pakeha Anglican leaders of Maori Anglican clergy and followers.

The first Maori bishop was appointed in 1928[25] but was suffragen to a diocesan bishop, and so was only able to exercise restricted episcopal leadership. No Maori was elected to General Synod for many years, and even when one was, he represented majority Pakeha interests anyway. Maori clergy were always subservient to Pakeha bishops, and while many were treated benevolently, very few were ever appointed to senior clerical positions. All institutional theological education for clergy was monocultural, monolingual and thus not only pedagogically and methodologically unjust, it was also largely contextually irrelevant for Maori clergy and congregations.[26]

In the secular world, the devastation wrought by colonial legislation and underpinned by the official policy of assimilation led to a popular belief that eventually through miscegenation[27] all that would be left would be a remnant Maori population. However, notwithstanding the overwhelming experience of cultural, spiritual, and economic desolation, the indigenous spirit of resistance and, I suspect, an irrepressible human yearning for gospel justice, has rendered the Maori spirit indomitable.

THE INDIGENOUS SPIRIT OF RESISTANCE

Throughout the years 1850 to 1975, there is much evidence of courageous, albeit mostly ineffective acts of political resistance, of defiance and struggle by Maori against Pakeha domination.[28] Maori have cried incessantly for representation in politics and in all aspects of public institutional decision and policy making; for equitable access to all public institutions, including those of higher education, and for recognition of the rights to exercise cultural preferences in terms of various social practices. All of these appeals are simply for those human and civil rights which were supposedly provided for by the Treaty of Waitangi.

While some minor gains were made, up until 1975 Maori interests remained subordinated and were, in fact, further eroded by the introduction and vigorous promotion of post-World War II government economic policies which effectively "seduced" the majority of Maori off our remaining rural tribal lands, away from close-knit, kinship-based and faith-based communities and into isolated and individualized urban dwellings.

As the inevitably negative outcomes of the rural-to-urban drift became more and more apparent (homelessness, unemployment, family dislocation, health problems, criminal involvement and poor educational achievement), Maori leaders continued to give voice to the anguish of the people. This post-war generation of leaders always "protested" in an extraordinarily dignified and peaceful manner.

However, by the mid 1970s a radically different spirit of protest was being engendered by international events. The civil rights movement in the United States, the feminist movement, the "hippie movement," the apartheid struggle in South Africa, and the Vietnam War were to have an impact upon our small South Pacific nation in quite dramatic ways. Previously peaceful and dignified protest by older Maori leaders was suddenly unceremoniously displaced by defiant, impatient, and aggressive protest by younger Maori (usually women), demanding restorative justice or else! During this period a small group of university-educated young Maori were galvanized into radical action by their exposure to Marxist analysis of the experience and outcome of colonization.[29] And so it was that indigenous protest in Aotearoa New Zealand became strident, articulate, youthful, dynamic, and well organized.

Political protest erupted frequently throughout the 1970s and 1980s over: Maori land rights, Maori language teaching in all educational institutions, Maori justice issues, institutional racism, police brutality, educational injustice, and poor housing conditions. Maori were and have remained at the forefront of emergent international indigenous protest groups. An international network of indigenous groups continues to exert pressure on governments and on churches; the two "colonial" institutions seen as being primarily responsible for creating and sustaining the conditions necessary for subverting and marginalizing indigenous interests throughout the colonized world.

Ironically, the "icon" or symbolic focus of protest in Aotearoa New Zealand has always been the Treaty of Waitangi, the original covenant document which recognized the right of Maori as a sovereign people, to "treat" honorably with another sovereign people for the terms essential to a future which envisaged peaceful and settled co-existence as co-equal partners in one land. In spite of the fact that history reveals an undeniable and sustained legacy of dishonor by one partner to the Treaty, the catch cry of the contemporary protest movement was usually always, "Honor the Treaty," or "Bring Back the Treaty," or "Aotearoa is Maori Land."[30]

By 1975, the virulence and legitimacy of Maori grievances could no longer be avoided nor denied. But perhaps of more immediate concern, many in the community were becoming extremely fearful of the potential which existed for gang violence[31] and the resultant social disruption. The time had come for a political response, and the first of these was the establishment by Parliament of the Waitangi Tribunal. This was followed some nine years later by the second largest national institution in this land, the Anglican church indicating its own willingness to take seriously the indigenous cry for restorative justice.

THE TREATY OF WAITANGI—A SYMBOL FOR REDEMPTION?

Remarkably, it was the Anglican church in Aotearoa New Zealand, the very same colonial institution whose representatives had assisted with the drafting, translating and promoting of the original Treaty of Waitangi, which responded most enthusiastically and most readily to the impassioned and unequivocal call by concerned Anglicans for the church to examine its own complicity in perpetuating social injustice, whether consciously or unwittingly. While Maori Anglicans were at the forefront of this initiative, the responsibility for its development and eventual success was one shared willingly by both Maori and Pakeha.

In 1984, the General Synod of the Anglican Church agreed to establish a Commission:

> To study the Treaty of Waitangi and to consider whether any principles of partnership and bicultural development are implied and the nature of any such principles that may serve as indicators for future growth and development, and, to advise General Synod on any ways and means to embody the principles of the Treaty in the legislation, institutions and general life of the church of the Province of New Zealand.[32]

Here, just sixteen years ago, was the executive decision-making body of the Anglican church taking an extraordinarily bold step, not only to revisit the Treaty of Waitangi, but also preparing itself for constitutional revision, a potentially transformative action, unprecedented, since the original Constitution was drafted and signed in 1857.

The intention behind the recommendations to General Synod was not simply for the church to acknowledge its role in past injustices; to say sorry; to seek forgiveness and then in a gesture of magnanimity, to offer a few extra key positions to Maori in senior decision making roles. This is simply a gesture of "token" representation, which is inherently unjust because it exists and is sustained in the interests of the dominant majority. Rather it was hoped that by revisiting the Treaty of Waitangi, it would be possible for the original model of partnership between equals to be restored.

Redemptive justice requires restoration and genuine opportunity for future flourishing, and this was the challenge confronting the Anglican church in 1984. It was a challenge confronted with utmost integrity.

Between 1984 and 1992, the General Synod Commission on the Constitution met with hundreds of Maori and Pakeha Anglicans throughout Aotearoa New Zealand. They undertook to complete some incredibly significant historical research tasks; they undertook to give honor to those whose stories and memories informed and influenced their understandings and eventually their findings; and they sought always to bring solid biblical wisdom and insight to the challenges they faced.[33]

In 1986, General Synod established a second commission. This Bicultural Education Commission was charged with the responsibility of devising educational programs and resources to help the church at large understand what was occurring within its leadership and decision-making structures.

As a member of that second commission, I recall well the profound sense of hope and the awesome sense of responsibility which combined to underpin our collective efforts, as two Maori and two Pakeha, men and women, lay and ordained, worked together, to "help our people understand" why the partnership model based on the Treaty of Waitangi was so vitally important. We saw the Treaty model offering a partnership relationship founded on a mutually agreed willingness to share; to each benefit and flourish from the existing gifts and resources; to ensure that protective measures were implemented to care for finite treasures; and to agree to contribute to the welfare of each other through proper governance and rules. The appeal went right to the heart of Christian understandings, right to the heart of the gospel imperative for justice, for peace and equality.

The two commissions traveled widely, consulted regularly, debated incessantly, agonized, theorized, and reflected endlessly and prayerfully upon the material gathered. In 1990 a revised constitution for one church with two partners was proposed to the General Synod. At that time a constitutional anomaly which would have excluded the Church in Polynesia was corrected, and the Constitution was finally officially revised in 1992. This Revised Constitution is I believe, unique in the worldwide Anglican Communion, and it is indeed radical in its insistence upon the principles of partnership and bicultural development within the one church.

THE CONSTITUTION OF THE ANGLICAN CHURCH IN AOTEAROA, NEW ZEALAND AND POLYNESIA

In spite of the unique story behind the development of the current Constitution of the Anglican Church in Aotearoa, New Zealand and Polynesia, in many respects ours is probably fairly standard as far as Anglican Constitutions go.[34] After all, as Anglicans no matter where we are from, we are all bound and obligated within the broad framework of the worldwide Anglican Communion. And so it is, that within our Constitution, we see reference to our fundamental belief in the Trinity, in our apostolic origins, and in the catholicity of our church.

We in Aotearoa, New Zealand and Polynesia also subscribe enthusiastically to the Anglican Consultative Council's Mission Statement, which calls us to mission as teachers and nurturers of believers; as workers for social justice; as proclaimers of the gospel of Jesus; as agents for the care of God's creation and as compassionate servants of those who suffer in our communities.[35]

There is also in the Preambles of our Constitution, a section worth quoting at length because it is here that are contained the historical facts to which I have alluded, and the subsequent rationale, which informed and influenced the 1992 revision.

Preambles 5-8 and 10-13 read thus:

> AND WHEREAS (5) this Church has developed in New Zealand from its beginnings when Ruatara introduced Samuel Marsden to his people at Oihi in the Bay of Islands in 1814, first in expanding missionary activity as Te Hahi Mihinare in the medium of the Maori language and in the context of tikanga Maori. Initially under the guidance of the Church Missionary Society, and secondly after the arrival of George Augustus Selwyn in 1842 as a Bishop of the United Church of England and Ireland spreading amongst the settlers in the medium of the English language and in the context of their heritage and customs and being known as the Church of England, so leading to a development along two pathways which found expression within tikanga[36] Maori and tikanga Pakeha;

AND WHEREAS (6) by the Treaty of Waitangi, signed in 1840, the basis for future government and settlement of New Zealand was agreed, which Treaty implies partnership between Maori and settlers and bicultural development within one nation;

AND WHEREAS (7) in 1840 there was also recognised the freedom of the inhabitants of New Zealand to hold and practice their religious faith within the several branches of the Church then present, or according to their own custom;

AND WHEREAS (8) on the 13th day of June in the year of our Lord, 1857, at a General Conference held at Auckland, the Bishops and certain of the Clergy and Laity representing a numerous body of the members of the said United Church, and including Missionary clergy but without direct Maori participation or the inclusion of tikanga Maori, agreed to a Constitution for the purpose of associating together by voluntary compact as a branch of the said United Church ...

AND WHEREAS (10) Clause Three of the Constitution made provision for the said Branch to frame new and modify existing rules (not affecting doctrine) with a view to meeting the circumstances of the settlers and of the indigenous people of Aotearoa/New Zealand;

AND WHEREAS (11) after the continuing development of Te Hahi Mihinare[37] the first Bishop of Aotearoa was appointed in 1928, and a measure of autonomy as te Pihopatanga o Aotearoa[38] was provided in 1978, and new forms of mission and ministry have emerged;

AND WHEREAS (12) the principles of partnership and bicultural development require the Church to;

(a) organise its affairs within each of the tikanga (social organisations, language, laws, principles, and procedure) of each partner;

(b) be diligent in prescribing and in keeping open all avenues leading to the common ground;

(c) maintain the right of every person to choose and particular cultural expression of the faith;

AND WHEREAS (13) Te Runanga o Te Pihopatanga o Aotearoa[39] and the General Synod, meeting together in General Conference in November 1990, covenanted with each other and agreed to certain amendments and revisions of the Constitution to implement and entrench the principles of partnership between Maori and Pakeha and bicultural development and to incorporate and extend the principal provisions of the Church of England Empowering Act....

ON BEING PARTNERS

Just as the first revision of our Constitution took one hundred and thirty-five years to achieve, so partnership relationships did not simply, nor immediately, take "new form" in 1992. The political, economic, spiritual and moral implications of the new Constitution are, in 2000, still being variously misinterpreted, newly recognized, often challenged and, in rare instances, rejected out of hand. All of these reactions point toward what I believe to be an overlooked necessity, which is the establishment by the church of a debating forum where these extant concerns might be addressed by the body corporate. In spite of this criticism, I believe however that as church, we have demonstrated to our national society and beyond, to the worldwide Anglican Communion, what it means to take seriously our mission statement to be involved in the "transformation of unjust structures." Beginning with our own institutional framework, which our church conceded was fundamentally unjust, we have set about devising and implementing a process of transformation.

The Anglican Church in Aotearoa New Zealand is now genuinely inclusive in terms of cultural diversity. Decision-making is now achieved in General Synod, and in all common life forums where the partners are represented, by consensus and not by majority vote. Representation is now achieved *as of right* because partnership cannot function in the absence of one partner. Resources are now distributed equitably according to identified need, and this takes account of historic disadvantage. Church leadership is now a shared function between those who represent the partners.

THEOLOGICAL EDUCATION

The previously elitist monocultural, monolingual Provincial Anglican Theological College is one of the key sites where the implications of the Revised Constitution have been perhaps most dramatically realized.

In 1992, the College of St. John the Evangelist was transformed into two distinctive societies or Colleges, one representing the autonomous interests of Maori Anglicans and the other Pakeha Anglicans, and yet each is also committed to a functional partnership relationship. And so as Dean or Ahorangi, I am at once solely responsible for Maori Anglican interests in institutionally based theological education, and equally responsible, together with the Dean for Pakeha Anglicans as my Constitutional partner, for the overall interests of all Anglicans and for those students who choose to participate in institutionally based, university associated theological education.[40] My colleague or co-Dean is similarly entrusted with the responsibility for Pakeha students. My College is known as Te Rau Kahikatea[41] and the Pakeha College is known as Southern Cross.[42]

In a recent article in which I was describing the evolving partnership relationship, I wrote the following:

> Together the two colleges still legally constitute the College of St John the Evangelist; together, the colleges still adhere to a common curriculum; together, all students are still taught by a 'common' Faculty; together and daily, all students worship and study together. The integrity of being Christian, of being sisters and brothers in Christ is thus honoured and celebrated.

> Within each partner college, cultural preferences in terms of language use, adherence to cultural tradition, extracurricular learning activities, expressions of hospitality, ministry formation practices, worship styles and theological responses are also nurtured and maintained—the integrity of cultural difference is thus also honoured and celebrated.

> The College is uniquely placed as an educational institution to model Treaty based partnership relationship understanding and practices. It can implement and monitor the ongoing internal structural transformations essential to ensuring a bilingual, bicultural teaching, learning and worshipping environment is developed and sustained. The model is intended to place the emphasis, first and foremost on engaged partnership relationships.

> In these relationships, Maori and Pakeha Anglicans can teach, learn and enact Christian theology as a common community of faith, we recognise that our human differences are only made visible in and through the experience of being together in community (through partnership with the other I find myself) and we understand and celebrate the blessings of unity in diversity in community, by acknowledging, accepting, respecting and delighting in our differences'[43]

The task of preparing future leaders for our church through the delivery of quality theological education is daunting. As indigenous Anglicans we have endured the educational experience of being a marginalized minority group for over 150 years, and the negative results of that experience are predictable.

When I began teaching at the College of St. John the Evangelist in 1992, out of fifteen faculty, there were no Maori teaching theology; there was no substantive Maori theological research material (either available or in process); no substantive Maori input across the theology curriculum; no attention was given to the teaching and learning needs of Maori students in terms of pedagogy, assessment or teaching methodology. The two Maori faculty then employed were perceived as teaching "Maori Studies" only—subjects on the periphery of the preeminent "theology" curriculum.

Today in 2000, we have two Maori theologians, one of whom as a senior priest teaches across the Pastoral curriculum, has sole responsibility for all Maori Studies courses, and is responsible for developing and supervising the Field Education and Ministry Formation programs for all Maori students. He is currently completing a Master's degree in Education and will undertake Doctorate in Ministry Studies at the completion of his M.Ed. I have sole responsibility for teaching a Maori research paper, for a Social Justice course on the Constitutional Revision, and for co-teaching in one or two of the Pastoral Studies courses. I will complete my Ph.D. in 2001, and have focused my dissertation in the area of Race Politics and Theological Education.

We have one full-time Maori faculty member who teaches four Maori-language papers and conducts seemingly endless tutorials for language learners! As an essential adjunct to the teaching of Maori language, we have employed one full-time Maori Educational Resources Development Manager who is in charge of the establishment and development of one of the most technologically sophisticated Languages Laboratory Centres in Aotearoa New Zealand. The center is utilized primarily for computer-enhanced teaching of Maori language but can also be utilized for instructing students and faculty in the use of interactive computer technology for teaching purposes. Given that Maori language and Maori studies are key to our uniqueness as an indigenous theological college, the highest priority has been given to the establishment of a strong, credible, and visionary teaching unit which accords high honor and status to this cultural treasure entrusted by God into our care. Both Maori-language faculty have Master's degrees with Honors in their fields of expertise, and both are being encouraged and given resources to undertake Ph.D. studies.

Te Rau Kahikatea have the only fully equipped research center on campus, for which we employ a part-time research assistant who is currently completing a Master's degree in History and Demography. All senior Maori students are required to produce a major research paper in their final year at college—and this is a way of (re)creating our own resource base of precious cultural narrative. Our legacy of educational disadvantage has left us as indigenous survivors, bereft of published material, stories, poems, songs, art, laments, hymns, prayers, speeches. The required research paper is intended to facilitate the very urgent task of cultural recovery.

Since 1995, we have graduated four Maori women with Bachelor's degrees in Theology, one of whom has since completed an M.A. in Theology at the Church Divinity School of the Pacific in Berkeley. Another is enrolled in the Feminist D.Min. program at the San Francisco Theological Seminary, and one is enrolled in a Master of Education program at Auckland University. Of these, two are ordained and one is a laywoman. Five Maori male priests have also graduated, all of whom have expressed interest in post-graduate studies. These graduates provide us with a small but growing pool of potential scholars of theology, from among whom we may target future faculty.

Until we are in a position to appoint fully qualified indigenous faculty, we have negotiated firmly and insistently with our tikanga partners for agreement that all non-Maori faculty who teach our students must now be demonstrably biculturally competent to do so. The implications of this requirement are slowly being seen in a couple of pioneering examples of tentative but irrevocable transformations of curricula and of the essential co-requisites of teaching pedagogy, methodology and assessment.

The struggle to build our indigenous institution is often fraught with both unknown delights and difficulties—delights, as previously seemingly immovable racist or sexist forces suddenly or unexpectedly begin to demonstrate uncharacteristic signs of graciousness or tolerance or sensitivity! Then there are times of deep disappointment, when the *oppositional* forces and faces are those of our own—the anti-intellectuals, the "cultural purists," whose romanticized ideologies threaten the very possibility of mutuality and interdependence in any form of partnership.

Notwithstanding the "delights" and the "difficulties," it is clear that without the mandate for partnership relationships provided for by the Revised Constitution, the struggle for equality of opportunity within theological education would have proven impossible to overcome.

As I stated at the outset, I see myself as being uniquely privileged by being entrusted with the responsibility of developing and sustaining an indigenous Anglican theological educational institution. The responsibility is not without its associated challenges, many of which arise inevitably as a result of our sustained legacy of disadvantage as indigenous Anglicans, and many of which arise inevitably as a result of our church being no less affected than any other in the Anglican world by an embedded patriarchal propensity for hierarchical power and control.

As a leader myself in this complex new South Pacific Anglican milieu, I am daily confronted with the interesting and sometimes impossible task of reconciling multiple accountabilities—those demanded by the privilege of autonomy and those demanded by the experience of engaged or shared partnership. I worry about the lack of institutional, let alone theological, critique of the racial imperatives which undergird our constitutional arrangements. I worry about the way in which the immediate transformation of theological education and ministry training in my own context is so constrained by the burden of colonial freight. I recognize that what are needed are critical-thinking theological educators, whose scholarship and teaching ministries are informed by a powerful sense of social justice and who are unapologetic advocates for the legitimacy and beauty of "cultural" knowledge.

Leadership, as a younger single woman within my own cultural context, is still a somewhat fraught experience, but I believe that with infinite patience, abundant humor and timely gestures of boldness, even the most intransigent indigenous sexist can be moved along! I prefer to see the responsibility of shared leadership as being a requirement to model generosity, not power; to engage, rather than to avoid tension (but to do so with humility and not arrogance); and to envision a just and open future, grounded in the best of our past and yet firmly attuned to the current realities.

I see that my leadership opportunity has arisen out of a specific and intentional redemptive gesture made by the Anglican church as a Christian religious institution, toward human reconciliation. I am unequivocal in recognizing the magnificent potential that this partnership model may provide in terms of assisting existing institutions to undertake similarly transformative action, or alternately for new institutions in terms of laying credible foundations for theological education that embodies, enacts, and thus exemplifies justice for all.

As an indigenous Anglican woman, it seems only fitting that as a descendant of both the original messenger missionaries and of those responsible for the establishment and nurturing of the original missionary church in Aotearoa, I would find myself poised as servant leader for a church which seeks now to model to itself and to the worldwide Communion within which it belongs, something of its prophetic claim of moral courage, of unending faithfulness, and of spiritual prosperity.

And so it is that my indigenous story concludes, not with any sense of finality or of completion, but rather with a profound sense of gratitude for the gift of liberation with which we have been entrusted, and an equally profound sense of hope and of faith that God's will for redemptive justice is done. This at the heart of the challenge and the opportunity of creating and sustaining Te Rau Kahikatea.

In conclusion, I turn to one of the prayers of thanksgiving from the New Zealand Prayer Book. This little prayer serves appropriately as a continual reminder to us all of the common legacy we share as sisters and brothers in the Christ who knows no distinction among us—for indeed we have been created to be above all else "as equals in the image and likeness of God."

> God of justice and compassion,
> you give us a work to do
> and a baptism of suffering and resurrection.
> From you comes power to give to others
> the care we have ourselves received
> so that we, and all who
> love your world, may live in harmony and trust.[44]

NOTES

[1] I use the term postcolonial in a somewhat tentative manner. I agree with Bart Moore-Gilbert in his assertion of "just how tangled and multi-faceted the term 'postcolonial' has now become in terms of its temporal, spatial, political and socio-cultural meanings," in *Postcolonial Theory: Contexts, Practices, Politics* (London: Verso, 1997), 10. I also remain unconvinced of the veracity of the populist definitions, most of which may be traced to those writing out of the experience of being colonial "beneficiaries," rather than colonial "victims." For an incisive and controversial critique of postcolonial theory, see E. San Juan Jr., *Beyond Postcolonial Theory* (New York: St. Martins Press, 1998).

[2] Aotearoa is the name commonly used by Maori and increasingly by non-Maori New Zealanders, to describe the country renamed after the 1642 visit of Dutch voyager Abel Janzoon Tasman, who wrote the name Staten Landt in his original journal records of his encounter with Maori people. Later historians abstracted the name Nouvelle Zelande from others of Tasman's journals.

[3] While some postcolonial critics, particularly Edward Said in *Culture and Imperialism* (London: Chatto & Windus, 1993), tend to describe colonial history as an uninterrupted narrative of oppression and exploitation, I tend more toward the position of Gayatri Chakravorty Spivak who, while not ever denying the destructive impact of imperialism, insists upon a recognition of the positive aspects of that legacy which she describes variously as either an "enabling violence" or an "enabling violation." See Spivak's *In Other Worlds: Essays in Cultural Politics* (New York: Methuen, 1987).

[4] I need to qualify my use of the term indigenous here, which is entirely dependent on the notion of authenticity in relation to the principle of originality. While there are indeed Anglican Theological Colleges in essentially sovereign countries such as Tonga, Samoa and Fiji, which are largely staffed by indigenous peoples, they were all originally established *by* colonial missionaries *for the* indigenous peoples of those lands. Te Rau Kahikatea, the subject of this paper, was established as a theological college, by Maori for Maori and the initiative for its establishment, arose out of the struggle against those vestiges of Anglican colonial imperialism which were unjustly constraining the emergence of an indigenous Anglican response.

⁵ The following texts provide compelling narrative examples of what I describe as "classic" colonial exploitation. For *Hawaiian* stories, see Michael Dougherty, *To Steal a Kingdom: Probing Hawaiian History* (Waimanalo, Hawaii: Island Style Press, 1992); and Keoni Agard and Michael Dudley, eds., *A Hawaiian Nation II, A Call for Hawaiian Sovereignty,* (Waipahu, Hawaii: Na Kane o Ka Malo Press, 1990). For *Canadian* First Nations peoples stories, see Howard Adams, *A Tortured People: The Politics of Colonization* (Penticton, B.C.: Theytus Books, 1995); and Thomas Berger, *A Long and Terrible Shadow: White Values, Native Rights in the Americas* 1492-1992 (Vancouver: Douglas & MacIntyre, 1992). For *Native American* stories, see Vine Deloria Jr., *Red Earth, White Lies: Native Americans and the Myth of Scientific Fact* (Golden, Colo.: Fulcrum Publishing, 1997); and Lois Crozier Hogle and Darryl Babe Wilson, *Surviving in Two Worlds: Contemporary Native American Voices* (Austin: University of Texas Press, 1997). For *Maori* stories, see Harry Evison, *The Long Dispute: Maori Land Rights and European Colonization in Southern New Zealand* (Christchurch: Canterbury University Press, 1997); Ranginui Walker, *The Maori People of New Zealand: 150 years of Colonization* (Auckland: Center for Continuing Education, 1975); and Hugh Kawharu, *Conflict and Compromise: Essays on the Maori since Colonization* (Wellington: A. H. & A. W. Reed, 1975).

⁶ Perhaps most indicative of this process of societal re-evaluation has been the emergence of public debates witnessed only in the past five years, on the idea of creating a Republic of New Zealand, thereby severing the last 'colonial tie' to the Commonwealth of Great Britain. See Brendon Burns, "Bolger Plays the Republican Card," *The Christchurch Press,* 19 March 1994, p. 23. Pete Barnao, "Dilemmas for Maoris if NZ Breaks with Monarchy," *Otago Daily Times,* 23 March 1995, p. 9, and Brian Rudman, "Kiwi Republic: A Cause Without a Rebel," *Sunday Star Times,* 29 May 1994, C7.

⁷ In 1975 Parliament passed the Treaty of Waitangi Act, which established the Waitangi Tribunal. This tribunal, which has always comprised both Maori and non- Maori members, was set up to investigate and report on claims by Maori against the Crown. It was empowered to make recommendations as to how historic prejudice to Maori might be overcome and in recent years, its influence has been profound.

[8] Up until 1997 a number of major claims for historic prejudice have been adjudicated by the Waitangi Tribunal and acted upon by the Crown. Douglas Graham notes that the combined total financial settlements agreed to by the Crown up until that time has been $600 m. See Graham's *Trick or Treaty* (Wellington: Institute of Policy Studies, Victoria University, 1997).

[9] San Juan, *Beyond Postcolonial Theory*, 168.

[10] The name used by the indigenous people of Aotearoa to describe ourselves.

[11] The name used by Maori to describe non-Maori New Zealanders.

[12] The two descriptives can and are used interchangeably throughout this paper, although it is probably more likely that New Zealand became commonly used *after* the signing of the Treaty of Waitangi in 1840.

[13] Geoffrey Rice, ed., *The Oxford History of New Zealand*, 2nd ed. (London: Oxford University Press 1992), 29-86.

[14] Maori words, which are literally translated as, tangata = person, whenua = land, thus the popularly accepted translation is "people of the land."

[15] Maori word that means a visitor or person from afar, a person belonging therefore, to somewhere else.

[16] See *Mission and Moko: The Church Missionary Society in New Zealand* (Christchurch: Olive Tree, 1992).

[17] The Anglican church was the first "denominational" church to establish itself in Aotearoa New Zealand and it remains to this day, statistically the largest and arguably, the most socially and politically significant.

[18] A. K. Davidson, *Christianity in Aotearoa: A History of Church and Society in New Zealand* (Wellington: EFM, 1991).

[19] Douglas Graham is instructive on this point. "Some New Zealanders believe the Treaty was a prototype, but in fact Britain had already a century of treatymaking in North America, Canada and other parts of the world. Nevertheless, it was a document of its times and reflected the political and juridical thought then prevailing.

Most treaties entered into by Britain sought to legitimise the assumption of sovereignty . . . When it became obvious to the Colonial Office that some definitive action would need to be taken with regard to New Zealand, the decision was made to treat with the Maori to seek their consent to British rule. So it was never intended that New Zealand would be annexed against their will." See *Trick or Treaty*, 9-10.

[20] New Zealand's colonial history is strewn with examples of unjust legislation intended to deprive Maori people of our land and traditional rights. Alan Ward records a very early example of colonial imperialism in respect to legislation which was ostensibly always enacted for the benefit of all citizens, "By its legislation of 1858 the Assembly further demonstrated how it proposed to use the law to promote policies, in regard to land, incompatible with the Maori aspirations . . ." See *A Show of Justice: Racial "Amalgamation" in Nineteenth Century New Zealand* (Auckland: University of Auckland Press, 1974), 107.

[21] See note 5.

[22] See W. P. Morrell, *The Anglican Church in New Zealand: A History* (Dunedin: John McIndoe Ltd., 1973).

[23] Selwyn's appointment as Bishop was heavily influenced by key associates of the New Zealand Company, the primary agency responsible for the push for colonization in New Zealand.

[24] Right from the earliest period of colonization, official policy was broadly assimilationist; the problem was that this policy was also racist in its uncontested assumptions. In his pioneering work, *A Show of Justice: Racial "Amalgamation" in Nineteenth Century New Zealand*, Alan Ward notes: "In that these policies . . . assumed a high level of capability in Pacific peoples and stood ready to meet their desire to participate in the institutions of the new order; they were liberal and progressive. Their very great weakness was that they were underlain by undoubted convictions of the superiority of the English institutions and conversely by a disastrously limited appreciation of local values and local peoples preferences for their own institutions . . ." (p. 36).

[25] Bishop George Augustus Bennett was Bishop of Aotearoa from 1928 to 1950.

[26] See the author's M.Ed. Thesis, Kua Whakatungia Ano A Te Rau Kahikatea An Historical Critical Overview of the Events that Preceded the Re-establishment of Te Rau Kahikatea (University of Auckland, 1993). This thesis provides substantive evidence of the injustices, which systematically accrued against those Maori selected by the church to undertake studies in theology. The study covers the period 1843-1992.

[27] In one of the very few references to New Zealand that I have encountered in contemporary postcolonial literature, Robert J. C. Young notes the following: "Until the word 'miscegenation' was invented in 1864, the word that was conventionally used for the fertile fusion and merging of races was 'amalgamation.' A writer on colonization in Australia and New Zealand, comments in 1838, that: 'It may be deemed a cold and mercenary calculation; but we must say, that instead of attempting an 'amalgamation' of the two races—Europeans and Zealanders—as is recommended by some persons, the wiser course would be to let the native race gradually retire before the settlers, and ultimately become extinct.'" See Young, *Colonial Desire: Hybridity in Theory, Culture, and Race* (London: Routledge, 1995), 9.

[28] Over the past decade there has been a proliferation of revisionist histories written, mostly in direct response to a more extensive public demand for knowledge of the facts of our colonial history. See Jamie Belich, *The New Zealand Wars and the Victorian Interpretation of Conflict* (Auckland: Auckland University Press, 1986); Judith Binney, *Redemption Songs: A Life of Te Kooti Arikirangi Te Turaki* (Auckland: Auckland University Press, 1995); Michael King, *Nga Iwi o Te Motu: One Thousand Years of Maori History* (Birkenhead, Auckland: Reed Books, 1997); M. P. K. Sorrenson, *Maori Origins and Migrations: The Genesis of Some Pakeha Myths and Legends* (Auckland: Auckland University Press,1979); Ranginui Walker, *Ka Whawhai Tonu Matou: Struggle Without End* (Auckland: Penguin Books, 1990).

[29] Nga Tamatoa was the name coined by this group—they modeled themselves very much upon the images and the ideologies of the Black Panthers and other radical black activists from the U.S.

[30] Donna Awatere, *Maori Sovereignty* (Auckland: Broadsheet, 1994).

[31] During the 1970s, groups of disenfranchised young predominantly but not exclusively urban Maori males began organizing themselves into gangs, modeled very closely upon those of the inner city black gangs of Los Angeles, Chicago and New York. Inter-gang violence became commonplace and unmitigated sexual violence also characterized the behavior of some gangs—the word 'gang-bang' was associated with one of the rights of initiation for new gang members who were required to provide evidence of having participated in the multiple rape of any woman.

[32] Report of the General Synod, Te Hinota Whanui 1984.

[33] See *Te Kaupapa Tikanga Rua : Bicultural Development* (Auckland: Anglican Church Publication, 1986).

[34] The Constitution of the Anglican Church in Aotearoa New Zealand and Polynesia (1992).

[35] These statements, while universal within the worldwide Anglican Communion, are also included in the preamble section of the Revised Constitution (1992).

[36] Maori word when literally translated meaning "culturally correct ways of being."

[37] Te Hahi Mihinare when literally translated means the Missionary Church.

[38] Pihopatanga o Aotearoa = Bishopric of Aotearoa. This episcopal jurisdiction is prescribed over Maori people wherever they are located throughout Aotearoa, rather than over a discrete geographic territory.

[39] The overarching decision making and controlling authority for Maori Anglicans in Aotearoa—it is accountable to General Synod.

[40] In 1998 the General Synod approved of the establishment of a third society, representing the interests of tikanga Polynesia. The relationships between the three Colleges are somewhat complex, and whilst they derive somewhat from the original Treaty arrangement, Polynesians are not regarded as Treaty partners in the same way Pakeha are.

[41] The name of the Theological College established originally in Gisborne, in 1883, by the CMS for Maori students.

[42] The name of one of the ships in which Bishop Selwyn traveled while establishing the church in Melanesia.

[43] See *Stimulus: The New Zealand Journal of Christian Thought and Practice* 6:2 (May 1998).

[44] Church of the Province of New Zealand, *A New Zealand Prayer Book* (Auckland: Collins, 1989), 478.

13

BEYOND THE MONARCH/CHIEF

Reconsidering the Episcopacy in Africa

SIMON E. CHIWANGA

FROM MONARCH/CHIEF TO MHUDUMU

It is very difficult to pinpoint exactly how I started groping for a shared leadership style. I was born in a poor and humble home. Both my parents were very hardworking peasants. They converted to Christianity just before they married and my father entered the full-time ministry of the church as a catechist before I was born. My mother came from a chiefly family. Because of this connection, in 1959 I was appointed Chief of our area but my parents strongly objected, for I would have to be the custodian of the ritual paraphernalia. I did not fully appreciate their intervention until three years later when the institution of Chiefs was abolished by the Independence Government. I wonder whether I would have had the same interest in servant leadership had I been made Chief in 1959.

In my seven years of ministry as a bishop, I have observed again and again a notorious problem facing both the Tanzanian church and Tanzanian society as a whole: a dependency mentality. This results, I believe, from the fear and an inferiority complex created during the colonial period. As a former President of Tanzania once said,

> In the past years and centuries, we were greatly intimidated and harassed by the colonialists. If you stood before a colonial leader to speak or to ask him a question, you would be harassed by his juniors, who would ask you why you spoke or asked questions. This practice instilled fear in the minds of many citizens. The people did not respect their seniors; they simply feared them.[1]

There is great need to build trust between the leaders and the people. In the church, the issue is seen most vividly in the relationships between ordained ministry and lay people. There are different perceptions of the role of the ordained ministry. Some see ordained ministers as "proprietors" of the church, while others see ordained ministers as the hired servants of the laity. In this view, laity want certain ministries to be performed in their congregation, but they are too busy earning a living, so they recruit clergy and catechists to carry out those ministries for them. Lay people who hold this view lay blame wholly on their clergy if parish life ebbs, attendance declines, the sick and prisoners are not visited, or the youth and women's programs stagnate.

Some clergy encourage these misconceptions too, when, on the one hand, they meekly and passively accept these roles, and likewise see the bishop as the proprietor of the diocese. On the other hand, some priests present themselves as indispensable at the expense of lay creativity and initiative. I also have made my own contribution to the mess by being too ready to offer solutions and by being impatient for the zeal of the vision that is consuming me. As Bishop Bennett Sims reflects:

> Responsibility for the performance of others in any system or organization acts as an impatient inner urge to use our power to compel compliance, whether we are a frustrated mother who is tempted to force oatmeal on a stubborn child at breakfast or an overworked bishop who would like nothing better than to expel an incompetent parish priest whose congregation is suffocating.[2]

The *mhudumu* model defined in this essay allows for a greater identification of the leader with the led, which is what Jesus advocated. *Mhudumu* is a Swahili word which means "minister," or better still, "server." It describes the facilitation of the desired goal: the act of enabling something to happen. This essay presents this sharing and serving *mhudumu* model as a vision of a postcolonial episcopacy, emerging from the Tanzanian context, a vision that reorients episcopal leadership toward servanthood and mutual responsibility.

This paper is not a theological study of episcopacy in general, nor even of episcopacy in Africa. Rather, it is a theological reflection on my own experience in the diocese of Mpwapwa. I know, however, that people in other churches and other locations face many of the same challenges we do in Mpwapwa. Should my reflections be of some relevance to others, I will be humbly grateful. Two larger concerns are behind this paper: the issue of Anglican identity in the context of Tanzania, where the predominant traditional communitarian values shape and are shaped by dynamic social change; and the issue of liberation from oppressive leadership forms we have inherited from our colonial past, from fear and a dependency mentality implanted in us by colonial history.

The nature and style of ministry is determined by the nature of the community; the mission of the community constitutes the ministry and not vice versa. The re-visioning of episcopacy necessarily calls for a definition of the nature of its community, whose mission needs a relevant ordained ministry. The context of Tanzanian Christians, like other Tanzanians, is that of practicing most of the traditional values of familyhood and extended-family connections in the midst of rapid social changes brought about by technology and globalization. It is my hope that ministry be reformed to become what the local church needs in all of its experiences of dynamic change: a serving rather than dominating ministry; a ministry which identifies itself with the community, rather than setting itself above it and dictating the kind of change the leadership needs. The *mhudumu* model of ministry is what the Tanzanian situation demands.

In calling for reform of episcopal and clerical ministry, I also hope for a reinvention of the local church. In view of the distorted expectations created by clerical domination over the years, many congregations have come to expect orders and initiatives for ministry from the top. Local churches should be aware of their local and wider mission imperative, and enable the participation of every member for the building up of the body of Christ. It is at this level of community that both the individual and the whole body are best nourished for mission. I call this new vision *ujamaa,* or "familyhood," ecclesiology which I will explain more fully in a moment. Important as this objective is, however, I pursue it primarily to provide the context, which gives birth to the need for a *mhudumu* model of *episcopé.* So in spite of *ujamaa* ecclesiology appearing like another major thrust in this essay, I still maintain the overall title of a call from Monarch/Chief to *Mhudumu:* a call from the foreign monarchical influences and the negative aspects of traditional African chieftainship in our leadership style. I tremble on reading the indictment of the shepherds who projected their horns.

> The weak you have not strengthened, the sick you have not healed, the crippled you have not bound up, the strayed you have not brought back, the lost you have not sought, and with force and harshness you have ruled them.... Because you push with side and shoulder, and thrust at all the weak with your *horns* (Ezek. 34:4, 20; emphasis added).

As we seek to understand Anglican identity in our present shift from a colonial Communion to a postcolonial Communion, I wish to point out the need for contextual discernment in our search, while avoiding what Professor John Pobee has described as the "Anglo-Saxon captivity" of Anglicanism. Re-visioning the episcopacy through the lens of *ujamaa* ecclesiology is an example of such contextual discernment. *Ujamaa* ecclesiology arises from two perspectives: the understanding of church as *koinonia* and the Tanzanian understanding of the primacy of communal life. *Ujamaa* ecclesiology is the product of the encounter of the gospel and *ujamaa* culture.

In Swahili, Tanzania's national language, *ujamaa* means "familyhood." It is a way of life such as can be found within a nuclear family or an extended family. Through belonging to a family, clan and tribe, the African learned to say, "I am because I participate." The life of the community was made possible through an interplay of three cardinal principles which permeated the customs, manners, and education of the people from birth to death: respect for everyone, hard work by everyone, and mutual caring by everyone. Most traditional Tanzanian families live by these principles, despite the great changes that have swept our country. When these principles inform ecclesiology, the church is understood in terms of community, the people of God, who are agents together in the mission of God, clergy and laity together acting as signs and bearers of God's saving love in a troubled world. The foundation of such a church is trust in the grace of God to perfect human nature. The ethos of such a church is that of a corporate world accustomed to movement and change, rather than an individualistic world which must be preserved and kept in order. Members in this community experience spontaneous expansion and corporate witness, rather than relying on officials to legitimate and parcel out activities. This church is an educated community of Christ-centered people going about God's work in mutual responsibility. An understanding of the church as *ujamaa* communion implies the nature of ministry is collaborative. The context of community life is the lens that shapes our understanding of scripture and theology and the mission and ministry of the church. Given the nature of *ujamaa* church, the most effective style of ministry is collaborative or sharing, as the principle of community life requires.

* * * * *

There's a land where the mountains are nameless
and the rivers all run God knows where,
There are lives that are erring and aimless,
There are deaths that just hang by a hair,
There are hardships that nobody reckons,
There's the valley, and plain, and the hill,
There's a land, oh, it beckons and beckons
And I want to go back, and I will.[3]

MHUDUMU EPISCOPACY

The kings of the Gentiles exercise lordship over them; and those in authority over them are called benefactors. But not so with you; rather let the greatest among you become as the youngest, and the leader as one who serves. For which is the greater, one who sits at table, or one who serves? Is it not the one who sits at table? But I am among you as one who serves (Luke 22:25-27).

The *mhudumu* model of leadership presented here flows out of the definition of *ujamaa* ecclesiology. A community-oriented ecclesiology demands a collaborative style of leadership. The discussion of *mhudumu* leadership that follows is not primarily a definition of personality traits such as attitudes, knowledge, or skills, even though they are important. The *mhudumu* model, episcopal or otherwise, is a relational model that has the greatest potential of transforming relational dynamics of authority, responsibility, support, information, and evaluation. Drawing from studies in Collaborative Ministerial Leadership, I describe a framework for practical application of the *mhudumu* episcopacy. I also highlight the shifts required by the move from chief to *mhudumu*. Then I offer concluding remarks by way of summary and to indicate areas for further exploration.

Definition of *Mhudumu*

In the Swahili translation of the Bible, *mhudumu* is used where the English translation uses "minister," and *mtumishi* for "servant." In Acts chapter 6, the apostles appeal for more people to serve *(kuhudumu)* at the tables, while they serve *(kuhudumu)* the word. Here the same word is used for both types of ministry. One might ask why I choose to use *mhudumu*, not *mtumishi*, and why do I not use "minister" or "servant," since I am writing in English anyway? While the words *mhudumu* and *mtumishi* are used interchangeably to refer to ministers of the church, lay and ordained, the latter has employment connotations, and less of that voluntary offering which is so critical in ministry. I do not use the English words "servant" and "minister" because, as English words, they do not evoke for Tanzanians all that is conveyed by the word *mhudumu*.

The New Testament Greek word that is translated *mhudumu* or *mtumishi* is *diákonos*, which, according to Beyer,[4] has various applications, but all centering around the idea of service. To the Greeks, as to an African chief or English prelate, service (*diákonein*) was undignified and subservient. To later Judaism, service was given as meritorious rather than sacrificial. Therefore Beyer comments, "By exalting service and relating it to love of God, Jesus both sets forth a completely different view from that of the Greeks and purifies the Jewish concept."[5]

Beyer gives four senses of service in the New Testament, relevant to the *mhudumu* concept which reflects the same transvaluation of the view of authority and power. First, the narrowest sense of waiting at table, which Christ himself does, assumes a new pattern of relationships, extending to the washing of feet. The table service of Acts 6:2, "to supervise the meal," involves the whole process of distribution, preparation, and organization. It was love in action rather than just a proclamation of love. It is interesting that the Swahili translation uses the same word *kuhudumia* (to serve) for the new deacons' table service as for the apostles' ministry of the word. So in Swahili translations, the ranking of ministries is not so pronounced as in English translations. Second, the wider sense "to serve" includes many activities, like those mentioned in Matthew 25:42-45. Serving others is serving Christ and involves personal commitment, even to the point of death itself (John 12:25-26). Third, the life of the community is a life of service. Charismata are gifts of action and gifts of word (Acts 19:22; Philem.13; 2 Tim. 1:18). Timothy, Erastus, Onesmus and Onesphorus are examples. "This service cannot be proud, self-righteous service; it is discharged only by God's power and to his glory."[6] Fourth, the sense of service as the collection for the saints (Rom. 15:31; 2 Cor. 8:1-4) is a corrective of the tendency to regard those called and assigned to administrative duties as less important.

THE NATURE OF *MHUDUMU*

The *mhudumu* concept conjures up most powerfully the image of a leader who renders service in a team, in collaboration with fellow servers who believe that gifts are given to everyone; a *mhudumu* is a leader whose heart is for service and not status; a leader who honors the personal dignity and worth of all who work with him or her; a leader who evokes as much as possible fellow members' innate creative power for leadership; a leader who is empowering. *Mhudumu* leadership is characterized not by privilege, but by service which promotes justice and peace and creates a spirit of self-reliance rather than dependency. Most likely women and children were the table servers at the time of Jesus, as it is in Tanzania today. When Jesus took the role of a server at table, he was taking the role of those who had less power. The image of a bishop serving at table where lay people, clergy, young and old, men and women are seated, is radical in some places, and is often dismissed theologically. Why, for example, do some of us theologize against the rite of footwashing on Maundy Thursday?

THE ROLE OF THE BISHOP AS *MHUDUMU*

The essential role of the bishop is to lead and enable the mission of the *ujamaa koinonia*. Therefore it is crucial for the bishop to be the pioneer in radically moving away from non-transforming ministerial structures in order to enhance the liberation of the people of God for ministry. The table-serving metaphor that is conveyed both by the Swahili concept of *mhudumu* and the Greek word *diakonos*, and the way Christ transformed it, is most consistent with the nature of leadership required under *ujamaa* ecclesiology. *Ujamaa* as *koinonia* shares a common memory, a common praxis, and a common hope. Leadership in such a community enables the sharing to take place, and as such, it must be collaborative.

The *mhudumu* bishop will facilitate sharing in three corresponding roles: first, just as a table server makes sure that food is available for everyone, so it is for *mhudumu*. Her or his role is to ensure that the memory of the community is made common, by making sure that it is interpreted. This is what Paul means when he says, "as servants of Christ and stewards of the mysteries of God" (1 Cor. 4:1). These mysteries have to be made common, shared, uncovered, and distributed equitably to members of the fellowship. Second, the *mhudumu* bishop makes sure that the body builds itself up through the contribution of the experiences (praxis) of everyone in the community. Paul calls this to "equip the saints for the work of ministry" (Eph. 4:11-16). Third, the *mhudumu* bishop makes sure that the hope of the community is kept alive. Paul said, "May the God of hope fill you with all joy and peace in believing, so that by the power of the Holy Spirit you may abound in hope" (Rom. 15:13). All three dimensions of the faith of the community are combined in the prayer of Paul found in Ephesians, "that you may know what is the *hope* to which he has called you, what are the riches of his glorious *inheritance* in the saints, and what is the immeasurable greatness of his *power* in us who believe, according to the working of his great might" (Eph. 1:18-19, emphasis added). Therefore, the *mhudumu* bishop enables the interpretation of the gospel, the building up of the members, and the inspiriting of hope in them.

I emphasize the role of the bishop of *ensuring*. Reading historical and current literature on the role of bishops in the West, since the patristic period, one gets an overwhelming picture of a bishop as a leader, first and foremost, in theological scholarship. I am not referring to everyday theology that every believer does, and especially if one is expected to teach or preach. I refer to a more academic and apologetic engagement in theology, such that has given us a wealth of high-level theological resources, and sometimes even heresy.

There was a time in the history of the church in Tanzania when a priest was the highest-educated person in the community. That time passed away long ago. More highly trained lay theologians are emerging. Unless we adopt a different interpretation of the bishop's theological leadership, we need to recognize that fact, and consequently appreciate the role of *ensuring* that various tasks are done by those with the relevant talents. This again calls for the humility to be led by those we lead, lay or clergy, when it comes to their area of specialization and to help them be better equipped for the common good. The bishop may be gifted in one area, and, therefore, take the lead in that one area. But the bishop and the church must resist the temptation to orient the entire mission of the church towards the bishop's gift so that his/her leadership may always be seen out front, even though that particular area is not a priority at the time.

I share the views expressed by Bishop Stuart Blanch and Father Vincent Donovan. In discussing the development of the "monarchical bishops" as a guarantee of authenticity of doctrine amidst conflicting schools of theology, Blanch notes that the bishops also came to be seen as repositories of learning and were often trained in the classical schools of the world: "philosophers in their own right who brought to the study of the Scriptures a scholastic rigor, which was to provide the church with a solid intellectual basis against which extravagances of thought and action could be judged." Blanch uses this as an example of the point he argues that "circumstances rather than theory ruled in the development of episcopacy as we know it today."[7] I like his theory of circumstances ruling in the development of episcopacy, because it is very much in line with my thesis of contextual discernment. Blanch makes another point that is also relevant to my thesis. "The danger is that a particular view of the past, conditioned by time and place, may unduly influence our reaction to the unprecedented changes in the church of the next millennium— if the Parousia is that long delayed."[8]

The second person whose definition of the minister agrees with my understanding of *mhudumu* is Vincent Donovan, who wrote from his experience of working with the Maasai of Tanzania.

> That man who called the community together; at the end of the instructions he would not be the one in the community who knew the most theology, the theologian. Wherever and

> whenever the community acted as Christian community he
> would be carrying out his function, the focal point of the
> whole community, building that community, holding it
> together, animating it to action, signifying its unity, enabling
> it to function.[9]

The table server makes sure that each one has food, but also that all have food, and that even those who are away are counted. I see in this picture the local and the catholic dimension of both the community and the *mhudumu* as a link person. This is a radical move away from a utilitarian, functionally centered (servicing) concept to a community-oriented, common humanity facilitator, and, therefore, liberating (serving) model. The *mhudumu* in this context serves the purpose or the mission of the *ujamaa koinonia* and is answerable to the community where he or she belongs. This means that the ordained ministers, which include the bishop, are firmly rooted in the community as one of them. The *Baptism, Eucharist, and Ministry* document of the World Council of Churches describes the relationship of the ordained misters and the rest of the people of God as follows:

> All members of the believing community, ordained and lay,
> are interrelated. On the one hand, the community needs
> ordained ministers.... They serve to build up the community
> in Christ and to strengthen its witness. On the other hand, the
> ordained ministry has no existence apart from the communi-
> ty. Ordained ministers can fulfill their calling only in and for
> the community. They cannot dispense with the recognition,
> the support and the encouragement of the community.[10]

THE NEED FOR CHANGE

The relational nature of clergy to the community in a family way of being made it natural for African Christians to address their clergy as "Father/Mother-in-God." It is this relationality that Bishop Leslie Brown observed while serving in Africa.

> There is however another most important factor which affects
> the style of episcopacy in Africa.... The bishop is seen not only
> as the ultimate authority in the church, but as a man in rela-
> tionship to church members. It is a family relationship and
> the church is analogous to an extended family. The universal
> way of addressing the bishop is, "Our Father in God." This
> implies a relationship of mutual trust and interdependence.[11]

However, what Bishop Brown is saying is as it should be. In some cases in the Anglican church, the "our Father in God" is hardly different, functionally, from the former "my Lord Bishop." It is given on demand, implicitly or explicitly. It is given as a way of winning favors, implicitly or explicitly. It is given to enhance paternalism and even maternalism. I am convinced that the Lord Christ would repeat the same injunction, which he gave to those who were misusing this radically relational address, "Call no man your father on earth, for you have one Father, who is in heaven. Neither be called masters, for you have one master, the Christ"(Matt. 23:9-10). My point here is to call for a return to the real basis of this address of "Father" or "Mother" which is in communal relationship and in rendering acceptable and humble service, *huduma*, to the community by the *mhudumu* leader. Another reason for change is that the underlying theology of ministry followed in the Anglican Church of Tanzania, even though it has not been deliberately articulated, is very hierarchical, and is based on the 1978 Lambeth statement on the functions of a bishop.

> In his function of exercising pastoral care over his Diocese, it is necessary for [the Bishop] so to discharge his own pastoral care of his Clergy that they in turn are truly pastors of the flock committed to him and them. When he delegates pastoral responsibility to the Clergy he must do so in such a way and in such a spirit that they in turn will delegate responsibility to those who work with them.[12]

The Lambeth statement on the authority of the ordained ministry shows a clear hierarchy of Christ–Bishop–Clergy–People, based on the principle of delegation. K.S. Chittleborough has observed that Anglicans, like the rest of the Western church, have from the fourth century, "inherited a fundamental change in church and ministry from the principle of organism in which the whole is greater than the sum of its parts, to the principle of hierarchy in which the 'greatest' is the sum of its parts."[13] I find this to be an apt description of the present Anglican model of episcopacy in Tanzania, which has distanced the ordained ministry from the rest of the people of God. Some of the negative results have been to view ordination or consecration to the ministry as "election" into membership of a "caste" within the church, and that the role and authority of the ordained ministers is located in membership to this "caste," rather than in the organic relationship with people.

The series of scandals surrounding elections of bishops in the last five years is a clear sign that people feel they are not heard.

The usual response by leadership that it is mere tribalism is superficial and not supported by reality. People desire a fundamental change in the way their leaders act, not just in what they say. A senior Roman Catholic missionary in Tanzania has noted a very serious desire of the people to see change in the style of leadership.

> We will have to ask ourselves whether we are really prepared to ... cast off the pyramidal pattern of hierarchy which ensures that the bishops are the extension of the people, the priests are the extension of the bishop, and the laity that of the priests.... The people of God take this very seriously. Some go so far as to call it a question of life and death for the church in Africa. They complain that some of the priests are inclined to become one-party leaders, that they are not transparent and do not listen to the spoken word of inculturation that is already taking place among lay members of the Christian communities.[14]

The need for change can be seen more clearly by comparing the two models. In the Monarch/Chief model the main features are: an ordained ministry independent though aware of the laity; an irreducibility of orders; and, a great stress on chain-link in the apostolic succession. On the whole the church is a pyramid in structure, and is seen as an institution governed and directed by clergy who shape the policy and make plans. Then the laity are enlisted to assist them in carrying out these plans. The ordained ministry consists of the bishop who has the "fullness of ministry," while priests, deacons, and the laity derive their ministries in descending ranks and functions from the bishop.

In the *mhudumu* or organic model, the main features are: historic orders located within the community; recognition of the integrity of each charism and ministry; apostolicity is of the whole church. In general the church is viewed as the people of God, the body of Christ, in which every member through baptism has a common though differentiated responsibility for the church and its ministry in God's mission. There is no thought of a *cursus honorum* by which one rises from lower to higher rank, status, and responsibility. Each ministry in the church has its own integrity, function, and type of authority which is derived not from the bishop, but from the community in the power of the Holy Spirit who bestows gifts. It is circular in structure.

Diagrammatically, we would represent the two models as follows:

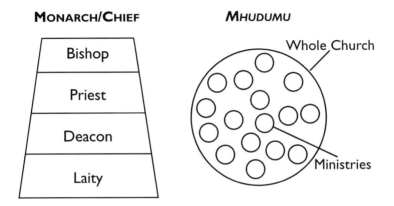

MHUDUMU AND SYSTEMS THEORY

The study of ministerial systems is well advanced in some churches of the Anglican Communion, drawing from the general sciences of management. The practical steps proposed here that a leader could take to implement the *mhudumu* model are derived from the study of collaborative ministerial leadership, which has benefited from the insights of systems theory. Systems theory can be described as a tool for analyzing organizational behavior in a way that allows different aspects of the organization, its players, and its environment, to be identified by how they relate systematically. Collaborative ministry theorist William Kondrath notes, "Systems theory attempts to gain an overview of the very complicated inter-relationships that constitute the unit under consideration."[15] Systems theory holds that every church leader operates in a theory of church organization which determines what he or she considers the most appropriate organizational structure and leadership, whether or not the leader in question is aware of it. Because leadership in the church is teamwork, it is not enough for each leader to have his or her own private theory separate from or unknown to others. This, then, calls for a deliberate choice of a theory which can be shared by everyone in the team, be it a congregation, parish, or diocese.

Ministerial systems are indeed complicated in four main aspects. First, they are organizationally complex because of the interdependency of the various parts of an organization, like a parish or diocese. Each part influences another part in the way things can develop, and feedback between each part of the ministerial system is crucial. For example, it is very important that the parish knows in advance what it is expected to contribute to the diocese so that it can budget properly. Second, the church's ministerial systems are open, and cannot be closed-in systems. It is the very essence of the catholicity of the church which requires internal (local) and external (universal) relationship and very often, accountability. Leadership has to relate with those inside the church and those outside. Third, the ministerial systems are adaptive, in that they do not allow conflict, tensions, or sudden changes of demography to crush them, but make use of these elements to adapt to the new situations. To an alert church, for example, these changes are considered opportunities to grow in directions not explored before. Fourth, ministerial systems are ready to receive new ideas, sift them and adapt them as appropriate. This involves also openness to God's Spirit, who can diverge into new paths and dimensions.

From the above description, ministerial leadership is essentially collaborative. The *mhudumu* concept, as it has been noted above, is essentially collaborative, because the *mhudumu* connotes a process involving more than one person. Two is the unavoidable minimum, in that even if it were possible to imagine an isolated *mhudumu* somewhere remote, that one *mhudumu* is with God, the very first collaborator. *Mhudumu* is collaborative in that the bishop or priest is located within the work, with labor, not apart from it. *Mhudumu* leadership saves a priest or bishop from becoming what Kondrath has described as "Rev. Solo's personal ministry rather than the ministry of the people of God gathered in that place."[16] From the social sciences again, Loughlan Solfield has observed,

> What is most significant for our purposes as we talk about leadership within the church is that people in the work-world are experiencing new forms of leadership and organization. The leader is no longer expected to be the expert but the team leader. New roles for leaders are support manager, coach, helper, and facilitator.[17]

One writer has also observed that "We are all engaged in the paradox that in order to be an individual we have to take on groupness."[18]

Of the four styles found in collaborative ministerial leadership, I briefly describe two of them, which offer a good comparative observation in identifying practical steps: the Sovereign and the Mutual styles. The other two, the Parallel and the Semi-Mutual, are not such crucial alternatives at the moment in Tanzania, where, given our history, the greatest need is to move from chief to *mhudumu*.

THE SOVEREIGN STYLE

The sovereign style is hierarchical and demands order, obedience, clear accountability and a uniform way of doing things. It is a domination model, and therefore relationships are of a dependent nature, in which "respect for those above, merely because they are above, is more common than trust. The system is closed. It exercises a high degree of control and is relatively self-sustaining."[19] It is vulnerable to the tendency to be rationalized on the basis of the divine right of the leader, in a unique possession of charismatic gifts.

THE MUTUAL STYLE

In this style, members of a team of ministers, (bishop and deans; priest and catechists or parish councils) work together in planning the activities and evaluation of performance of each member of the team, which includes the leader. While the division of responsibility is made, members do not hold rigidly to their pigeonholes, but are willing to step in and help in case of an absence or difficulty in other positions. There is more emphasis on integration and sharing of authority, and the language is more of "our parish," "our diocese," "our project," or "our idea."

Table 2 shows a comparison between two styles in several facets of interpersonal relationships, in outline form.

TABLE 2. COMPARISON BETWEEN TWO STYLES OF LEADERSHIP[20]

	SOVEREIGN	MUTUAL
EXAMPLES	Chain of command: Bishop, Priest, Curate, Lay	"Shared Ministry" Teams
IDEALS	Order and obedience Clear accountability Uniformity	Shared authority, accountability, labor Autonomy not stressed Integration Diversified unity
CHARACTERISTICS	Authority is indivisible Real delegation is not common	Consensus on goals, objectives Joint responsibility for tasks Ongoing interaction
RELATIONSHIPS	Authority Obedience Dependence No peer relationship Respect rather than trust	Strong sense of shared peers Interdependence Authority shared High Trust
ACCOUNTABILITY	Obedience to authority Support for agenda of authority To immediate supervisor	About wide range of issues To oneself first, rather than to colleagues
SUPPORT/SUPERVISION	Controlled by system Often not given When given: informal; depends on person, not system; priest centered	Built in systematically Ongoing, consistent Formal, informal Given for both planning and tasks
FEEDBACK/EVALUATION	Confined to authority's feedback Based on limited observation Judgmental	Built-in Growth and development of staff shared Assess performance Creates supportive climate
TRAINING: KNOWLEDGE	Hierarchical	Personal development and relationship dynamics
TRAINING: ATTITUDE	Hierarchical	Values collaboration as such
TRAINING: SKILLS	Specific skills for ministry in institutional church	Interpersonal and group insti dynamics Theological reflection
TRAINING: ROLE	Competent Reliable Subordinate	Full-time team

CONSEQUENTIAL SHIFT: FROM EPISCOPOCENTRIC TO POLYCENTRIC LEADERSHIP

We must leave behind the idea of ministry as the monopoly of the bishop who then delegates tasks to others, and instead travel toward an understanding of ministry and leadership as the responsibility of every baptized Christian. I am convinced, as Miroslav Volf argues, that the church is a communion of interdependent subjects; that the way salvation is received by members is not only through the ordained ministers, but also through all other members of the church gathered together; and, that the Holy Spirit constitutes the church when the communal confession of faith is made by Christians as they gather to share the word of God between them. "From these three basic theological convictions, it follows that the life of the church cannot be episcopocentric … but rather fundamentally a polycentric community;"[21] hence, the move from the position of "episcopacy is primary" to that of the "primacy of the community," from the concept of indelible "church orders" to that of "ordering the church" for mission.

The most important ordination to the ministry of all the people of God is baptism. "Baptism, not ordination, is where the calling to a life of mission originates. The work of mission and leadership of the entire church belongs to the *laos* as the people of God. It is not the exclusive domain of one group of people or another."[22] It is in this sense that we can speak of the priesthood of all believers. The model of *mhudumu* calls upon the bishop to move from the royal stool to the kitchen steward apron; from preoccupation with status to that of humble service, in order to be able to say, as St. Augustine said in his sermon 340,

> For you I am a bishop, but with you I am a Christian. The first is an office accepted; the second is a gift received. One is danger; the other is safety. If I am happier to be redeemed with you than to be placed over you, then I shall, as the Lord commanded, be more fully your servant.

The *mhudumu* model, genuinely followed, liberates the leader from even the thought of being placed "over" others. For the office is for a shared responsibility with laity and clergy. Diversity of functions are not turned into degrees of power and privileges; nor is there a thought of qualitative difference between various functions.

PRACTICAL APPLICATION AND AN EXAMPLE

SHARING IN TRAINING PROCESSES

A mutual style calls for creativity in training processes, and this requires trust that each member of the team has an important contribution to make. Each member is therefore given the opportunity to lead training, and the leader must sit in class and actively participate as a learner. I have found through experience that when I ask a participant, say one of the deans, to lead a session and I use that time to attend to other concerns away from the session, it works against empowerment. It gives the signal that the team member cannot teach me anything.

MUTUAL EVALUATION

Evaluation is always threatening. A mutual style of collaborative leadership can minimize the element of threat by developing an instrument of evaluation which involves every member of the team, including the leader of the team. The bishop should offer to be evaluated by those forming the team of assistants, the deans in my case, or committee participants, in the case of events of that nature.

THE EXAMPLE OF THE EAST AFRICAN REVIVAL MOVEMENT

The East African Revival Movement was a mighty experience of spiritual renewal which resulted in breaking of all sorts of barriers, as everyone involved felt humbled and reconciled to those they despised or dominated. It could truly be said "like people like priest." A regular feature was the weekly fellowship meeting at which everyone felt free to share and to learn from others, regardless of position. The leadership was mainly lay, while bishops and clergy happily accepted that situation and felt greatly affirmed. It was the Revival Movement that accentuated the principle of self-extending to a degree that has never been surpassed. Bishop Alfred Stanway noted,

> The church was in some ways poorly equipped, but nevertheless it had one great asset. The Revival Movement in East Africa had given to a large number a deep desire to propagate the Gospel, and whatever their lack of knowledge they were alive with a sense that Christ had come into their lives and wrought a change, and so through the witness of these within the life of the church, it was possible to have available the evangelists who were required to push back the frontiers and gather in the harvest.[23]

The revival movement provided the ideal model of a mutual style of leadership. The principle of transparency applied to every member, regardless of age, gender and position. Whenever paternalism ruled, clerical or lay, fellowship meetings disintegrated.

Conclusion

As I have formulated the idea of a *mhudumu* episcopacy, some of my assumptions have been effectively challenged; my conviction on collaborative leadership has been deeply impressed; my commitment to serving God's people for God's mission has been invigorated; my horizons as to the questions I should be asking myself and fellow sojourners have been greatly expanded; and my love and devotion to my God, my family, and to all God's people has been deepened.

The reality of the context of Tanzania, of the nature of human beings, of the trends of business management even in the West today, and the gospel of a Triune God, all demand a serious engagement with communitarian and collaborative leadership models. Talking about community as the goal of development intervention, Norman Kraus says:

> To be is to be part of and participate in the whole web of existence. Thus, by definition, being involves interdependence and process. It involves doing and relating. This challenges modernization's concept of individualism and independence as the final value and suggests community (shalom) as the goal of our intervention.[24]

The *mhudumu* leader in *ujamaa koinonia* is one who values community, develops the power of listening, empowers others, facilitates a shared vision, and advocates learning and changing. Above all, the *mhudumu* bishop is always aware of the Chief Server's words, "But I am among you as one who serves."

The *mhudumu* model demands an urgent reorientation of our clergy formation systems, especially theological colleges, so that we turn out people who have the passion for, and are trained in, the art of equipping the people of God for mission and ministry at the grassroots. The polycentric participatory model of the church has to be our focus as we search for better ways to reform our ministry and election processes of various office holders, especially bishops, in the church.

When you have done all that is commanded you, say,
"We are unworthy servants;
we have only done what was our duty" (Luke 17:10).

NOTES

[1] J. K. Nyerere, *Freedom and Socialism* (Dar es Saalam: Oxford University Press, 1968), 139.

[2] Bennett J. Sims, *Servanthood: Leadership for the Third Millennium* (Cambridge, Mass.: Cowley, 1997), 7.

[3] Author unknown (Mpwapwa: Diocesan Archives).

[4] H. W. Beyer, "Diakonein, Diakonos," in *The Theological Dictionary of the New Testament, Abridged in One Volume*, ed. Geoffrey W. Bromiley (Grand Rapids: William B. Eerdmans Publishing Company, 1985), 154.

[5] Ibid., 153.

[6] Ibid., 153.

[7] Stuart Blanch, *Future Patterns of Episcopacy : Reflections in Retirement* (Oxford: Latimer House, 1991), 10-11

[8] Ibid. 7.

[9] Vincent J. Donovan, *Christianity Rediscovered* (Notre Dame: Fides/Claretian, 1976), 144-45.

[10] Max Thurian, ed., *Churches Respond to BFM: Official Responses to the "Baptism, Eucharist, and Ministry" Text* (Geneva: World Council of Churches, 1986) 11, 12.

[11] Leslie Brown, "Episcopacy in Africa," in *Bishops—But What Kind?* ed. Peter Moore (London: SPCK, 1982), 141.

[12] Robert Runcie, *1988 Lambeth Report* (London: Anglican Communion Office, 1988), 20.

[13] K. S. Chittleborough, "Towards a Theology and Practice of the Bishop-in-Synod," *Authority in the Anglican Communion*, ed. Stephen Sykes (Toronto: Anglican Book Center, 1987), 157-58.

[14] Hugo F. Hinfelaar, "Evangelization and Inculturation,"*Africa Ecclesial Review* 36:1 (1994): 11-12.

[15] William M. Kondrath, "Collaborative Ministerial Leadership" (D. Min. Thesis, Andover Newton Theological School, 1987), 11.

[16] Ibid., 3.

[17] Loughlan Sofield, *Collaborative Leadership* (Notre Dame: University of Notre Dame Press, 1994), 98.

[18] Kenwyn K. Smith and David N. Berg, *Paradoxes of Group Life* (San Francisco: Jossey-Bass, 1987), 96.

[19] Kondrath, "Collaborative Ministerial Leadership," 61.

[20] Adapted from Kondrath, "Collaborative Ministerial Leadership," Appendix 5.1.

[21] Miroslav Volf, *After Our Likeness: The Church as the Image of the Trinity* (Grand Rapids: William B. Eerdmans Publishing Company, 1998), 224

[22] Ibid., 436.

[23] Alfred Stanway, "Rapid Church Growth among the Wagogo of Tanzania, 1876-1967" (paper presented at Theory and Practice in Church Life: Studies in East and Central Africa over the Last Hundred Years at Nairobi, Kenya, 1968), 484.

[24] C. Norman Kraus, *Christian Mission in the Postmodern World: An Intrusive Gospel?* (Downers Grove: InterVarsity Press, 1998), 23.

14
CULTURE, SPIRIT, AND WORSHIP

JACI MARASCHIN

The Brazilian Episcopal Anglican Church is a Province of the Anglican Communion representing a valiant venture of being that church in a non-English world. It is not alone in that venture. There are all around the world churches and Provinces attempting to be Anglican in what could be understood as a "foreign" land—for example, in South America, Central America, Mexico, the Philippines, French Africa, Japan and the rest of Asia. The Anglican church in these places does not use the English language nor does it share the colonial history of such places as the United States of America, Canada, parts of Africa, India and Australia, among others. This, of course, presents a challenge to the Communion as a whole.

I will try to discuss the relationship of culture to spirit and worship from the perspective of Brazil. I shall divide this presentation into three parts: the first one will deal with the question of culture in a global civilization taking into account the resisting function of the experience of contextualization, the understanding of spirit in this global civilization and the meaning of the loss of the spirit in what I will call the dumbing down of culture, and with the way worship works as the expression of a spiritual culture. The second part will examine the relationship of culture to ideology and will try to understand how the Anglican Communion acts as an ideological society. It will see spirit as utopia, against ideology, functioning as the possibility of opening the church to the new. This is going to be related to our ecumenical commitment. Worship, as cultural creation, will be dealt with as the possibility of bringing together ideology (to be redeemed) with utopia (to be actualized). The third part of this paper will deal with the relationship of culture to modernity and shall criticize the traditional theology of essences, viewed particularly in the theology of culture of Paul Tillich. Spirit will be related to postmodernity and will show possibilities of a new approach to liturgy through fragmentation, emotion, poetry and the arts. Finally I will try to relate worship to mysticism and will set it into the new understanding of the end of philosophy according to Martin Heidegger. The conclusion will show some possibilities of a fresh approach to liturgy in the non-English world.

The organizers of this symposium asked me to "feel free to push the horizon of issues as much as possible, looking in a visionary way toward what we would hope for in a multicultural church in the coming century."[1] I am well aware that our horizons depend on the place we are. They move as we move. Horizons are related to space and space to bodies. Although I live in Brazil, I have had the opportunity to share in the life of many other Provinces of our Communion from North to South and from East to West. But I will take, as a matter of methodology, my experience at the last Lambeth Conference as a starting point, since all our Provinces were represented in Canterbury with their liturgies. And I will try to see what happens in Brazil in the light of what I experienced at the University of Kent in mid-1998. All this, of course, is seen from the background of my understanding of culture, spirit, and worship. It goes without saying that this may be a too ambitious task for me to undertake in the short time at my disposal in this plenary.

I

CULTURE IN A GLOBAL CIVILIZATION

What is culture? It is that which is cultivated. It depends on drives. In my context the first cultural drive is apollonian. It depends on reason, measure, correction, and symmetry. Culture is then that which persons acquire through study, research and experience transformed into a body of knowledge. It is a possession related to power. This concept started backed by the idea that rationality was the basic element in human life and history. This is why universities and schools played a decisive role in the making of this level of culture. However, this was contrasted with another level of culture emerging from the popular classes. If the first moment is apollonian the second, in turn, is dionysian. Popular culture is the development of skills and knowledge much more related to the body and the emotions than to the mind. This kind of culture may be seen in our popular festivals, like Carnival, popular religious festivals, and processions, accompanied by the creation of typical costumes and music.

Culture is always the product of human beings. We make culture and are influenced by it. As there are many layers of production as there are classes, some forms of culture appear to be more important than others. For instance, from the time of Constantine until the eighth century, culture meant for the church, in the first place, the uses and customs of the court. It is for this reason that the liturgical culture of those days was very similar to the imperial model. But there was also another layer of culture that was the character of Roman life, with the accent on sobriety and order. These two types of culture had resonance in the shape of the medieval liturgy.

I can, certainly, speak of a Brazilian culture. But this affirmation has to be explained. Brazilian culture, which may be apollonian and dionysian in its different features, is today inserted into a global culture. As I said before that culture is power, in the capitalist world it is dependent on economic power. Globalization is the mark of this ending century. The prophecy of Marshall McLuhan that the world was going to become a global village has been accomplished by now. The global culture is centered in the First World. The temple is the World Bank, the Bible, the Internet, and the liturgical songs, the powerful rhythms of rock music. If you go to any village in Brazil you may not (yet!) find computers and Internet installations in every home, but you will certainly find their acolytes, television and radio. Someone, hidden somewhere, is the great Messenger. The message comes through many channels, the sacraments of modernity. It comes through soap opera, news, interviews, fashion, mega-shows and preaching. Culture becomes the culture of domination, in other words, the culture of the dominant powers. It is centripetal.

As in the Constantinian church, the people in our villages adopt the style of the dominators. Their dress is the same as is found in New York or London. They sing the same hit songs and buy the same CDs that you may buy in Tower or in Virgin. This is much truer of the new generation. It is not the case that we in Brazil do not dance the samba anymore. But our popular songs are relegated to a sort of second-class art: rock is the thing. You will find in almost all the large cities of Brazil, McDonald's, Dunkin' Donuts, Pizza Hut, and so on. With the popularity of information science, all students now use the English language of computers in their everyday lives.

Our questions are: How can contextualization still mean anything in this global culture? Could it be a kind of counterculture? Is it possible to be a citizen of our time retreating to some kind of desert? Do such deserts still exist? How could we try to make a dialogue between contextualization and globalization?

SPIRIT IN A GLOBAL CIVILIZATION

In the traditional and apollonian culture of Brazil, spirit means that which opposes matter. This is evident throughout all Latin America. But this is a misleading opposition. In the apollonian culture the value of reason according to the Platonic tradition was always affirmed at the expense of matter and, consequently, of body. Religion in Brazil is rooted in that conception of life. From the perspective of the liturgy of the church, this understanding of spirit has created a very formal and lifeless kind of worship. The primacy of reason has given priority to the word, making worship a sequence of speeches, explanations, readings, homilies and sermons.

But spirit means something else. Starting from the Bible it is the *ruach* of God, breathing upon the waters in order to create life. Spirit is the creator of life. The life created by God through the Spirit was the material life. Woman and man were created from the dust of the earth. The Spirit was a new quality brought into the matter, in such a way that we now have a spiritualized matter. When we understand Spirit as the quality of creativity, the whole picture changes. We do not have spirit as a sort of substance opposed to matter, but matter in a new dimension.

The notion of spirit as creativity and life is related to the experience of beauty. And here we have to make a clear distinction between a rational concept of beauty and a spiritual one. The rational concept of beauty thinks of beauty from the outside. It starts from rules and that which is outside beauty. It is always subject to interpretation and explication. If we know the canons of beauty, then through them we should be able to judge any appearance of beauty in our experience. But note, it is not beauty in itself that we judge but the application of rules and canons to a given subject. The spiritual concept of beauty is free from the rules of reason. It is the emergence of the thing in its newness and surprise. In a way it means the avoidance of all which is not the thing in itself as a pure being there in the world. This is precisely the aim of painters like Mondrian in their visionary seeking of the purity of art as beauty and nothing else. Artistic expression has been the privileged place for this kind of experience. It is not the face of the Mona Lisa that is beautiful. It is the event in which that face lost itself as a referent, to become a thing by itself free from the image as such. The image is still there, but it is in a way absolutely independent of its appearance that counts. This means creativity.

Heidegger once said that the gods have deserted the world and as a result the world has become dark and without spirit. This abandonment of the world by the gods is best seen in the dumbing down of the culture. It is very hard to sense the presence of the Spirit in the mass-media pageantry offered to billions of human beings through the media as the only food for their spirits. It seems that the globalization of culture dispenses with the Spirit in favor of a technological reason for the benefit of the world market.

WORSHIP AS THE QUALITY OF A SPIRITUAL CULTURE

We are living in the culture of plastics. With this culture comes the tendency to look for disposable things. Packages are enormous and many, and soon we will not know what to do with the remains of our plenteousness transformed into garbage. As Dorothee Sölle has put it, "the situation in which we find ourselves today can be described as one in which there no longer exists a language to express the notions of meaning, existential unconditionedness, and faith.... We have been exposed to a manipulation of needs that has also transformed the need for uniqueness, novelty, and meaning into an obsession with possessions. Domination, the manipulation of consciousness, schooling in the destruction of one's own interests are no longer performed by religion and the church but by production and advertisement." And she concludes: "The new religion is consumerism."[2]

It seems to me that worship is a possible counterpart to this culture. It is not the only existing force to face the situation. As we shall see later in this paper, worship stands alongside music, poetry, dance, and theater, which are experiences linked to mysticism. But worship does not always show that quality. In my country, as elsewhere, the mainline churches are facing a threatening decline in their membership. Church attendance is poor and priests and pastors feel somehow paralyzed when facing it. Traditional Pentecostal churches represent the other side of the picture. They gather together thousands and thousands of persons for their services which are alive and full of movement. In turn, they have generated new movements, which can be called neo-pentecostalism. In general they are churches belonging to a charismatic leader who is also the owner of the church. They have been successful in their "missionary" efforts and have conquered large TV audiences. One of them owns a TV channel and another one owns half of the interests of another very popular Brazilian TV channel. The Roman Catholic Church, in turn, also has a TV channel, called "Rede-Vida" (life net). We wage in Brazil through the media a sort of electronic war of religion. Many churches do not hesitate to employ all the devices used by other commercial channels to boost their audiences.

The liturgical life of most of our churches reflects the quality of popular Brazilian culture as far it has been globalized and banalized. The old method of opposing apollonian culture to dionysian culture does not apply for analyzing this new situation. These liturgies are apollonian as far as they are still based on a logocentric form of communication and rule themselves by codes and ideals. But they are also dionysian as far as they use the body in a very free way, dancing and moving through the use of different types of choreography. That choreography tends to imitate the worst TV shows of our commercial networks. The Roman Catholic Church has also embarked in this kind of liturgical show, through the charismatic movement. I wonder if you have heard about Father Marcelo Rossi. He gets together, weekly, some thirty to fifty thousand persons in São Paulo to listen to his pop preaching and to sing and dance what he calls "the Lord's aerobics." His songs (sort of pop/rock style) occupy the first rank in the hit parade of Brazil.

In that situation context means very little. Yes, of course, the language is Portuguese and the people are Brazilian. Even if Father Marcelo does not reproduce foreign paraphernalia, what he is doing reflects what is going on in some forms of popular religion in the United States, along with the open acceptance of many of the gestures of most of the Pentecostal churches.

On the other side, the mainline Protestant churches, as well as the Anglican, still hold strongly to their inherited traditions. They don't grow as their Pentecostal brothers and make no impact on the Brazilian society as a whole. They think that their liturgies represent a purer form of religion and show the spiritual quality lacking in most of the popular movements in the country. What is the rule to govern such a judgment?

II

CULTURE AS IDEOLOGY

The things we do depend on imagination. Social institutions live through the power of symbolic action. This means that we carry a little of ourselves as a sort of externalization of our inner being. When, for instance, I compose a song or write a novel, preach a sermon or write a book, something of myself goes into the work. This is what we call style. It was not without reason that George Buffon wrote once that "style is man." Symbolic action is communal. It is related to the way we behave and with the way this affects the other. Personal and social behavior is meaningful. The meaning we give to it, or apprehend from it, is what we might call "ideology." According to Marx, the function of ideology is always negative. It is a distorted vision of reality as if it were upside down, originated in the unconscious need to dissimulate the real causes of our actions and thoughts in order to hide our real interests, and is neither candid nor good.

Applying the concept of "ideology" to our understanding of culture I would say, following Paul Ricoeur, that we try to build a self-image of ourselves. Churches and denominations are always going back into history to appeal to their founders in order to maintain their self-image. But this is, in the end, paradoxical, because the situation lived by our founders is no longer relevant in our situation. When we apply this to culture, spirit and worship, we are led to say, ideologically, that we have to reinterpret the "origin" of Anglicanism to fit in to a completely different situation no longer related to the founding event. In this moment "ideology" becomes a justifying principle. We are used to speaking of marks. What are the marks of our liturgy? What is distinctive in Anglicanism? Do we have a proper culture to be followed and developed? So, we are always speaking of our Anglican identity. Why not extend it to the identity of our liturgy?

When we start this way, we want to know, ideologically, what is the reason for being the way we are. Note that this is very rationalist. It shows our dependence on illuminist thinking. This ideological disease turns frequently into sectarian apologetics. You all have heard in one moment or another of our "incomparable Book of Common Prayer." Thanks to God we are now moving towards the "unbinding of the book," the "Anglican worship beyond the Prayer Book." According to Ricoeur all ideology is reductionism. It expresses itself by slogans. Is not the Prayer Book a reductionist factor in our ecclesial life?

Ideology also functions for dissimulation. We think from it and not on it. This means that all ideological thinking lacks the prophetic principle so powerfully present in the Old Testament and in the preaching of Jesus. We act as if from a direct linguistic revelation, and are unable to apply to our words any self-criticism. Ideology, then, fixes us in the past. There is not any possibility for the new. In Ricoeur's words, "the new can only be received through the typical." This is why it has been so difficult for Anglicans to experiment with new ways of worship, church life and thinking. We are always threatened by orthodoxy and intolerance.

Ideology manifests itself in culture in the way it affirms and reaffirms authority. Latin American culture has a long tradition of authoritarianism. This is widely reflected in the life of our churches. Our liturgies have been in chains. Liturgy, then, needs liberation from such authoritarian chains. We live in a church organized under specific powers. But they are ideologically dissimulated. We say, for instance, that the church is the body of Christ called together from all levels of our faithful people, but we are not or have not been so far able to show this in our actual practice. One of the functions of ideology is "domination," related to several "hierarchical aspects of social organization." Ricoeur quotes Max Weber to say that "all authority seeks its own legitimization ... which depends on some kind of belief...." The problem is that there is much more pretension from the side of authority than from the side of believers in relationship to the same authority. Ricoeur thinks that "there is an excess of demand from the side of authority than the possibility we have to bear it." This is what Karl Marx would call "plus-value." For him, the character of inversion present in all ideology (for him primarily seen in religion) means that reality (i.e., life in itself) is no more the basis for action, but the substitution of reality for something we built with the help of imagination. Then, we take the image for the real. This is very clear in the way we act as a church: we take metaphors for historical fact, doctrines about God as if they had the power to explain and describe the being of God, and so on.[3]

As liturgy is part of culture, global and contextual, it is also touched by ideology. When we start our liturgical reforms from our allegiance to our historical liturgical past and see it as definitive and unavoidable, this is, I dare to say, idolatrous. Ideology is idolatrous. The ideological aspect of religion and of denominations in particular can be seen in the history of religion in general and of the Christian church in particular. And it is highly ideological to avoid this kind of reading. As Anglicans, we have a past and a history. I always think that it is very good that our past is not so clean and perfect. It cannot be a perennial model for subsequent generations. We should thank God, humbly, that we did not have great theological heroes in the first days of our tradition, so that we cannot fall into the temptation of being followers of particular theologians or reformers, being open to read the Bible and to look at tradition in a free way. But we should not be deceived. Ideological procedures are always around us, "for the devil, our enemy, is always around us looking for someone to devour."

The question left for us is the following: Is it possible to express liturgically our religiosity and theology from a non-ideological place? Is not any criticism of ideology *a priori* ideological?

SPIRIT AS UTOPIA

Could utopia be the answer to the previous question? Or, at least, could it be a way to open to us the direction of the kingdom of God when the Prayer Book will be no more? Utopia means that which has no place. It belongs to the realm of wishes, desires, expectations, and dreams. It hides nothing, shows no dissimulation, wears no masks. The history of our world is a history of utopias. According to Ricoeur the first function of utopia is social subversion. And "social" in this context includes institutions, relationships, and partnerships. This function is somehow symmetrical to the character of social integration seen in ideology. In the second place utopias tend to denounce all systems of legitimization revealed in the way power is exercised. This element is also symmetrical to the function of legitimization of authority visible in ideologies. Some authors think that utopias may, sometimes, show signs of schizophrenia. Utopia tends to perfectionism and is unable to see reality as it is. As it belongs to the realm of imagination it may suffer from blindness and become pathological.

What is the origin of utopia? It is born from the real experience we have in society. According to Ricoeur, it is "an exercise of imagination in order to think of a different mode of being for the social." Imagination, of course, comes from real experience. It is the escape of intelligence amidst the impossibilities of finding solutions to our problems. It grows out of situations of despair in social, political, economic, and religious situations. In other words, utopias are the other side of experience. Our human history shows a variety of utopias starting from ancient times until today. They have the forms of mythology, of sacred saga, of political visions, of religious realization, and most frequently express themselves in liturgy. As we have seen, they start with the experience of reality and grow out of human disenchantment with that reality. In the secular realm, utopian patterns of the future are not fruits of revelation but of deception. Utopian imagination comes from a very precise place and goes to what has no place. When I read people like Habermas or Horkheimer from the former school of Frankfurt, I realize the fragility of their utopian visions in relation to society.

It seems to me that there are two kinds of utopias: visions based on our frustrated desires and visions coming up from possibilities and promises. The difference between secular utopias and Christian (or religious) utopias should be seen in the difference between mere wishful thinking and a well-based promise, even if dependent on faith. In the first case we have idealistic utopias. History is full of them. In the second case we have hope and the experience of people of a historical kind. Karl Manheim (*Ideologie und Utopie*)[4] has taught us that utopia always represents a threat. But it is only a threat when it leaves the mere field of literary expression and comes down to the social and political life. In this perspective Manheim prefers to analyze utopia taking as an example Münzer, through the eyes of Ernst Bloch. Ricoeur quotes this in his book on text and action, saying: "With Thomas Münzer utopia represents the extreme form of claiming some kind of actualization, here and now, of all dreams brought about by human imagination, from Judaism to Christianity, in the representations of the end of history."[5] In theological terms utopia becomes realized eschatology. Ricoeur goes on to say that "everything preached by Christians to be reached at the end of history, Münzer wants to realize in the midst of history." I think Ricoeur tends to be a little bit fundamentalist when he says that. For where is the "end of history"? Is it in itself a historical reality or is it the coming down of the Spirit in what Paul Tillich would call "kairotic moments"? I think we have to criticize Ricoeur at this point because the "end of history" talk cannot be seen as something at the end of times, so to say, but the momentary realization of the kingdom of God which can already be amongst us in the dialectical experience of the "already" and the "not yet."[6]

How can we bring our Anglican liturgies from the bondage of ideology into the freedom of utopia?

WORSHIP AS TRANSCENDENCE AND IMMANENCE: LIBERATION FROM IDEOLOGY

What are the ideological traces threatening liturgical renewal in our Anglican Communion and especially in Brazil? As I said before, I started this reflection from my experience during the last Lambeth Conference where almost all Provinces had the chance to celebrate according to their ways and cultures. From that experience I am convinced of the existence of the following traces:

- We were all bound to the Book of Common Prayer in one way or another. It seems that all celebrants came from the same place, wearing the same white albs, the same colored stoles, and performed almost the same gestures. There were some local elements such as music (Africa and Brazil) and of course language, but these differences were not that significant.

- As they were bound to the Book of Common Prayer they depended heavily on the spoken word. These liturgies were logocentric liturgies. The organizers of Lambeth had the fine idea of providing a large screen behind and above the altar to be used for whatever kind of visual aids the Provinces chose. But it served to show, most of the time, flashes of the congregation as if it were the proper icon to underline what was going on upon the altar.

- These liturgies were heavily clerical. We can argue that Lambeth is a gathering of bishops. But also it was affirmed that the bishops would bring to Canterbury their own dioceses. Where and how did they bring them?

- Homilies and sermons were traditional, and most of the time fundamentalist and moralist. There were, of course, exceptions, but they were few. This is related to the manner in which we employ scriptures in worship. The Bible is taken, ideologically, as if it were the "real" word of God.

- These liturgies were deeply male-oriented at different levels: predominance of male celebrants, male preachers and male language. (It is not the case to hand over the ceremonial to women, as if that would by itself transform our liturgies into inclusive events.) Male ideology is still very strong and, as ideology functions, our congregations take it for granted.

The unbinding of the Book of Common Prayer means the revision of, or perhaps the recreation of, our liturgical practices under the light of the Spirit. Immanence and transcendence are to be related as contextualization and globalization, apollonian culture and dionysian culture, in order to produce a new spiritual quality in our worship.

III

CULTURE AND MODERNITY

Modernity (which could as well be called "enlightenment") means that reality is always something else than that which it appears to be. If it is so, that which is, the Dasein as Heidegger would say, the "being there," is not the being there. It should stand for another thing. This is precisely what Plato wanted to say through his Myth of the Cave. We are not what we think we are. Matter is pure illusion. The body is a lost piece of reality falling down from the real world of ideas. Descartes was responsible for enforcing that position in the beginning of our modern world when he stressed the *cogito* as the basis of reality. Rational thinking was, then, the root of life. Rationality works with the *a priori* scheme. Paul Tillich applied this idealistic principle to build his theology of culture. For him culture does not stand by itself. It is the form of religion, and religion, in turn, is the substance of culture.[7] This is an affirmation of faith. No one can experience this as a historical truth. The failure of that kind of thinking is the negation of culture as a reality in itself. It needs the "substance" of religion in order to exist. But religion is also culture unless we decide that it be part of revelation. But even in the most traditional forms of theology revelation is never religion, but the word of God, or the same God. If we want to maintain Tillich's position we shall arrive at the paradoxical conclusion that religion is its own substance.

Modernity also stands for globalization. I have friends who believe globalization to be a sign of the kingdom of God. Globalization sees behind scientific and technological advances a "substance" which gives support to it. It is operationality. In modern society our leaders do not seek for justice or for truth, but for results in the form of profit. In ancient societies wisdom was what it was: an experience of pleasure. The wise man was wise for the sake of wisdom.

Should I say that liturgy by its own nature cannot be modern? But in most of our churches and especially in the Pentecostal movement liturgy is modern. It stands for another thing outside of itself. It is a means working for the growing of the religious group. It has aims which are not liturgical. But what is liturgical in liturgy? *Mediator Dei*, n. 25, defines liturgy as "the public worship which our Redeemer as head of the Church renders to the Father, as well as the worship which the community of the faithful renders to its Founder, and through him to the heavenly Father. In short, it is the worship rendered by the Mystical Body of Christ in the entirety of its head and members." Liturgy, then, is worship. The Roman Catholic definition of liturgy sees it as a mystical affair. It has to have the spiritual quality absent in most of the new experiments of our day. Liturgy exists for the glorification of God and, consequently, for the sanctification of the worshiping community. To think of the liturgy of the church in these terms means to protest against modernity with its accent on utilitarianism and technology. We still can ask if technology could not be transformed by the spiritual quality of liturgy. Are the electronic churches unfaithful to the real character of Christian worship? Should we not bring to the altar the gifts of information science? Could we not worship God through computers?

SPIRIT AND POSTMODERNITY

Mark C. Taylor makes this bold declaration:

> In the end, it all comes down to a question of skin. And bones. The question of skin and bones is the question of hiding and seeking. And the question of hiding and seeking is the question of detection. Is detection any longer possible? Who is the detective? What is detected? Is there anything left to hide? Is there any longer a place to hide? Can anyone continue to hide? Does skin hide anything or is everything nothing but skin?[8]

In the previous section I said that modernity is always looking for something else than that which appears to be. Postmodernity challenges this. It asks if we have really to look under every surface for their depths.

Postmodernity not only stresses surface but also criticizes globalization in favor of fragmentation.

Globalization is an impossible venture. It represents the aim of domination by certain central powers in order to homogenize culture at the expense of context. It is built upon the logic of profit and for that reason looks always inside the components of the global. Fragmentation, on the contrary, sees that which appears to have a face value, let us say. Perhaps the case of contemporary art illustrates better what I want to say. Let us remember the effort of Hegel in dealing with the dialectic of surface and depth. According to him, the vocation of art is to "unveil truth." In order to do so, when we visit an art gallery or contemplate a painting or any other type of visual arts we should make a trip from the outward to the inward. The work of art should then be like an onion. We would descend from one layer into the other, hoping to attain the immaterial truth hidden down there. But for contemporary art there is no distinction between surface and depth. The spiritual is the material, that which we can see and touch. The attempt to go down to the inner center of the work would only destroy the work. Postmodern thinkers would agree that there is nothing under the surface. If you take out the surface you create a new surface.

What would be the impact of postmodernity for liturgy? In the first place it gives back to liturgy its own reality. It is a fragment of culture, which stands on its own value. It is its own substance. It does not need a global forum to decide how liturgy should be performed in different places of the world. Fragmentation relates to contextualization. Some scholars prefer to call this inculturation. Inculturation, however, may be a misleading term. It could suggest precisely what postmodernity avoids: the existence of a cultural model to be reproduced. The impact of modernity on liturgy unbinds liturgy and calls it to the experience of freedom.

WORSHIP AND MYSTICISM

Mysticism is not a bad word. Heidegger in his book on Nietzsche affirms: "With the end of philosophy, thinking does not end, but enters in transition for a new beginning."[9] Philosophy and thinking are seen as different matters. In the long history of the world, philosophy only appeared among the Greeks in a particular time and place. Before philosophy, thinking was related to myths, sagas and mystical religion. The Greeks, however, built a monumental system of thinking known to us as philosophy and exported it to Europe and to the rest of the world. But the time of philosophy has ended. Thinking is trying to flourish in other ways and for new purposes.

What activity may take the place of philosophy? For Heidegger, two things: poetry and mysticism. Some other thinkers would prefer to speak of art and mysticism, to be more precise. Modernity looks for competence. Postmodernity, for beauty. It tends to the side of dionysian culture instead of the apollonian. Beauty has no interest beside itself. It is very similar to the concept of "art for

334 BEYOND COLONIAL ANGLICANISM

art's sake." Beauty functions on a level different from the rational. This is the reason why Angelus Silesius, a seventeenth-century poet, heavily influenced by Meister Eckhart, wrote that "the rose has no why." It means that being precedes logos. Kant once wrote that aesthetics shows "a purposiveness without purpose."[10] It is probable that ritual is the best way to understand this statement. Liturgical worship is fundamentally ritualistic. It depends on ritual. Ritual is like play. You do not play for purposes outside the pleasure of playing.

This leads us into mysticism as the spiritual quality of staying in pure contemplation in the divine presence. This is completely different from current theologies of prosperity, through which you challenge God to do things for you based on the exchange of favors. Myticism is based on love, which is complete "disinterestedness." Eckhart wrote a small treatise on this to state that detachment (*separatus*) is the highest of the virtues. All human virtues depend on it. For Eckhart we are called to be cut off from all affections, from ourselves and from the world. Ritual as detachment means rejection of everything which hinders it from being a state of contemplation and adoration. It is a matter of feeling, not of reason.

And this is beauty. This is music. Do not ask Beethoven what he wanted to say with his sonatas for violin and piano. He was not interested in the rational discourse. He had no foreign referent besides sounds, intensity, rhythm, fantasy, emotion and creativity. The first mark of beauty, and also its condition, is pleasure. Pleasure relates to joy. It is not for any other reason that C. S. Lewis described his conversion as being "surprised by joy." Global society has repressed beauty as a spiritual quality, because that type of society is puritan. Beauty starts with the experience of pleasure as a sensual element, only possible when we are free.

CONCLUSION

The liturgical life of the church is always related to a particular culture. It is true that particular cultures suffer from the influence of globalization and find it difficult to offer consistent resistance in the face of it. The problem is that non-English Anglicans have inherited their liturgical forms from a very distinctive culture, which is English. Somehow that English culture is reflected today in the contemporary global culture. Whereas the church in Brazil has had some awareness of this situation, it has been unable to experiment at the national level with autochthonous and creative forms of cultural expressions in liturgical life. We still hold to a poor translation of portions of the Book of Common Prayer of the American church.

I once proposed a liturgical moratorium for our Province. Bishops would release clergy and lay people from our regular bondage to the Book of Common Prayer to experiment and create. I was called subversive and irresponsible. I still think that this is one of the things we need. Liturgists would organize that moratorium, and the results would be analyzed by committees all around the country. The synthesis of it could, perhaps, bring some good surprises to the Province. This should be seen as transcending the stage of translation.

In order to stretch Anglican worship beyond the Book of Common Prayer we should also develop a contextualized theological thinking open to the new trends of postmodernity, i.e., relating it to the arts and to mysticism. This new theological thinking would take into consideration the place of beauty, and therefore pleasure, in the liturgical life of the church.

We should pay attention to the dionysian aspects of our Brazilian culture and experiment with dance, gestures, and colors. The celebration of the eucharist by the Brazilian Province in Lambeth had a few Brazilian songs, played with mistaken rhythms and badly sung by a non-trained audience. The bodies of the celebrants were just like the bodies of our English brothers. They did not carry the marks of our culture. We still have to ask what being Brazilians does to our body posture.

As we propose to transcend the Prayer Book we are released to enter into dialogue with our fellow Christians belonging to other churches and denominations. It would be good for us and for them if we could try to do together some of the experiments we need in worship. It is obvious that we are most divided when we stress our distinctive characteristics.

A new liturgy should not be a monster. What we are proposing is to continue in the long tradition of the church, trying to learn with history how the church in different contexts, ideologies and pressures solved its liturgical problems. But this is not sufficient. The look into the past has to be critical and somehow detached. It is more important to sense the methodology than the actual results visible in practice. In other words, I am not proposing that we should copy earlier church achievements.

Music is a crucial element in any liturgical experiment. When I speak on the liberation of liturgy from old bondages, I am thinking of the liberation from English and American hymnals currently in use in Brazil. Happily there are already some experiments with Brazilian music, like samba, modinhas, and bossa nova; but our congregations still think that in order to be sacred, music has to be English. Although Brazilian music is important, I do not think that we should limit the music of the liturgy in this part of the world to our own music. There is a marvelous richness all around the world, ancient and contemporary, that we should share for the sake of beauty and pleasure.

Any liturgical reform should also be related to mission, and should be based in a new theology relating mission to joy and freedom. Liturgy and mission are sisters dancing together in the direction of the beauty of the kingdom of God.

NOTES

[1] This essay was presented at the symposium "Unbound! Anglican Worship beyond the Prayer Book" hosted by the Church Divinity School of the Pacific, Berkeley, in January 1999.

[2] Dorothee Sölle, " 'Thou Shalt Have No Other Jeans before Me'," in *Observations on "The Spiritual Situation of the Age,"* ed. Jürgen Habermas (Cambridge, Mass.: MIT Press, 1984), 159.

[3] Cf. Paul Ricoeur, *Interpretação e ideologias* (Rio de Janeiro: Francisco Alves, 1977), 67-75.

[4] Karl Manheim, *Ideologie and Utopie* (Bonn: Cohen, 1929).

[5] Cf. Paul Ricoeur, *Du texte à l'action* (Paris: Collection Esprit/Seuil, 1986), 228-36.

[6] Ibid., 389.

[7] Cf. Paul Tillich, *Theology of Culture* (New York: Oxford University Press, 1959).

[8] Mark C. Taylor, *Hiding* (Chicago: University of Chicago Press, 1997), 11.

[9] John D. Caputo, *The Mystical Element in Heidegger's Thought* (New York: Fordham University Press, 1986), 1. Chapter 1 discusses the problem of mysticism, philosophy, and thought.

[10] Ibid., 188-92.

15
TOWARD A POSTCOLONIAL RE-VISIONING OF THE CHURCH'S FAITH, WITNESS, AND COMMUNION

CHRISTOPHER DURAISINGH

The following essay, the last in this collection, seeks to further the rethinking of the nature of the faith, the witness, and the communion of churches around the world from a postcolonial mode. It calls for a decolonization of imagination in Christian faith and worship and a reconstruction of the interchurch relationships across the world. What I seek to do in the following pages is first to identify some theoretical lessons from the use of the term "post-colonial" in the writings of several postcolonial theorists. Then I shall proceed to identify the possible direction of a re-visioning of three interrelated but distinct aspects of the life of the church from a postcolonial vantage point. They are namely the nature of Christian faith, the mode of Christian witness, and the shape of the communion among churches across the world.

The term "post-colonial" is used in this essay, as in much of the recent postcolonial studies, in a double sense. First it seeks to indicate a historical process of the systematic dismantling of European colonization from the middle of the last century and the end of the "Christendom" mind-set. The term is a historical marker; it is a going "beyond" all that was entailed in the socio-political and economic exploitation of the colonized people and their countries. Second, it is also an affirmation of a new mode of imaging, a new cultural logic, posited over against the eurocentric monologic and the colonial manner of thinking and visioning reality. It is a process of supersession of outmoded philosophical, aesthetic, and political thought forms and theories shaped by centuries of colonial hegemony. Therefore, any re-visioning of the faith, life and relationships of the churches today must also take these two dimensions seriously. On the one hand, theology needs to address the hegemonic forces of colonialism and its structural consequences. On the other hand, the rethinking needs to be undertaken in terms by which the colonial mind-set is countered and dismantled and an alternative postcolonial knowledge and vision of reality are framed. In the light of these two factors, it may be significant to make use of the form, "post-colonial,"—with a hyphen—to indicate primarily the historical marker of the end of the formal European colonial era, which began almost five hundred years ago. Consequently, the term, "postcolonial"—without the hyphen—may be used mainly to connote the new decolonized manner of thinking and defining reality.

It is also important to bear in mind that the lessons that we might learn in this paper from the use of the term postcolonial in recent critical theory, particularly in literary criticism, are rather ambiguous. For the term has both positive and negative values, as we shall see below. While it is important to celebrate the positive breakthrough, it is equally important that in a serious theological engagement with the post-colonial context and thought, we must also question and avoid the pitfalls of many studies.

The Post-colonial Context

That the European colonial rule has come to an end and many former colonized people are politically independent and free to govern themselves, more or less successfully, is a fact. The churches in the former colonial lands, too, have been making a slow and painful journey toward the "de-Europeanization" of their theologies, worship, and ecclesial life. There are many signs of the shift. For one thing, we may legitimately speak of the church as truly global at the turn of the twenty-first century. Perhaps a striking way to explore the shift is to compare the first and the most recent ecumenical world mission conferences. The meeting in Salvador at the end of 1996 stands in stark contrast to the first conference in 1910 in Edinburgh. Edinburgh took place at the pinnacle of colonialism, for the colonial process reached its apogee with the turn of the twentieth century, when the proportion of the earth's surface controlled by European powers rose from 67 percent in 1884 to 84.4 percent in 1914. The participants at Edinburgh—all but a handful of them white, male and North-Atlantic—its leadership, and its confidence in the progress of the Christendom project were sure and certain tokens of the colonial era that shaped much of mission thinking at the turn of the century. At the heart of the two conferences that followed Edinburgh, namely Jerusalem (1928) and Tambaram (1938), was the continued conviction of an intrinsic relationship between Christianity and the history of Western civilization. An *"unthinking eurocentrism"*[1] was at the root of the tendency to interpret the expanding European history as the sign of God bringing into being a single universal history for all peoples everywhere through the agency of Western colonialism. This tendency was characteristic of the ecumenical vision and the ecclesiastical mind-set even into the late fifties. The following statement from a Faith and Order meeting in Bristol in 1967 spells out this point further:

> So God's history must sooner or later give birth to the conception of universal history, in the sense that all groups, tribes, nations, imperial, races and classes are involved in one and the same history…. The universalizing and unifying history started in the ages of mission and colonialism, and is now in this generation penetrating human minds everywhere as never before.[2]

A blatant and secular version of the same eurocentric mind-set is the statement by Francis Fukuyama with reference to the process of globalization: "What we may be witnessing is not just the end of the cold war, or the passing of a particular post-war history as such: that is, the final point of humankind's ideological evolution and the universalization of Western liberal democracy as the final form of human government."[3]

Over against that picture, at the conference in Salvador, a city in Brazil with the majority of people of African descent, the participants came from well over one hundred countries. Seventy percent of them were from countries outside the North Atlantic region. The majority of those who had speaking or leadership roles at the conference were from the former colonized world. The most poignant reminder that we were on a threshold of something new was the visible and articulate presence of indigenous peoples from around the world. A group of them felt it important, for example, to vocally protest against the policy of using in the conference proceedings five official languages, which were all European and colonial. Salvador thus was a historical marker of the post-colonial shift in mission thinking and practice and in interchurch relationships.

Moreover, the enormous growth of the churches in Africa and Latin America has brought about "a jarring demographic metamorphosis that is dismantling the thousand-year-old idea of 'Christendom'."[4] As we step into the first decades of this millennium, well over 60 percent of Christians live in the South, and worship and witness to Christ in idioms previously unimaginable in Christian history. In spite of the continuing financial power of many Western churches, the creative theological strength and the vitality of Christian faith in areas outside the traditional Christendom are remarkable. In fact, while there is a clear lack of confidence in the gospel in much of the West and the churches are increasingly marginalized from the mainstream public life, in the South the gospel is lived out and witnessed to vibrantly with renewed strength and confidence.

Just as a large number of intellectuals from the former hinterlands of the empire now play distinct and decisive roles in the Western institutions of higher learning, a number of creative theological and ecclesiastical leaders from the churches in the South are in responsible positions in the denominational and ecumenical institutions in the North.

The Anglican Communion is no exception. While the birth of the quest for Pan-Anglicanism, and later the Anglican Communion, must be located squarely at the pinnacle of modern colonialism, today the Communion is indeed global. Lambeth 1998 is a dramatic manifestation of this reality. As one who was present at both Lambeth 1978 and 1998, I can testify to the visible change within the Anglican Communion. From the colorful and multicultural opening worship, through the daily eucharistic celebration in the tradition and cultural idioms of one or another of the member churches, to the closing moments, Lambeth 1998 bore evidence to the irreversible fact that the Anglican Communion is postcolonial.

But this is not the whole story. In reality, the geo-political context today is marked by the ever-increasing "neo-colonial" exploitation of most of the former colonized peoples by the European nations and the former white settler-nations such as the United States and Australia. These oppressive power relations have taken new modes and new forms, for example, the more disturbing "interventionist economic policies" of global economic structures such as the International Monetary Fund and the World Bank and the interventionist politics of superpowers. But the geo-economic hegemony has not been superseded. As Gayatri Chakravorty Spivak succinctly puts it, "Three hundred years have passed, and territorial imperialism had changed to neo-colonialism."[5] Therefore, we cannot let the term "post-colonial" carry with it the implication that colonial exploitation is now a matter of the past, and thus, "undermining colonialism's economic, political and cultural deformative-traces in the present."[6] Moreover, in the light of the continuing oppressive positions of power in the world, our rethinking of the churches' faith and witness must take seriously several other factors as well. Let me identify a few.

First, we cannot allow the term "post-colonial" as one more universalizing category to flatten and neutralize significant differences and contradictions between colonial experiences of different colonized peoples. Colonial experience in Africa is not the same as that of Asia. The experience of the indigenous peoples in the Americas is not the same as those in South Asia. Nor can we let the term mask the real asymmetric power relations that continue to exist between different colonized peoples—for example, between the white settlers in Australia, South Africa, and the Americas on the one hand, and the Aborigines, blacks, and indigenous peoples, on the other. There is the danger that by describing our context as post-colonial, some may "mask the white settlers' colonial racist-policies toward indigenous peoples not only before independence but also after the official break from the imperial center, while also de-emphasizing neocolonial global positionings of First World settler-states."[7] My sense is that much of the post-colonial writings, particularly by immigrant literary critics from South Asia and the North Atlantic academia, do not take the difference seriously, and that racism, a colonial project, is seldom a crucial factor. But any theological rethinking that is worth its name cannot afford to fall into that trap.

Second, the term cannot be detached from the decolonized spaces and the disadvantaged persons who continue to struggle against the economic and political oppression in the former colonies. But the social location of many of the "postcolonial" theorists is the diaspora in Western academia.[8] As Jenny Sharpe rightly observes, "although the objective of a post-colonial approach was to bring the Third World into the imperial centres, its effect has been to further marginalize the ex-colonies."[9] In rethinking the church's faith and witness, we need to bear in mind that these diasporic intellectuals in Western universities cannot adequately represent the post-colonial issues and the problems among the former colonized people.

This leads to my third point. Experience of both colonialism in the past and of neocolonialism today implies economic and racial oppression and the possibility of resistance against it. Therefore, we cannot let the prefix, post, in "post-colonial" blunt an *activist* orientation and the actual practice of resistance and struggle which accompany the efforts of many oppressed people, the "subaltern," in the colonized spaces even today. But I wonder whether the quest for justice among the post-colonial theorists, primarily the new immigrant intellectuals in Western academia, is to find what Spivak calls "justice under capitalism." I wonder too whether, in much of the postcolonial writings, there is a tendency to transcend dichotomies such as the colonizer/colonized in a way that there is no clear articulation of continuing domination and the consequent call for resistance, opposition, and transforming praxis at the margins. If so, there is a serious discrepancy and even a conflict between the post-colonial interests of those who live and struggle in former colonies, and the identities and interests of the first– and second-generation diasporic intellectuals in the West.

The challenge before the theological community is, then, how to avoid in our post-colonial conversation a similar discrepancy between the church's identity and commitment and those of the marginalized, with and for whom the church is to live and serve. It would also imply our searching for a "hermeneutic from below," as it were. It is a call to reread the gospel story inductively from its function within the life and struggles of God's people. Therefore, the proper starting point for a hermeneutic from below is not an academic exercise in postcolonial theory within our seminaries, but rather a concrete *decolonizing commitment in solidarity* with those who struggle for freedom, fuller life, and a radical transformation of their subjugated histories. It is from below, because its starting point is not an *a priori* theological dogma, but rather a historically discerned understanding within the life and discipleship of the believing community, as it expresses its solidarity in the name of Christ with people, particularly the marginalized.

Fourth, the post-colonial context is described as one in which various forms of cultural syncretism are generated by the interaction between the new immigrants from the former colonies and the colonizers. It is inevitable. For as Shohat observes, "'Hybridity' and 'syncretism' allow negotiation of the multiplicity of identities and subject positionings which result from displacements, immigrations and exiles without policing the borders of identity along essentialist and originary lines."[10] However, the celebration of hybridity and transnationalism has two possible dangers, and avoiding them is critical for a re-visioning of a liberative framework for thought and theology. First, too easy a celebration of hybridity might hinder a genuine exploration of the particularity of the local knowledge and cultures of the formerly colonized peoples. The search for origins and identities is important for authentic selfhood. Second, as Shohat puts it, "A celebration of syncretism and hybridity per se, if not articulated in conjunction with questions of hegemony and neocolonial power relations, runs the risk of appearing to sanctify the *fait accompli* of colonial violence."[11] Or again as Aijaz Ahmad asks trenchantly,

> ... speaking with virtually mindless pleasure of transnational cultural hybridity, ... amounts, in effect, to endorsing the cultural claims of transnational capital itself....It is not at all clear how the celebration of a postcolonial, transnational, electronically produced cultural hybridity is to be squared with this systematic decay of countries and continents, and with decreasing chances for substantial proportions of the global population to obtain conditions of bare survival, let alone electronic literacy and gadgetry.[12]

The challenge before us is how can we take seriously the process of fluid and hybrid identity formation on the one hand, and at the same time the oppressive neocolonial forces that destroy local knowledges and particularity of local cultures, in our re-thinking the church's faith and witness in a postcolonial mode.

Finally, it is also the case that the term "post-colonial" has a decentralizing function. It successfully points to the fact that decolonization involves a deconstruction of a unilateral and monocentric power relationship. The colonial power has been primarily centripetal, in drawing all that is at its periphery to the center for the sole benefit of the center. It has bifurcated the world into the West and the rest. The dynamic behind imperial colonialism was in its singular desire to bring into being a single "universal regime of truth and power." As someone put it, colonialism, in this sense, "is ethnocentrism armed, institutionalized and gone global." It is important to remember that even now in the "post" colonial days when the hegemonic powers are rather dispersed, the hierarchical power relations generated by the colonizing process continues. While colonialism imposed boundaries, the post-colonial cannot and should not be speaking about some abstract "transnationalism," but about dismantling those boundaries and racist constructions. Therefore, the post-colonial theorists powerfully portray the alternative as the *"decentering the center"* of power in Europe, as the title of a recent book suggests.[13] This alternative is to envision the power relationship as polycentric and multilayered and to struggle for it. But churches in their relationship with each other still betray an uneven power relationship with the centers of identity, resources, and at times even decision-making in the West, as in Canterbury, Rome, or headquarters of Western mission agencies. Churches in the South are spoken of as outposts and "provinces"! Therefore, any task of re-visioning a post-colonial relationship between the churches should follow a polycentric and relational paradigm. The power of polycentrism is precisely in the decolonizing of power relations between communities and decentering roles and representations.

THE POSTCOLONIAL IMAGINATION

The use of the term "postcolonial"—without the hyphen—is to indicate that we are here talking about a different *logic*, and a different manner of visioning reality and relationships in terms of a decolonized imagination. The postcolonial in this sense introduces a *decolonization of imagination*[14] and *decolonizing methodologies.*[15] Here, the term postcolonial functions almost in the same way as the terms postmodern and poststructuralist function in the production of knowledge. It is to image and articulate reality not in a monologic and eurocentric mode, but rather from a dialogical and a polyphonic perspective. What we call the colonial mind-set permeates and structures much of contemporary practice in church and society, even long after the formal end of imperialist colonialism. In countering such vestigial thinking, we need to begin with identifying the features of an alternative logic and mental processes proposed by the postcolonial frame of mind. It is here one finds a significant similarity between much of recent feminist theory and that of postcolonial theory. What then are some of the features of a decolonized imagination and postcolonial mind-set?

First, eurocentrism denies its own historical particularities and therefore universalizes its concepts, values, and beliefs as the norm for all else. The European standpoint becomes now the singular defining categorical scheme. In a sense it is a "point-of-viewlessness." Derrida and others consistently warn us that at the core of the Western tradition, the colonial included, lies the search for something unitary and fundamental that could provide a stable center on which to hang all our understanding, and in the light of which, boundaries and exclusions can be erected. It is a search for a single meta-narrative. But the postcolonial alternative stresses the inevitability of the historicality of every particular. Western colonial thinking is essentialist. It reduces reality, selves in particular, into autonomous, simply-located substances, as in Newtonian metaphysics. While the former can speak therefore in meta-concepts and essentialist language, the latter sees each context or constituent body through its social location and its multilayered relationships to others. Everything has meaning only as it is located both in its particularity—whether social, cultural, gender, racial, or economic power relationship—and within "a densely woven web of relationality." Therefore, no single nation or part of the world or race can be privileged over against others, whatever may be their economic or political power.

Second, once the world is seen in terms of privileges and possession of power, as in eurocentric thinking, it is easy to bifurcate reality and organize everyday life and discourse in terms of binaries such as the white/black, civilized/uncivilized, the West/the rest, etc. But the postcolonial imagination rejects this oppositional and binary thinking and the consequent hierarchical organization of reality and relationships. It rejects identities as unified and fixed, but rather sees them as "multiple, unstable, historically situated,"

the products of "differentiation and polymorphous identifica-
tions."[16] Further, the binary thinking that undergirds the colonial
mind-set necessarily leads to a hierarchical ordering of reality and
to an erecting of borders in the name of authenticity and purity.
It privileges the first or the dominant term in any of the binary
oppositions, including the white over the people of color, male
over female, North over South. But the postcolonial celebrates
the popular, the marginal, and the syncretic. Border-crossing too
is a central feature of the postcolonial. We shall return to some of
these motifs more fully when we consider the nature of Christian
faith and witness in a postcolonial mode.

Third, eurocentrism values unity over diversity and sameness
over difference. Its essentialist description of reality and its val-
orizing of the homogenous over the diverse seem to be significant
features of much of Western thought and culture even today. A
dominant tendency in the eurocentric metaphysical and theological traditions has been to privilege and valorize unity, harmony,
totality, and thereby to denigrate, suppress and marginalize multiplicity, contingency, and particularity.[17] Much of Anglicanism is
not free from such an essentialist perspective either. But as Cornel
West powerfully puts it, the postmodern and the postcolonial
alternative seeks "to trash the monolithic and homogenous in the
name of diversity, multiplicity and heterogeneity; to reject the
abstract, general, and universal in light of concrete, specific, and
particular; and to historicize, contextualize and pluralize by highlighting the contingent, provisional...."[18]

Fourth, eurocentrism has been marked throughout its history
by a "providential" sense of its historical destiny to civilize the rest
of the world by its power and control. One needs only to look at the
numerous statements of colonial representatives in the British Raj
in India in the late eighteenth and nineteenth centuries, or the
statements of Christian missionaries. Let me give just one example,
more tempered than many others. Macaulay, who was chiefly instrumental in introducing the teaching of English in Indian schools,
stated in a speech before the House of Commons in 1835:

> What is power worth ... if we hold it only by violating the most
> sacred duties, which as governors we owe to the governed ...
> to a race debased by three thousand years of despotism and
> priest-craft. We are free, we are civilized to little purpose, if we
> grudge to any portion of the human race an equal measure of
> freedom and civilization.[19]

But the alternative postcolonial logic begins not with privileging those in power. Nor does it tolerate some liberal pseudo-equality. Instead, it allows the voice of the other, particularly the suppressed and the colonized, to shape the direction of their own history. It affirms what Foucault calls "the epistemological privilege of the subjugated." Or as Shohat and Stam put it,

> It thinks and imagines "from the margins" seeing minoritari-an communities not as interest groups to be added on to a pre-existing nucleus but rather as active, generative participants at the very core of a shared, conflictual history.[20]

Finally, eurocentric thinking is monologic and monocultural. Its hegemonic power inhibits and limits dialogue. But the postcolonial approach to reality is multicultural, reciprocal and dialogical. Since it envisions selves not as windowless monads and self-sufficient, discrete and bounded, but rather as permeable, open to the other, mutual and multivoiced, genuinely promoting verbal or cultural exchange so that all those involved in the relationship are changed or enriched. Here, Mikhail Bakhtin's notion of the polyphonic nature of discourse is significant. Each voice, as Bakhtin insists, exists only in dialogue with other voices. As he states it, "Utterances are not indifferent to one another, and are not self-sufficient; they are aware of and mutually reflect one another."[21] In the postcolonial vision of things, persons do not exclude each other, they simply do not co-exist nor are they assimilated into a sameness. Rather, social diversity is fundamental to a fruitful dialogue through which each member of the community helps the constitution of the other.

I have identified a few of the features of the "post-colonial movement" beyond the colonial structures and the "postcolonial paradigm" of describing reality. Much of what has been said above may be summed up in three terms. A postcolonial way of visioning things is multicultural or, better, *multivoiced* (where each voice matters and has a say), *dialogical,* and *polycentric.* In the light of the ambiguity surrounding the use of the term postcolonial and the dangers that a soft version of it—particularly that of the South Asian immigrant intellectuals in Western academia—poses to a continuing of our resistance to neocolonialism, I wonder whether one should continuously substitute the phrases "polycentric, multicultural, and dialogical" for the term "postcolonial."

TOWARD A RE-VISIONING OF THE CHURCH, ITS FAITH, WITNESS, AND COMMUNION

The post-colonial scenario and the postcolonial frame of thought seem to involve three distinct factors. They are: (1) a relational epistemology or founding of knowledge multiculturally, or multivocally; (2) a dialogical mode of communication for the constitution of social selves; (3) a structure of power relationship which is polycentric, and fluid for mutual empowerment. Therefore, I intend to develop a re-visioning of the church in terms suggested by these three aspects of postcoloniality. Hence the rest of the essay seeks to explore the gospel as *multivoiced* story, the *dialogical* witness and the *polycentric* communion.

THE GOSPEL AS MULTIVOICED STORY

As we have discussed above, a key characteristic of the colonial articulation of any reality is in monologic and universal categories. As Edward Sampson puts it, "In monologism lies the heartland of domination."[22] Many recent feminist theorists have powerfully established that there is an unmistakable correlation between domination and a kind of disembodied, abstract and transcendent form of knowledge, applicable everywhere and to everyone.[23] Or as Jane Flax states, the colonial logic demands that "only to the extent that one ... group can dominate the whole can reality appear to be governed by one set of rules, be constituted by one privileged set of social relations, or be told by one story."[24]

From this colonial standpoint, it is not too difficult to move into an articulation of a form of monotheism in which the theme is of a wholly Other self-sustaining God at "His" fiat creating all-else for which "He" has no need. This omnipotent and self-sufficient Being has of "His" own will revealed "Himself" once and for all in a singular revelation which excludes every other claim to truth. No wonder much of eurocentric Christian theology has tended to tame diversity, denied the uniqueness of each contextual expression of God's love in Christ, conceived Christian revelation as exclusive truth, and proclaimed that outside the church there is no salvation. It turns the *truth of a revealing God* whose being and nature are constituted by a dynamic relation into a formal *system of revealed truths*, allegedly unchanging over time.

The biblical images of Babel and Pentecost are highly suggestive for our purpose at this point. Look for a moment at the image of Babel, a quest for the monological. The search is for a single language, a singular and unitary truth in terms of which the rest could be excluded. The very language of those who want to build the tower is oppositional in intent, against God, against other humans and creation. Their language values the unitary and homogenous. It orders reality hierarchically. It cannot tolerate being at the margins. It celebrates the self-sameness. It is the symbol of domination, and possessive power over everything else.

But the story of Pentecost overturns this monologism. Look at the context of Judea at the time of the death of Christ. Two elements, two opposite forces, were at work. There was the expanding colonial rule of Rome. Along with the imperial presence came the forces of globalization from the North. In the culture of the *polis*, the state, with the promise of unifying the world in one monolithic order, Rome offered what in today's language we may call the McWorld culture. All peoples are to be united under one rule, one culture, and one market. Over against that is the struggle of the "each," the political aspiration and the struggle among the people of Israel, for example, to be a free people. Hence, there were those who struggled to reassert their identity, their national and ethnic culture, in the name of their blood and of belonging. The battle between the power of the *polis,* spreading from the North, and the forces of *local civil relationships,* built on the passions of the Jewish identity. How much of this is true even in our times around the globe! The world everywhere is split asunder by the forces of the neocolonial capitalist market with the promise to unify its peoples, and the forces of *ethnic fragmentation* and struggles of local identities that often turn violent and separatist. Here are the two key characteristics of the world at the turn of this millennium: *Jihad vs. McWorld*[25] as the title of one book suggests: the *McDonaldization,*[26] on the one hand, and interethnic, fundamentalist and local struggles for identity, the *Balkanization*[27] of society, on the other. Humans across the world are caught between the promise of community for "all" that allows no room for the local identity of "each," and the forces that struggle for the identity of "each" at the expense of the community of "all." The declaration of Pentecost is that the outpouring of the Spirit takes place precisely in the midst of these two forces. Babel offers a promise of unity for all through one language, one culture. It allows no room for the identity of each language, each culture.

Pentecost is the reversal of Babel, holding together both "all" and "each." Local identities are affirmed within a larger community.

In the place of a single monologic tradition, vernacularization takes place on the day of Pentecost. All traditions and languages are destigmatized and affirmed. While Babel excludes, Pentecost embraces. At the same time, no single language is given a central place. There *is* no central place. All are included, and yet each is decentralized, relativized. The Spirit aims not for a homogenous or homogenizing unity, but for a differentiated unity of all people, Jews, Arabs, and gentiles.

In the spirit of Pentecost, may we not say with certainty that the hegemony and centrality of the European model of Christianity is dead, and with it all Western claims to cultural dominance in the Two-Thirds World? How would an Anglican Communion look when it seems to be a "de-centering" force of eurocentric cultural and theological dominance, of a free expression of the gospel in a variety of cultural ways?

Perhaps the most powerful image of the Pentecost story is the richness of diversity. As the passage opens before us, the first thing that strikes us is the fact of a milling crowd, of masses of people, a sea of humanity in the narrow streets of Jerusalem on the day of Pentecost. They come in different colors, speaking different languages—Arabs and Libyans, Romans and Iranians, a microcosm of the then known world. The gospel is heard in the interwovenness of the plurality of peoples, in cultures in collision. A mark of post-colonial world is migration. Ours is an era of immigration, particularly from the former colonies to the colonizers' metropolitan centers. The biblical image is that in the midst of the reality of immigration and all the promise and pain that it entails in our postcolonial times, we discern the Spirit. The meaning and content of the gospel story are to be found in the interwovenness, the intermingling, of the plurality of people. That is the proper locus of the gospel.

Diversity is not something to be afraid of. But for many theologians, particularly in the West, diversity is unsettling. All defenses go up, as though the intermingling of the gospel with different cultures is a weakening of faith and a destruction of its purity. But the Spirit breaks forth in the midst of color, contrasts and plurality; and it is there that the gospel is made known as the transforming power of God brings the new into being. The words of Lamin Sanneh, the Yale missiologist, are strikingly relevant at this juncture. He says, "For all of us pluralism can be a rock of stumbling, but for God it is the cornerstone of the universal design."[28]

Analogously, it is only as the gospel is read and reread in a variety of cultures that its multifaceted splendor is drawn out. Is not the gospel also like a diamond, raw and uncut? It is only as it is shaped and illumined by a plurality of cultures that the priceless beauty of its many facets is manifested. While all cultures are valid instruments with which to cut and sharpen the gospel stone, no single culture can exhaust its richness. Let me use yet another metaphor. The story of God's love in Jesus Christ is like the bud of a fragrant flower, fully ripe but as yet only in the process of opening fully. As we read and hear the book from the variety of our languages and perspectives, multivoicedly, to use my phrase, each interpretation opens one petal of the gospel-flower. As each petal of the flower opens, we come to behold the loveliness of the blossoming flower and smell its fragrance. But it is an *unending process*. Its fullness is in the end, in the eschaton. Only through a process of a multicultural, or multivoiced, opening up shall we discern that love in all its fullness.

The colonialist approach to the Acts of the Apostles understands it as the story of *the expansion* of a conquering church, or the planting of it into every corner of the world. But it is equally valid to read the book as the story of *the unfolding of the gospel*, its nature being increasingly revealed *as it is appropriated and reappropriated by culture after culture*. It is through the encounter of the Jewish Christians with the cultures of people like Cornelius that the horizon of theology is expanded. It is in facing the religio-cultural milieu of Athens that Paul's grasp of the gospel is enriched. As the cultures of Jewish and Gentile Christians collide in the first council meeting in Jerusalem, as older theological assumptions and ritual practices are called into question, the church is liberated from forms of dogmatism, and the gospel is released as a force of liberation for many. Acts dramatically portrays for us what the Bangkok world mission conference said, "Culture shapes the voice that answers the voice of Christ." Such shaping began on the day of Pentecost. It continues to this day. The truth of the Christian faith in this sense is dynamic, processive and *multivoiced*—that is, it comes to be known in its fullness only as it is constituted and reconstituted in diverse ways and in multiple voices—of women and men, young and old, those of diverse sexual orientation, and those from the North and South. It is only as the multiplicity of traditions that mark the global church are recognized and brought into dialogue with each other that the church can discern and witness to "the multi-colored wisdom of God" that the author of the letter to the Ephesians speaks of. As the Fourth World Conference on Faith and Order in Montreal in 1963 stated, "the truth that the more the tradition is expressed in the varying terms of particular cultures, the more will its universal character be fully revealed."[29]

Mikhail Bakhtin's concept of heteroglossia is helpful to counter the monologism of the colonialist discourse. Bakhtin argues convincingly that not only among different languages, but even within a single language, there is a diversity of speech styles and genres of professions, classes, ethnic groups, and diverse orientations. Hence language is heteroglot, a term which refers to the diversity of *speechedness*.[30] "Utterances are not indifferent to one another, and are not self-sufficient; they are aware of and mutually reflect one another," says Bakhtin.[31]

This implies that we have many different voices in and through which we speak, think, and hear others, and in and through which we relate to the world. "We are 'the voices that inhabit us.'"[32] Our many voices of heteroglossia offer us a richness of thinking, knowing, and experiencing ourselves and all that is around us. It is through this multivoicedness that we are constituted as social selves. The absence of multivoicedness—a biblical symbol of which is Babel—leads to dominant modes of discourse and definitions of truth in static and ahistorical terms.

The Pentecost experience points to the possibility of perceiving the truth of the faith of the church as multivoiced, processive, and emergent. Its catholicity is precisely in the process of God's people from diverse contexts sharing their appropriation of God's love in Christ. Does not the very word, catholic, *kata'holon*, imply this? As the word means "according to the whole," the catholicity of truth comes to be as contextual expressions of the faith, from every tribe and nation, are shared, contested, and allowed for mutual challenge and enrichment.

Therefore, it is critical to become aware how many of us uncritically share the monologic mind-set of the colonial past and tend, sometimes unconsciously, to reduce the dynamic and multi-voiced stories of the gospel to a unitary, unchanging, and static substance. Essentialist discourse, in which every dynamic and open-ended meaning is atomized and made ahistorical, seems to be a trap, particularly in Christian theological circles. As David Hardy puts it:

> Through long habits instilled into western patterns of thought by figures of the past, we are inclined to think in terms of dualities. Whenever, therefore, we need to identify something, we do so by differentiating it from what it is not. We tend therefore to see everything as sharply atomized, this from that, you from me, God from the world, and so on. These differentiations quickly turn into sharp distinctions, and the distinctions into oppositions or confrontations, and it soon seems paradoxical to suppose that there is some fundamental unity between those which/who have been disjoined.[33]

Monologic definitions of reality, in our instance the Christian faith from the colonial period, have functioned as instruments of domination in the hands of the powerful. But in so far as multi-voiced hearing of the Christian story allows room for the restoration of the voices of the silenced and the "subaltern"—yet another postcolonial term—such as women, people of color, and the indigenous peoples, the articulation of Christian faith takes those at the margins seriously. In fact, a central aspect of the story of Jesus is that he refuses to play the role of the dominant hero, but always moves to the margin and to places of solidarity with the oppressed. So the multivoiced gospel is not smooth and soapy; it does involve contestations and conflict when liberative praxis is at stake. Therefore, what we call for here is not a liberal co-existence of plurality nor an innocuous pseudoequality of viewpoints. All these marginalize and disempower certain voices, and seek to avoid contestations, and silence the conflictual ones. The multi-voicedness of the gospel story is that which does not fall into a cheap harmony; but rather, in letting the plurality of voices speak, it addresses creatively the deep structural issues of social life in solidarity and, in the midst of the brokenness of relationships, it points to the possibility of liberated and liberating life for all. The mission of the Christian people everywhere is to witness to the multivoiced richness of the gospel story as they dialogically listen to other voices about God's multi-colored wisdom and love.

THE DIALOGICAL WITNESS OF THE CHURCH

Of all aspects of the life of the churches around the world, it is in the area of Christian witness that the churches manifest predominantly what we have described above as the colonial mind-set to this day. What Keith Bridston said in1965 rings true even at the present time. Referring to mission thinking and practice of churches, he suggested that "they embody a response to a world that no longer exists and express a theological understanding of the relation of the world to God that is now fallacious."[34] Imperialist colonialism has ended. It is true that there has been considerable rethinking in mission in many of the mainline churches, the churches of the Anglican Communion included. However, the larger number of Protestant missionaries today are from churches outside the mainstream and para- church agencies. Besides this, a number of Christian movements in the South have begun to undertake missionary enterprises, almost repeating the style and theology of the late eighteenth– and nineteenth-century missions. Therefore, Bridston's judgment would still apply. Hence, the postcolonial challenge for a re-visioning of the nature of Christian witness is critical and urgent.

A *post-colonial* challenge to the mission of the church comes at several levels. Let me identify only three of them below. First, there is the continuing notion that the primary missionary frontier is geographical. Such a frontier lies "out there" beyond the home front, often overseas. It is a mission primarily shaped by "the territorial 'from-to' idea."[35] The goal of mission is seen essentially as the physical extension and the numerical increase of the church. The passage in Matthew 28:19 has been interpreted to confirm the colonial and imperialistic interpretations of the churches' mission. Therefore, in many churches in the West, Christian witness in the neighborhood is called *evangelism*, in distinction from mission proper, which is carried overseas. However, already this notion is critiqued by many. Bishop Leslie Newbigin and David Bosch have been pioneers in such a critique. Recently those who belong to the "Gospel and our Culture Network" in the U.S. have called attention to the fact that North Atlantic countries are also the fields for mission today. Ian Douglas, one of the editors of this volume, has tirelessly pointed out that a central tenet in the Book of Common Prayer of the Episcopal Church USA is that the mission of the church is to restore "all people to unity with

God and each other in Christ."[36] However, in spite of the theological breakthrough among many ecumenical missiologists, one may boldly say that the geographical frontier still looms large and the planting of the church is seen as the primary goal for many. A negative indicator of such a malaise is the fact that many churches within the ecumenical tradition are little concerned about mission in any form at all today, primarily because for them mission is the sending of persons "from here" to "there."

In a *post-colonial* context in which the center-periphery dichotomy is challenged, it would be significant for Christian witness to recover the import of the popular slogan, "The end of a missionary era but the beginning of world mission," for our thinking about and practice of Christian witness. The slogan implies that the church has no meaning, no reality of its own apart from the world. The church is what it is only as it is located within and for the sake of the world. The slogan implies also that Christian witness takes place everywhere, in all places. It is multidirectional. It is a witness from "within." We are accustomed to hypostatizing culture as something fixed and outside the gospel, into which the Christian witness enters like a divine intervention in order to confront and convert. But the post-colonial ethos challenges us to discover an incarnate form of witness to God's love, incarnate *within* human history. A witness from "within" is the only proper mode of evangelism worthy of a God who does not control history from "without," but rather enters into it, suffers within, and transforms it by participating in it fully and really.

Second, in a post-colonial context, the still rampant notion that the church is the primary agent of mission needs to be challenged. When God is conceived in the image of an omnipotent Emperor, as Elaine Pagels tells us, it is natural to envision the church as God's sole agent. "If God is one, then there can be only one representative of God in community."[37] Within such a concept, witness cannot be exercised in a dialogical mode. But biblical testimony reminds us that mission, first and foremost, is God's. Mission is a predicate of God and God alone, not of the church. Hence mission is not a function of the church, certainly not one among many of its functions. The church cannot domesticate mission and manage it. It simply "gets-in-behind" the Spirit of God who is witnessing from within the world and within human hearts

356 BEYOND COLONIAL ANGLICANISM

to the movement of the new creation that God incessantly brings about. Mission as God's implies that discernment of the movement of the Spirit is the first and prior act to witness. In dialogue with the Spirit, and in dialogue with all others who discern the movement of the Spirit in their own contexts and in their own way, Christians can get ready for witnessing to their own story.

This also implies that Christian witness cannot be reduced to a duty, a burden we need to carry. As Leslie Newbigin put it so well, much of our concern for mission seems to show "as though mission were part of the law rather than part of Gospel.... There is an atmosphere of anxiety ... fortified—in England at least—by well-publicized statistics.... All this is very remote from the New Testament. The fact that mission is a gift rather than a task, that it belongs to the gospel rather than to the Law, is also repeatedly brought out in the gospels. Witness is primarily the work of the Spirit himself; the role of the Church is secondary...."[38] Christians who seek to discern the movement of the Spirit in the world, and to participate in that movement first, will necessarily be in a dialogical relationship with the Spirit and, in the Spirit, with all those, including people of other faiths and no faith, for a fuller discernment of God's movement in the world. Their witness will indeed be dialogical.

In a dialogical witness, there is room for surprises. For the movement of the Spirit in mission is always fresh and takes place in unheard-of places and through the agency of unheard-of people in unknown and ever-new ways. The stories of the early church testify to this fact, often taking those who respond to the Spirit, for example Peter or Philip, to places and people for genuinely dialogical witness. In such a witness, all those involved are transformed and enriched. It is never a one-way mission. Nor is there any room for a fixed order; things are turned upside down.

Finally, a dialogical witness to the gospel in a *postcolonial* context also challenges colonial definitions of reality and truth. We have described above that a monologic definition of reality is, among other things, essentialist, and oppositional or binary. Colonial forms of mission were characterized by an understanding of the truth of the gospel as fixed for all times and places. The historically and culturally particular understanding of the missionary became universalized as the sum and substance of Christian faith. It implied that there was no possibility of witnessing dialogically with those who were adjudicated as "heathens" and without God. The oppositional logic led to binary thinking. If what I know is truth, then that which does not resemble it must only be false. Then, the only option is to conquer them on the one hand and to convert them with the other hand, to displace their religious and cultural experiences with mine. In fact this is what happened, for example, in India. Listen to one of the British missionaries almost at the turn of twentieth century in India:

> In the case of many a Hindu, the first thing to be done is to empty him. His head is crammed with loads of learned lumber and his heart is the birthplace of vices, which the English language will not fitly describe. No man [sic] would attempt the subversion of a system he did not to some extent understand....[39]

Therefore the missionaries are encouraged to learn Sanskrit and Indian philosophies so that they can be subverted. The best among the missionaries were able to grant at least some credit to the three-thousand-year-old philosophical and religious systems of India and locate them somewhere in the lowest rung of a ladder. They could speak of the possibility of their development and eventual change. If Christianity could be presented as the crown of Hinduism, then there was a chance that India might be won both for Christ and the crown! We know that to this day Christians in India are only about 2.3 percent of the population. How important, then, is the role of dialogical witness?

Positively, the postcolonial logic describes reality as relational, dynamic or processive, and multilayered, as we have seen above. It is suggested here that authentic Christian witness too is relational, participatory, processive and multilayerd. It is this characteristic which makes a Christian witness in the postcolonial mode dialogical. Some brief comments are in order.

Any witness which does not arise out of a genuine participation in the socio-political and cultural ethos and life of those among whom one witnesses cannot adequately make sense. However, in Christian mission, often the concern to preserve the "truth"—understood in essentialist and static terms—has led to the alienation of the Christian from his/her hearers. In a highly imaginative essay, C. S. Song calls for a mission born out of love and not truth. I am citing him extensively below, for he captures what I seek to portray as dialogical witness in a postcolonial mode.

He begins by caricaturing those practices in mission where truth is understood in an essentialist and universalist sense:

> Christian mission has been very much a truth affair of Christians with the world. Truth is its noble commodity. Being a noble commodity, truth cannot mingle with less noble things. It must stand out. It must stand above. And it must stand apart. Truth is a unique vocation. Being a unique vocation, truth does not recognize other truths. It cannot have equals. It explains itself and explains others. Truth is a universal claim. Being a universal claim, it cannot tolerate other truth claims.... All in all, a truth affair is a judgmental affair. It judges, and is not to be judged. It conquers, and is not to be conquered.[40]

Having offered a powerful critique of defining Christian mission as a truth affair, in almost the kind of categories that I have suggested as colonial, he moves on to speak of mission as a dialogical, participatory love affair. Song continues:

> ... Christian mission in essence should be a love affair of the church with other human beings with whom God has already fallen in love.... It is Christian believers building with them a community in the power of God's love. If this is what Christian mission is, then Christian mission is God's mission.[41]

A dialogical witness is a love affair, ready to participate in the life of others, ready to make oneself vulnerable in love even as Christ himself did. Often the practice of mission tends to forget this central affirmation of Christian mission. We need to remind ourselves again and again that the last "commission" of Christ to go into all the world needs to be interpreted only within the basic framework of the great commandment to love one another as Christ loves all. Mission in essence is thus an expression of what Song calls God's "pain-love" demonstrated in Jesus Christ. "Pain-love language is the deepest kind of language. Jesus is God's pain-love Word. God's mission is pain-love mission. This is the Word and the mission that truly communicates."[42]

There is no doubt that such a word and witness will necessarily be dialogical. But those of us who are called to this form of witness in pain-love need to learn vulnerability at the crucible of dialogical encounters. Much will be demanded of us; we will be called upon to leave aside our cherished doctrines and dogmas and much more, in order that Christian witness indeed be a "love-affair."

I have used the terms "dialogical" and "dialogue" in a fairly broad sense, meaning a genuine openness of listening to the

other and the different in such a way that both partners in dialogue are challenged and deepened. Such dialogue requires an
intentional posture of permanently being open to the other. The
outcome surpasses, is greater than its parts, and hence does not
depend upon what two or more partners bring to the dialogical
relation. In this sense, dialogue is distinctly different from dialectics. Raimundo Panikkar says that "it befits the *kairos* of our time
to have liberated dialogue from the tutelage of dialectics."[43] To be
dialogical, therefore, is not to adopt a technique or a method, but
to be in a particular way of relating. As the prefix "dia" suggests, it
is not as much a speaking as a letting the subject matter sought
disclose itself through the words shared. In this process, witness
has a significant role. For in witnessing, one seeks to be so present
or so transparent to and before the dialogical partner, that the disclosure of the subject matter comes to be the disclosure that the
dialogue partners seek. Panikkar helpfully points out that the
Latin term *testimonium* is derived from *testis,* that is, *tr-stans,* literally meaning the one who "stands for the *third.*" [44] In the context
of a theological or interreligious dialogue, one may say that the
Spirit, the word of truth, makes itself known, and it is that truth
the Spirit discloses which possesses both participants.

The implications of such a dialogical lifestyle for Christian witness and mission are enormous. How significant it will be if churches within the Anglican Communion can assist each other in discerning the way forward and practicing such a dialogical witness.

THE POLYCENTRIC COMMUNION OF THE CHURCH

Let me now turn, albeit rather briefly, to the third aspect of
the life of the church that needs to be re-visioned in a postcolonial mode. It is the nature of the relation between the churches
across cultural and other divides. This re-visioning entails a move
away from the colonial to post-colonial, and from the eurocentric
to polycentric, in the structures and power relationships among
churches in general and the churches within the Anglican Communion in particular. Churches around the world have reached a
critical point in the movement from being more or less homogeneous in faith, worship and life, to a situation of theological and
liturgical heterogeneity, rooted in a profound commitment to
express Christian faith and witness in terms of particular local,
cultural idioms. This movement is accompanied by a refusal to

allow distinct local formulations of the good news in Christ to be reduced or conformed to a single paradigmatic perspective shaped elsewhere. The question is, how can our local churches challenge and help the Anglican Communion and Lambeth celebrate and worship God, given the diversity, multiplicity, and heterogeneity born out of Christian experiences in concrete, specific and particular contexts?

The term "polycentric" points not only to the reality that there are many churches around the world but also to a systematic principle of differentiation, diversity in life and witness, theological formulation, and dialogue and communion. Polycentrism signifies a refusal to accord epistemological privilege and adjudicating power to any single church, whatever its intellectual, economic or political strength, however rich its historical background and heritage. A polycentric reality of churches as we move into the twenty-first century also entails genuine reciprocity among the churches—for no church in any culture has a unitary and fixed identity. All are bound together in a communion that allows them to be permeable, interactive, mutually enriching.

As in the experience of Pentecost, there is a going beyond individualism and somehow allowing many different perspectives to count equally. A great number of different common identities come into view, which nevertheless become transparent to each other and able to communicate with each other. Only with this plurality of distinctive identities, modes of communication and structures of relationships are authentic identities preserved, while communion is sustained.

Pentecost is a symbol of people moving from a mere plurality to genuine pluralism. If the concept of plurality refers to "the state of being plural," the notion of pluralism refers to a state or relationship that recognizes the legitimate presence and role of more than one position, and allows genuine interaction among them for mutual critique and enrichment.

Can the Anglican Communion become a movement away from eurocentrism to a Communion of genuine pluralism through acknowledgement of its plurality? The point of the Pentecost experience and of the outpouring of the Spirit is the promise and the provision of power to be just, that without dissolving or suspending the different loyalties and local traditions and customs, a differentiating and differentiation-protecting experience of community.

The mind-boggling theological point behind Pentecost is the affirmation that the presence of the Spirit is inseparable from differentiated identities sharing in common the gifts of God in community with God. May it imply that a church or a communion that does not affirm and protect pluralism and differentiation does not know the Spirit as made manifest at Pentecost?

The Pentecost narrative in the Acts of the Apostles draws together two terms: "one" and "diverse." The word "one" within the biblical tradition need not mean a numerical oneness or unicity, but rather points to unity, integrity, communion—something which is unfragmented, unifying, shared. How significant and urgent today is such a communion, which affirms different identities on the one hand, and yet holds them in relationship. For the world today is characterized in part by increasing fragmentation—the struggle for particular cultural, ethnic, linguistic, and religious identities. All around us at this turn of the millennium, we are witnessing the birth and development of violent and separatist tendencies. In the U.S. alone, there are said to be no fewer than four hundred "hate groups" with home pages on the Internet! At the same time, dangerous alliances are being forged between religion/culture and exclusivistic expressions of national/ethnic identities. The legitimate search for diversity and difference, a hallmark of our postmodern age, has turned many parts of the world into the nightmare of "killing fields."

It is in such a context that the church is called to be a sign and instrument of the hope of one shared communion of diversities, setting up pointers to the possibility of human community, even as groups seek to affirm their own identity. As Philip Potter has said, a central ecumenical question for all churches is how can they "cooperate with God making the *oikoumene* an *oikos*, a home, a family of men and women ... of varied gifts, cultures, possibilities, where openness, trust, love and justice reign."[45] In a world being torn apart by centrifugal forces of fragmentation, the churches are called to witness to God's call for the unifying, reconciling, one hope of the gospel. How can the Anglican Communion be a sign and witness to the promise of the gospel that God in Jesus Christ wills for a community of diverse identities, distinct but bonded together in fellowship, a sign of "otherness in communion"?

It could be said that the central problematic of our era is that of "the other," particularly those who are pushed to the periphery of society. Hence it is of paramount importance that Christians recapture the vision of the gospel story of God in Christ as that which gives hope both by affirming the "otherness," the integrity and identity of peoples and groups, and by building them into community. The synoptic gospels portray Jesus' eating and drinking with "tax collectors and sinners" as a central symbol of the coming of God's reign. Not only does Jesus free and name people, giving identity and worth to those whose identity has been systematically denied; he also draws them into a circle of companionship with himself and each other, binding them together in community. Liberation in and for community is the hope of the gospel of the coming reign of God in Christ. "Otherness in communion" (to borrow a phrase from the Metropolitan Zizioulas) is therefore an unavoidable imperative for the life and witness of the church. The vision is clearly one of reconciled diversity. In recent times the churches have rediscovered the vision of the being of the Triune God, a communion of three Persons, as the ground of and pattern for human communion in "otherness."

Such a vision is beautifully portrayed in one of the eschatological passages in the book of Zechariah. Zechariah 2:1-5 reads:

> I looked up and saw a man with a measuring line in his hand. Then I asked, "Where are you going?" He answered me, "To measure Jerusalem, to see what is its width and what is its length." Then the angel who talked with me came forward, and another angel came forward to meet him, and said to him, "Run, say to that young man: Jerusalem shall be inhabited like villages without walls, because of the multitude of people and animals in it. For I will be a wall of fire all around it, says the Lord, and I will be the glory within it.

The man with a measuring line suggests to me the normal desire in each of our local churches, or for that matter for a world confessional family such as the Anglican Communion, to be certain about their strength and power, their stability and influence. It is as if each seeks to count and measure our ramparts, towers, and moats around us. But the wiser angel warns that in the eschatological vision and God's order of things, such an isolated measurement of the church is no more possible. For now Jerusalem itself is described as a communion of diverse "villages without walls." The time of Zechariah was not the safest and securest time for Jerusalem. Danger was around the corner. But each village, in the midst of its vulnerability, differences and even contestation, must seek to be permanently open to others.

But let us look for a moment at the reality of the interrelationship among the churches of the Anglican Communion. Many are concerned about the limits of Anglican diversity. There is evidence of the fear of plurality within the fellowship. The desire for unity at times leads some to call for the old colonial form of centralized authority located in a central place. In the process, the identity and rights of people in local churches, particularly those who are marginalized—women, people of different sexual orientation, those of different theological persuasion—are trampled under. Others who are suspicious of the calls for greater centralization at times are prepared to go their separate ways, thus with little concern for the health of the Communion. It is in this context that the postcolonial mode of reflection calls us to discover a genuinely polycentric Communion. Therefore the question is how the Anglican Communion can be broken open, and its ramparts so leveled, that genuine policentricity among the local churches within the family, and with churches outside it, may be made manifest for the glory of God.

This may involve learning to engage in genuine border crossings. As in the incarnation, when Christ, the very self of God, crosses borders, so are the churches across the world called today to empty themselves and cross borders that appear to be so different and strange. A fuller understanding of the calling of the church to be the signs of a unifying and shared hope in Christ helps local churches to become "cross-border spaces," where the "otherness" of the other may be understood on its own terms, and where new, and holistic, and corporate Christian identities may be formed together in solidarity. I have elsewhere identified some of the conditions and criteria for such border crossing across diverse cultures.[46]

A significant element in a polycentric Communion is the manner in which resources are shared and decisions that affect the common life are made, particularly when many members of the Communion in the South do not hold the same economic and political power as those in the North. What is needed is that the member churches seek to open themselves to each other across their differences so that they may learn to "share a rich diversity of the Christian faith; discover the unity that binds these together; and affirm together the Christological centre and Trinitarian source of our faith in all its varied expressions."[47]

NOTES

[1] Ella Shohat and Robert Stam, *Unthinking Eurocentrism: Multiculturalism and the Media* (London: Routledge, 1994).

[2] *New Directions in Faith and Order, Bristol 1967: Reports - Minutes - Documents* (Geneva: WCC, 1968), 25.

[3] In "End of History?," *The National Interest* (Washington, D.C., 1989), 3-18.

[4] Harvey Gallagher Cox, *The Silencing of Leonardo Boff: The Vatican and the Future of World Christianity* (London: Collins, 1988), 12.

[5] Gayatri Chakravorty Spivak, " Poststructuralism, Marginality, Postcoloniality and Value," in *Contemporary Postcolonial Theory: A Reader*, ed. Padmini Mongia (London: Arnold, 1996), 203.

[6] Ella Shohat, "Notes on the 'Post-colonial'," in *Contemporary Postcolonial Theory*, 326.

[7] Ibid., 324.

[8] It is significant to note that many of the post-colonial pioneers are intellectuals from the South, particularly from South Asia, teaching in North Atlantic countries primarily in literary studies and criticism. However, Spivak seems to tirelessly remind her fellow postcolonial theorists of this danger.

[9] Henry Schwarz and Sangeeta Ray, *A Companion to Postcolonial Studies* (Malden, Mass.: Blackwell, 2000), 123.

[10] Shohat, " Notes on the 'Post-colonial'," 329.

[11] Ibid., 330.

[12] "The Politics of Literary Postcoloniality," *Race and Class* 36:3 (1995):12-13 as cited in E. San Juan, Jr., *Beyond Postcolonial Theory* (New York: St. Martin's Press, 1998), 6. Also see Aijaz Ahmad, *In Theory: Classes, Nations, Literatures* (London: Verso, 1992).

[13] Uma Narayan and Sandra Harding, eds., *Decentering the Center: Philosophy for a Multicultural, Postcolonial, and Feminist World* (Bloomington: Indiana University Press, 2000).

[14] Title of a book edited by Jan Nederveen Pieterse and Bhikhu Parekh (London: Zed books, 1995).

[15] Title of another on research and indigenous peoples by Linda Tuhiwai Smith (London: Zed books, 1999).

[16] Shohat and Stam, *Unthinking Eurocentrism*, 49; I am indebted to Shohat and Stam's useful way of identifying the marks of polycentric thinking, see ibid., 46-49.

[17] See Richard J. Bernstein, *The New Constellation: The Ethical-Political Horizons of Modernity/Postmodernity* (Cambridge, Mass.: MIT Press, 1992), 58-60.

[18] Cornel West, "The Cultural Politics of Difference," in *The Cultural Studies Reader* (New York: Routledge, 1993), 203-4.

[19] Cited in Gauri Viswanathan, *Masks of Conquest: Literary Study and British Rule in India* (New York: Columbia University Press, 1989), 16-17.

[20] Shohat and Stam, *Unthinking Eurocentrism*, 48.

[21] Cited in Robert Stam, *Subversive Pleasures: Bakhtin, Cultural Criticism, and Film* (Baltimore: Johns Hopkins University Press, 1992), 231.

[22] Edward E. Sampson, *Celebrating the Other: A Dialogic Account of Human Nature* (London: Harvester Wheatsheaf, 1993), 158.

[23] For example, see Lorraine Code, *What Can She Know?: Feminist Theory and the Construction of Knowledge* (Ithaca: Cornell University Press, 1991); Catherine A. MacKinnon, *Toward a Feminist Theory of the State* (Cambridge, Mass.: Harvard University Press, 1989).

[24] *Thinking Fragments* (Berkeley: University of California Press, 1990), 28, as cited in Sampson, *Celebrating the Other,* 10.

[25] Benjamin R. Barber, *Jihad vs. McWorld: How Globalism and Tribalism Are Shaping the World* (New York: Times Books, 1995).

[26] George Ritzer, *McDonaldization of Society* (London: Routledge, 1994).

[27] Stjepan G. Mestrovic, *The Balkanization of the West: The Confluence of Postmodernism and Postcommunism* (London: Routledge, 1994).

[28] Lamin Sanneh, *Translating the Message: The Missionary Impact on Culture* (Maryknoll: Orbis Books, 1989), 27.

[29] P.C. Rodger and L. Vischer, eds., *The Fourth World Conference on Faith and Order* (London: SCM Press, 1964), 59, as cited in Martin Conway, "A Universal Faith in a Thousand and One Contexts," *International Review of Mission* 84 (January-April, 1995), 133.

[30] See particularly *Speech Genres and Other Late Essays,* trans. Vern W. McGee (Austin: University of Texas Press, 1986), 60-62.

[31] Ibid., 91.

[32] Gary S. Morson, *Mikhail Bakhtin: Creation of a Prosaics* (Stanford: Stanford University Press, 1990), 213.

[33] David Hardy, "The Future of Theology in a Complex World," in *Christ and Context,* ed. Hilary Regan and Alan J.Torrance (Edinburgh: T&T Clark, 1993), 22.

[34] Keith Bridston, *Mission, Myth and Reality,* (New York: Friendship Press, 1965), 17.

[35] Andrew Walls, *The Missionary Movement in Christian History* (Maryknoll: Orbis Books, 1996), 258.

[36] See his *Fling Out the Banner* (New York: The Church Hymnal Corporation, 1996) and several of his articles in *Witness.* The quote is from *The Book of Common Prayer* (New York: Church Publishing Incorporated, 1979), 85.

[37] Cited in Sampson, *Celebrating the Other,* 113. Elaine Pagels continues, "As God reigns in heaven as master, lord, commander, judge, and king, so on Earth he (sic) delegates his rule to members of the church hierarchy, who serve as generals, who command an army of subordinates. . . judges who preside in God's place."

[38] "The Holy Spirit's Witness," in *Madras Diocesan News and Notes* 16 (May 1982), 4.

[39] *Harvest Field,* September 1892.

[40] *Tell Us Our Names: Story Theology from an Asian Perspective* (Maryknoll: Orbis Books, 1984), 106.

[41] Ibid., 108.

[42] Ibid., 114.

[43] Raimundo Panikkar, *Myth, Faith, and Hermeneutics* (Bangalore:

Asian Trading Corporation, 1983), 242-43.

[44] Ibid., 238. This idea is analogous to Mikhail Bakhtin's notion of the "middle-third" in his dialogism.

[45] Report of the General Secretary, WCC Central Committee, Geneva, July-August, 1977, 9.

[46] "Contextual and Catholic: Conditions for Cross-cultural Hermeneutics," *Anglican Theological Review* 82 (Fall 2000), 679-703.

[47] David Gill, ed., *Gathered For Life* (Geneva: WCC, 1983), 33.

CONTRIBUTORS

DENISE M. ACKERMANN, a feminist theologian with a particular interest in Christian spirituality, lives in Cape Town, South Africa, where she is the Professor of Practical Theology at the University of the Western Cape. She has lectured at various other universities, including a year in the Women's Studies in Religion Program at Harvard Divinity School. In 1996 she was elected a Procter fellow at the Episcopal Divinity School, Cambridge, Massachusetts and in 2000 held a fellowship at the Center of Theological Inquiry in Princeton, New Jersey. She has served on various commissions dealing with doctrinal matters and theological education in the Church of the Province of Southern Africa and in 1998 accompanied Archbishop Njongonkulu Ndungane to the thirteenth Lambeth Conference as theological consultant. Her interests in Cape Town include serving as a Trustee on the Desmond Tutu Peace Trust, being a council member of the University of Cape Town, and participating in the Circle of Concerned African Women Theologians. Otherwise, she enjoys walking in the mountains and playing with her grandchildren.

SIMON E. CHIWANGA is Bishop of the Diocese of Mpwapwa in the Anglican Church of the Province of Tanzania. Dr. Chiwanga was educated at St. Paul's United Theological College, Limuru, Kenya; the University of Dar es Salaam, Tanzania (B.A., M.A.); and the University of London (M.Th.). He completed his Doctor of Ministry at the Episcopal Divinity School in 1999. Ordained in the Diocese of Central Tanganyika, he served as parish priest and school chaplain before becoming MP and Minister of Education for the Government of Tanzania in 1975. Working closely with

President Julius Nyerere, Dr. Chiwanga helped to greatly advance access to education for all Tanzanians. He also served his country as Director of the Government's Development Institute from 1976-1984. In 1985, Dr. Chiwanga returned to full-time ministry in the Anglican church, serving as Provincial Secretary of the Church of the Province of Tanzania for five years before being elected bishop of his home Diocese of Mpwapwa. Dr. Chiwanga has been a member of the Anglican Consultative Council (ACC) for over a decade as both a priest and bishop representative from Tanzania. He is currently Chairman of the ACC. An internationally respected church leader and widely sought-after preacher, Dr. Chiwanga has preached at the central eucharist of both the 1998 Lambeth Conference of Bishops and the 2000 General Convention of the Episcopal Church USA. He and his wife Gladys are the parents of five children.

KORTRIGHT DAVIS is an Anglican priest from Antigua, West Indies, who is currently serving as Professor of Theology at Howard University School of Divinity, Washington, D.C., and Director of the Doctor of Ministry Program. He has also been rector (part-time) of Holy Comforter Episcopal Church in the Diocese of Washington since 1986. Dr. Davis was appointed by the Archbishop of Canterbury to the Anglican–Roman Catholic International Commission II, and he has also been a member of the Faith and Order Commission of the World Council of Churches. He is the author of numerous articles, chapters, and books, and continues to function as a consultant and resource person for various ecclesiastical and academic institutions. Dr. Davis' more recent books include: *Can God Save the Church?* and *Serving With Power: Reviving the Spirit of Christian Ministry*. He has previously published: *Emancipation Still Comin': Explorations in Caribbean Emancipatory Theology*; *Cross and Crown in Barbados: Caribbean Political Religion in the Late 19th Century*; and *Mission for Caribbean Change: Caribbean Development as Theological Enterprise*. Dr. Davis holds the D.Phil. degree from Sussex University, UK, and has been awarded honorary doctorates (D.D.) from the General Theological Seminary, New York, and St. Paul's College, Virginia. He is also an honorary Canon of the Diocese of the Windward Islands, the Church in the Province of the West Indies.

GLAUCO S. DE LIMA is Bishop of Sao Paulo and Primate of the *Igreja Episcopal Anglicana do Brasil* (IEAB). Dr. de Lima was born in Pelotas, Rio Grande do Sul, in a lower-middle-class family. He was educated at the University of Rio Grande do Sul and at the Theological Seminary of the IEAB. He was ordained in the Missionary Diocese of Southern Brazil in 1956. Dr. de Lima pursued graduate theological studies at the Episcopal Theological School (currently Episcopal Divinity School) receiving an M.Div. in 1961. He was later awarded an honorary Doctor of Divinity from the same school. Dr. de Lima has served as rector of various parishes in Rio de Janeiro, often while supporting himself and his ministry through secular employment in the fields of education and training. He has also been a Professor of Pastoral Theology at his church's National Theological Seminary. Dr. de Lima was elected Bishop of Sao Paulo in 1989 and Primate of *Igreja Episcopal Anglicana do Brasil* in 1994. He is a passionate speaker and preacher on the injustices of globalization and capitalism and is committed to helping people to encounter God through the exercise of solidarity and social justice. Dr. de Lima and his wife Helen are the parents of four children.

IAN T. DOUGLAS is Associate Professor of World Mission and Global Christianity and the Director of Anglican, Global, and Ecumenical Studies at the Episcopal Divinity School. Dr. Douglas holds degrees from Middlebury College, the Harvard Graduate School of Education, Harvard Divinity School, and a Phd.D. from the Boston University Graduate School. He has served as a Volunteer for Mission in *L'Eglise Episcopale d'Haiti* and as Associate for Overseas Leadership Development at the Episcopal Church Center in New York City. Dr. Douglas is the Convener of the Episcopal Seminary Consultation on Mission, a member of the Inter-Anglican Standing Commission on Mission and Evangelism and past Secretary and Chair of the Standing Commission on World Mission for the General Convention of the Episcopal Church USA. Dr. Douglas writes and lectures extensively on mission and contemporary Anglicanism and is author of *Fling Out The Banner: The National Church Ideal and the Foreign Mission of the Episcopal Church.* He is married to Kristin Harris and they are blessed with three children, Luke, Timothy, and Johanna.

CHRISTOPHER DURAISINGH, a presbyter of the Church of South India, has taught at the United Theological College, Bangalore. He holds degrees from the United Theological College in Bangalore, the Episcopal Theological School and a Doctor of Theology from Harvard Divinity School. Dr. Duraisingh was formerly the director of the Commission on World Mission and Evangelism of the World Council of Churches. While at the WCC, he edited the *International Review of Mission* and directed a global study process on gospel and cultures. His recent publication is *Called to One Hope: Gospel in Diverse Cultures.* Currently he is the Otis Charles Professor of Applied Theology at the Episcopal Divinity School and is working on a cross-cultural and dialogical approach to theology.

JEFFREY M. GOLLIHER is the Canon for Environmental Justice and Community Development and pastoral supervisor of the healing ministry at the Cathedral of St. John the Divine, New York City. He is also program representative for the environment with the Office of the Anglican Observer at the United Nations. Dr. Golliher received a Ph.D. in cultural anthropology from the State University of New York at Buffalo in 1989. Before entering the General Theological Seminary in 1979, he taught cultural anthropology, worked as the director of youth and young family programs for an ecumenical agency, and lived in the Talamanca Rainforest in Costa Rica and on the Isle of Iona, a pilgrimage site in Scotland. He co-edited *Crisis and the Renewal of Creation: Church and World in the Age of Ecology* and contributed to *Cultural and Spiritual Values of Biodiversity* published by the United Nations Environmental Program.

LAURIE GREEN is a Londoner who studied in London and New York before working in urban Anglican parishes for twenty years. He has been an Industrial Chaplain to the British Steel Corporation and also had his own BBC Radio program for young people. His special interest in adult education led to his becoming the principal of a national theological course for Anglican ordinands before returning to inner-city London to become team rector of Poplar. In 1993 Laurie moved to Essex as Bishop of Bradwell. He has written on the nature of contextual theology, international debt, and urban mission. He is the Chair of England's Churches' Network for Housing Estate Ministry and also serves on the Urban Bishops' Panel of the Church of England. He is currently engaged in the setting up of an Anglican Urban Network.

DAVID HAMID is a Canon of the Diocese of Niagara, the Anglican Church of Canada. For ten years he was the Anglican Church of Canada's Mission Secretary for Latin America and the Caribbean, in charge of partnership relations with Anglican churches and ecumenical councils and institutions in the Americas, and responsible for a number of programs in the region ranging from the exchange of missionary personnel to advocacy on issues of justice and human rights. Since 1996 Canon Hamid has been the Director of Ecumenical Affairs for the Anglican Communion and is the Anglican co-secretary of the major international ecumenical conversations, including Anglican–Roman Catholic International Commission and the International Commission of the Anglican–Orthodox Theological dialogue, as well as secretary of the Inter-Anglican Theological and Doctrinal Commission. Born of a Scottish mother and a Burmese father, David's upbringing was culturally diverse: European and Asian, Christian and Muslim. He was educated at McMaster University in Hamilton, Ontario, and Trinity College, Toronto. Canon Hamid lives in London with his wife Colleen and their two sons, Jonathan and Michael.

JOHN HAMMOCK is currently Director of the Feinstein International Famine Center in the School of Nutrition Science and Policy and Associate Professor of Humanitarian Studies at the Fletcher School of Law and Diplomacy at Tufts University in Medford, Massachusetts. Dr. Hammock has a Ph.D. in international relations from the Fletcher School of Law and Diplomacy (Tufts), and an Honorary Doctor of Laws degree from Denison University, Ohio. Born and raised in Havana, Cuba, he has lived in various Latin American countries and has traveled extensively throughout Asia, Africa, and Latin America. Dr. Hammock was President of Oxfam America, a private, nonprofit international agency that funds self-help development in poor nations in Africa, Asia, Latin America, and the Caribbean. An expert in economic and community development in the global South, particularly Latin America, Dr. Hammock has served as Executive Director of ACCION International, which provides credit and technical assistance to micro-enterprises in South America and the Caribbean. He has consulted with the Inter-American Development Bank and the *Instituto Nacional de Servicios de Entrenamieto* in the Dominican Republic. Working with Women's World Banking, Dr. Hammock helped organize programs in Colombia, the Dominican Republic, and Haiti. He has advised the Government of Costa Rica's National Office of Community Development and has worked with a number of U.S. groups on community-development and micro-business programs. Dr. Hammock lectures and writes extensively on international relations, social science research, and a variety of development issues. He has served as a Visiting Professor at both the University of Costa Rica and the Universidad del Valle in Cali, Colombia. A life-long Episcopalian, he is an active lay leader in the Diocese of Massachusetts.

ANURADHA HARINARAYAN works with Save the Children-U.S. as a technical specialist in the Food Security Unit, providing support for programs in East Africa and Latin America. Prior to that, Anuradha was a researcher at the Feinsten Famine Center, Tufts University. She has a Master's in International Affairs from the Fletcher School of Law and Diplomacy and a graduate degree in Nutrition from the School of Nutrition Science and Policy at Tufts University.

RENÉE L. HILL is the Senior Associate for Peace and Justice at All Saints Episcopal Church in Pasadena, California. She is a graduate of Bryn Mawr College and earned both her M.Div. and Ph.D. at Union Theological Seminary in New York City. Dr. Hill has served parishes in both Harlem and the South Bronx and is a former member of the faculty at Episcopal Divinity School, where she was Assistant Professor of Theology and Director of Studies in Feminist Liberation Theologies. Dr. Hill is a participant in the International Young Women's Leadership Project and a grant recipient from the E. Rhodes and Leona B. Carpenter Foundation for a project on "Emancipatory Liturgies for Liberative Churches." Her research interests include contemporary liberation theologies, religion in the African diaspora, postcolonial and feminist theory, and community/congregation-based education. Dr. Hill has widely published in the fields of Black Theology and Womanist Theology and is completing a book entitled: *Which 'Me' Will Survive All these Liberations: Identity, Theology, and Feminist Theory*.

KWOK PUI-LAN is William F. Cole Professor of Christian Theology and Spirituality at the Episcopal Divinity School. Born in Hong Kong, she received her doctorate from Harvard Divinity School and has published extensively in Asian feminist theology, biblical hermeneutics, and postcolonial criticism. Her recent books include *Discovering the Bible in the Non-Biblical World* and *Introducing Asian Feminist Theology*. She has co-edited *Women's Sacred Scriptures* and *Postcolonialism, Feminism, and Religious Discourse* and is co-editor of the *Journal of Feminist Studies in Religion*. As an Anglican, she is active in the ecumenical movement, especially in the discussion of Justice, Peace, and Integrity of Creation and Gospel and Culture of the World Council of Churches. She also serves on the Outreach Committee of the Asian Task Force against Domestic Violence in Boston.

JACI MARASCHIN was born in Bage, RS, Brazil. He was educated in philosophy at the University of Rio Grande do Sul and received his theological training at the Brazilian Episcopal Seminary. Dr. Maraschin's graduate degrees include a Master in Theology from the General Theological Seminary in New York; a Doctor in Sciences of Religion, University of Strasbourg, France; a Diploma in Music, Musical Institute of Porto Alegre, Brazil; and graduate studies in Communication, University of Sao Paulo, Brazil. Dr. Maraschin is a priest in the *Igreja Episcopal Anglicana do Brasil,* Diocese of Sao Paulo. He has served as a consultant for the 1988 and 1998 Lambeth Conferences and is a former member of the Inter-Anglican Theological and Doctrinal Commission, the Anglican Consultative Council and the Standing Commission of Faith and Order, World Council of Churches. An author of many books and articles, a songwriter and poet, Dr. Maraschin is currently Professor of the School of Philosophy and Sciences of Religion at the Methodist University of Sao Paulo.

NJONGONKULU NDUNGANE is Archbishop of Capetown and Primate of the Anglican Church of the Province of Southern Africa. Dr. Ndungane was educated at the Federal Theological College in South Africa as well as at the University of London (B.D., M.Th.). He received an honorary doctorate from Rhodes University in 1997. Dr. Nudungane served as a priest, rector, and chaplain in various parishes in Cape Town before becoming Provincial Liason Officer for the Synod of the Church of the Province of Southern

Africa (CPSA) in 1981. In 1985, Dr. Ndungane became Principal of St. Bede's Theological College, Umtata, until his appointment as Chief Executive Officer of the Synod of the CPSA in 1987. From 1981-1990, Dr. Ndungane was a member of the Anglican Consultative Council from Southern Africa. In 1991, he became Bishop of the Diocese of Kimberly and Kuruman and then Archbishop of Capetown in 1996. Dr. Nudungane is a tireless advocate for justice and reconcilition and was imprisoned on Robben Island for his struggle against apartheid. He is widely seen as one of the most outspoken leaders in the Anglican Communion and in wider political circles for both his stand against the burden of international debt and his efforts to overcome the AIDS crisis in Africa.

JENNY PLANE TE PAA is *Ahorang*i or Dean of *Te Rau Kahikatea*, indigenous constituent of the College of St. John the Evangelist in Auckland, New Zealand. Appointed in 1995 as *Ahorangi* when she was forty-one years old, Dean Te Paa is the first lay, indigenous, and single woman ever to be appointed as dean of an Anglican theological seminary in the Anglican Communion. Her "qualifications" for the position include a lifelong commitment to the Anglican faith, extensive service to local parishes and vestries, a serving member of General Synod of the Anglican Church in Aotearoa, New Zealand and Polynesia since 1994, leader of many women's and community social-service projects, and member of church-based research projects. Dean Te Paa was the first Maori person to complete an academic degree in theology, and in 1994 she completed a Master's degree with Honors in Educational Administration. Dean Te Paa is finishing her Ph.D. through the Graduate Theological Union in Berkeley, California where she is writing on race politics and theological education. In her "spare" time, she serves on the Executive Steering Committee of the Anglican Peace and Justice Network, the World Council of Churches Commission on Ecumenical Theological Education and Ministry Formation, and is Moderator of the Working Group, responsible for funding faculty development and ecumenical theological educational projects on an international basis. Dean Te Paa belongs to the Anglican Indigenous Network and has written many articles for publication in various theological journals throughout the world.

FREDRICA HARRIS THOMPSETT is Mary Wolfe Professor of Historical Theology at the Episcopal Divinity School. She holds a Ph.D in History from the University of Chicago. Dr. Thompsett has served on the Executive Council staff (1978-83) of the Episcopal Church USA, as the Academic Dean at the Episcopal Divinity School (1986-1999), and as one of the Episcopal Church's representatives to the Inter-Anglican Theological and Doctrinal Commission (1993-98). Her most recent book, *Living with History,* is part of the New Church's Teaching Series of the Episcopal Church USA. Other publications include *Courageous Incarnation* and *We Are Theologians: Strengthening the People of the Episcopal Church.* Her current projects focus on the ministries of laity at work in the world, and on historical vocations of Episcopal women.